# Multi-Party Redress Mechanisms in Europe: Squeaking Mice?

Editors:
V. Harsági
C.H. van Rhee

# Multi-Party Redress Mechanisms in Europe: Squeaking Mice?

intersentia

METRO

Ius Commune Europaeum

Editors:
V. Harsági
C.H. van Rhee

Multi-Party Redress Mechanisms in Europe: Squeaking Mice?

Intersentia Ltd
Sheraton House | Castle Park | Cambridge | CB3 0AX | United Kingdom
Tel.: +44 (0)1223 370 170 | Email: mail@intersentia.co.uk

ISBN 978-1-78068-277-8
D/2014/7849/161
NUR 822


Cambridge – Antwerp – Portland
www.intersentia.com | www.intersentia.co.uk



British Library Cataloguing in Publication Data. A catalogue record for this book is available from the British Library.

## CONTENTS

## LIST OF AUTHORS

**Neil H. Andrews**, Professor of Private Law and Civil Justice, University of Cambridge, Cambridge, United Kingdom

**Michael Bakowitz**, Research Fellow at Max Planck Institute Luxembourg for International, European and Regulatory Procedural Law, Luxembourg

**Gyula Bándi**, Jean Monnet Professor of EU Environmental Law, Pázmány Péter Catholic University, Faculty of Law, Jean Monnet Centre of Excellence, Budapest, Hungary

**Laura Ervo**, Professor of Procedural Law, Örebro University, Sweden; Associate Professor (docent), Universities of Turku, Helsinki and Eastern Finland, Finland

**Frédérique Ferrand**, Chair of Civil Procedure and Comparative Law, University Jean Moulin Lyon 3, Faculty of Law, Lyon, France

**Viktória Harsági**, Chair of Civil Procedure Law, Pázmány Péter Catholic University, Faculty of Law, Budapest, Hungary

**Burkhard Hess**, Director of Max Planck Institute Luxembourg for International, European and Regulatory Procedural Law, Luxembourg, Honorary Professor, Université du Luxembourg, Luxembourg, University of Heidelberg, Germany

**Robert Kulski**, Chair of Civil Procedure II, Lodz University, Faculty of Law and Administration, Lodz, Poland

**Richard Marcus**, Coil Chair in Litigation, University of California, Hastings College of the Law, USA; Associate Reporter, Advisory Committee on Civil Rules, Judicial Conference of the USA

**Elisabetta Silvestri**, Associate Professor of Civil Procedure and Comparative Civil Procedure, University of Pavia, Department of Law, Pavia, Italy

**Ákos Szalai**, Economist, Associate Professor, Pázmány Péter Catholic University, Faculty of Law; Fellow of the Institute for Legal Studies (Hungarian Academy of Sciences, Centre for Social Sciences), Budapest, Hungary

**Pál Szilágyi**, Director of the Competition Law Research Centre, Pázmány Péter Catholic University, Faculty of Law, Budapest, Hungary

**Tihamér Tóth**, President of the Scientific Board of the Competition Law Research Centre, Pázmány Péter Catholic University, Faculty of Law, Budapest, Hungary

**Ianika Tzankova**, Chair of Mass Claim Dispute Resolution, University of Tilburg, Faculty of Law, Tilburg, The Netherlands

**Alan Uzelac**, Chair of Civil Procedure, Zagreb University, Faculty of Law, Zagreb, Croatia

**Remco (C.H.) van Rhee**, Chair of European Legal History and Comparative Civil Procedure, University of Maastricht, Faculty of Law, Maastricht, The Netherlands

**Stefaan Voet**, Postdoctoral Fellow, Flanders Research Foundation, University of Ghent, Faculty of Law, Belgium

## LIST OF ABBREVIATIONS

| | |
|---|---|
| ADA | Anti-Discrimination Act |
| ADR | Alternative Dispute Resolution |
| AGB-Gesetz | Gesetz zur Regelung des Rechts der Allgemeinen Geschäftsbedingungen (Act on Standard Contract Terms) |
| ATCA | Anti-Counterfeiting Trade Agreement |
| CAE | Conseil d'analyse économique |
| CCC | Contrats Concurrence Consommation |
| CCP | Code of Civil Procedure |
| CDC | Cartel Damage Claims |
| CFA | Conditional Fee Agreement |
| CFF | Croatian Football Federation |
| CJC | Civil Justice Council |
| CNB | Conseil National des Barreaux |
| CNC | Conseil National de la Consommation |
| CPA | Consumer Protection Act |
| CPC | Code de procédure civile |
| CPR | Civil Procedure Rules |
| DG | Directorate-General |
| DGCCRF | Direction générale de la concurrence, de la consommation et de la répression des fraudes |
| EC | European Commission |
| ECJ | European Court of Justice |
| ECtHR | European Court of Human Rights |
| EU | European Union |
| GDP | Gross Domestic Product |
| GKG | Gerichtskostengesetz (Court Fees Act) |
| GLO | Group Litigation Order |
| GPA | Group Proceedings Act |
| GVG | Gerichtsverfassungsgesetz (Courts Act) |
| GVH | Gazdasági Versenyhivatal |
| GWB | Gesetz gegen Wettbewerbsbeschränkungen (Act against Restraints on Competition) |
| HCA | Hungarian Competition Act |

| | |
|---|---|
| HUF | Hungarian Forint |
| JVEG | Justizvergütungs- und Enschäditungsgesetz (Judicial Compensation Act) |
| KapMuG | Kapitalanleger-Musterverfahrensgesetz (Capital Markets Model Act) |
| MoJ | Ministry of Justice |
| MP | Member of Parliament |
| NCA | National Competition Authority |
| NGO | Non-Governmental Organisation |
| OJ | Official Journal |
| OLG | Oberlandesgericht |
| OTKA | Hungarian Scientific Research Fund |
| TFEU | Treaty on the Functioning of the European Union |
| AGCM | Autorità Garante della Concorrenza e del Mercato |
| UCPA | Hungarian Act on the prohibition of unfair business-to-consumer commercial practices |
| UKlaG | Unterlassungsklagengesetz (Prohibitory Injunctions Act) |
| US | United States |
| USA | United States of America |
| UWG | Gesetz gegen den unlauteren Wettbewerb (Act Against Unfair Competition) |
| VKI | Verein für Konsumenteninformationen (Association for Consumer Information) |
| WpHG | Wertpapierhandelsgesetz (Securities Trading Act) |
| ZPO | Zivilprozessordnung (Code of Civil Procedure) |

## ACKNOWLEDGEMENTS

This volume is the result of the conference 'Public Interest Litigation & Group Litigation: Comparative Perspectives' hosted by the Law Faculty of Pázmány Péter Catholic University in Budapest on 7-8 November 2013. The conference was organised by Viktória Harsági within the framework of a research project financed by the Hungarian Social Renewal Programme (TÁMOP Project No. 4.2.1.B-11/2/KMR-2011-0002) and the Hungarian Scientific Research Fund (Project No. OTKA K 105559). The organiser of the event is grateful to the sponsors of the conference, namely the Hungarian Chamber of Civil Law Notaries and the Hungarian Bar Association. The Hungarian Chamber of Civil Law Notaries and Maastricht University, Faculty of Law in the Netherlands (Research Programme 'Principles and Foundations of Civil Procedure in Europe' of the Ius Commune Research School), sponsored the publication of the present volume. The volume aims at providing information as regards recent developments in Collective Redress Mechanisms in the European Union with the view of assisting Hungary and other jurisdictions in the reform of their civil justice systems.

The editors would like to thank Mrs Marina Jodogne from the Maastricht European Institute for Transnational Legal Research (*Maastrichts Europees Instituut voor Transnationaal Rechtswetenschappelijk Onderzoek* or METRO) for her help and advice in editing the present volume. They are also grateful to Mr Randolph W. Davidson (Pavia) for revising the English text of the contributions of the non-native English speakers to this volume.

The subtitle of the present volume was inspired by J. Goldsmith, 'European Collective Redress', *The Law Gazette*, 20 June 2013.

V. Harsági & C.H. van Rhee
July 2014

V. Harsági
C.H. van Rhee

## COLLECTIVE REDRESS IN THE EUROPE UNION - COMPARATIVE PERSPECTIVES

### Introduction

The story of collective redress in the European Union up to the present day may be qualified as a story of missed opportunities and small steps forward. This is due to an (overly?) cautious approach to the topic at the European and national levels, a fear of American-style class actions (often due to a certain degree of unfamiliarity with the specific features of these class actions as opposed to those of the American system of civil litigation in general) and lobbying against the introduction of such mechanisms by those who might become subject to them as defendant parties. As a result, many of the collective redress mechanisms introduced so far in the various EU Member States may rightly be qualified as 'Squeaking Mice'.[1] This does not only appear from the contributions to the present volume, but also from the considerable number of studies that have been published on collective redress mechanisms in Europe during the last few years. Indeed, the topic of collective redress has become very fashionable in academic literature (one only has to consult the bibliographies accompanying the contributions to this book), and the amount of writing contrasts sharply with the limited progress that has been made in this area at the European and national levels so far.

The editors of the present volume hope that the future of collective redress in Europe will be brighter than the past. They hope that this volume will contribute to the discussion on collective redress in Europe, and that this discussion will lead to the implementation of effective collective redress mechanisms in the various EU Member States, mechanisms that cannot be qualified as stillborn, as is the case with many of the reforms that until today have been introduced in a variety of European countries.

At the outset of this volume it should be remembered that the legal terminology used in the area of collective redress in Europe is sometimes

1 See J. Goldsmith, 'European Collective Redress', *The Law Gazette*, 20 June 2013.

bewildering.[2] Although this is not necessarily the case in all contributions to this volume, the present introduction uses some of the terminology of the recent EU Commission Recommendation of 11 June 2013 on common principles for injunctive and compensatory collective redress mechanisms in the Member States concerning violation of rights granted under Union Law (*OJ* 2013 L201/60). Since this Recommendation does not cover all types of collective redress mechanisms in depth, e.g. legal mechanisms to obtain declaratory judgments or ADR in the area of collective redress, it cannot be used to solve all terminological problems.

The volume is divided into two parts. The first part (I) starts with two contributions on developments at the EU level, and they are followed by a contribution on developments in the United States of America (the latter contribution is included since the American class action is often used as an argument for a cautious approach in Europe). The fourth and fifth contributions of Part I discuss collective redress from the perspective of EU Member States with an inefficient and ineffective Judiciary and from a Law & Economics perspective respectively.

The second part (II) of this volume is devoted to a selection of European jurisdictions (Belgium, England & Wales, France, Germany, Hungary, Italy, the Netherlands, Poland and Sweden). These encompass, on the one hand, jurisdictions where, at least for the moment, limited progress has been made with the introduction of effective collective redress mechanisms and where usually a vertical or sectorial approach has been chosen, meaning that collective redress mechanisms are only available in limited areas (e.g. only in consumer cases, capital market transactions and the environment). These jurisdictions often exhibit a cautious approach to the subject matter, especially where they combine a vertical approach with a preference for opt-in mechanisms, which often results in the available collective redress mechanisms hardly ever being used in practice. On the other hand, there are more audacious European jurisdictions, jurisdictions where collective redress has proven to be more successful. These jurisdictions have often adopted a horizontal approach to matters, meaning that collective redress is not limited to some areas of the law only, and some of them combine this approach with opt-out mechanisms and creative ways of funding collective redress,[3] something that is especially important where the individual harm caused is of limited value.

2 A few examples inspired by the terminology used in this volume: Group actions are also referred to as aggregate litigation, class actions, collective actions and multi-party litigation. Subtypes of group actions are called *actio popularis*, association suits, test case litigation, model case litigation, representative collective actions and substitutional collective actions. The representative action itself has various subtypes as well, and the terminology used is e.g. traditional representative action, collective representative action and joint representative action. Obviously, in Europe there is also the terminology in other languages (which may sometimes give rise to interesting translations into English when non-English authors write in English), such as the Italian *azione di classe* and in French e.g. *recours collectif, action de groupe* and *action collective*, the latter having as one of the various possible subtypes the *action collective de substitution*.

3 Funding is not discussed in depth in the present volume.

**Part I: EU & USA**

Part I of this volume opens with a contribution by the current director of the Max Planck Institute for International, European and Regulatory Procedural Law in Luxemburg, Professor Burkhard Hess, on the latest developments in the context of the European Union. These developments are influenced by the fact that, as the learned author holds, most Member States of the European Union favour representative collective redress mechanisms, meaning that only representative entities have standing in such actions, preferably entities that have a non-profit character and that are subject to certification (approval) by a court of law. Group actions in the sense of actions brought by those who claim to have suffered harm jointly are not favoured. Within this context, Professor Hess discusses the recent EU Directive on the Compensation of Cartel Damages, and the EU Recommendation on Collective Redress. The author concludes that the proposals of the EU Commission cannot be considered as ambitious legislative undertakings and that the Commission has largely renounced its initial ambition of introducing a modern and comprehensive legislative instrument of collective redress. Ironically, this is underlined by the positive reactions from the business world as regards the EU initiatives. Since collective redress mechanisms may impact the business world to a large extent as defendant parties, they may favour the cautious and non-binding approach chosen at the EU level. The Directive on Cartel Damages can be considered the 'worst' example of the cautious approach taken. According to Professor Hess, it replaces the concept of private enforcement of rights (i.e. by way of collective redress mechanisms) with a concept giving preference to public enforcement (i.e. enforcement by the Member States' authorities), and therefore undermines to a certain extent the whole idea of collective redress. This is slightly less problematic as regards the EU Recommendation which, combined with the EU Communication on a Horizontal Framework for Collective Redress, provides recommendations for EU Member States in developing collective redress mechanisms. Nevertheless, also these documents are rather conservative in their approach, since they provide for a restricted model of collective redress based on the standing of representative entities only, opt-in and strict control of the funding of collective litigation. Cross-border collective redress and ADR (although mentioned) are not covered in depth by these documents. Professor Hess states that the EU initiatives may be too reluctant in promoting effective collective redress mechanisms, and it is very likely that some of the Member States will implement more effective instruments incompatible with the principles of the Recommendation. This is certainly true for some of the jurisdictions discussed in the second part of this volume.

The second contribution to Part I is written by Professor Bándi from Budapest and discusses collective redress mechanisms in environmental protection cases, more specifically the influence of the Aarhus Convention as part of EU law. Here we are not dealing with representative actions for safeguarding an aggregate of individual interests, but with a representative action for safeguarding general interests of the public at large (according to one definition, this may be qualified as an *actio popularis*). The idea behind this development is to involve the public in protecting the environment (public participation rights) by providing access to justice in cases which, according to the ordinary rules of procedure, would result in the inadmissibility of the claim because of lack of individual interest. Unfortunately, at the EU level a legislative proposal to provide access to justice under the Convention has not yet been implemented even though the proposal has been pending for about 10 years. This means, according to Professor Bándi, that action needs to be taken at the level of the individual Member States.

Professor Bándi also discusses the role of the Court of Justice of the European Union in interpreting the public participation guarantees encompassed in EU legislation. Given the fact that the European Legislature is not very successful in introducing new rules providing access to justice under the Aarhus Convention, activity by the Court of Justice may be welcomed. The learned author holds that 'one may see a very clear message [in the case law of the CJEU], which is, to give life to effective access to justice standards'. The starting point is the *Janecek* judgment which noted that the concept of 'interested party' should not be interpreted too narrowly at the national (German) level. It seems that the number of cases in which the CJEU finds that support of the public in the enforcement of environmental law is needed is on the rise, which is demonstrated by the large number of cases discussed by Professor Bándi. According to the author, the Commission believes that public participation in enforcement may become a strong collaborator in the proper implementation of environmental law, but the debate is still open. In the meantime, CJEU case law has turned more and more towards the guarantee of effective remedies within the judicial system, in order to grant better representation to environmental interests in general.

The contribution following that of Professor Bándi is written by a scholar involved in rule-making in the area of class actions in the United States of America, Professor Richard Marcus. At the end of his contribution, Professor Marcus states that 'those tempted to reject the American model out of hand might consider whether the features of American class actions they dislike are really a consequence of features of American litigation more generally.' For the informed observer, but apparently not for those in Europe who are afraid of American-type class actions, this seems obvious, since broad discovery, punitive damages, contingency fees and so on are evidently not features of the American class action itself, but of civil litigation in the US in general. At the same time, the American class action provides examples of deviations from the general American procedural framework which European opponents might embrace, since for example in some class actions the American rule on attorney fee recovery (meaning that each party has to bear its own costs) is abandoned in favour of the European rule that the loser has to pay the expenses of the winner, as is shown by Professor Marcus.

Nevertheless, Professor Marcus demonstrates that there is some concern about class actions in the US as well. These concerns have given rise to a series of changes in the original approach to class actions since the introduction of the modern rule on class actions in 1966 (Rule 23 of the Federal Rules of Civil Procedure). In 1996, for example, a new provision was introduced allowing an immediate review of decisions whether to certify a class, which gave rise to important case law on standards of class certification. Furthermore, the US Congress provided 'that the "group" with the largest potential claim should become the "lead plaintiff" in securities fraud class actions, and that this lead plaintiff should hire class counsel and take other actions instead of leaving those to the lawyer, under the review of the court, as in ordinary class actions'. Amendments that became effective in 2003 'clarified', amongst other things, 'that, when certifying a class, a judge had to define the class and the claims asserted, and also appoint class counsel' and they increased the powers of the judge when reviewing proposed class settlements. In 2005, Congress decided to change the rules on jurisdiction, expanding the jurisdiction of the federal courts in order to have more class actions litigated at that level so as to avoid state courts' certifying nationwide class actions while applying their own state law. This last approach was thought to give rise to unfair results due to the fact that state law in these actions differed from state to state. Although Europe does not have a system of federal European courts, this development might be of interest for Europe too, for example since some national courts of the Member States assume jurisdiction in collective redress cases over foreign nationals even where the majority of interested parties are from a state other than that of the national court. Another American amendment that, although not introduced in practice is interesting nevertheless, suggested that the judge should have the possibility to order an opt-in regime instead of the usual opt-out regime in class actions. Finally, the US Supreme Court has influenced the approach to class actions to a significant extent, although according to Professor Marcus one should be cautious in drawing general conclusions from individual cases. It seems that the Supreme Court is not favourable to an expansive use of class actions and class certification has become more difficult to obtain. For the rest, it is worthwhile repeating here what Professor Marcus has to say about class settlements – which occur much more often in the US than litigation by way of class actions – since it may eliminate some of the concerns of European observers. The learned author remarks that in these settlement situations the standards for certification on some particulars are much higher than the standards in litigation certification, and therefore it is not so likely that entities are forced into unfavourable settlements within the American system of class actions.

The fourth contribution in the first part of this volume is written by Professor Alan Uzelac from Zagreb in Croatia, the latest EU Member State, who has been involved in law-making as regards group litigation in his country of origin. This author qualifies his own jurisdiction as problematic in the sense that the Judiciary in Croatia is subject to many systemic and procedural failures. Litigation takes too long, the possibilities for appeal are extended and the career judges lack experience and are not used to teamwork in order to solve some of the more problematic factual and legal issues. Although this may be the result of the Socialist heritage of present-day Croatia, the author holds that the same problems also exist in some of the old European Union Member States of which Italy is of course the proverbial example. Professor Uzelac claims that within the context described by him, in which courts have problems in deciding ordinary cases in an efficient and timely manner, the introduction of collective redress mechanisms is a bridge too far; it will not improve access to justice and might even be harmful. The existing mechanisms in Croatia (e.g. an association suit inspired by the German *Verbandsklage* and collective redress based on the 2009 Croatian Anti-Discrimination Act) are not particularly successful. At the same time the author states that instead of private enforcement by way of collective redress mechanisms, public enforcement by public state entities does not work well in Croatia either. Unfortunately, the same may be true for several other European jurisdictions, and this raises questions about the possible success of any new collective redress mechanisms. A conclusion might be that the introduction of collective redress mechanisms in various EU Member States is impossible without a considerable reform of the existing judicial framework in order to have it reach the high standards that may be observed in some other EU Member States. But obviously this is a much more daunting task than the publication of an EU Recommendation on collective redress mechanisms and a Directive on Collective Litigation in the area of Cartel damages.

The final contribution in the first part of this volume deals with Law & Economics. The author, Professor Szalai from Budapest, formulates a series of important propositions within the context of the Law & Economics approach to collective redress mechanisms. He discusses various issues that may arise in collective redress litigation, such as why the members of a group would participate in a collective action. Within this context the author addresses the so-called 'free-rider problem'. This problem arises in situations where the results of collective redress are available to all, even to those who have not contributed to bringing the action, meaning that these results can be classified as public goods. The free-rider problem is dominant especially when a collective action is brought in order to obtain injunctions, since once an injunction is given, e.g. as regards noise produced by a dance hall in a heavily populated neighbourhood, no one can be excluded from enjoying the benefits of the injunction. In the case of compensatory collective actions the situation may be different, according to the learned author, at least if the *res iudicata* effect of the collective action only applies to group members who have participated in the action, and not to others. However, even if non-participants can or will not be excluded from the benefits of these actions, there are possibilities to create incentives to use collective redress mechanisms. These incentives may not be very much needed in cases in which the compensation available for individual group members is high (in these cases, bringing a group action within a short amount of time might also be interesting for individual group members in order to obtain compensation within a reasonable time, given the relatively low costs of such litigation; these group members will opt for a group action instead of an individual action – because especially when the case settles, the benefits might be higher where a group action has been brought than in case of an individual action only), but in low value cases it might be necessary to create so-called club-incentives: those who are involved in the action should receive some additional benefits in comparison to those who profit from the group action but who have not participated.

Professor Szalai also discusses the opt-in and the opt-out systems in collective litigation. He claims that opt-in and opt-out should not be considered as each other's opposites. The actual opposite of an opt-in system is a system in which group membership is established automatically. The author claims that a system with automatic group membership results in the highest settlement awards if such a system does *not* allow parties to leave the group (i.e. opt-out). This is due to the fact that such a settlement is very interesting for the liable party since only in this situation does he know for sure that he will not be confronted with additional individual actions when the case has been settled collectively. The author also underlines that the present trust in representative actions in which non-profit organizations are given standing (this is the case, for example, in Belgium, as emphasized by the contribution on this jurisdiction in the present volume but also in many other jurisdictions) is not justified. Just like profit-making entities, non-profit organizations may have interests that interfere with the interests of those in whose interest the collective action is brought.

**Part II: National Perspectives**

As stated, Part II of the present volume deals with national jurisdictions. Obviously, a distinction could be made between jurisdictions where, at least for the moment, limited progress has been made with the introduction of effective collective redress mechanisms and where often a rather timid sectorial approach is chosen, and jurisdictions that appear to be more successful in introducing solid, often horizontal collective redress mechanisms. Jurisdictions discussed in the present volume that have chosen the timid, sectorial approach (even though the relevant legislation may be 'state of the art') are Belgium, France, Germany, Hungary, Italy and Poland (although the results in practice in the last country are relatively promising). Bolder, horizontal approaches can be found in England & Wales, the Netherlands and Sweden. However, even within the latter group success in the sense of high numbers of court cases is not guaranteed. Sweden, for example, has chosen for a bold, horizontal approach but the number of cases is very limited. Better results were achieved in, for example, the Netherlands.

*Belgium*

As Stefaan Voet from the University of Ghent states in his contribution, until very recently Belgium had no or very limited tools to resolve mass cases. The available injunctive or declaratory collective actions could only be used in the area of consumer protection, the environment, and discrimination and racism, and they were rarely used in practice. A new Belgian Act which entered into force on 1 September 2014 should change this situation. The Act introduced a consumer collective redress action and is accompanied by another Act, also from 2014, concerning the out of court resolution of consumer disputes (meant to implement the EU Consumer ADR Directive). Obviously, in Belgium one has opted for a sectorial approach, but after the evaluation of the Act in 2017 the number of areas covered by the Act might be enlarged. In this sense, Belgium is following the example of France and Germany, which also will consider enlarging the ambit of their collective redress mechanisms after an evaluation in the near or not so near future. Interestingly, Dr Voet argues that this sectorial approach may be found problematic by the Belgian Constitutional Court since it may qualify this approach as constitutional discrimination. If indeed the Belgian Constitutional Court were to qualify this approach as such, this might be an example in Europe of a Constitutional Court facilitating collective redress mechanisms instead of hampering their development, for example by arguing that opt-out systems are against the constitutional guarantee of access to justice, an argument that the Amsterdam Court of Appeal is unwilling to accept, claiming that opt-out mechanisms are – when certain requirements are met – in line with the requirements of Article 6 of the European Convention on Human Rights (it should be noted that the Netherlands, like the United Kingdom, does not have a constitutional court).

The new Belgian collective action is a representative action in the sense that only consumer associations and authorized non-profit organizations, of which the statutory aim corresponds with the collective harm, have standing in court. The Belgian Consumer Ombudsman Service only has standing to initiate a collective action and to negotiate a collective settlement. If a settlement cannot be reached, and the court has to decide the merits of the case, a consumer association has to step in to continue the procedure. The Belgian law has opted for what Stefaan Voet calls 'ideological plaintiffs' such as non-profit organizations, since they have 'no private cause of action or grievance against the defendant' and will thus focus only on the interests of the group. Whether indeed this choice can be applauded, as the learned author claims, is a matter of debate, especially when taking into consideration what has been stated in the Law & Economics contribution by Professor Szalai in Part I of this volume.

In Belgium, the lawmaker has realized that for collective redress mechanisms to work well, courts need to be specialized. Therefore, the courts in Brussels have been given exclusive jurisdiction in these matters. Unfortunately, the Brussels Court of Appeal, where most cases will end up according to the author, is a court with considerable backlogs, and therefore one may already start to worry about the successes in actual practice of the new Belgian Act, especially taking into consideration the findings of Professor Uzelac in the first part of this volume.

Apart from this worrying aspect of the new Belgian scheme, other elements look promising. Fortunately from the perspective of success in practice and contrary to the EC Recommendation, opting-in is not the default rule for group actions in Belgium. Stefaan Voet states, 'In its certification decision, the Belgian court can freely choose between an opt-in or opt-out system', with the exception of cases where the class members are not residing in Belgium; in that case only an opt-in regime is allowed.

Very complicated and rather bureaucratic is the enforcement of a collective settlement or a decision on the merits of the case in Belgium under the supervision of a collective claims settler. Again, this is one of the weak points of the Belgian Act.

Although Dr Voet holds that Belgium is a European front runner in collective consumer redress, this might only be true on paper and not in actual practice, as is also acknowledged by the learned author.

*England & Wales*

According to the learned author of the contribution on England & Wales, Professor Neil Andrews from Cambridge, England knows several types of multi-party litigation: test case litigation, representative proceedings and Group Litigation Orders. The fourth mechanism mentioned by Professor Andrews, the consolidation and joinder of co-claimants, would in most jurisdictions only be considered to be a 'surrogate' for collective redress, and therefore we will not discuss it here.

The test case procedure is available for public bodies which have 'legal power disinterestedly to seek legal declarations (or other relief) on behalf of the community or segments of it'. Test case procedures result in a stay of individual lawsuits until the High Court has issued a decision in the test case. This decision may give rise to appeals to the Court of Appeal and the Supreme Court, and this may, at least for foreign observers, appear to be a problematic aspect of this procedure in light of the duration of the proceedings (similar observations can be made about the test case ('model case') procedure in Germany; see below).

The other two collective redress mechanisms in England & Wales are not without flaws either. In representative proceedings the representative claimant brings an action on behalf of himself and others (these others are known as 'the represented class'). The members of the represented class will not become parties to the action but they will enjoy the benefits of a *res iudicata* decision and are bound by it unless they opt out. Representative proceedings for pecuniary relief do not occur frequently and most cases are brought to obtain a declaratory judgment or injunctions. This may change in the future due to a change in traditional restrictive case law concerning the requirement 'where more than one person has the *same interest* in a claim' (emphasis added). The new case law allows more cases to be brought by way of a representative action and as a result the Group Litigation Order discussed below may become less popular in the future according to Professor Andrews.

The Group Litigation Order was introduced in 2000 and can be defined as 'an order to provide for the case management of claims which give rise to common or related issues of fact or law'. It is currently popular for the recovery of pecuniary claims, but this may change due to the abovementioned relaxation of case law as regards representative proceedings. The procedure is started by the court's approving the order and by its ratification. Subsequently, interested parties may opt in. By doing so, they will become full-fledged parties to the action. The court will exercise extensive case management powers and, in the event the group loses, all members of the group will be liable for their 'share of the common costs of the proceedings and for any individual costs specifically incurred' with respect to their claim. When they win, however, they can recover their costs due to the applicability of the loser pays principle. The number of Group Litigation Orders that have been issued to date is limited (when Professor Andrews wrote his contribution to this volume 63 GLO's had been issued, but currently this number has risen to 81), which may amongst other things be due to problems with funding and the presence of an opt-in system instead of the more efficient opt-out system as was adopted in some other common law jurisdictions. According to the editors of this volume, it is for this reason unfortunate that a proposal for the introduction of a generic opt-out class action in England for compensatory claims was opposed by the British Government in 2009.

*France*

The French story of collective redress is rather gloomy. According to Professor Ferrand, it can be characterized as a story of 'stillborn reforms'. Whether things will be different with the recent Act that was adopted in 2014 is yet to be seen, but prospects are not encouraging. The Act introduces collective redress for the compensation of damage caused to the collective interests of consumers only and in some cases also for the compensation of individual harm, and is an example of a rather timid sectorial approach to matters. Also, the procedure is rather complicated, only approved consumer associations with often limited means may bring the action, while the effective opt-out system is rejected. Sadly, it may be doubted whether this reform will indeed increase the international legal competitiveness of France as is hoped by the French Government. It might first of all be a reaction against developments in other EU Member States, notably the Netherlands, which have expanded the collective redress mechanisms extensively internationally. After all, Professor Ferrand states that the French Government is of the opinion that a French model of group litigation should be built 'in order to avoid that national disputes be indirectly dealt with by foreign courts pursuant to rules that would not necessarily be compatible with the principles of the French legal system'.

The 2014 Act introduces what is called an 'action de groupe'. The qualification of the new collective redress mechanism is problematic, but it can most likely best be qualified as an 'action de substitution' (this qualification was made by E. Jeuland), although there is discussion about this issue in France. The action is brought by an approved national consumer association and it consists of 'exercising the individual actions of the (not yet known) substituted consumers'. The consent of these consumers is not needed. The scope of the action is rather limited: it covers the financial damage suffered by consumers (natural persons) as a result of illegal practices of a professional. There is no national register of these group actions, and no preliminary stage for certification. Whether or not the action is admissible is determined in the judgment on liability.

Professor Ferrand mentions that the opt-in approach of the Act is criticized in France. She refers to the model code of the Instituto Ibero-americano de Derecho Procesal for an alternative approach, where group members will only be subject to the judgment in the group action if the court admits the claim (*res iudicata secundum eventum litis*). Another approach would be to allow a new group action where the first action was rejected because of lack of relevant evidence (*res iudicata secundum eventum probationem*).

*Germany*

For some readers it may be surprising that just as in France, the approach to collective redress in Germany is rather timid. According to Michael Bakowitz, who is a fellow at the Max Planck Institute for International, European and Regulatory

Procedural Law in Luxemburg, there are currently two sectorial mechanisms in place, the so-called association suit or (in German) *Verbandsklage* and the Capital Markets Model Case Act (KapMug) which provides for test case proceedings or, as the Germans have it, model case proceedings.

The association suit is an action brought by an association on behalf of a group of victims and was introduced in 1976. By way of this action, prohibitory injunctions can be obtained. Only in competition cases does the association suit allow for additionally claiming that the undertaking suspected of infringements surrenders the economic benefits obtained at the expense of consumers or competitors. If the claim is successful, this money is *not* used for the benefit of those who have brought the action, but is paid into the federal budget which, to say the least, may not serve as an incentive to bring the association suit. Therefore, Mr Bakowitz holds that in practice the association suit is mostly used to obtain prohibitory injunctions.

The other collective redress mechanism in Germany, the KapMug, was introduced on 1 November 2005. Originally it contained a sunset clause of 1 November 2010, which has been expanded to 1 November 2020. During this (very long) period (the German legislator seems to be extremely cautious) the Act is being tested and for the time being it only covers damages regarding wrong or misleading public capital markets information. According to Mr Bakowitz, this might change at the end of the period allowed for testing since it has been announced that in case of positive results horizontal model proceedings might be introduced.

The procedure is complicated, usually takes a very long period of time and consists of three stages at different courts of law. The first stage takes place at the Regional Court or *Landgericht*. In an individual lawsuit for damages, a party (claimant or defendant) may ask for the commencement of a test case. This application is published in a complaints registry on the Internet and nine other claimants have to join the application. If the necessary requirements are met, the Regional Court will submit a specific subject matter to the competent Higher Regional Court or *Oberlandesgericht*. In the second stage, the Higher Regional Court will select a model claimant, decide on the matter and issue a binding ruling. Injured parties with pending lawsuits in other courts may register their claims, resulting in periods of prescription to stop running. Finally, in the last stage, cases are dealt with on an individual basis at the Regional Court, taking into consideration the binding ruling of the Higher Regional Court.

The KapMug allows neither opting-in nor opting-out even though initially the nine claimants who need to join the application for a model case ruling clearly have to opt in. However, once this is done and the case is being dealt with at the Higher Regional Court, other pending cases that concern the same subject matter are stayed automatically (this may be qualified as automatic group membership without an option to opt out; see the contribution of Professor Szalai in this volume). Given the long duration of the proceedings, this may be problematic for them.

Finally, it should be mentioned that the model claimant and model defendant may also make a proposition for a settlement or the court itself may suggest a settlement. This settlement is valid for all those who have joined the model case, but this only if less than 30 per cent of them decide to opt out of the settlement. Mr Bakowitz, however, notes that '[i]t is another question whether the model defendant will agree to a settlement when it has to expect ongoing proceedings with up to 30 per cent of the claimants'.

All in all, it is rather doubtful whether indeed the KapMug will be successful. Especially the rather complicated procedure, the absence of the possibility to opt in or to opt out, the long duration of the proceedings and the limited number of decided cases appear to be rather problematic, at least to the editors of this volume.

*Hungary*

In her contribution to this volume, Professor Viktória Harsági from Budapest states that multi-party litigation is sporadic in Hungary. It is only available vertically in certain sectors and then only by way of an *actio popularis*. The number of organizations that may bring these actions is limited and established by law. Apart from representative actions, there is no alternative in Hungary other than the traditional means of joinder of parties or joinder of actions and the assignation of claims. The author, who in her contribution to this volume discusses the available representative actions in Hungary in detail, is currently involved in drafting legislation to change this situation and advocates a comparative approach while paying attention to the particularities of the Hungarian legal system and an opt-out system in cases where the value at stake per individual is low. The author claims, however, that the basic model in Hungary should be based on the opt-in model. The only problem could be that the Hungarian Judiciary might not be able to face the challenges of multi-party litigation, something that especially appears from the contribution of Professors Tihamér Tóth and Pál Szilágyi from Budapest, a contribution that seems to prove several of the statements of Professor Uzelac in Part I of the present volume.

The learned authors claim that there are serious concerns in Hungary about American-style class actions. Collective redress in competition cases in Hungary tries to avoid the perceived problems with American-style collective litigation. The representative action that may be brought in Hungary in such cases can only be instituted by the Hungarian Competition Authority, and both injunctions and damages may be claimed. Only a single case has been litigated so far. The authors claim that the situation will not improve after Hungary has implemented the EU Directive on Cartel Damages, and they identify the lack of opt-out class actions and the absence of contingency fees as a problem. Additionally, they note that Hungarian courts are inexperienced in the application of EU or Hungarian competition law, and even if they had experience the procedural rules and the legal environment do not really favour group litigation in competition cases. Apparently, Hungary belongs to the group of countries identified as problematic by Professor Alan Uzelac in his contribution in Part I of this volume, which is underlined by the statement of the authors that especially the slow pace of litigation in Hungary is a problem where it concerns follow-on competition litigation: it takes years to reach a final decision. Hungarian courts will certainly not be favoured in matters of international collective redress according to the authors. They identify criteria for a positive choice of forum that potential litigants may use: the language capabilities of the judges, the duration of litigation, an understanding of economic reasoning and a positive attitude towards and an understanding of EU law. Professors Tihamér Tóth and Pál Szilágyi claim that these criteria are not met by the Hungarian Judiciary.

*Italy*

Italy originally knew only collective redress mechanisms meant to implement EU law. Although there had been discussions as early as the 1970s, only in the early years of the new millennium were new discussions on the need to introduce group actions for damages started. This resulted in January 2010 in a statute (amended in 2012) regulating what is called a 'class action'(in Italian: *azione di classe*) for consumer cases only (the Italian approach is sectorial). In her contribution, Professor Elisabetta Silvestri from Pavia states that this action (the name of which is a 'glaring misnomer' in her opinion since it has nothing to do with the American class action) is meant for groups of individuals that claim damages as compensation for the harm suffered as a result the wrongdoing of the same defendant. A public class action was also introduced which may be brought against public bodies that do not take action even though they have a duty to act.

In Italy, individual group members may start the class action. Associations and committees may do so as well provided that they have been named by one or more class members as representative of the whole class. The Italian class action is an opt-in procedure, and requires that the individual rights of the consumers are 'homogenous' in nature. The action may also be brought to safeguard collective interests. According to the learned author, it is hard to define what 'homogeneous' interests are, and this is one of the reasons why the Act is difficult to apply. Furthermore, the fact that it provides for an opt-in procedure is according to the author not very class-friendly (few class members opt in), whereas here again appears a problem with class actions that has been identified by Professor Uzelac in his contribution to this volume as detrimental for the success of collective actions (Part I): the excessive length of procedure in Italy in general. As regards statistics, Professor Silvestri provides the following details: 40 class actions have been introduced since 2010. Fifteen were declared inadmissible, 9 admissible, 23 are still pending and only 1 class action has been decided on the merits. It seems that Italian collective redress mechanisms can rightly be described (to borrow terminology of the author) as a series of 'empty boxes'.

The editors realize that by now the reader may have become pessimistic about the future of collective redress in the European Union. Very few successes can be mentioned so far. Therefore, it may be a relief that the Netherlands, which forms the topic of the present section, and Poland, which will be discussed afterwards, provide a more positive story (although the Polish story should be qualified as moderately successful only because of the few successful cases).

*The Netherlands*

In 1994, the Netherlands was one of the first European countries to provide for collective redress by way of an action brought in court. The approach is horizontal in the sense that there are no limits to the type of cases that may be subject to the collective proceedings, although damages may not be asked (currently, however, a legislative proposal is pending to change this situation). A non-profit organization such as a foundation or an association with full legal personality may bring this collective action. The claim is not admissible if 'in the given circumstances' a sufficient attempt to achieve a settlement has not been made. The action is brought in the foundation's or association's own name but nevertheless in the interest of a group. Legal persons under public law are also allowed to bring a collective action. Interestingly, the group members are *not* a party to the action. Therefore, the final judgment in the case does *not* have *res iudicata* effect for them and the Dutch group action can therefore not be qualified as a representative action. Nevertheless, group members may use the judgment as a kind of precedent in their subsequent individual lawsuits, e.g. for damages.

An innovation is the new legislation that introduced a preliminary ruling procedure at the Supreme Court of the Netherlands which is very relevant in case of collective litigation (the procedure is not available in the collective settlement procedure discussed below).

According to Professors van Rhee and Tzankova, the Dutch collective action may be called a success. For a relatively small country with a population of about 17 million inhabitants, the number of collective actions that have been brought since 1994 is large and many of these actions were successful.

Apart from collective litigation, the Netherlands has known a collective settlement procedure since 2005. Again the approach is horizontal and not sectorial. Within the procedure, natural or legal persons having caused harm and a foundation or association (or the Consumer Authority) representing the interests of those who have suffered harm may reach an agreement which can be submitted to the Court of Appeal in Amsterdam (only a single court is competent to allow for specialization) in order to have it sanctioned as an agreement binding for all who have suffered harm in the context of the agreement (except for those who decide to opt out). This has to be done by way of a mutual petition of the organization(s) acting in the interest of the victims and the natural or legal person(s) being responsible for the harm. The submission of the petition to the court stops periods of prescription from running. At the request of the party from whom damages are being claimed the Amsterdam Court of Appeal may decide to stay pending individual actions for damages, including those which are started during the collective settlement procedure.

Again according to Professors van Rhee and Tzankova, the Dutch collective settlement procedure can be described as successful. Soon the eighth largest case might be settled by way of the 2005 collective settlement procedure, and a number of these settlements have also provided the necessary relief for foreign parties who might not have been able to obtain redress at home due to the lack of effective collective redress mechanisms (this progressive attitude of the Dutch Judiciary has, ironically, given rise to concern in other European jurisdictions where effective collective redress mechanisms are not available).

It is important to note that Dutch collective redress procedures should not be looked at in isolation. Although until now collective litigation cannot result in an award of damages (as stated, this may change in the near future), the judgment resulting from such litigation may help parties in subsequent individual litigation for damages (or in litigation after the assignment of claims to a third party) and may also be an incentive for reaching an individual or a collective settlement, the latter being certified - as stated - by the Amsterdam Court of Appeal.

*Poland*

Poland introduced an Act on group actions in 2010. Apparently, the Polish legislator was not as bold as his Dutch counterpart, since Polish group actions only cover specifically defined categories of cases. This was not the original idea, but limitations were introduced in the discussions resulting in the new Act. Consequently, group actions are now only available in Poland when they concern consumer protection, liability for damage caused by a dangerous product and claims arising from prohibited acts (torts). Further requirements for admissibility are that the claims be of the same type, be brought by at least 10 persons and arise from the same or an identical factual basis. Pecuniary claims are also allowed. In this event unification of the amounts claimed is needed but if unification is not possible, a group action is still possible, but then only for establishing liability. An opt-in approach is chosen since it is felt in Poland that an opt-out approach would not be in line with the right of access to court as encompassed by the Polish Constitution (as stated above, whether this is also problematic from the perspective of the European Convention on Human Rights is doubtful; in Strasbourg, an opt-out mechanism might not be considered to be problematic for access to justice).

The action needs to be brought by a representative of the group, and this can be a group member or a District Consumer Advocate when it concerns claims related to consumer protection. There is a preliminary stage in which the admissibility of the group action is considered. The group action is announced in the Polish national mass media and indicates up to what point in time potential group members can join the group. The group representative (on whom the members of the group have to agree) is responsible for compiling a list of persons who have joined the group. Group members may decide to opt out up until a decision on the composition of the group is issued by the competent court.

From the chapter by Professor Kulski in this volume one may conclude that the Polish Act has proven to be moderately successful. In the period 2010-2013, 102 group actions were filed. Forty-one of them were unsuccessful. Most of the other cases are still pending and up to now claimants have been successful in only a few court decisions.

*Sweden*

In Sweden, group actions were introduced in 2003. Sweden has chosen a horizontal approach in the sense that group actions are available for all civil cases that can be brought before the general first instance courts as well as for those cases concerning environmental damage which can be brought before the environmental courts.

Three types of group actions can be distinguished in Sweden according to Professor Laura Ervo: private or individual group actions, public or governmental group actions and actions brought by consumer organizations (these last actions will not be discussed here). Private group actions are brought by an individual that is a natural or legal person who is a member of the group concerned. Public group actions are available in cases where no private group action has been brought. In that situation, the Consumer Ombudsman may bring a public group action or, in environmental cases, the conservation authorities. Private group actions are favoured in Sweden since public group actions are only allowed if no private group action has been brought in a particular case.

According to Professor Ervo, Swedish group actions can be defined as actions brought by a plaintiff as the representative of several persons who will be bound by the judgment even though they will not become parties to the suit. An opt-in mechanism is used, and group actions are only available for small claims cases even though the definition of a small claim seems to be flexible. The following criteria are amongst those that need to be met for bringing a group action: (1) the action is founded on circumstances that are common or of a similar nature, (2) the claims of the group members do not differ substantially from each other, (3) a majority of claims cannot be pursued equally well in the individual lawsuit, (4) the group has an appropriate size and is properly defined, and (5) the plaintiff is the appropriate person to represent the members of the group, also in light of his financial situation. Enforcement of a judgment in group litigation is the task of the group members and not of their representative. The enforcement procedure is qualified as bureaucratic by Professor Ervo.

Finally, it should be mentioned that friendly settlement and mediation are allowed in group actions in Sweden, but Professor Ervo states that it seems that the Swedish legislator has not put much effort into this.

The number of cases that have been subject to group litigation is very small: to date only 17 cases can be mentioned. Therefore it seems that the Swedish approach to group actions has not been as effective as was hoped (albeit more effective than in another Nordic country, Finland, where only public group actions brought by the Consumer Ombudsman are allowed and where, according to Professor Ervo, to date no (!!) group actions have been brought even though group actions have been available since 2007 in that country). Various reasons for this can be mentioned, for example funding problems and the choice for an opt-in mechanism. It seems that as regards the latter issue the Swedish legislator should pay attention to Professor Per Hendrik Lindblom from Uppsala, who once stated, 'Opt-in is out and opt-out is in', which, perhaps, might be phrased differently in light of the various contributions to this volume as, 'Opt-in *should* be out and opt-out *should* be in'. However, in light of the general attitude towards group actions in the majority of EU Member States, this is probably only a consummation, devoutly to be wished.

**Final Remarks**

Within the European Union, limited progress has been made with the introduction of effective collective redress mechanisms. Many EU Member States opt for a sectorial approach only and plaintiff-friendly opt-out mechanisms (or a combination of opt-in and opt-out mechanisms) are not very popular. Recovery of damages by way of collective litigation is often not available. The incentives for bringing collective actions are usually limited and frequently only non-profit representative entities have standing, which is especially problematic if these entities do not have the means to fulfil their tasks as for example consumer organizations. Funding of collective redress litigation in general is a problem, since many of the more 'creative' ways of financing such litigation are considered to be inappropriate in Europe (e.g. contingency fees, although this might change in the future given the fact that some European Union Member States are currently embracing this concept due to the fact that publicly funded legal aid systems have become unaffordable). In Europe, the sometimes unjustified belief in the blessings of the enforcement of rights by public authorities (a strong belief in the State) also hinders the development of effective private enforcement mechanisms. As a result of these and other reasons many EU Member States currently have collective redress mechanisms that sometimes look good on paper but that are not used very often in actual practice. Under these circumstances one would expect the European Union to take the lead in developing more vigorous collective redress mechanisms. Unfortunately, the opposite is true. When considering the latest European initiatives in this field one cannot be but disappointed in what has been produced. The Recommendation on Collective Redress is so cautious that it will most likely not produce any positive effect. It should for example have provided real alternatives for the opt-out mechanisms that many EU Member States dislike, but instead it advocates the often not so effective opt-in mechanism. Even worse is the Directive on Cartel Damages which in a way discourages private enforcement for the sake of encouraging public enforcement mechanisms. Therefore, states that are thinking about reforming their legal system and introducing effective collective redress mechanisms should in our opinion not look too hopefully at the EU for guidance, but would do better to study successful collective redress mechanisms available in the world at large. Obviously, the American class action is problematic in a variety of respects, but it deserves more serious attention than the superficial expressions of dislike which one often encounters. Furthermore, attention to developments in EU Member States that have succeeded in introducing effective collective redress mechanisms may be worthwhile. Studying black letter law only should be avoided since there are obviously no guarantees that mechanisms that look good on paper do actually work in practice. Instead, empirical studies are needed. Unfortunately, the number of such studies to date is limited. Ideally, empirical studies should not only focus on the collective redress mechanisms themselves but should also focus on the legal environment in which they have to function. Collective redress will not blossom in an environment where courts are not able to process ordinary individual lawsuits in an efficient and timely manner and where relevant knowledge of complex legal issues is missing. Unfortunately, there are still too many of these jurisdictions in the European Union and coordinated action is needed to change this situation. For collective redress the best option might be to concentrate these cases at specialized courts which are manned by judges that are enthusiastic about collective redress and that are provided with incentives to handle these cases successfully based on clear legislation that avoids vague concepts such as 'homogeneous claims' and the like. But, obviously, this needs more than a timid

European Recommendation on collective redress and a European Directive that hinders collective litigation.

# PART I: EU & USA

B. Hess

# EUROPEAN PERSPECTIVES ON COLLECTIVE LITIGATION

## 1. Introduction: Regulating Collective Redress in the European Union

One of the most controversial debates in the field of the European law of civil procedure relates to collective redress. This topic has been on the agenda of the EU Commission since the 1980s. At this time, several specific EU instruments on consumer protection prescribed the introduction of collective action brought by consumer associations. In 1998, the European Union adopted Directive 98/27/EC on injunctions for the protection of consumers' interests.[1] This comprehensive instrument was aimed at facilitating cross-border injunctive relief against infringements harmful to the collective interests of consumers.

However, after the millennium the EU Commission engaged in the preparation and elaboration of legislative instruments on collective redress mechanisms aimed at the compensation of damages. This discussion started in the context of cartel law. In 2003, the EU Commission (DG Comp) commissioned the famous Ashurst Study on the conditions of claims for damages in case of infringement of EC competition rules which drew a picture of the redress systems in Europe as 'one of astonishing diversity and total underdevelopment'.[2] This study triggered a heated debate on the pros and cons of collective litigation and of private enforcement in the European Union.[3] In this chapter, I do not want to reiterate the numerous initiatives, studies, consultations and impact assessments, the Green and White Papers on cartel damages, on consumer protection and on collective redress which have been published during the last years.[4] For political scientists, the never ending story of introducing collective redress mechanisms at the EU level will serve as an interesting example of the influence of different stakeholders and powerful lobby groups in European lawmaking.

1 *OJ* 1998 L166/51.
2 Ashurst Study 2004, p. 1.
3 *Cf.* Hodges 2014, p. 68 *et seq.*
4 A brief description is found in the EU Commission's Communication on Collective Redress of 11 June 2013, COM(2013) 401 final, p. 4-7.

The political debate at the European level must be seen against the backdrop of legal developments in the EU Member States on the one hand and of developments at the transatlantic level on the other hand. Let's briefly look at the national level: During the last decade, most Member States reformed their respective domestic procedures and introduced – heterogeneous – collective redress procedures. In some Member States, these mechanisms were primarily based on opt-in mechanisms, although other Member States[5] (still a minority) took up the American model which is based on opt out and entrepreneurial lawyering. However, the situation in Europe is mainly marked by the intervention of public bodies like ombudsmen and by the involvement of consumer protection associations. Consequently, most of the EU Member States strongly favour the involvement of qualified bodies in collective redress mechanisms.

At the transatlantic level, European businesses experienced the 'nightmare' of being a defendant in class-action litigation in the United States. These lawsuits were considered and described more or less as a kind of legal blackmail.[6] Yet, the first negative experiences in the late 1990s must be distinguished from the legal developments in the last decade: According to recent case-law of the US Supreme Court (*Morrison*[7] and *Kiobel*),[8] forum shopping to the US is not an easy task and so-called F-cub class actions are permitted only in exceptional circumstances. However, it must be stated that the political discussion in Europe on the introduction of collective redress mechanisms was mainly influenced by the model of the American class action.[9]

In June 2013, the debate on collective redress and on private enforcement in Europe came to a provisional end when the EU Commission issued two legislative proposals: one for a Directive on the Compensation of Cartel Damages[10] and another one for a Recommendation on Collective Redress.[11] Compared to the initial approaches, the final proposals of the EU Commission cannot be considered as ambitious legislative undertakings – at first sight, it appears that the EU Commission largely renounced to its initial ambition of introducing a modern and comprehensive legislative instrument of collective redress and took a step back.

In the political debate, the documents of June 2013 have triggered mixed reactions. A first comment described the Recommendation as 'a squeaking mouse

5 Mainly Portugal and the Netherlands.

6 *Cf.* Behrendt & Freiin von Enzberg 2014, p. 253 *et seq.*; Van den Bergh 2013, p. 26 *et seq.*

7 *Morrison v National Australia Bank Ltd.*, 561 U.S. 247 (2010).

8 *Kiobel v Royal Dutch Petroleum Co.*, 133 S.Ct. 1659 (2013).

9 Buxbaum 2013, p. 1443 *et seq.*

10 Proposal for a Directive of the European Parliament and of the Council on certain rules governing actions for damages under national law for infringements of the competition law provisions of the Member States and of the European Union, COM(2013) 404 final of 11 June 2013.

11 Commission Recommendation of 11/06/2013 on common principles for injunctive and compensatory collective redress mechanisms in the Member States concerning violation of rights granted under Union Law, *OJ* 2013 L201/60.

hurrying over the floor of the EU Commission, frightening no one'[12] and *Chris Hodges* from Oxford asked the question of whether the Recommendation was a 'breakthrough or damp squib'[13] (and I would assume that he tends rather to the second alternative). However, positive reactions came from the business world[14] – this is no surprise as the final legislative initiative of the EU Commission adopted a cautious and even non-binding approach: the directive on cartel damages replaces the concept of private enforcement by a concept giving preference to public enforcement and with regard to collective redress, the EU Commission refrained from proposing any binding legal instrument.

Before making an assessment of the recent proposals, I would like to briefly present the EU Commission's documents.

## 2. The EU Commission's Package of 11 June 2013

The EU Commission's proposals consist of a package of three linked documents: First, a sectorial proposal for a Directive on Cartel Damages (focusing in particular on issues of evidence and of substantive law), and, second, a Recommendation on Common Principles for collective redress which is, thirdly, accompanied by a 'Communication on a Horizontal Framework for Collective Redress'.

The proposed Directive on cartel damages[15] deals primarily with substantive law issues of this specific area of law, as the joint and several liability of the members of the cartel (with the aim of protecting leniency recipients), the passing-on of overcharges,[16] the quantifying of the harm and, finally, the assessment of damages. With regard to procedural law the proposed instrument addresses primarily the access of claimants to information held by public authorities.[17] However, contrary to the main objective of improving the claimants' access to evidence the directive establishes limits to the disclosure of evidence held by public authorities engaged in the public enforcement of EU anti-trust law. This restrictive approach corresponds to the general objective of the instrument which aims at giving a clear preference to the public enforcement of cartel law, at least with regard to follow-on lawsuits for damage claims.[18] Accordingly, the proposal limits the access of private litigants to documents which are considered to be crucial for

12 Goldsmith 2013 – it appears that this author does not know the premises of the EU Commission (DG Justice) in Brussels where a survival of mice seems to be almost impossible.

13 Hodges 2014, p. 67.

14 BDI 2011.

15 Art. 9 of the proposed Directive on certain rules governing actions for damages under national law for the infringements of the competition law provisions, COM(2013) 404 final.

16 As a matter of principle, this defense shall be permitted, see Arts. 12-13 of the draft Directive, COM(2013) 404 final.

17 Arts. 5-8 of the draft Directive, COM(2013) 404 final. The proposed Articles are mainly based on the structure of the Enforcement Directive 2004/48/EU.

18 Similarly, para 33 of the Recommendation on Collective Redress (2013/396/EU) states that 'collective redress actions should, as a general rule, only start after any proceeding of the public authority.'

leniency programs and settlements proceedings.[19] Furthermore, it intends to protect leniency recipients in the context of joint liability by providing for a kind of immunity.[20] As a result, the access of victims of cartel infringements to information obtained in the course of the administrative proceedings will be considerably limited.[21] Finally, the EU Commission refrains from making any binding proposal on the introduction of collective redress mechanisms in the sector of cartel damages by giving preference to a horizontal framework of collective redress mechanisms in all areas of EU law as addressed in the Recommendation of the same day.[22]

With regard to collective redress mechanisms, the Recommendation (2013/396/EU) provides for a set of definitions and of common principles for both injunctive and compensatory relief. The starting point of the instrument is twofold. According to its first operative paragraph (No. 1), the purpose of the Recommendation is to 'facilitate access to justice ... while ensuring appropriate procedural safeguards to avoid abusive litigation.' Obviously, the EU Commission tries to balance the interests of the parties involved, but the focus seems to be more on the avoidance of abuses by setting 'safeguards' than on facilitating collective redress.[23] The Recommendation contains legislative guidelines for the Member States with regard to the enactment of collective redress procedures in their respective procedural systems.[24] It provides for a set of definitions of different collective redress instruments (para 3: 'collective redress', 'mass harm situation',[25] 'representative action' etc.) aimed at delineating the scope of the instrument. The next part contains common principles to injunctive and compensatory collective redress with regard to 'standing' (paras 4 7), 'admissibility' (paras 6-9), the dissemination of information on pending actions (paras 10-12), reimbursement (according to the 'loser pays'-principle), funding (paras 14-16) and standing in cross-border cases (paras 17-18).[26] The subsequent section addresses briefly injunctive collective redress urging expedient and efficient procedures (paras 19-

19 According to the case-law of the ECJ, the conflicting interests must be balanced, ECJ, case C-360/09, *Pfleiderer*, ECR 2011 I-5161, para 24; case C-536/11, *Bundeswettbewerbsbehörde v Donauchemie* (nyr), paras 29 *et seq*.

20 Art. 11(2) of the draft directive, COM(2013) 404 final.

21 Arts. 5-8 of the draft directive, COM(2013) 404 final.

22 The introduction of collective redress was a major objective of the Green Paper on Cartel Damage Claims of 2005, *supra* at fn. 4.

23 However, the general presumption that collective litigation might be 'abusive' seems to be too far reaching.

24 *Cf.* Recommendation on Collective Redress (2013/96/EU), No 2: 'Member States should ensure that the collective redress procedures are fair, equitable, timely and not prohibitively expensive.'

25 The definition of a 'mass harm' (para 3(b)) is obviously misleading as it describes a 'mass harm' as a situation where two (sic!) or more natural or legal persons suffered harm. Here the Recommendation does not sufficiently delineate the joinder of proceedings and mass torts.

26 Surprisingly, the Recommendation addresses the relationship to the Brussels I Regulation in very general terms. No. 3.7. of the Communication states that 'the existing rules (...) should be fully exploited.' It goes without saying that this statement does not sufficiently address the difficulties of cross border collective relief, see Hess 2010a, p. 116 *et seq*.

20).[27] With regard to compensatory collective redress, Sec. V of the recommendation strongly advertises the introduction of opt-in instruments (paras 21-23), encourages settlements (paras 25-28), prohibits contingency fees (para 30) and punitive damages (para 31) and corresponding third party funding (para 32). Finally, the Recommendation provides that follow-on actions in cartel law should be commenced after the definite closure of the respective administrative proceedings (paras 33-34).

In contradiction with its title, the Recommendation does not provide for general principles of collective redress, and rather contains a kind of legislative toolbox aimed at assisting the Member States in implementing national procedures. With regard to the political preference, the EU Commission considerably changed its original strategy: The current proposal strongly prefers public enforcement – even to the detriment of private enforcement by collective actions.[28] Against this backdrop, one may wonder whether the EU Commission finally abandoned its initial preference of promoting private enforcement and refrained from proposing a mandatory instrument implementing collective redress mechanisms.[29] Obviously, the resistance of many national governments, of the EU Parliament[30] and the diversity of the national systems prevented a top down approach to collective redress. However, the Regulation provides for a restricted model of collective redress based on the standing of representative entities, opt in and a strict control of the funding of collective litigation. All in all, the new legislative approach seems to be defendant oriented and, therefore, too reluctant in promoting effective collective redress mechanisms. It may turn out that Member States will implement more effective instruments incompatible with the 'principles' of the Recommendation.[31]

## 3. The New Legislative Approach

### 3.1. *Public v Private Enforcement*

The most important shift of the EU Commission's policy relates to the relationship of private and public enforcement. According to the Communication the proposed legislative parcel is clearly aimed at 'protecting public enforcement' and at strengthening the position of public authorities, especially when negotiating

27 Injunctive collective relief is already addressed by the Directive 2009/22/EC, *OJ* 2009 L110/30.

28 Explicitly paras 33 and 34. According to Recital 22, follow-on lawsuits for damage do not implement public interests and do not serve the purpose of enforcing EU law: 'Moreover, in the case of collective actions following a decision by a public authority (follow-on actions), the public interest and the need to avoid abuse can be presumed to have been taken into account already by the public authority as regards the finding of a violation of Union law.'

29 This equally demonstrates strong influence of lobbying groups in Brussels and Strasbourg.

30 European Parliament Resolution of 2 February 2012 on 'Towards a Coherent European Approach to Collective Redress' (2011/2089(INI)).

31 One example is the Dutch Act on Collective Settlements which serves as a model for similar redress procedures in other EU Member States, Tzankova & Van Lith 2012, paras 4.37 *et seq.* See also the contribution of Van Rhee & Tzankova in the present volume.

leniency in order to protect cooperative businesses which were involved in cartels.[32] However, favouring public enforcement seems to be questionable with regard to the capacity of public authorities to efficiently sanction infringements of cartel law. As the practice and the debates during the last decade demonstrate, national authorities usually do not dispose of sufficient working power to investigate and to sanction infringements of cartel law. On the other hand, the deterrent effect of follow-on lawsuits for damages should not be underestimated. Thus, the underlying policy of the EU Commission does not seem to me entirely convincing. It remains to be seen whether the ECJ will equally adopt this approach. At present, there is a preliminary reference pending at the Court where the referring court openly addressed issues of private enforcement in the context of the Brussels I Regulation.[33]

It appears that the present proposal was mainly influenced by recent case-law of the ECJ on the disclosure of evidence obtained by public authorities to the parties in civil litigation.[34] As a result, the balance seems to go too far in the direction of favouring public enforcement. The EU Commission seems to fear and tends to prevent adverse effects of civil litigation on pending administrative proceedings. However, the proposed directive on cartel damages not only precludes claimants and courts from information obtained in the administrative proceedings, but also impedes negotiations (and settlements) between the claimants and the 'whistleblower' (who might also be inclined to provide for information to the claimants). In this respect, the 'double shielding' of undertakings granting immunity from fines by an authority with regard to information and with regard to liability does not appear to balance appropriately the conflicting interests of the victim and the tortfeasors. Victims of cartel infringements should be able to obtain the full compensation of their damages – in this respect the proposed regime of limited liability of the 'whistleblower' imposes a heavy burden on the potential claimants who cannot longer freely seek compensation from all members of the cartel.

## 3.2. *Horizontal and Sectorial Approaches*

The second shift of the EU Commission's policy with regard to collective redress relates to the adoption of a horizontal approach.[35] Initially, the EU Commission proposed a sectorial instrument for collective redress in cartel damage cases. Since the joint statement of the Commissioners in 2011, the EU Commission preferred a horizontal approach in order to avoid parallel (and contradictory) legislative activities in different DGs.

However, as Chris Hodges correctly pointed out, at the level of the EU Member States a horizontal (or comprehensive) coverage of collective redress

32 Communication, COM(2013) 401 final, at 3.6 (p. 13).

33 Case C-352/13, *CDC Hydrogen Peroxide*.

34 ECJ, case C-360/09, *Pfleiderer*, ECR 2011 I-5161, para 24; case C-536/11, *Bundeswettbewerbsbehörde v Donauchemie* (nyr), paras 29 *et seq*.

35 Positively Behrendt & Freiin von Enzberg 2014, p. 255; reserved Koch 2013, p. 1068 *et seq*.

mechanisms is still an exception. It is found in Sweden, the Netherlands and England (with regard to the group litigation order); and it was discussed in Germany. Yet, the German lawmaker recently declined to extend the German Capital Markets Model Case Act (KapMuG) to other disputes than securities litigation. Compared to the situation in the EU Member States the broad approach of the EU Commission with regard to private enforcement seems to be ambitious and 'top down'.

On the other hand, a sectorial approach (i.e. addressing only cartel damages) might entail positive consequences. An example of a successful expansion of EU law making is the Directive 2004/48/EC on the enforcement of intellectual property rights. This instrument provides for minimum procedural standards regarding the preservation of evidence, access of the parties to (necessary) information; it provides for injunctive relief. Although the scope is limited to proceedings on the infringement of intellectual property rights, it has been extended to other areas as cartel damages.[36] In some of the Member States, the directive even influenced reforms of the national procedures.[37]

The example of the Enforcement Directive does not only demonstrate the virtues of sectorial lawmaking, but also its dangers: The transposition of a legal solution adopted in a very specific area of law is not always the appropriate solution.[38] Furthermore, Member States may be reluctant in accepting innovative sectorial instruments as they fear the extension and the generalisation of an innovative solution to other areas of law.[39] Finally, a legal solution developed for a specific area of law might not be the appropriate tool for a general approach - and, sometimes, the EU Commission might rely on existing provisions for tactical reasons - i.e. to avoid resistance in the Council and the Parliament. Against this backdrop, there are good reasons for a horizontal approach, although the latter entails the adoption of a non-binding instrument by the EU Commission.

### 3.3. *Non-binding and Binding Instruments*

At first sight, the adoption of a non-binding instrument might appear as a step backwards - a non-binding instrument does not oblige the EU Member States to introduce new legislation, nor to adapt existing legislation to the guiding principles

36 Another example of expanding sectorial approaches is found in the Recommendation on Collective Redress (20137396/EU), where recital 23 refers to provisions of the Aarhus Convention on access to information which shall be generally applied to collective redress.

37 E.g. Germany - the Enforcement Directive also influenced the case law on the interpretation of Sec. 142 German Code of Civil Procedure (on the general obligation of parties to give information to the court and to the opponent).

38 The extension of the regulatory concept of the Enforcement Regulation by the Anti-Counterfeiting Trade Agreement (ATCA) was rejected by the European Parliament as this international instrument did not sufficiently balance the diverse interests of the holder of IP rights and the users of the Internet.

39 The discussion on the adoption of an EU instrument on collective redress in cartel damage cases was mainly influenced by concerns regarding the extension of the new instrument to other areas of law.

of the Recommendation. However, the smooth approach of the EU Commission may also entail positive reactions in the Member States as the Recommendation will certainly influence the political debates at the national level. First reactions from the Member States show that at least national ministries closely look at the guiding principles in order to be prepared for future legislative initiatives at the EU level.

Therefore, it would be premature to conclude that the legislative process has come to an end. In fact, it seems to me that the EU Commission, quite to the contrary, carefully changed its political strategy to collective redress, but without giving up its principal ambition. The current instruments must be seen against the backdrop that the term of the Barroso II-Commission will come to an end in the course of 2015 and that the elections of a new EU Parliament took place in May 2014. At present, there is not sufficient time for the initiation of comprehensive legislative initiatives which are considered to trigger controversial political reactions. Consequently, the EU Commission opted for the implementation of a limited instrument on cartel damages and for a comprehensive, non-binding recommendation on collective redress which does not need any adoption by the EU Parliament and the Council.

Moreover, the current preference of the EU Commission for a non-binding instrument does not preclude the implementation of binding instruments at a later stage. This strategy was recently successfully implemented in the field of consumer ADR. In this area of law, the EU Commission initiated in the 1990s two recommendations on minimum procedural and fairness standards for consumer dispute resolution which were finally accepted by all stakeholders.[40] In 2011, the EU Commission made the second and decisive step by proposing a directive for a comprehensive framework on consumer ADR. This directive, which was recently adopted by EU Parliament and Council, endorses the principles of the former recommendations and implements a binding framework for consumer ADR to be provided by the EU Member States. If one looks at the final part of the Recommendation on Collective Redress, there appear some parallels to the Consumer ADR Directive: In the final part of the Recommendation, EU Member States are urged to adopt corresponding domestic remedies and to report within two years their legislative activities to the EU Commission. According to para 41 of the Recommendation (2013/396/EU), the EU Commission will assess the implementation of the instrument and propose further legislative action, if necessary. This provision clearly demonstrates that the EU Commission still envisages further legislative action.

## 4. Left-overs of the EU Commission's Recommendation

### *4.1. Cross-border Collective Redress*

There is one major leftover in the current parcel of the EU Commission: the coordination of cross-border collective relief has not been sufficiently addressed by

[40] Hess 2010b, § 10 VI.

the Recommendation[41] - in this area, further coordination is urgently needed.[42] At present, there is an open and growing competition between several 'market-places' for cross-border collective redress in Europe, especially the Dutch Act on Collective Settlements has become a matter of concern. This instrument is based on the model of the American class action and has been used as a tool for implementing opt-out settlements under the Brussels I Regulation and the Lugano Convention. However, the application of the Brussels I Regulation to court-approved settlements is still an open issue which is also discussed in the context of the English scheme of arrangement. In this area of law, clarification by the European lawmaker seems to be needed. With regard to pre-insolvency proceedings the EU Commission proposed to enlarge the scope of the Insolvency Regulation to these instruments. However, there is at present some resistance in the Council against these proposals - some EU Member States seem to be more inclined to export their national models under the Brussels I Regulation than to elaborate a solution which permits a coordination of the heterogeneous proceedings at the European level. However, maintaining the current situation would entail an increased competition among the judicial systems of EU Member States and an increase of forum shopping[43] - a model which is not in line with the objective of a sound administration of justice and a balanced coordination of the national procedural systems by European instruments.

## 4.2. *An Area Uncovered: Collective Redress and ADR*

Another leftover of the Recommendation can be found in the text of the instrument itself: According to its No. 1, the purpose of the Recommendation is to 'facilitate access to justice and to stop illegal practice and to enable injured parties to obtain compensation in mass harm situations caused by violations of rights granted under Union law.' No. 25 of the Recommendation refers to the Mediation Directive and urges the EU Member States to encourage out of court settlements of mass claims. At first sight, these provisions seem to be convincing: on the one hand, the Recommendation is aimed at the enforcement of EU rights by providing for compensation. On the other hand, mediation has become a recognised tool of dispute resolution in Europe, as the Mediation Directive clearly demonstrates.

Yet, an article in the Frankfurter Allgemeine Zeitung of 5 November 2013[44] demonstrates that the law enforcement and mediation of mass claims are not easy to reconcile. According to this article, the main Austrian consumer association (VKI - *Verein für Konsumenteninformation*) recently settled a major case concerning the sale of life insurance policies (*Swiss Life*) by a German company to Austrian consumers. The Austrian consumer association collected 2,500 claims and filed five

41 The existing legal framework proved to be insufficient as the Brussels I Regulation is suited for two-parties litigation and does not address the coordination of cross-border collective actions, Stefanelli 2012, para 9.05.

42 Hess 2010a, p. 120.

43 Behrendt & Freiin von Enzberg 2014, p. 259.

44 Seiser 2013, p. 15.

parallel lawsuits for around 40 million €. Litigation was funded by Fortis AG, a company specialising in process financing. As proposed by the court, the case was finally settled by a team of mediators. The parties agreed that the damage amounted to 23 million € and settled the case for 11.1 million €. This amount included the costs to be paid to the mediators, the lawyers, the VKI and, finally, around 7 million € were paid out to the individual plaintiffs. The Frankfurter Allgemeine Zeitung called this outcome an elegant resolution of the dispute. This evaluation might correspond to the expectation of the board of the corresponding defendant where an unpleasant case was finally settled for half of the sum due. However, the individual plaintiffs cannot really be happy with this outcome. They only get one third of the real damage and the costs of the mediation amounted to 40 per cent of the sum of the settlement.

In my opinion, this example demonstrates a need for closer scrutiny with regard to the objectives of collective litigation, the proceedings applied and the standards to be respected. The Recommendation seeks the effective enforcement of subjective rights granted by EU law. Its aim is to implement mandatory and binding provisions. However, commercial mediation is about the settlement of individual cases, not the enforcement of mandatory law. The outcome of the *Swiss Life* case demonstrates that the interest of the parties and the judges to bring litigation to an end finally prevailed over the interests of the represented parties who had invested large parts of their income in the policies and were left with only one third of the invested money. From this perspective, I cannot consider the result of the mediation as an 'elegant' outcome, but would urge for a broader discussion about the objectives of collective redress, the procedures to be applied and the results to be expected. In this respect, the Recommendation only offers a potpourri of diverging topics without giving any guidance or indicating any priority. It demonstrates that the introduction of collective redress remedies deserves a thorough preparation and a discussion of the values and objectives of collective litigation, the underlying concepts (private and public enforcement), the procedural tools and the suitability of the judicial system for the implementation of the new proceedings.

## Bibliography

**Ashurst Study 2004**
Ashurst, Study on the conditions of claims for damages in case of infringement of EC competition rules, 31 August 2004, <http://ec.europa.eu/competition/-antitrust/actionsdamages/comparative_report_clean_en.pdf>.

**BDI 2011**
Bundesverband der Deutschen Industrie, 'Stellungnahme. "Kollektiver Rechtsschutz: Hin zu einem kohärenten Ansatz"', 29 April 2011, <www.bdi.eu/download_content/RechtUndOeffentlichesAuftragswesen/Red_Dot_StN_Sammelklagen_final.pdf>.

**Behrendt & Freiin von Enzberg 2014**
Behrendt, P. & Freiin von Enzberg, D., 'Auf dem Weg zur Class Action in Europa?', *Recht der Internationalen Wirtschaft (RIW)*, 2014, p. 253-259.

**Buxbaum 2013**
Buxbaum, H.L., 'Class Actions, Conflict and the Global Economy', in Bruns, A., Kern, C., Münch, J., Piekenbrock, A., Stadler, A. & Tsikrikas, D. (eds.), *Festschrift für Rolf Stürner zum 70. Geburtstag*, Band II, 2013, p. 1443-1454.

**Goldsmith 2013**
Goldsmith, J., 'European Collective Redress', *The Law Gazette*, 20 June 2013.

**Hess 2010a**
Hess, B., 'Cross-border Collective Litigation and the Regulation Brussels I', *Praxis des Internationalen Privat- und Verfahrensrechts (IPRax)*, 2010, p. 116-120.

**Hess 2010b**
Hess, B., *Europäisches Zivilprozessrecht*, Heidelberg: C.F. Müller, 2010.

**Hodges 2014**
Hodges, C., 'Collective Redress: A Breakthrough or a Damp Sqibb?', *Journal of Consumer Policy*, 2014, Vol. 37, p. 67-89.

**Koch 2013**
Koch, H., 'Europäischer kollektiver Rechtsschutz vs. amerikanische, class action': die gebändigte Sammelklage in Europa?', *Wirtschaft und Wettbewerb (WuW)*, 2013, p. 1059-1070.

**Seiser 2013**
Seiser, M., 'Österreich löst die Sammelklagen gegen AWD auf elegante Weise', *Frankfurter Allgemeine Zeitung*, 5 November 2013, p. 15.

**Stefanelli 2012**
Stefanelli, J.N., 'Parallel Litigation and Cross-Border Collective Actions under the Brussels I Framework: Lessons from Abroad', in Fairgrieve, D. & Lein, E. (eds.), *Extra-territoriality and Collective Redress*, Oxford: Oxford University Press, 2012, 9.01-9.72.

**Tzankova & Van Lith 2012**
Tzankova, I. & Van Lith, H., 'Class Actions and Class Settlements Going Global: The Netherlands', in Fairgrieve, D. & Lein, E. (eds.), *Extraterritoriality and Collective Redress*, Oxford: Oxford University Press, 2012, 4.01-4.72.

**Van den Bergh 2013**
Van den Bergh, R., 'Private Enforcement of European Competition Law and the Persisting Collective Action Problem', *Maastricht Journal of European and Comparative Law*, 2013, Vol. 20, p. 12-34.

Gy. Bándi

## ACCESS TO JUSTICE IN ENVIRONMENTAL PROTECTION CASES*

### 1. Class Actions and Environmental Group Actions – Similarities and Specialities

The concept of *class actions* is wide-ranging and covers various types of group procedural devices used before civil courts. According to one authoritative American dictionary of legal usage, a class action is 'a lawsuit instituted by one or more parties on behalf not only of themselves but also of many other parties, when common questions of law and fact are involved'.[1] This is a simple and broad definition, which may encompass very diverse types of actions. The legal setting, the conditions, the parties and the procedures may vary in line with the nature of the dispute. I will not focus on class actions as such below, but only on group litigation in environmental matters, especially as it is known in Europe. First, though, I would like to identify the common roots of environmental group actions in general.

As an example, one may refer to the ongoing European harmonisation process related to some elements of class actions, which is far from being a complete legislative proposal covering all aspects of such actions.

> 5. The current European debate focuses on two areas: consumer redress and competition damages. These two areas are distinct and *different solutions* are needed for each of them. This is because (a) the current arrangements for public and private enforcement differ between those two areas (and any other areas), and (b) evidence of the need for and effectiveness of existing systems is different between each sector.[2]

The Appendix of the above study undoubtedly points to the large pool of variations:

* This chapter was written within the framework of OTKA (Hungarian Scientific Research Fund) research project (registration number K-105559).

1 Garner 1995.

2 Hodges 2010, p. 2.

> There is a considerable variation in the purposes of the class action procedures around the world. For example, some are intended to provide injunctive relief, whilst others are to deliver damages. Some address environmental issues, others address investor protection, or consumer protection, or competition law. These (and many other) different purposes will affect the design of the procedure, and the relevance of the controls and restrictions that are included.[3]

Thus, while some forms of class actions focus on the compensation in money for a loss or damage suffered – sometimes numerous, relatively minor individual cases of loss or damage such as in connection with consumer protection actions – other forms may have a totally different philosophy and turn towards the enforcement of legal requirements on behalf of the public.[4] This latter form is characteristic for the environmental protection actions.

There are many different matters that may be discussed in connection with class actions. A detailed list of topics is given in a recent survey[5] covering 14 so-called 'General Collective Action Safeguards', each of which answers some specific question relating to class actions. From this list, here I mention those that may have some specific significance to environmental protection:

- *the subject matter of claims* is environmental issues and within this our centre of attention is direct intervention, or injunctive relief, and less compensation for loss or damage (i.e. damages), simply because the major interest is the possible reinstatement of the original environmental conditions. Of course this does not mean that there is no way to use class actions in connection with environmentally originated loss or damage, but this option is much closer to the other means and types of redress schemes than to public interest group litigation in connection with an injunction;
- *standing in environmental issues* is mostly restricted to the representation of *public interests* – meaning usually the action of environmental NGOs and sometimes other official representatives of such interests, like the public prosecutor or an ombudsman-type person or organisation. As the subject matter is mostly connected to public interests and not to the aggregate interests of numerous individuals, the focus is also on intervention and not on compensation, plus there is a great need for specific knowledge, etc. – all these arguments support the above delineation of standing;
- *other pathways or procedural options* – such as the different means of ADR – may also appear in connection with environmental protection, but there is less need for a so-called 'pathway prioritisation' in this respect;

3 Hodges & Money-Kyrle 2010, p. 14.
4 See, e.g., Response of European Justice Forum to the Commission Staff Working Document Public Consultation: Towards a Coherent European Approach to Collective Redress (the 'CR Consultation Paper') 29 April 2011, <http://europeanjusticeforum.org/storage/-EJF%20Summary%20Response%20to%20EC%20Consultation%20on%20CR%20.pdf> (last accessed on 7 May 2014).
5 See *supra* note 3.

- we should also look at one of the most challenging issues – whether *the form of procedure* should be an *opt-in* or an *opt-out system*. In public interest environmental actions the question of how to form a group litigation entity[6] is not a core issue, there is no real chance nor need to focus on individual claims. In our understanding, public interest group litigation in the field of environmental law is not simply a summary of plentiful individual claims having the same or similar certification criteria, but *the representation of relatively homogenous public interests*; thus there is no need to join or leave the class, which here means a larger group or the society or even more the environment itself;
- there is a great need for *special expertise* in most environmental actions, which may prolong the proceedings and will also require some assistance in funding the proceedings.

## 2. Modelling Class Actions within the EU

Environmental claims of this type constitute a specific kind of class action. The prospective European collective redress mechanism, as it is highlighted in the European Parliament resolution,[7] takes the following as the starting point: '[W]hen a group of citizens are victims of the same infringement, individual lawsuits may not constitute an effective means of stopping unlawful practices or obtaining compensation, in particular if the individual loss is small in comparison with the litigation costs ...' The resolution also adds the specific enforcement element: '[P]rivate enforcement should only supplement, but not replace, public enforcement ...'

The resolution is the basis of the Commission Communication[8] that, in my understanding, clearly draws a distinction between two major forms of collective redress:

> 1.2. Collective redress is a procedural mechanism that allows, for reasons of procedural economy and/or efficiency of enforcement, many similar legal claims to be bundled into a single court action ... Depending on the type of claim, collective redress can take the form of injunctive relief, where cessation of the unlawful practice is sought, or compensatory relief, aimed at obtaining compensation for damage suffered.

In connection with which, environmental protection is one major example:

> 1.3. In the area of environmental law, the Aarhus Convention requires Member States to ensure access to justice with regard to infringements of environmental standards.

6 Cofee 2000, p. 382-384.

7 European Parliament resolution of 2 February 2012 on 'Towards a Coherent European Approach to Collective Redress' (2011/2089(INI)).

8 Communication from the Commission to the European Parliament, the Council, the European Economic and Social Committee and the Committee of the Regions, 'Towards a European Horizontal Framework for Collective Redress' (COM/2013/0401).

> All Member States thus have procedures in place which allow claimant parties, acting in a collective or representative way, to seek an injunction to stop illegal practices.

No wonder our next focus is on the Aarhus Convention. The Communication takes two arguments as basic reasons to extend such mechanisms. These are access to justice and stronger enforcement of EU law. It is also clear from the Communication that options such as environmental protection are somewhat different from the general conditions of collective redress.[9]

Additionally, there is a clear distinction in connection with legal standing. In the 'general' class action cases, the joint action is brought by a legal representative, agreed - either in an opt-in or in an opt-out system - by the parties themselves. Contrary to this, the other type of actions - 'representative actions' - is different, which needs different guarantees.

> 3.3. Legal standing. A representative damages action is an action which is brought by a representative entity (which in some systems can also be a public authority) on behalf of a defined group of individuals or legal persons who claim to have been harmed by the same alleged infringement. The individuals are not parties to the proceeding; only the representative entity acts on the claimant side. It should therefore be ensured that the representative entity acts genuinely in the best interest of the group represented, and not for own profit.

These actions somehow provide some assurance of those human rights that are reflected - directly or indirectly - in the Charter of Fundamental Rights.[10]

## 3. Right to Environment[11] and Access to Justice

There is a reference to environmental protection already in the Preamble of the Charter, namely to sustainable development and to the interests of future generations. Environmental protection is a part of Title IV on solidarity, although the specific article does not mention 'right' in its definition. The article itself is, rather, a summary of the objectives and principles of environmental protection of the Treaty and does not really resemble a formulation of a right:

9 '3.2. Admissibility of collective redress ... Some collective actions are available for all types of civil damages claims; others are only available for claims concerning damages for alleged breaches of specific legal rules: consumer protection rules, environmental protection, investor protection, competition law, etc.'

10 Decision of the European Parliament, 29 November 2007, on the adoption of the Charter of Fundamental Rights of the EU, *OJ* 2010/C 83/02.

11 'Right to environment' is the basic term which refers to a right whose definition has not yet been universally agreed upon but which is generally used to express acknowledgement of and support for the right of all human beings to enjoy a safe, clean, healthy and sustainable environment.

> Article 37 - Environmental protection. A high level of environmental protection and the improvement of the quality of the environment must be integrated into the policies of the Union and ensured in accordance with the principle of sustainable development.

Although legal certainty and clarity, but also the unambiguity of the concept, would serve the interests of environmental protection better,[12] most probably these principle-like formulations can provide the chance for individuals to argue with the help of these provisions.[13] In any event, the concept of the right, either directly or indirectly, may provide better arguments for developing a class action or collective redress mechanism. The right to environment as a specific right does not appear, however, in the important global - principally UN[14] - and European human rights conventions, but still there are many references to this right, most of them being connected with case law.

The right to environment as a potential human right has also been mentioned by judges of the International Court of Justice, such as Weeremantry in his separate opinion to the *Gabčikovo-Nagymaros* judgment:

> b) Environmental Protection as a Principle of International Law - The protection of the environment is likewise a vital part of contemporary human rights doctrine, for it is a sine qua non for numerous human rights such as the right to health and the right to life itself. It is scarcely necessary to elaborate on this, as damage to the environment can impair and undermine all the human rights spoken of in the Universal Declaration and other human rights instruments.[15]

Nonetheless, the attempts by different UN bodies to find a proper formulation have not resulted in an agreement in this respect. There is nothing more concrete than the set of different studies and resolutions, such as the UN Commission on Human Rights resolution which affirms that 'the protection of the environment and sustainable development can ... contribute to human well-being and potentially to the enjoyment of human rights.'[16] The same consideration has been reaffirmed,[17] but this has not added very much to the outcome of the process.

In Europe, the situation is somewhat more promising due to the fact that there is an active judicial mechanism - the European Court of Human Rights. The ECtHR began to extend first of all Articles 2 and 8 of the European Convention on Human Rights plus Article 1 of the Protocol of 1952 on the right to property to encompass environmental interests. In connection with Article 8 - Right to respect for private

12 See, e.g., Ermacora 2003.
13 Craig 2006, p. 511-512.
14 See, e.g., <www.un.org/en/documents/udhr/> (last accessed on 10 May 2014).
15 Weeremantry 1997.
16 'Human rights and the environment as part of sustainable development', UN Commission on Human Rights, Resolution 2003/71.
17 'Human rights and the environment as part of sustainable development', UN Commission on Human Rights, Resolution 2005/60.

and family life – the first important case proved to be *López Ostra v Spain*,[18] followed by *Guerra and Others v Italy*,[19] *Fadeyeva v Russia*,[20] *Moreno Gomez v Spain*,[21] *Dubestka v Ukraine*[22] and others. All these cases applied Article 8, with some restrictions or conditions – in *Fadeyeva*: '70. Thus, in order to fall within the scope of Article 8, complaints relating to environmental nuisances have to show, firstly, that there was an actual interference with the applicant's private sphere, and, secondly, that a level of severity was attained.' One of the best examples for the use of Article 2 – Right to life – and Article 1 of the Protocol of 1952 is the *Öneryildiz* case.[23] Thus the Court could extend the field of duties of the states in the direction of the protection of the environment and towards the active role of the state.

All these examples may provide a good chance for the implementation of Article 37 of the EU Charter of Fundamental Rights, which is in a better position than the European Convention, having direct references to the environment, although with relative ambiguity. Given the proactive role of the Court of Justice of the European Union (CJEU) in the field of environment, it is very likely that this imprecise formulation may even be implemented if necessary. The situation is much better than in the case of the European Convention, which does not have any direct reference to environmental protection; however, the CJEU simply could not disregard its principal importance.

As we move closer to implementation, probably the most fundamental of all the dilemmas is either to go for the possible substantive content and try to figure out exactly what the right really means or to move towards the procedural guarantees supporting the implementation of the right. Postiglione notes: 'Therefore, with the human right to the environment, whilst the procedural element is clear and extremely important (information, participation and access), it is difficult to define its "substantive" content (such as the "acceptable" quality of the air and water and food).'[24] The same is articulated by other authors, for example Pedersen:

> [T]wo strong trends are emerging in relation to environmental rights in Europe. First, the strong focus on procedural environmental rights to access to information, public participation and access to review procedures at the regional level, as embodied in the jurisprudence from the European Court of Human Rights, the Aarhus Convention, and environmental policy and law from the EC, has led to these rights today enjoying the status of regional customary law. Second ... the recognition of a substantive human

18 *López Ostra v Spain,* Case No. 41/1993/436/515 (ECtHR, 9 December 1994).
19 *Guerra and Others v Italy,* Case No. 116/1996/735/932 (ECtHR, 19 February 1998).
20 *Fadeyeva v Russia,* App. No. 55723/00 (ECtHR, 9 June 2005).
21 *Moreno Gomez v Spain,* App. No. 4143/02 (ECtHR, 16 February 2005).
22 *Dubestka v Ukraine,* App. No. 30499/03 (ECtHR, 10 February 2011).
23 *Öneryildiz v Turkey,* App. No. 48939/99 (ECtHR, 18 June 2002).
24 Postiglione 2010, p. 527.

> right to the environment on a regional level in Europe is taking place in a cautious and step-by-step process, ...[25]

As a consequence, the different procedural guarantees, such as the third pillar of the public participation regime - access to court - are vital for the implementation of the right to environment. This feature gives a different weight to class actions of this category, because in environmental protection usually not merely the cumulative individual - and predominantly material, financial - interests are involved, as happens in most class action issues, but the protection of a human right is at stake. Also, these procedural guarantees, due to the lack of or at least the ambiguity of clear-cut substantive provisions, may be taken as the key apparatus of protection. And we should not forget that the right to environment is a collective right, covering present and future generations, nor should we forget the importance of the protection of the environment in its wider context.

## 4. The Aarhus Convention and its Article 9

The Aarhus Convention[26] is the best example in the course of setting up the system of guarantees. The Convention, while also finding its foundations in the concept of the right to environment, clearly refers to the three pillars of public participation, from among which the third is connected with litigation:

> Article 1. Objective. In order to contribute to the protection of the right of every person of present and future generations to live in an environment adequate to his or her health and well-being, each Party shall guarantee the rights of access to information, public participation in decision-making, and access to justice in environmental matters in accordance with the provisions of this Convention.

The Convention provides the right to access to the 'public concerned', which in the set of definitions means:

> Article 2. Definitions. 5. The "public concerned" means the public affected or likely to be affected by, or having an interest in, the environmental decision-making; for the purposes of this definition, non-governmental organizations promoting environmental protection and meeting any requirements under national law shall be deemed to have an interest.

25 Pedersen 2008, p. 111.

26 Convention on Access to Information, Public Participation in Decision-Making and Access to Justice in Environmental Matters, done at Aarhus, Denmark, on 25 June 1998. See: <www.unece.org/fileadmin/DAM/env/pp/documents/cep43e.pdf> (last accessed on 10 May 2014). For further details, it is also worth studying *The Aarhus Convention: An Implementation Guide,* 2nd edn., 2013. See: <www.unece.org/environmental-policy/treaties/public-participation/publications/public-participation/2013/aarhus-convention-implementation-guide-second-edition-text-only-version.html> (last accessed on 10 May 2014).

The meaning, the content of this definition is carefully analysed in the Implementation Guide, the most important elements of which are the following:

- While narrower than the "public," the "public concerned" is nevertheless still very broad. With respect to the criterion of "being affected", this is very much related to the nature of the activity in question.
- With respect to the criterion of "having an interest", the definition appears to go well beyond the kind of language that is usually found in legal tests of "sufficient interest" ... In particular it should be read to include not only members of the public whose legal interests or rights guaranteed under law might be impaired by the proposed activity.
- Potentially affected interests may also include social rights such as the right to be free from injury or the right to a healthy environment.
- It is significant that article 2, paragraph 5, does not require that a person must show a legal interest to be a member of the public concerned. Thus, the term may encompass both "legal interest" and "factual interest"...

There is a special role assigned for NGOs:

> Parties may set requirements for NGOs under national law, but in the light of the integral role that NGOs play in the implementation of the Convention, Parties should ensure that these requirements are not overly burdensome or politically motivated, and that each Party's legal framework encourages the formation of NGOs and their constructive participation in public affairs. Moreover, any requirements should be consistent with the Convention's principles, such as non-discrimination and the avoidance of technical and financial barriers. Within these limits, Parties may impose requirements based on objective criteria that are not unnecessarily exclusionary.

When defining access to justice, the above considerations answer the most challenging question of conditions of legal standing.

Access to justice is carefully regulated in Article 9 of the Convention, covering the following requirements in a nutshell:

- paragraph 1: requires access to review procedures relating to any legal disputes which may arise in connection with information requests under Article 4 of the Convention;
- paragraph 2: requires access to review procedures relating to decisions, acts or omissions subject to Article 6 and other relevant provisions of the Convention;
- paragraph 3: requires access to review procedures for public review of acts and omissions of private persons and public authorities concerning national law relating to the environment;
- paragraph 4: sets general minimum standards that apply to all relevant review procedures, decisions and remedies; and finally
- paragraph 5: requires parties to facilitate effective access to justice – 'to remove or reduce financial and other barriers to access to justice'.

The Implementation Guide lists some additional general conditions of the same kind, requiring that access to justice regulations

- must be fair, equitable, timely and not prohibitively expensive, and
- must provide adequate and effective remedies; furthermore
- that information on administrative and judicial review procedures must be disseminated to the public, and that the Parties be encouraged to establish appropriate assistance mechanisms to remove or reduce financial and other barriers; and finally
- that as far as court or court-like bodies are concerned, parties have flexibility in deciding how to structure their appeal systems.

It is not my purpose here to analyse the Convention itself and its Implementation Guide, as there are also several studies available.[27] The most important and detailed studies in connection with the Convention and its implementation within the EU are:

- Access to Justice in Environmental Matters under the Aarhus Convention, Justice & Environment Position Paper, May 2010, and its background document: Report on Access to Justice in Environmental Matters, Justice and Environment;
- Access to justice in Europe: an overview of challenges and opportunities, FRA – European Union Agency for Fundamental Rights, 2011;[28]
- Studies on the question of environmental justice and the synthesis report by Jan Darpö: Effective Justice? (Synthesis report of the study on the Implementation of Articles 9.3 and 9.4 of the Aarhus Convention in Seventeen of the Member States of the European Union, November 2012);[29] and
- A study on the socio-economic implications of access to justice by Maastricht University, Faculty of Law, METRO in 2013.[30]

## 5. Access to Justice in Environmental Protection Cases within the EU – Facts and Proposals

If we now turn to the EU, it becomes clear that while the first two pillars of public participation have a relatively extensive history and presence in European

27 <http://ec.europa.eu/environment/aarhus/> (last accessed on 10 May 2014).

28 <http://fra.europa.eu/sites/default/files/fra_uploads/1520-report-access-to-justice_EN.-pdf> (last accessed on 10 May 2014).

29 See the studies in: http://ec.europa.eu/environment/aarhus/access_studies.htm and the synthesis report: <http://ec.europa.eu/environment/aarhus/pdf/synthesis%20report%20-on%20access%20to%20justice.pdf> (last accessed on 10 May 2014).

30 <http://ec.europa.eu/environment/aarhus/pdf/access%20to%20justice%20%20economic-%20implications%20-%20study%202013.pdf> (last accessed on 10 May 2014).

integration – the first access to information Directive originated in 1990[31] and has been amended substantially in the meantime, with several additional specific conditions listed in the different legal regulations as well as numerous different provisions related to participation in decision-making[32] – comprehensive legislation of access to justice is still missing, although the first proposal was already made soon after the EU became a party to the Aarhus Convention.[33] There are of course some examples for such legislation, among others the just-mentioned Industrial Emissions Directive, in its Article 25,[34] but these types of provisions should be general rather than specific.

The access to justice proposal in its Explanatory Memorandum clearly refers to the specific importance of this kind of action in connection with the need 'to eliminate shortcomings in the enforcement of environmental law', accordingly also describing the role of this legal instrument within the entire set of class actions. This special feature delineates the essential conditions of access.

The words of the Memorandum underline why the major characteristic of access to justice is the focus on enforcement, which needs to be strengthened:

> These shortcomings are due to, among other things, the lack of a financial private interest in enforcing environmental law, in contrast to other areas of Community law where economic operators require the correct application of legislation, such as internal market and competition. Moreover, the failure to fully enforce environmental laws can distort the functioning of the internal market by creating unequal terms of economic competition for the economic operators. ... In addition, the lack of enforcement of environmental law is too frequently due to the fact that legal standing is limited to persons directly affected by the infringement. A way of improving enforcement is hence to ensure that representative associations seeking to protect the environment have access to administrative or judicial procedures in environmental matters. Practical experience gained from granting legal standing to environmental non-governmental organisations indicates that this can enhance the implementation of environmental law.

31 Council Directive 90/313/EEC of 7 June 1990 on the freedom of access to information on the environment, *OJ* L158 of 23 June 1990, 0056-0058.

32 A good example is Directive 2010/75/EU of the European Parliament and of the Council of 24 November 2010 on industrial emissions (integrated pollution prevention and control), Text with EEA relevance, *OJ* L334 of 17 December 2010, p. 17-119. Here Art. 24 covers the details of 'Access to information and public participation in the permit procedure'.

33 COM(2003) 624 final, 2003/0246 (COD), Brussels, 24 October 2003, Proposal for a Directive of the European Parliament and of the Council on access to justice in environmental matters.

34 This access option of the Directive uses the same language as the Convention, providing access to 'members of the public concerned', if there is either a sufficient interest or they maintain the impairment of a right, where administrative procedural law of a Member State requires this as a precondition. Art. 25 gives a wide margin of discretion to the Member States regarding the interpretation of this general formula. NGOs by definition are taken as meeting the requirements. Also, this article refers to the possibility of an intermediate review before an administrative authority.

Consequently, the features are largely dependent upon this function of class actions in the field of environmental protection.

The EC and later the EU always articulated the role of the public as a potential collaborator in environmental protection implementation and enforcement. Even the First Action Programme[35] more than 40 years ago underlined: 'The success of an environment policy presupposes that all categories of the population and all the social forces of the Community help to protect and improve the environment.' The same has been repeated by the Second[36] and Third[37] Action Programmes, placing environmental information in the centre. The Fourth Action Programme[38] refers to the need for effective implementation of environmental legislation, taking also the role of the public as a device to help better implementation of environmental legislation or as an ally in promoting compliance. The Fifth Action Programme[39] – Towards Sustainability – describes for the first time in the history of such programmes the three pillars of public participation.

Public participation is a priority issue of the Sixth Action Programme,[40] taking again the whole as an important condition for better implementation. Article 3 defines strategic approaches to meet the environmental objectives and within this, in its Paragraph 9, provides the details of public participation: access to information, the raising of environmental awareness and also the mention of justice.

The Seventh Action Programme[41] has nine priority objectives, within which environmental democracy is a major constituent in the fourth objective, that is, according to Article 2(1) d), 'to maximise the benefits of the Union's environment

35 Declaration of the Council of the European Communities and of the Representatives of the Governments of the Member States Meeting in the Council of 22 November 1973 on the Programme of Action of the European Communities on the Environment, *OJ* C112 of 20 December 1973.

36 Resolution of the Council of the European Communities and of the Representatives of the Governments of the Member States Meeting within the Council of 17 May 1977 on the continuation and implementation of a European Community policy and action programme on the environment, *OJ* C139 of 13 June 1977.

37 Resolution of the Council of the European Communities and of the Representatives of the Governments of the Member States Meeting within the Council of 7 February 1983 on the continuation and implementation of a European Community policy and action programme on the environment (1982 to 1986), *OJ* C46 of 17 February 1983.

38 Resolution of the Council of the European Communities and of the representatives of the Governments of the Member States, meeting within the Council of 19 October 1987 on the continuation and implementation of a European Community policy and action programme on the environment (1987-1992), *OJ* C328 of 7 December 1987, 0001-0044.

39 Resolution of the Council and the Representatives of the Governments of the Member States, meeting within the Council of 1 February 1993 on a Community programme of policy and action in relation to the environment and sustainable development, *OJ* C-138 of 17 May 1993.

40 Decision No. 1600/2002/EC of the European Parliament and of the Council of 22 July 2002 laying down the Sixth Community Environment Action Programme, *OJ* L242 of 10 September 2002, 0001-0015.

41 Decision No. 1386/2013/EU of the European Parliament and of the Council of 20 November 2013 on a General Union Environment Action Programme to 2020 'Living well, within the limits of our planet', *OJ* L354 of 28 December 2013, 0171-0200.

legislation'. The concept itself is presented in the Preamble: '(20) Engagement with non-government actors is important in ensuring the success of the programme and the achievement of its priority objectives.' The main purpose is to improve the implementation of EU environmental law. The five areas of Paragraph 65 of the fourth priority objective are connected with public participation, within which point (e) focuses on access to justice: '[T]he principle of effective legal protection for citizens and their organisations is facilitated.' The details later refer, among many other things, to the case law of the Court of Justice of the European Union as an imperative source of legal development.

The Commission has confidence in cooperative efforts and considers the public a partner in the improvement of the proper implementation of environmental law.[42] As a consequence, public participation becomes a more and more essential component of the implementation of European environmental policy and law.

Turning back to the access to justice proposal, the most comprehensive summary may be found in its Point 6 – Detailed explanation of the proposal: 'The proposed directive grants legal standing to certain members of the public, enabling them to have access to judicial or administrative proceedings against the actions and omissions of public authorities which contravene environmental law. This approach incorporates the Aarhus Convention and is based on the administrative and judicial proceedings existing in Member States.'

There are two major bases for determining standing in such cases:

- Article 4 covers the *general legal standing for members of the public* – having a sufficient interest in the related administrative act or omission or maintaining the impairment of a right. Here the proposal provides a definite explanation on the foundation of standing: '[T]he Commission decided not to opt for the possibility of a general right of legal standing for every natural persons because the generalised requirement of "actio popularis" is incompatible with the principle of subsidiarity, in the light of the fact that the Aarhus Convention leaves the possibility of laying down criteria under national law.'
- The *legal standing of qualified entities* – actually NGOs – is provided for in Article 5. This privileged legal standing also requires the qualification of characteristics, as such groups will not be required to have a sufficient interest or to maintain the impairment of a right. Article 8 prescribes the criteria for recognition of qualified entities and Article 9 contains the procedure for recognition, using a mixed approach combining a preliminary procedure and a case by case recognition.

42 Communication from the Commission to the European Parliament, the Council, the European Economic and Social Committee and the Committee of the Regions: Improving the delivery of benefits from EU environment measures: building confidence through better knowledge and responsiveness, Brussels 7 March 2012, COM(2012) 95 final.

The 2012 studies on environmental justice[43] and the synthesis report clearly underline the need to use the proposal of 2003 as the proper basis, and also the need to adopt as soon as possible the 'missing link' for the appropriate implementation of the Aarhus Convention in the EU, although the EU has not promised that all the issues of access to justice could be regulated by EU level legislation. The Council Decision of 2005, in connection with the conclusion of the Convention, in its Annex states that upon

> the implementation of the obligations resulting from Article 9(3) of the Convention ... Member States are responsible for the performance of these obligations at the time of approval of the Convention by the European Community and will remain so unless and until the Community, in the exercise of its powers under the EC Treaty, adopts provisions of Community law covering the implementation of those obligations.[44]

Thus there is no specific time-limit which requires the EU to adopt a complex scheme of access to justice.

## 6. The Role of CJEU Case Law in Opening up Access to Justice Possibilities

In the last several years the CJEU has become more and more active in interpreting the public participation guarantees of EU legislation, focusing principally on the Aarhus Convention as part of European law. One may see a very clear message, which is, to give life to effective access to justice standards.

Many studies and authors take the *Janecek* judgment[45] as one of the first steps of the more active involvement of the Court in supporting the improvement of access to justice requirements within the EU. Jans-Vedder mentions: 'The Court of Justice seems to require the German Court to apply a wider interpretation of the concept "interested party" than is usual in German law.'[46] In the given case, the Court agreed that a private person has the right to request that the authorities undertake their obligations, and this may also be challenged in court: '39 [T]he natural or legal persons directly concerned by a risk that the limit values or alert thresholds may be exceeded must be in a position to require the competent authorities to draw up an action plan where such a risk exists, if necessary by bringing an action before the competent courts.' Still, in this judgment the direct

43 See *supra* note 28.

44 Council Decision of 17 February 2005 on the conclusion, on behalf of the European Community, of the Convention on access to information, public participation in decision-making and access to justice in environmental matters (2005/370/EC) – Annex: Declaration by the European Community in Accordance with Art. 19 of the Convention on Access to Information, Public Participation in Decision-Making and Access to Justice in Environmental Matters.

45 C-237/07, preliminary ruling from the Bundesverwaltungsgericht, in *Dieter Janecek v Freistaat Bayern*, 25 July 2008, Reports of Cases 2008 I-06221.

46 Jans-Vedder 2012, p. 231.

interest – 'directly concerned' – of the individual is a core element of the dispute, while this direct interest is relatively remote, as the given omission affects the wider public and not only the particular person.

The Commission itself agrees with the importance of the new line of CJEU practice, among others in the preparatory assessment of the proposal for the Seventh Action Programme:

> CJEU case-law has moved in a direction of confirming an entitlement to access – see in particular Case C-237/07, *Janecek*, where the Court recognised a citizen's entitlement to challenge the absence of an air quality management plan (despite German law considering that the citizen had no standing to bring such a case) and Case C-240/09, *Slovak Bears*, where the Court found that Article 9(3) of Aarhus had no direct effect but that Member States courts must nevertheless facilitate access by NGOs.[47]

This specific aspect of public participation was articulated by Advocate General Sharpston in the *Slovak Brown Bear* case: 'Indeed, the Court appears to be keen on providing EU citizens with *effective remedies before national courts* ...'[48] This reference also points to the fact that this access is mostly granted in connection with the national Judiciary.

In more and more cases the Court accepts the need for supporting public enforcement in environmental law, representing public interests and the wider context of environmental interests. First of all, the major reason for this attitude towards public participation and its active role will be discussed, using the argument of Sharpston again: 'No one can act on behalf of the environment itself.'[49] That is the most important reason to enforce public participation rights. This has been reinforced in other procedures. Advocate General Kokott formulated likewise: 'Recognition of the public interest in environmental protection is especially important since there may be many cases where the legally protected interests of particular individuals are not affected or are affected only peripherally. However, *the environment cannot defend itself before a court, but needs to be represented,* for example by active citizens or non-governmental organisations ...'[50] But *who* shall be entitled to represent environmental interests? It is clear from the legal positions mentioned above that the *actio popularis* has never been considered as a viable option, so the optimum result has proven to be to give rights to environmental

47 Commission Staff Working Document Impact Assessment Proposal for a Decision of the European Parliament and of the Council on a General Union Environment Action Programme to 2020 'Living well, within the limits of our planet' (COM(2012) 710 final) (SWD(2012) 397 final), Brussels, 29 November 2012 SWD(2012) 398 final, Annex 6, p. 120.

48 Opinion of Advocate General Sharpston, delivered on 15 July 2010, Case C-240/09 *Lesoochranárske zoskupenie VLK v Ministerstvo životného prostredia Slovenskej republiky*.

49 Opinion of Advocate General Sharpston delivered on 16 December 2010, Case C-115/09 *Bund für Umwelt und Naturschutz Deutschland, Landesverband Nordrhein-Westfalen eV v Bezirksregierung Arnsberg Trianel Kohlekraftwerk Lünen (intervening)*.

50 Opinion of Advocate General Kokott delivered on 18 October 2012, Case C-260/11 *The Queen, on the application of David Edwards and Another v Environment Agency and Others*.

NGOs - Kokott's opinion already mentioned it. This has been articulated again by Advocate General Sharpston.[51] First there is a reference to the Aarhus Convention, which

> 63. … decided to strengthen the role of non-governmental organisations promoting environmental protection. That formula was adopted in an attempt to steer a middle course between the maximalist approach of the *actio popularis* and the minimalist idea of a right of individual action available only to parties having a direct interest at stake. Giving special standing to non-governmental organisations reconciles these two positions. It seems to me to be a very sensible compromise.

And what is the exact role and significance of the function of NGOs in this situation? - '62. … they bring together the claims of many individuals in a single action.' It is worth adding that in this kind of representative function they also play an important role in the settlement of legal disputes: '[T]he overall result of this policy is to create a filter which, in the long run, assists the work of the courts. In addition, as I have just indicated, these associations often have technical knowledge that individuals generally lack.'

The *Djurgården* case[52] also makes reference to the Convention - protecting the rights of NGOs from the setting up of such national legislation for NGO participation that would substantially limit their participation in decision-making or access to justice. The finding was that there are '49. ... very restrictive conditions in Swedish law'; and the final outcome was: '52. Accordingly, the answer to the third question is that Article 10a of Directive 85/337 precludes a provision of national law which reserves the right to bring an appeal against a decision on projects which fall within the scope of that directive solely to environmental protection associations which have at least 2,000 members.'

The same type of arguments was also used in other analogous cases, such as *Trianel*,[53] where the major conclusion was: '44. … Member States ... cannot ... deprive environmental protection organisations, which fulfil the conditions laid down in Article 1(2) of that directive of the opportunity of playing the role granted to them both by Directive 85/337 and by the Aarhus Convention.' Moreover, *Trianel* contains a final serious criticism towards domestic legislation:

> 59. … non-governmental organisations promoting environmental protection, as referred to in Article 1(2) of that directive, can derive from the last sentence of the third paragraph of Article 10a of Directive 85/337 a right to rely before the courts, in an action contesting a decision authorising projects "likely to have significant effects on

[51] Opinion of Advocate General Sharpston delivered on 2 July 2009, Case C-263/08 *Djurgården-Lilla Värtans Miljöskyddsförening v Stockholms kommun genom dess marknämnd.*

[52] Case C-263/08, preliminary ruling under Art. 234 EC from the Högsta domstolen (Sweden), in *Djurgården-Lilla Värtans Miljöskyddsförening v Stockholms kommun genom dess marknämnd*, 15 October 2009, Reports of Cases 2009 I-09967.

[53] Case C-115/09, preliminary ruling in *Bund für Umwelt und Naturschutz Deutschland, Landesverband Nordrhein-Westfalen eV v Bezirksregierung Arnsberg*, 12 May 2011, Reports of Cases 2011 I-03673.

the environment" for the purposes of Article 1(1) of Directive 85/337, on the infringement of the rules of national law flowing from Article 6 of the Habitats Directive, even where, on the ground that the rules relied on protect only the interests of the general public and not the interests of individuals, national procedural law does not permit this.

A typical example of the recent judgments of the CJEU was the previously mentioned *Slovak Brown Bear* case,[54] which on the one hand summarizes the most important conclusions – based upon the international obligations formulated by the Aarhus Convention – related to the need to have a wide access to justice option available and on the other hand refers the final decisions back to the domestic Judiciary, but with a very strong message. The applicants in the given case were eager to prove the direct effect of the Convention, in order to guarantee the best outcome for public access to courts. Their attempt failed *pro forma*, but has been supported in context. Although the Convention does not provide the necessary conditions of direct effect, still the access rights shall be granted:

30. ... according to settled case-law, the provisions of that convention now form an integral part of the legal order of the European Union ...
44. In that connection, a provision in an agreement concluded by the European Union with a non-member country must be regarded as being directly applicable when, regard being had to its wording and to the purpose and nature of the agreement, the provision contains a clear and precise obligation which is not subject, in its implementation or effects, to the adoption of any subsequent measure ...
45. It must be held that the provisions of Article 9(3) of the Aarhus Convention do not contain any clear and precise obligation capable of directly regulating the legal position of individuals. ....
52. Article 9(3) of the Aarhus Convention does not have direct effect in EU law. It is, however, for the referring court to interpret, to the fullest extent possible, the procedural rules relating to the conditions to be met in order to bring administrative or judicial proceedings in accordance with the objectives of Article 9(3) of that convention and the objective of effective judicial protection of the rights conferred by EU law, in order to enable an environmental protection organisation, such as the "zoskupenie", *to challenge before a court a decision* taken following administrative proceedings liable to be contrary to EU environmental law.

The different public participation rights, among them the access to justice provisions, all serve a major interest, going far beyond the protection of numerous and cumulative individual interests. This is much more than a procedural

54 Case C-240/09, preliminary ruling from the Najvyšší súd Slovenskej republiky (Slovakia), in *Lesoochranárske zoskupenie VLK v Ministerstvo životného prostredia Slovenskej republiky*, 8 March 2011, Reports of Cases 2011 I-01255.

guarantee, or relief; this is the guarantee offered by public or common goods. The main conclusion is given by another judgment:[55]

> 31. ... the objective of the European Union Legislature is *to give the public concerned 'wide access to justice'*.
> 32. That objective pertains, more broadly, to the desire of the European Union Legislature to preserve, protect and improve the quality of the environment and to ensure that, to that end, the public plays an active role.

Of course, there are several issues, most of them are procedural, which must all be addressed, such as

- the scope of 'environmental' issues;
- the review procedure in case of acts or omissions of the public administration;
- the initiation of direct actions against breaches of environmental law, without direct interest;
- the definition of standing – from narrow to broad standing, and the reasonable conditions that must be met (for example, only NGOs that are entrusted to represent environmental public interests);
- other details of standing, such as, for example, the definition of qualified entities, the necessity to participate in a previous action, etc.;
- the conditions of review (legality?);
- the costs which should not be prohibitively high; and
- many practical issues, such as timeliness and effectiveness.

## 7. Summary

In class actions the most important distinction is that between those whose major intent is to provide injunctive relief and those whose focus is on damages. The first type mostly means the enforcement of legal requirements in the name of the relatively homogenous public interest, while the second type is generally an aggregate interest of numerous individuals. In public interest cases with an environmental focus therefore, the distinction between opt-in or opt-out models does not have real significance. Accordingly, these types of actions concern private enforcement, attached to or reinforcing – and sometimes supplementing – public enforcement. In the field of environmental law, besides the attempts of the EU to develop collective redress mechanisms, the major focus is on access to justice, as the third pillar of public participation, provided for among others in the UN Economic Commission for Europe Aarhus Convention, Article 9. Public participation – and consequently access to justice in the field of the environment – means the practical

55 Case C-260/11, preliminary ruling in the proceedings *The Queen, on the application of: David Edwards, Lilian Pallikaropoulos v Environment Agency, First Secretary of State, Secretary of State for the Environment, Food and Rural Affairs*, 11 April 2013, Reports of Cases – not yet published.

implementation of the concept of the right to environment. Given the actual difficulties of developing the substantive approach to this right, procedural guarantees are vital.

Perhaps the best way forward is to build on the representation provided by environmental NGOs, instead of accepting a general *actio popularis* attitude. In the EU, with a legislative proposal at the EU level still pending after ten years, the main burden of implementation lies on the individual Member States. The Commission believes that public participation in enforcement may become a strong collaborator in the proper implementation of environmental law, but the debate is still open. In the meantime, CJEU case law has turned more and more towards the guarantee of effective remedies within the judicial system, in order to grant better representation to environmental interests in general.

## Bibliography

**Cofee 2000**
Cofee, J.C., Jr., 'Class Action Accountability: Reconciling Exit, Voice, and Loyalty in Representative Litigation', *Columbia Law Review*, March 2000. Vol. 100(2), p. 370-439.

**Craig 2006**
Craig, P., *EU Administrative Law*, Oxford: Oxford University Press, 2006.

**Ermacora 2003**
Ermacora, F., 'The Right to a Clean Environment in the Constitution of the European Union', in Jans, J.H. (ed.), *The European Convention and the Future of European Environmental Law*, Groningen: Europa Law Publishing, 2003, p. 27-42.

**Garner 1995**
Garner, B.A., *A Dictionary of Modern Legal Usage,* 2nd edn., Oxford: Oxford University Press, 1995.

**Hodges 2010**
Hodges, Chr., 'Towards a Coherent European Approach to Collective Redress', Centre for Socio-legal Studies, Manor Road, Oxford, 28 April 2010, <http://ec.europa.eu/competition/consultations/2011_collective_redress/university_of_oxford_en.pdf>.

**Hodges & Money-Kyrle 2010**
Hodges, C.J.S. & Money-Kyrle, R., 'Appendix Safeguards in Collective Actions', <http://ec.europa.eu/competition/consultations/2011_collective_redress/university_of_oxford_en.pdf>.

**Jans & Vedder 2012**
Jans, J.H. & Vedder, H.B., *European Environmental Law*, Groningen: Europa Law Publishing, 2012.

**Pedersen 2008**
Pedersen, O.W., 'European Environmental Human Rights and Environmental Rights. A Long Time Coming?', *Georgetown International Environmental Law Review*, 2008, Vol. 21(73), p. 73-111.

**Postiglione 2010**
Postiglione, A., 'Human Rights and the Environment', *The International Journal of Human Rights*, 2010, Vol. 14(4), p. 524-541.

**Weeremantry 1997**
Weeremantry, C.G., 'Separate Opinion of Vice-President Weeremantry', to the 25 September 1997 judgment of the ICJ, <www.icj-cij.org/docket/files/92/7383.pdf>.

R.L. Marcus

## THE BIG BAD WOLF: AMERICAN CLASS ACTIONS

For many, American class actions are like the Big Bad Wolf,[1] something to be avoided. Thus, Professor Hodges began his study of European techniques for affording relief to groups by explaining that such European efforts need not depend on 'a US-style court-based mechanism'.[2] Somewhat similarly, Professor Walker introduced a panel on alternative group litigation procedures by suggesting that 'everyone, at least outside the United States, seems also to agree that they do not want to adopt US-style class actions in their systems'.[3] On the other hand, some European innovations have built on the American model.[4]

For those seeking to emulate the US model, or seeking to avoid it, some background on that model should be of use. That is the purpose of this contribution – to report briefly on where the Big Bad Wolf came from, and also on where the stresses for American litigation have been felt most recently.[5] The key event in this history is probably the adoption in 1966 of revisions to Rule 23, the federal class-action rule. To begin that study, however, it is important to recognize that American civil litigation is itself exceptional in other ways, and that those features of US

1 According to Wikipedia, '[t]he Big Bad Wolf is a fictional wolf appearing in several precautionary folkloric tales, including some of *Aesop's Fables* and *Grimms' Fairy Tales*. Versions of this character have appeared in numerous works, and it has become a generic archetype of a menacing predatory antagonist, sometimes referred to as *Big Bad*'. Available at: <http://en.wikipedia.org/wiki/Big_Bad_Wolf> (last accessed on 15 August 2014).

2 Hodges 2008, p. 1.

3 Walker 2012, p. 414.

4 Thus, Van Rhee & Tzankova in the present volume, report that the Dutch collective settlement procedure 'has been inspired by the US class settlement procedure'. For further discussion of the Dutch procedure, see Krans 2014.

5 On this subject, I should note that I serve as Associate Reporter of the US Judicial Conference Advisory Committee on Civil Rules. This body is responsible for evaluating and developing possible amendments to the American Federal Rules of Civil Procedure. I am Reporter to the Rule 23 Subcommittee of that body, which is engaged in a study of possible areas for reform of American class actions. In this chapter, however, I speak only for myself and not for the Advisory Committee.

litigation also affect American class-action practice. One who contemplates US class-action procedures need not expect that similar procedures would produce identical results in another legal system.

Additionally, it is important to appreciate that the current American reality was not entirely the result of conscious effort. To a significant extent, it resulted instead from a confluence of factors of which American class-action practices are only a part, perhaps only a relatively small part. Nonetheless, like several other features of American procedure, the US class action is very definitely controversial in contemporary American legal and political circles. Some appreciation of those controversies – which are unlikely to be entirely resolved soon – also may prove useful to those contemplating US class actions from a safe distance.

## 1. US Litigation and Private Enforcement

Besides beginning his study of European group litigation experimentation with an acknowledgement that many seek to avoid the US model, Professor Hodges also noted that 'it is not widely understood that the law plays a function (in America), in combining compensatory goals with "private enforcement", which is fundamentally different from that which it performs in Europe'.[6] This is a key starting point.

Across an array of procedures, the US is singularly plaintiff-friendly when contrasted with other legal systems, particularly European ones. Unlike most other legal systems, it eschews exacting pleading requirements and does not insist that claimants show what evidence they will use in order to get their cases into court. Uniquely among legal systems, it affords claimants broad opportunities to use discovery to force other parties and non-parties to turn over large quantities of information – much of it often confidential – at no cost to the party seeking the information. Unlike almost all other countries, the US affords civil litigants a jury trial, with the ultimate decision after trial by a non-professional body guided by a professional judge. And those decisions may include very substantial monetary awards for losses that other countries would not regard as supporting large recoveries, such as pain and suffering, or (even more aggressively) punitive damages. Moreover, the American permission for contingency fee contracts with lawyers can make those large recoveries very remunerative for lawyers.

Together, these features of the American litigation system underwrite litigation to an extent not known in other countries, and those differences unnerve many other countries, including several in Europe. I am not urging that other countries adopt this peculiar American arrangement. As Professor Kagan has emphasized, it is a distinctly American way of handling litigation.[7]

Instead, the point is only one that Professor Gidi made in discussing the distinctive Brazilian class action procedure:

6 Hodges 2008, p. 1. See also Burbank, Farhang & Kritzer 2013.

7 See generally Kagan 2001.

> 'Some civil law lawyers have a negative opinion of American class actions, typically arguing that class actions are expensive and wasteful, that they generate high attorneys' fees, huge compensatory and punitive awards, and allow courts to create public policy and usurp the legislative function of societal regulation ... What the critics fail to understand is that these aspects are not necessarily related to class-action litigation, but to the peculiarities of American legal culture, civil procedure, and the constitutional role of its Judiciary'.[8]

## 2. The Background of the Modern American Class Action

The American class action was not always such a big or bad wolf. Historically speaking, the class action emerged from the English practice in the Court of Equity. More particularly, it involved a recognition of the role of recognized groups in society. Thus, the villagers of the village of *X* might file a lawsuit in their combined interest regarding matters affecting the village; in such circumstances there was an existing social bond among these villagers independent of litigation[9] likened to modern recognition in some civil law systems of suits by organizations on behalf of their members; the critical feature might be that the organizations owe their existence to some feature other than litigation and involve some element of voluntariness among those included in the membership.

That historical lineage was reflected in the original version of the American class-action rule, adopted in 1938. Thus, original Rule 23 of the Federal Rules focused mainly on 'true' class actions, which were said to be suits involving rights that were 'joint, or common, or secondary in the sense that the owner of the primary right refuses to enforce that right and a member of the class thereby becomes entitled to enforce it'.[10] Such situations might result from organizational arrangements gone awry. An example was a Supreme Court case from before the US Civil War involving the split of a church between opponents of slavery and supporters of slavery, where the issue was division of church property.[11] Much as this effort to identify 'true' class actions may have had theoretical appeal, it presented practical difficulties; Professor Chaffee criticized it on the ground that he had as much difficulty distinguishing 'common' from 'separate' rights as in deciding whether some ties were green or blue.[12]

These difficulties led the rule makers to reconsider the original framework of the class-action rule in the 1960s. From the perspective of some, the entire effort might profitably have been abandoned on the ground that class actions were used so rarely that trying to adapt to them would not be useful.[13] But others had a more ambitious attitude, and a new Rule 23 on class actions was adopted in 1966.

8 Gidi 2003, p. 315.

9 For a discussion of this evolution of the class action, see generally Yeazell 1987.

10 Fed. R. Civ. P. 23(b)(1) (as adopted in 1938).

11 *Smith v Swormstedt*, 57 US 288 (1853).

12 Chaffee 1950, p. 257.

13 For a thorough review of the revision of the federal class-action rule, see Rabiej 2005.

Professor Kaplan, then Reporter of the committee considering rule changes, urged shortly after the new rule went into effect that the class action had an important role to fill:

> 'We hear talk that it all belongs not to the courts but to administrative agencies. But by hypothesis we are dealing with cases that are not handled by existing agencies, and I do not myself see any subversion of judicial process here but a fine opportunity for its accommodation to new challenges of the times. The class action takes its place in a larger search for pliant and sensitive procedures. I confess that I am exhilarated, not depressed, by experimentation which spies out carefully the furthest possibilities of the new Rule'.[14]

The new Rule 23 did open up new possibilities, most particularly by adding the 'common question' class action provision in Rule 23(b)(3).[15] In the view of Professor Kaplan, Reporter of the amendment project,

> '[t]he entire reconstruction of the Rule bespoke an intention to promote more vigorously than before the dual missions of the class-action device: (1) to reduce units of litigation by bringing under one umbrella what might otherwise be many separate but duplication actions; (2) even at the expense of increasing litigation, to provide means of vindicating the rights of groups of people who individually would be without effective strength to bring their opponents into court at all'.[16]

## 3. The Emergence and Evolution of the Modern American Class Action

Despite Professor Kaplan's optimism, it is at least uncertain what most observers in 1966 expected the revised class-action rule would produce.[17] As the world now knows, the class action turned out to be a potent device fairly often. That is probably why it is regarded by many as the Big Bad Wolf. But the reason it is so big and bad recalls points made by Professors Hodges and Gidi – the prominent role of civil litigation in the US as a device to enable 'private enforcement' and the distinctively pro-plaintiff features of American procedure more generally.[18]

Those distinctive features of American litigation became more prominent and important during the period when the American class-action rule was revised and

14 Kaplan 1969, p. 500.

15 As presently written, this rule provision directs that a class action is proper if it satisfies the requirements of Rule 23(a) (numerosity, commonality, typicality, and adequacy of representation) and 'the court finds that questions of law or fact common to the class members predominate over any questions affecting only individual members, and that a class action is superior to other available methods for fairly and efficiently adjudicating the controversy'.

16 Kaplan 1969, p. 497.

17 For a review of this history of ups and downs of American class actions in the late 20th century, see Marcus 2013, p. 149-153.

18 See *supra* text accompanying notes 6-8.

strengthened. For a variety of reasons, both the federal and state governments in the 1960s and 1970s enacted many statutes to protect citizens against a variety of risks, including discrimination and consumer fraud. At the same time, common law doctrines such as product liability and punitive damages also experienced expansion. Coupled with the class action, these provisions of substantive law could resemble nuclear weapons when wielded by a lawyer armed with the American class action.

In most countries, the principal responsibility for regulation rests with agencies of the state, but in the US that is not so widely true. Even when there is a public agency with responsibility to enforce legal protections, a major part of the enforcement may be left to private legal actions. As Professor Farhang has explored, that tendency can be traced, in federal laws in the US, to the 1964 decision to place primary enforcement authority for Title VII of the 1964 Civil Rights Act, forbidding discrimination in employment on basis of race, religion, or national origin, on injured individuals rather than on the agency created to enforce the Act, the Equal Employment Opportunity Commission.[19]

When this sort of legislation began to appear in the 1960s, it may have seemed to be only a dream that a cadre of lawyers would emerge to embrace and enforce the regulatory measures eligible for private enforcement. But because the legislation changed features of American procedure for cases to which it applied, such a cadre began to emerge. Probably the most important deviation from conventional American procedure was the frequent abandonment of the American Rule on attorney fee recovery; many such laws authorized prevailing plaintiffs to recover their attorney fees. In addition, some authorized enhanced recoveries (like the 'treble damages' authorized under US antitrust laws) or minimum recoveries in cases with small damage potential (such as consumer claims).

During the 1970s, 1980s, and 1990s the cadre of lawyers who relied significantly, mainly, or entirely on this sort of litigation increased. At least some of these lawyers did very well indeed. At the same time, they could profess that they were doing important work for the public.[20] But on occasion, it seemed that this good work could lead to overkill. A consumer protection statute designed to ensure that a successful plaintiff would obtain a modest recovery and that the lawyer would also be paid - designed to empower the public to coerce those who violated the legal protection into respecting it - could become a fearsome instrument if class actions raised the stakes to many millions of dollars instead of a few hundred or thousand dollars.

An example illustrates the concern. The US Congress passed legislation to protect against identity theft by forbidding merchants from including any but the last four numbers of a credit card number on the customer's receipt. Those customers who received receipts that did not comply were authorized to sue for a

19 See Farhang 2011.

20 For a review of this flowering of 'private attorney general' activity, see generally Rubenstein 2004.

small guaranteed recovery and attorney fees if successful. No proof of actual identity theft was required to support this recovery under the Act. For a merchant with many customers, a class action on behalf of all of them could threaten huge liability, perhaps far out of proportion with the enforcement goals Congress had in mind. A state agency interested in obtaining compliance with the statute might take such matters into account, but a private lawyer interested in the profitable potential of a class action need not.

A federal case in California illustrates the problem. The federal appellate court in California had already ruled that class actions to enforce this statute were allowed,[21] but in 2012 a district court judge refused to go along when a customer at a municipal parking lot in a small city sued the city, seeking to represent a class consisting of all customers at the parking lot, on the ground that its receipt machine had not been retooled in time to comply with the new requirement regarding credit card numbers. Thus aggregated, the claims would total about $15 million. Noting that the city did not have 'the financial wherewithal to satisfy and survive an adverse $15 million judgement', and that paying such a judgment would 'compromise [the city's] ability to respond to emergencies and provide necessary public services', the judge simply refused to allow the case to proceed as a class action.[22]

At least here, the American class action seems to have become a Big Bad Wolf in the eyes of an American judge. Other American voices have expressed concern about the actual results of the 1966 expansion of the class-action rule, producing important changes.

## 4. Recent Revisions by Rule, Statute and Supreme Court Decision

Whatever the expectations were in 1966, the actual results of expanded class-action practice have heartened some and perturbed others. Along the way, courts have adopted broad and narrow views of the class-action procedure put in place in 1966. Whatever the views of others about American class-action practice, it seems useful to identify some of the pressure points that have emerged in America.

### 4.1. *Rule Revisions*

For a quarter century after the 1966 amendment went into effect, the committee responsible for developing rule amendments did not attempt to make further changes to the rule. During that time, judicial interpretation of the rule identified and attempted to address a variety of emerging issues.[23]

21 See *Bateman v American Multi-Cinema, Inc.*, 623 F.3d 708 (9th Cir. 2010).

22 *Rowden v Pacific Parking Systems, Inc.*, 282 F.R.D. 587, 587 (C.D. Cal. 2012).

23 As noted below in relation to Supreme Court interpretations, owing to the role of judicial precedent in clarifying or modifying procedural law, judicial interpretations could change things without a formal rule amendment or action by Congress.

In 1991, in response to a caseload crisis particularly identified with mass torts, and more particularly with asbestos personal-injury litigation, the Advisory Committee on Civil Rules began considering rule changes. Various fairly aggressive ideas were advanced, and in 1996 an amendment package was circulated with suggested changes to the criteria for certifying 'common question' class actions.[24] The proposals prompted an avalanche of public commentary, and eventually all the possible changes to the criteria for certifying class actions were shelved. But one important change was adopted – a new rule provision that permits immediate review of decisions whether to certify a class.[25] This rule change paved the way for a considerable growth in case law on standards for certifying class actions.

After the 1996 proposals were shelved, the Advisory Committee turned to concerns about the procedures used in class actions, and sought to build on judicial experience since the 1996 amendments. A key concern had been the handling of proposals to settle class actions. Whatever the expectation in 1966, the reality thereafter was that class actions were settled in the great majority of cases in which judges certified them for litigation as a class action, and in many cases in which judges had not yet ruled on whether class certification would be justified in the case. A further reality was that lawyers were sometimes accused of disregarding the interests of the class members and exploiting the class-action device for profit. This risk gave rise to concerns about 'reverse auctions', situations in which defendants sued in multiple class actions would pit the various plaintiff lawyers against each other in a 'bidding' contest on who would settle for the smallest amount, providing the case yielded a substantial attorney fee. Altogether, these developments indicated that greater attention might profitably be paid in the rule both to the review of proposed settlements of class actions, and to the choice and payment of class counsel.

A further package of proposed amendments was therefore published in 2001 and, after revisions, adopted effective 2003. These amendments clarified that, when certifying a class, a judge had to define the class and the claims asserted, and also appoint class counsel.[26] They also substantially expanded the rule's treatment of the responsibilities of the judge in reviewing a proposed class settlement.[27] The

24 See Proposed Rules, 167 F.R.D. 523 (1996). Included in the package of possible amendments were proposals to empower the judge to decide whether class certification would be worth the effort in light of the likely returns for class members, authorizing the judge to direct that the case proceed on an 'opt in' rather than an 'opt out' basis, and suggesting that the judge consider the 'maturity' of individual litigation of the issues involved in the proposed class action in deciding whether to certify a class.

25 Fed. R. Civ. P. 26(f), implemented in 1998, provides: 'A court of appeals may permit an appeal from an order granting or denying class-action certification under this rule if a petition for permission to appeal is filed with the circuit clerk within 14 days after the order is entered. An appeal does not stay proceedings in the district court unless the district judge or the court of appeals so orders'.

26 Fed. R. Civ. P. 23(c)(1).

27 See Fed. R. Civ. P. 23(e).

amendments introduced new subdivisions of the rule dealing with appointment of class counsel[28] and awards of attorney fees to class counsel.[29]

## 4.2. *Statutory Changes*

The rule makers have not been the only ones concerned about revising class-action practice. The development of procedural rules in the US is handled both by the Advisory Committee on Civil Rules and the US Congress. On at least some matters, such as federal-court jurisdiction, only Congress has authority to act. And it has acted at least twice in recent years to change the way certain types of cases were handled.

The first time was in 1995, when Congress enacted the Private Securities Litigation Reform Act.[30] This legislation resulted from concerns that class actions enabled lawyers too often to sue for securities fraud based on '20-20 hindsight' when there was a drop in stock price. Some contended that the 'bet the company' prospect of a class-action judgment meant that defendants felt they had no choice but to settle such cases, even though they probably would win on the merits.[31] At the same time, those lawyers might sometimes 'sell out' the class when the case was strong by settling for 'cosmetic' changes to company bylaws in return for handsome attorney fees. Prompted in part by a law review article,[32] the Act directed that the 'group' with the largest potential claim should become the 'lead plaintiff' in securities fraud class actions, and that this lead plaintiff should hire class counsel and take other actions instead of leaving those to the lawyer, under the review of the court, as in ordinary class actions. This 'empowered plaintiff' model might have held promise for other sorts of litigation, but would not have been of use in most class actions.[33]

In 2005, Congress adopted the Class Action Fairness Act[34] to respond to a somewhat different set of concerns. These concerns resulted from the peculiarity that the US has not only a federal court system, but every state also has a state court system. Particularly for claims based on federal law rather than state law, that arrangement meant that a state court might certify a 'nationwide' class action on behalf of customers from around the country and apply its own law to decide the claims presented. Because state law might differ in significant ways from state to state, such aggressive actions might produce unfair results, which seemed to have occurred in some cases.[35] The Act's solution was to change jurisdictional rules to

28 See Fed. R. Civ. P. 23(g).
29 See Fed. R. Civ. P. 23(h).
30 Private Securities Litigation Reform Act of 1995, 109 Stat 737 (1995).
31 See Alexander 1991.
32 See Weiss & Beckerman 1995.
33 For discussion, see Fisch 2002.
34 Class Action Fairness Act of 2005, 119 Stat. 4 (2005).
35 A prime example was *Avery v State Farm Mut. Auto. Ins. Co.*, 835 N.E.2d 801 (Ill. 2005), a class action in an Illinois state court. Plaintiffs asserted that State Farm violated Illinois law by →

expand federal-court jurisdiction for many more cases that formerly could only be litigated in state court. It is unlikely that similar issues would arise under the jurisdictional arrangements of many other countries.

### 4.3. *Supreme Court Class-Action Decisions*

In the American judicial arrangement, court decisions themselves may be regarded as making significant changes in procedure. One recent example of that sort of thing relates to the controversy resulting from Supreme Court decisions on pleading that seem to have made it more exacting although not comparable to the pleading requirements in many other countries.[36]

Class action decisions by courts can also have major impacts. In the 1970s, several Supreme Court decisions about class actions were criticized as significantly weakening the device. In 1997[37] and 1999,[38] the Court made further decisions that curtailed latitude that had been adopted by lower courts in employing class actions. But for about a decade thereafter, the Court had remained relatively quiet in the field.

Since 2010, however, the Court has again taken up a number of class-action cases.[39] By and large, these decisions have tended to favour those opposing class-action certifications. These decisions have also prompted an outpouring of academic commentary, which need not be repeated here. One important set of cases has expanded the effectiveness of arbitration provisions in contracts to divert cases from court and prevent class-action resolution either in court or in arbitral settings.

Overall, it is clear that the judicial reaction has not been favourable to more expansive use of class actions in court. In part, that development might have resulted from the expanded right to immediate review of certification decisions brought about by the 1998 amendment to Rule 23.[40] One goal of that rule change was to permit the appellate courts to take a more active role in supervising class-action jurisprudence, and a more cautious attitude might naturally have been expected to emerge as a result of this supervision. Besides that, there seems to have

insisting that cheaper substitute parts be used for car repairs rather than replacement parts manufactured by the maker of the car. Whatever the validity of the contention that Illinois law prohibited such a requirement, State Farm showed that many other states not only permitted the use of cheaper replacement parts but required using them. Eventually, the Illinois Supreme Court reversed the lower court's decision imposing this regime on State Farm, but the point was that class actions could have this potential.

36 The reference is to the results of the Supreme Court's decisions in *Bell Atlantic Corp. v Twombly*, 550 US 544 (2007), and *Ashcroft v Iqbal*, 556 US 662 (2009). These two decisions appear to say that judges can dismiss cases when they think the claims made are not 'plausible'. They have prompted an enormous response, particularly in the academic literature.

37 *Amchem Products, Inc. v Windsor*, 521 US 591 (1997).

38 *Ortiz v Fibreboard Corp.*, 527 US 815 (1999).

39 For discussion of several of these issues, see Kane 2012.

40 See *supra* note 25.

been something of a change in climate in the federal courts, making the Class Action Fairness Act provisions expanding federal-court jurisdiction more significant.

An example may suffice to convey the attitude. In a recent decision refusing to certify a class action in a securities fraud suit, a federal district judge remarked on

> 'the steady departure by federal courts away from a presumptively favourable approach toward class certification to a more sceptical view coupled with a more exacting review process. Courts employing the former, presumptively pro-plaintiff approach, permitted plaintiffs to obtain class-certification based solely on the pleadings or only on a modicum of evidentiary support ... . Going forward, the clear directive to plaintiffs seeking class certification – in any type of case – is that they will face a rigorous analysis by the federal courts, will not be afforded favourable presumptions from the pleadings or otherwise and must be prepared to prove *with facts* – and by a preponderance of the evidence – their compliance with the requirements of Rule 23'.[41]

## 5. Further Reform Initiatives?

Given the variety of sources for class-action reform in the US, it's worthwhile to reflect briefly on what those reforms might be in the future, or where they may come from. It must be stressed, however, that significant changes in US class-action practice are hard to predict, and there is no basis for predicting any at this time.

Congress could, as it has twice since 1990,[42] enact class-action changes. From time to time, it is urged to do so. A recent example was a bill proposing to insulate companies that participate in an energy conservation program from class-action suits asserting that their claims of energy efficiency are untrue.[43] Opponents of the proposed legislation argue that governmental regulators cannot do the full job of policing the energy conservation program, and that 'consumers need that backstop of the courts to get redress', adding that class-action litigation is particularly important when 'it's lots of small injuries', as in a situation where an appliance cost a few extra dollars to operate each year because it's not as efficient as claimed.[44] Although Congress may sometimes modify procedures for certain kinds of suits (like securities fraud actions) or for certain governmental programs, it does not often do so. And as the opponents of this proposed legislation emphasize, legislators may also consider the importance of private litigation, including class actions, in enforcing governmental directives like the energy conservation program.

Further procedural evolution may also emerge from court decisions, as suggested above.[45] As noted, the general trend of Supreme Court decisions has been to make class certification more difficult to obtain. But that is not a universal result. In 2010, the Supreme Court held that federal Rule 23 authorized a class action based

41 In re *Kosmos Energy Ltd. Securities Litigation*, 299 F.R.D. 133, 138-39 (N.D. Tex. 2014).

42 See *supra* text accompanying notes 30 and 34.

43 See Wald 2014.

44 *Ibidem.*

45 See *supra* text accompanying note 41.

on a state law that created a penalty for failure to pay insurance benefits in a timely manner even though the state Legislature that had created this claim also directed that there be no class actions asserting it.[46] That decision surely did not please opponents of class actions. Ironically, the case was in federal court only because the Class Action Fairness Act had widened federal court jurisdiction, emphasizing that even measures sought by opponents of class actions do not always produce the results they want.

In 2014, the Court rejected an effort to hobble securities fraud class actions under Rule 23(b)(3). That rule permits class actions only when the common issues predominate over issues relevant to individual claimants. But ordinarily fraud claims depend on proof of reliance – that the plaintiff was aware of and relied on the misrepresentation. In a securities fraud class action, that could mean that each purchaser or seller would have to testify, precluding class-action treatment. For the last 40 years, however, the US courts have recognized an exception to requiring proof of individual reliance when plaintiffs can demonstrate 'fraud on the market' – that the misrepresentation was material and the market in which the securities traded was 'efficient'. Then the efficiency of the market supported the assumption that all traders relied on the market to set a fair price, obviating proof they did so. Stressing academic criticism of this theory, defendants tried to persuade the Court to reverse course and reject it, which might have spelled death for securities fraud class actions. But by a 6-3 vote the Court refused to do so.[47]

Although the Court continues to take class-action cases, it is therefore dubious to predict that it will make major further changes in class-action law. Indeed, it is dubious to credit recurrent claims about whether its past decisions have done so. Regularly, when the Court announces a class-action judgment parties with class actions before the lower courts take aggressive positions about what the Court's decisions really mean. Very frequently, those positions overstate the real impact of the Court's decisions. So even if observers in Europe hear from US lawyers that our Supreme Court had definitively taken a step in a certain direction regarding class-action law, it may be wise to be cautious about accepting that assertion.

What remains, then, is the rulemaking process. That, of course, is where the modern American class action was born in 1966. As we approach the 50th anniversary of its creation, it is possible that there will be further proposals for change. In 2011, the Advisory Committee on Civil Rules created a Rule 23 Subcommittee, and during 2014 that Subcommittee began to study possible subjects for draft rule changes. It must be stressed that all such work is preliminary and exploratory,[48] but nonetheless it offers some indication of what problems seem to

46 *Shady Grove Orthopedic Associates, P.A. v Allstate Ins. Co.*, 559 US 393 (2010).

47 *See Halliburton Co. v Erica P. John Fund, Inc.*, 134 S.Ct. 2398 (2014).

48 I serve as Reporter of the Rule 23 Subcommittee. As noted above, however, I speak only for myself in this contribution, not for the Subcommittee or anyone else.

exist and what reactions may be possible.[49] Subject to those caveats, here are some areas of concern.

### 5.1. *Settlement Class Certification*

As noted above, most American class actions are settled rather than tried to judgment. (Many proposed class actions are dismissed or abandoned, as well.) Under a 1997 Supreme Court decision,[50] the standard for certifying a class for settlement purposes may differ from that used to certify for litigation purposes, but on some particulars the judicial scrutiny may be higher than it is for litigation certification.

At least some regard this attitude as too exacting for purposes of settlement certification, and fear that it retards productive settlements. The American Law Institute (ALI), for example, has proposed a set of criteria that might be written into Rule 23.[51] At the same time, at least one prominent scholar has argued that the whole idea of settlement class certification should be abandoned because adequate representation can only be assured when a case is certified for full litigation purposes.[52] As should be apparent, then, there is a range of views on this subject. But for those familiar with the Dutch settlement class procedure[53] this potential development may be of interest.

### 5.2. *Class Certification and Scrutiny of the Merits*

Under a 1974 Supreme Court decision,[54] the American courts long thought that they could not take account of the merits of plaintiffs' claim until after they had decided whether the case was properly certified as a class action. But that often produced difficulty if the court was to determine whether common questions existed and predominated over individual questions. As noted above,[55] the courts have shifted markedly from that view.

Whether any change to the rule might be appropriate in light of this development is an open question. To some extent, this development in the case law can be traced to some changes in Rule 23 made in 2003, but it resulted also from a number of other factors not controlled by changes in the rule since 1966. And

49 For those interested in more information, one source is a memorandum about possible topics for work of the Rule 23 Subcommittee in the Agenda Book, Advisory Committee on Civil Procedure Rules (22-23 March 2012), at 449-75, available at: <www.uscourts.gov/-RulesAndPolicies/rules/archives/agenda-books/committee-rules-civil-procedure.aspx> (last accessed in August 2014).

50 *Amchem Products, Inc. v Windsor*, 521 US 591 (1997).

51 American Law Institute 2010, §3.06.

52 See Erichson 2014.

53 See *supra* note 4 and accompanying text.

54 *Eisen v Carlise & Jaquelin*, 417 US 156 (1974).

55 See *supra* text accompanying note 41. See also Marcus 2011.

whether the question of class certification can really be separated from some evaluation of the merits of the case is quite uncertain.

## 5.3. *'Issue' Classes*

Since 1966, there has been a tension in the rule. Rule 23(b)(3) says that a class can be certified only if common questions predominate over individual questions. But Rule 23(c)(4)[56] seems to permit certification only as to certain issues even if those common issues don't predominate overall in the case. The federal courts of appeals have disagreed about whether 'issue' classes can be certified when common questions do not predominate.[57]

Given the split in lower court interpretation of this rule provision, there may be considerable force in favour of changing the rule to resolve the split. There are strong arguments that the 'issue' class procedure adds flexibility to class actions for courts and lawyers. At the same time, those concerned that Rule 23(b)(3) class actions (with their opt out feature) go too far may urge that this is too much flexibility.

## 5.4. *Criteria for Settlement Review*

Besides questions about the showing necessary for certifying cases only for purposes of settlement, concerns have been expressed about whether the criteria and techniques specified in the rule for judicial review of settlement proposals could be improved.

In 2003, the settlement-review provisions of Rule 23(e) were amplified quite considerably.[58] But the ALI criticized current practice as employing too many factors, and argued that the courts' handling of those factors is in disarray as a consequence.[59] So a further review of those factors may be in order even though they have recently been examined fairly thoroughly.

## 5.5. *Use of 'Cy Pres' Remedies*

As a feature of class action settlements, particularly of small claim cases, American courts have fairly frequently employed what we call a 'cy pres' solution to the problem of distributing relief to class members or dealing with a residue left in a

56 Rule 23(c)(4) says: 'When appropriate, an action may be brought or maintained as a class action with respect to particular issues'.

57 Compare *Castano v The American Tobacco Co.*, 84 F.3d 734, 745-46 n.21 (5th Cir. 1996) (saying that 'nimble use' of Rule 23(c)(4) may not be employed to 'manufacture predominance') with In re Nassau County Strip Search Cases, 461 F.3d 219, 230 (2d Cir. 2006) (rejecting the Fifth Circuit view and holding that 'district court may employ Rule 23(c)(4) ... to certify a class on a designated issue regardless of whether the claim as a whole satisfies the predominance test').

58 See *supra* text accompanying note 27.

59 See ALI 2010, §§3.03, 3.05, 3.11.

settlement fund after all submitted claims are satisfied. The idea has been for the court to authorize the remaining money (or perhaps all the money) to be used for a purpose that accords with the supposed objectives of the suit. For example, if the suit claims that defendant failed to protect the class members' privacy, the money might be provided to an organization that seeks to further customer privacy.

This is a striking example of American judicial creativity. Brazil, for example, has by statute adopted something like that for its class actions; money recovered is paid into a fund administered by the government.[60] California has by statute adopted a provision for class actions in its state courts directing something similar.[61] But even without authority in a statute or rule, federal judges have employed a similar strategy in a significant number of cases. This creativity has created considerable uneasiness in some quarters, and raised questions about the legitimacy - even in the US - of such judicial activity.

It bears emphasis that no provision of Rule 23 directly addresses 'cy pres' remedies. The ALI has proposed criteria for using this sort of remedy,[62] that at least some federal courts have adopted.[63] In addition, Chief Justice Roberts, concurring in denial of certiorari in a case involving some such questions, voiced serious concerns about the practice and observed that '[i]n a suitable case, this Court may need to clarify the limits of the use of such remedies'.[64] Rule changes may be another way to deal with these issues.

## 5.6. *Other Issues*

This tentative list of possible issue hardly exhausts all those that might occupy the rule makers in the future. For one thing, additional proposals have been formally submitted to the rule makers by members of the public.[65] For another thing, the Rule 23 Subcommittee will surely engage in outreach to identify further issues and evaluate the importance of various issues.

60 See Gidi 2003, p. 339-340.

61 See Cal. Code Civ. Proc. §384, which declares the intent of the Legislature to be that 'the unpaid residuals in class action litigation are distributed, to the extent possible, in a manner designed either to further the purposes of the underlying causes of action, or to promote justice for all Californians.'

62 ALI 2010 §3.07.

63 See *Klier v Elf Autochem North America, Inc.*, 658 F.3d 468, 474-75 (5th Cir. 2011).

64 *Marek v Lane*, 134 S.Ct. 8 (2013).

65 For those interested in seeing what has been formally proposed, all such proposals are posted on a federal courts website (collected on an annual basis) available at: <www.uscourts.gov/RulesAndPolicies/rules/archives/archived-rules-suggestions/civil-rules-suggestions.aspxm> (last accessed in August 2014). These suggestions relate to all the rules, not only the class-action rule. One interested only in that should look for proposals about Rule 23.

## 6. Taming the Wolf?

At least some American eyes have been paying attention to developments regarding group litigation in Europe.[66] Perhaps this contribution will assist some in Europe to consider what can be learned from the American arrangement as they evaluate possible provisions of this sort in their own systems. Owing to the distinctive role private enforcement of law plays in the US,[67] there is likely always to be some divergence between any measures adopted in Europe and the technique used in the US. But those tempted to reject the American model out of hand might consider whether the features of American class actions they dislike are really a consequence of features of American litigation more generally. If that's so, it may be that US class actions are worth a second look even for those who adamantly reject the other features of American litigation that can make our class action the Big Bad Wolf.

[66] For a very thorough study of developments in the European Union, see Strong 2012.
[67] See *supra* text accompanying notes 6-8.

## Bibliography

**Alexander 1991**
Alexander, J., 'Do the Merits Matter? A Study of Settlements in Securities Class Actions', *Stanford Law Review*, 1991, Vol. 43, p. 497-597.

**American Law Institute 2010**
American Law Institute, *Principles of the Law – Aggregate Litigation*, St. Paul, MN: American Law Institute Publishers, 2010.

**Burbank, Farhang & Kritzer 2013**
Burbank, S., Farhang, S. & Kritzer, H., 'Private Enforcement', *Lewis & Clark Law Review*, 2013, Vol. 17, p. 637-722.

**Chaffee 1950**
Chaffee, Z., *Some Problems of Equity*, Ann Arbor: University of Michigan Press, 1950.

**Erichson 2014**
Erichson, H., 'The Problem of Settlement Class Actions', *George Washington Law Review*, 2014, Vol. 82, p. 951-989.

**Farhang 2011**
Farhang, S., *The Litigation State*, Princeton & Oxford: Princeton University Press, 2011.

**Fisch 2002**
Fisch, J., 'Lawyers on the Auction Block: Evaluating the Selection of Class Counsel by Auction', *Columbia Law Review*, 2002, Vol. 102, p. 650-728.

**Gidi 2003**
Gidi, A., 'Class Actions in Brazil – A Model for Civil Law Countries', *American Journal of Comparative Law*, 2003, Vol. 51, p. 311-408.

**Hodges 2008**
Hodges, C., *The Reform of Class and Representative Actions in European Legal Systems*, Oxford & Portland, Ore.: Hart Publishing, 2008.

**Kagan 2001**
Kagan, R., *Adversarial Legalism*, Cambridge, MA & London: Harvard University Press, 2001.

**Kane 2012**
Kane, M.K., 'The Supreme Court's Recent Class Action Jurisprudence: Gazing Into a Crystal Ball', *Lewis & Clark Law Review*, 2012, Vol. 16, p. 1015-1047.

**Kaplan 1969**
Kaplan, B., 'A Prefatory Note', *Boston College Industrial & Commercial Law Review*, 1969, Vol. 10, p. 497-501.

**Krans 2014**
Krans, B., 'The Dutch Act on Collective Settlement of Mass Damages', *Pacific McGeorge Global Business & Development Law Journal*, 2014, Vol. 27, p. 281-301.

**Marcus 2011**
Marcus, R., 'Reviving Judicial Gatekeeping of Aggregation', *George Washington Law Review*, 2011, Vol. 79, p. 324-373.

**Marcus, 2013**
Marcus, R., 'America's Dynamic and Extensive Experience With Collective Litigation', in Stadler, A. & Hodges, C. (eds.), *Resolving Mass Disputes: ADR and Settlement of Mass Claims*, Cambridge: Edward Elgar, 2013, p. 148-171.

**Rabiej 2005**
Rabiej, J., 'The Making of Class Action Rule 23 – What were We Thinking?', *Mississippi College Law Review*, 2005, Vol. 24, p. 323-392.

**Rubenstein 2004**
Rubenstein, W., 'On What a "Private Attorney General" Is – And Why It Matters', *Vanderbilt Law Review*, 2004, Vol. 57, p. 2129-2173.

**Strong 2012**
Strong, S.I., 'Regulatory Litigation in the European Union: Does the U.S. Class Action Have a New Analogue?', *Notre Dame Law Review*, 2012, Vol. 88, p. 899-972.

**Wald 2014**
Wald, M., 'Whirlpool Wants Congress to Ban Class-Action Suits Tied to Energy Star Program', *NY Times*, 21 July 2014, at B3.

**Walker 2012**
Walker, J., 'General Report', in Maleshin, D. (ed.), *Civil Procedure in Cross-Cultural Dialogue: Eurasia Context*, Moscow: Statut Pub. House, 2012, p. 413-458.

**Weiss & Beckerman 1995**
Weiss, E. & Beckerman, J., 'Let the Money Do the Monitoring: How Institutional Investors Can Reduce Agency Costs in Securities Class Actions', *Yale Law Journal*, 1995, Vol. 104, p. 2053-2129.

**Yeazell 1987**
Yeazell, S., *From Medieval Group Litigation to the Modern Class Action*, New Haven: Yale University Press, 1987.

A. Uzelac

# WHY NO CLASS ACTIONS IN EUROPE? A VIEW FROM THE SIDE OF DYSFUNCTIONAL JUSTICE SYSTEMS

## 1. Introduction

In Europe, collective redress is increasingly becoming a popular topic, both for learned scholars, and for international organizations. Not surprisingly, the European Union has joined this trend.[1] Political dictate and academic curiosity are powerful driving forces, therefore it can be safely predicted that further exploration of various forms of collective litigation and their introduction in the legislation and practice of European countries will continue to gain momentum.

All the same, the optimistic wave of pro-collectivist procedural activism needs to have a reality check. In this chapter, we will point to a few reasons why it is not likely that class actions and similar forms of collective (aggregate, multi-party) litigation will ever develop into a serious procedural vehicle in a number of European countries. The primary focus of the analysis will be the institutional and organizational (in)capacity of the European civil justice systems, particularly in the (not so small) number of countries that experience difficulties with the efficiency and quality of their judiciaries. Some typical difficulties with the introduction of various forms of collective litigation (very modest ones, indeed) will be illustrated in the example of Croatia and its association suits (*Verbandsklagen*) in the area of consumer protection and anti-discrimination.

In conclusion, it will be questioned whether the very intentions of the introduction of collective redress mechanisms are clear and well thought out, and whether they, to the extent that they are clear, have the capacity to satisfy those intentions. Ultimately, the chapter will attempt to prove that a movement in favour of private enforcement of public interest matters in a European context does not have a chance of improving access to justice. On the contrary, it might work harmfully, both for the achieved level of public enforcement of legal rights, and for

1 See for an update of European developments in the area of collective redress Silvestri 2013 and the contribution of Hess to this volume.

the achieved level of judicial protection of rights in 'conventional', individual civil litigation.

Before entering into the merits, a small disclaimer: the topic of this chapter is not an 'American style' class action. In the title of this chapter 'class actions' refers to the most extreme form of complex, multi-party civil actions with elements of public interest. But, the notion of 'class actions' epitomizes in a certain way all forms of collective or aggregate litigation,[2] including large consolidated litigation, representative proceedings, test-case litigation, *Verbandsklagen*, group litigation orders, model cases and the like.[3] By pointing to difficulties and problems regarding several much softer forms of collective redress, *argumento ad maiori ad minus* we hope to say something about class actions in the narrow sense of the term as well.

## 2. Alice Meets the White Rabbit: Discovery of Collective Litigation by a (Southern) European Judiciary

The history of group litigation in Europe is certainly long.[4] But after a surge that corresponded to the collectivist nature of medieval feudal societies, in modern times group litigation has only been 'a temporary phenomenon', confined to a narrow substantive range. In essence, the exceptional cases of group litigation in the 19th and 20th centuries were 'dictated by the concerns of the particular groups momentarily occupying social and judicial interest' and lasted only so long as such groups either gained sufficient political power to change legislation in their favour or 'lost their claim on public attention and faded both from reports and social consciousness'.[5]

The re-discovery of group litigation in Europe in the 2000s was not a product of an organic development. It was also not an original invention aimed to improve the range of services offered by national judicial systems.[6] In its largest extent, the European developments in favour of group litigation were the product of fascination with the 'curious animal' of American class actions. Even today, a discussion among European lawyers about American practices of collective

2 A good definition of aggregate litigation as 'litigation that undertakes some manner of unified resolution with regard to related civil claims held by multiple persons' is given by ALI - see *Principles of the law of aggregate litig.* § 1.02 cmt. a (Council Draft No. 2, at 12, 18 November 2008), cited according to Nagareda 2009, p. 4-5. It may be important to note that all general points of this chapter are limited to litigation, as opposed to mediation, collective negotiation and consumer ADR, which in the view of the author have much better potential as dispute resolution devices than aggregate litigation.

3 For various forms of aggregate litigation in Europe see, in addition to the chapters assembled in this book, Andrews 2013, p. 621-656 (for England); Baetge 2007 (for Germany); Kulski 2011 (for Poland); Lindblom 1997 (for Sweden). See also Eliantonio *et al.* 2013.

4 For a detailed account on the historical development of group litigation see Yeazell 1987.

5 *Ibidem* at p. 195-196.

6 Before the 2000s, forms of group litigation in Europe were more interesting to American than European scholars (see Fisch 1979), with the exception of Mauro Cappelletti, who was a pioneer also in this field, see e.g. Cappelletti 1975.

litigation resembles the encounter of Alice with the White Rabbit from the famous 1865 novel of Lewis Carroll: the main characters are transported into a strange but fascinating world of inexplicable logic, with some creatures - like opt-out class actions - possessing stranger charm than others. Playing with the curiosities and spectacular creatures of Wonderland is indeed wonderful, but transposing the adventure into the real world may be more of a challenge. In the following text, I will illustrate this in the examples of the (very modest) uses of the new means of collective litigation in Croatia.

### 2.1. *Collective Litigation in Croatia or How Croatia Completed the EU Accession Homework and Devised the 'Most Modern' Legislation for Group Litigation*

Certain, very specific forms of proceedings regarding diffuse, fragmentary and collective rights existed in the period of the Socialist Federal Republic of Yugoslavia (fuelled by the doctrine of the self-managed socialist economy run by 'associated labour').[7] In the transition period in the 1990s the practice of litigation in most post-Yugoslav states attempted to escape 'homemade' procedures and return to conventional practices of individual litigation. The interest in collective and public interest litigation therefore occurred relatively late, and only in recent times under the influence of the EU accession process, during which it was perceived that the introduction of collective redress is part of the homework that has to be completed prior to joining the EU.[8]

If we disregard some relatively exotic forms that were primarily of academic interest, the first law that introduced a version of 'association suits', inspired by the German *Verbandsklage,* was the Consumer Protection Act of 2003 (hereafter: CPA, Off. Gaz. 96/03).[9] The action was granted for suppression of unfair contractual and business practices and illicit advertising to consumer associations against companies and telecom operators. This form of action was further reshaped in CPA 2007 (Off. Gaz. 79/07 *et seq.*), allowing additional organizations and entities the right to bring claims in the interest of consumers. The new CPA was at the time of its promulgation declared to be 'one of the most modern in Europe', but at the same time everyone conceded that the broad guarantees and rights were not converted into real life.[10]

Another law that introduced a similar form of *Verbandsklage* was the Anti-Discrimination Act of 2009 (hereafter: ADA, Off. Gaz. 85/08). That law provided for an even broader *locus standi* for claims relating to discrimination, that was defined to include 'associations, public bodies, institutions and other organisations in

7 See e.g. Rakić-Vodinelić 1982, p. 60.

8 See Tomljenović 2008.

9 See Dika 2003a; Dika 2003b; Baretić 2009; Triva & Dika 2004, p. 824.

10 See a typical journalist's report on 'good law, but consumers' interests still violated' at: <www.poslovni.hr/mobile/hrvatska/dobar-zakon-a-potrosaci-osteceni-80916> (last accessed in January 2014).

accordance with the law and [which] have legitimate interests for the protection of the collective interest[s] of a particular group or deal with the protection of the right to equal treatment'.[11]

Finally, as a part of the final stage of alignment of national legislation with EU law, the government added in the 2011 Amendments to the Code of Civil Procedure (hereafter: CCP, Off. Gaz. 57/11) another chapter, titled 'Actions for the protection of collective interests and rights'.[12] However, instead of supplying new, specific forms of the 'horizontal' framework of collective redress, the new CCP rules provided only a general definition and a few general rules for 'collective rights and interests claims', which apply under the condition that such claims are expressly provided in legislation regulating the specific sector (such as CPA or ADA).

Apart from these options, there are no other specific public interest multi-party proceedings, at least not in the area of civil litigation. In the domain of administrative disputes, the new Act on Administrative Disputes (hereafter: AAD, Off. Gaz. 20/10 and 143/12), written under the influence of German experts from an EU project, provided for an option of representative litigation (Croatian: *ogledni spor,* German *Musterverfahren*),[13] which has been available since 2012 when a new network of administrative courts was established. However, this instrument has not yet been transplanted to the CCP and the domain of civil litigation.

At the purely technical level, the new multi-party litigation devices may be assessed as state-of-the-art pieces of procedural legislation, with most issues regulated similarly to some other European countries (mainly Germany and Austria). For instance, the 'associational' anti-discrimination suits, just as the individual ones, introduce shifting the burden of proof and *prima facie* proof of discrimination. On the side of the plaintiffs, multiple entities may initiate the proceedings, but they can also join the proceedings in individual anti-discrimination suits as auxiliary intervenors (*Nebenintervenienten*). But, in order to produce legal effect as to all members of the group, the litigation needs to be instituted by a collective action, upon petition of an organization that has legitimate interests for the two sectors (consumer protection or the fight against discrimination). In such cases, the relief sought has to be limited to the establishment of violation (e.g. declaration of unfair standard contract terms in consumer contracts, or finding of discriminatory practices). While possible claims include the petition for injunctive relief (reinstatement of the *status quo ante,* prohibition of further illicit practices and the court order to publish the text of the judgment), no compensatory relief is available within the group litigation proceedings. In order to seek monetary damages, all members of the affected group need to bring individual actions. In those actions, the findings of the court in the

11 Art. 24, para 1 ADA. The author of this chapter was a member of the drafting group of that Act, contributing mainly to the procedural scheme described above.

12 See more in Dika 2011; Menđušić Škugor 2012.

13 Art. 48 ADA enables the Administrative Court to select a representative case if 10 or more administrative suits with the same factual and legal background are pending before it. The 'model suit' in such a case proceeds, while the other pending proceedings are stayed.

collective proceedings, if final and binding, would also have preclusive effect in the individual litigation, where it would have force of *res iudicata* which resolves in and of itself preliminary issues such as the existence of illicit business practices or the presence of discrimination.[14]

All these topics may be elaborated at considerable length, and they have been indeed extensively commented upon by a number of academic lawyers.[15] More informative, however, is an insight into the practical use of the new procedural vehicles. Admittedly, some of these vehicles have been available only for a few years, but the doors were opened for the first collective consumer litigation already over a decade ago – and this should be a period of sufficient length to justify inquiry into the real life of collective litigation in Croatia.

Not surprisingly, there is not much to show. Admittedly, the two outlined multi-party devices are not in their entirety 'empty boxes' (to borrow an expression from Professor Silvestri), but it might have been better had it been the case. Namely, that small content that filled the normative framework ('boxes') for collective litigation in everyday judicial practice turned out to be very different from the optimistic expectations of the lawmakers. We will first demonstrate this in the example of anti-discrimination legislation, and then in the context of collective consumer protection cases.

## 2.2. *In the Quest for Gay Rights: First Anti-Discrimination Verbandsklagen and Their Meagre Success*

First, as to the quantity. In anti-discrimination cases, according to reports of various citizens' associations, only six collective anti-discrimination suits were filed in 2009 and 2010, in spite of thousands of registered complaints filed with civil society organizations, and several hundreds of complaints submitted to offices of various ombudspersons. Official data is until the present day incomplete, as the Ministry of Justice failed to publish forms required for adequate monitoring, and therefore individual and collective anti-discrimination suits could not be separately reported.[16] But, the aggregate results are interesting as well: according to Ministry of Justice (MoJ) data for 2012 (the last published report at the time of the writing of this chapter), there were 116 pending individual and collective anti-discrimination cases, but only 16 cases were finally disposed of, 'out of which 1 anti-discrimination claim was accepted, three denied, and 12 cases otherwise disposed of'. The rest, exactly 100 cases, are 'still pending'.[17] In short, even after four years of application, anti-discrimination litigation has resulted in very few final and binding judgments that found discrimination (3 in 2011 and 1 in 2012).

14 See more in Uzelac 2009, p. 95-109.
15 See *supra* n. 9 and 12 above.
16 Ombudsman Discrimination Report 2012, p. 25.
17 *Ibidem*, p. 29.

Among the interesting examples of 'successful' collective anti-discrimination suits, we can mention two publicized cases regarding 'gay discrimination in playing football'. One of them was initiated by an alliance of gay and lesbian associations (LBGTQ Rights Protection Alliance) after media statements of the President of the Croatian Football Federation (CFF) that 'gay football players as sick persons would never play for the national team'. Similar statements were echoed by the informal boss of the Zagreb football club *Dinamo*, and they were also the subject of other collective anti-discrimination proceedings. Interestingly, in both cases, in spite of loud public outcry and close monitoring by the Ombudsperson's office, trial courts found no discrimination, holding that anti-gay statements were 'personal opinions'. In one of these cases, the first instance court judgment was reversed by the Supreme Court, and the President of the CFF had to publicly apologize for his statement. But, the same court upheld upon appeal the dismissal of the second anti-discrimination suit; today, almost four years after the controversial statements were made, the secondary appeal against this decision is still pending. On the other hand, collective anti-discrimination suits filed by gay and lesbian associations against a nun who taught, within her classes of religious education in primary schools, that homosexuality is a sickness, was finally dismissed based on lack of evidence, as well as on the basis that the nun was only teaching the official catechism. Another similar suit against a priest who praised anti-gay violence against 'perverts' at the Gay Pride in Belgrade in his internet blog was more successful, and resulted in a finding of discrimination and an order for removal of the discriminatory content from the internet.[18]

To complete the picture of anti-discrimination proceedings in Croatian civil courts, another case may be noted, though formally not a collective one. It was lodged as an individual anti-discrimination suit, in which several gay associations and the Gender Equality Ombudsman acted as intervenors (*amici curiae*). The case dealt with a junior university professor who was exposed to mobbing and mockery by his senior faculty colleagues on account of his sexual orientation, which in the end resulted in failure to put him up for promotion. The peculiarity in that case was that the trial court ultimately found discrimination on some accounts of the civil suit, but in the end the claimant was ordered to pay the quite substantive costs of the other side (the Faculty of Organization and Informatics in Varaždin), because the court held that the claimant succeeded in only 20 per cent of his claims.[19] As the claimant only got symbolic satisfaction, with no compensatory relief, he ended up paying for his own success. Although the decision was successfully appealed, the whole matter finally resulted in the plaintiff's quitting his job and leaving the country after issuing a public statement that the harassment at his workplace continued.

18 For a good case study of the association suits in Croatia see Poretti 2014, p. 7-42.

19 OS Varaždin, 18 P-3153/10-89, judgment of 12 July 2012.

### 2.3. *Interim Victory of Bank Loans Consumers in Swiss Franc Appreciation Case*

Apart from a few collective suits for the protection of rights of sexual minorities (which almost entirely covered all case law in collective anti-discrimination suits)[20] the *Verbandsklagen* only occurred in the context of consumer protection. Technically, the consumer protection collective actions were supposed to be the 'big brother' of actions under ADA, but they were overshadowed by the anti-discrimination cases described in the previous section. In fact, for about eight years, there were no association suits for consumer protection whatsoever, for various reasons.

Some of the hidden restrictions to collective consumer protection claims were apparently inspired by EU law. So, for instance, as EU Member States are required to give notices to the European Commission concerning qualified entities that may request an injunction for the protection of consumers' interests,[21] the CPA provides that only those entities that are listed by a special government decree have *locus standi* to submit collective consumer rights' protection claims. The actual government decree, however, contained a rather short and inconsistent list of qualified bodies that mentioned more governmental bodies than associations for the protection of consumers' interests.[22] To that extent, the *locus standi* rules of the CPA were different from those of the ADA, which contained an open formula ('any organization or body …') – and this led to a much smaller volume of litigation in this area.

The story about the (so far) unique (and therefore even more famous) collective consumer litigation case in Croatia known as 'Swiss franc litigation' also began by the dismissal of the action for reasons of lack of standing. This association suit was the consequence of the sharp rise in the value of the Swiss franc after the global financial crisis, which caused monthly instalments for consumers of bank loans indexed to the Swiss franc to rise on average by around 50 per cent. The claimant, the association for the protection of the interests of consumers of bank loans *Franak*, managed to circumvent the restriction of *locus standi* by linking to another association (*Potrošač*) that was among the qualified entities on the

20 Due to a number of collective redress cases initiated by gay and lesbian organizations, one researcher has argued that a false impression is created among the general public that collective anti-discrimination redress exists only for the use of the LBGTQ community. Poretti 2014, p. 30.

21 See Directive 98/27/EC (now Directive 2009/22/EC), Art. 4(3). It should be noted that the Directive only applies to cross-border disputes, and that it does not bind the Member States in national disputes, but the national legislator may nevertheless chose to use it as a model.

22 E.g. among the qualified bodies the Decree lists the Ombudsperson for Child Protection (but not the general Ombudsman office), and only two consumer protection organizations. See *Uredba o određivanju osoba ovlaštenih za pokretanje postupaka radi zaštite kolektivnih interesa potrošača*, NN 124/09. The list also authorizes various government ministries to institute proceedings, which is not in line with the EU Directive that requires qualified bodies to be 'independent' – see more in Poljanec 2013.

government list.[23] In the second try, the case was declared admissible, and resulted in one of the most well-known and controversial judgments in recent Croatian history. The Commercial Court in Zagreb, namely, ordered on 4 July 2013 that the eight biggest commercial banks (selected by the claimant as those that gave most loans with Swiss franc indexation clauses) had to recalculate the loans in favour of the consumers.[24] In his judgment, Judge Radovan Dobronić found that loans given in Croatian national currency (*kuna*), but linked to the Swiss franc, were governed by contracts that allowed banks to change the interest rates in a non-transparent manner, thereby violating the consumer protection rules.

The final destiny of this decision is still uncertain. It was appealed to the High Commercial Court, which is unlikely to decide on the appeal until the end of 2014. The comments on the decision were mixed, ranging from sharp criticism to fervent approval. It also caused political reactions, and partly motivated a change in legislation that provided a statutory recalculation that lowered the interest rates for the consumer loans indexed to the Swiss franc.[25]

This case also attracted international attention.[26] Not entirely unconnected to this Croatian case was a series of litigations in courts in Serbia and Bosnia & Herzegovina. There, the procedural device was not collective, but individual litigation. Some reported first instance judgments decided that agreements on variable interest rates indexed to the value of the Swiss franc were null and void, some found illegality of contract terms, or rejected claims. None of the decisions in these countries has, at the time of submission of this chapter, become *res iudicata*.[27] Meanwhile, different judgments regarding the same matter have been reported from Austria and Hungary.

## 3. Why Not? Inferences from Particular Southern European Examples

The experience from about a decade of very modest forms of collective litigation in Croatia, which were used in real life in an even more modest way, may be limited and incomplete. Yet, some inferences may be drawn, partly exactly because of the scanty reception of collective litigation in practice. I will first suggest several conclusions based upon the presented developments in Croatia that may be relevant especially for some European judiciaries that experience difficulties with

[23] Yet, *Franak* remained the main factual claimant which continued to control the litigation, issuing public statements, providing its own lawyers, and financing litigation from its own funds, while *Potrošač* acted only as the formal plaintiff, bringing the façade necessary for the admissibility of the claim. See *inter alia*: <http://udrugafranak.hr/index.php/stavovi-udruge/item/572-slučaj-franak-sažetak> (last accessed in January 2014).

[24] Judgment of the Commercial Court in Zagreb of 4 July 2013, 26.P-1401/2012.

[25] See Amendments to Act on Consumer Loans from November 2013 (*ZID Zakona o potrošačkom kreditiranju*, Off. Gaz. 143/13).

[26] <www.reuters.com/article/2013/07/04/croatia-banks-idUSL5N0FA1DZ20130704> (last accessed in January 2014).

[27] See *inter alia*: <http://danas.net.hr/svijet/susjedi-slave-krediti-u-svicarcima-proglaseni-nistetnima>; <www.vesti.rs/counter.php?id=4982694> (last accessed in January 2014).

the functioning of their civil justice systems. While less relevant for a number of more effective and flexible European judicial systems, some points may still apply to them as well. Further, more general arguments will be added in the last part of this chapter.

The three inferences from Croatian experience that I suggest may be summarized as follows:

1. If a judicial system is not capable of securing litigation within a reasonable time in conventional, 'one-on-one' litigation, it will not be able to do any better in collective litigation.
2. If the effectiveness of judicial protection is limited due to the excessive availability of means of recourse that impede finality and prevent final enforcement, collective litigation cannot fulfil its main purpose.
3. If a civil justice system does not dispose of organizational and procedural mechanisms and case-management techniques for handling complex multi-party and multi-claim matters, any collective litigation device will be inappropriate and will be perceived as 'legal irritant'.

These statements will be briefly explained below.

### 3.1. *Slow Individual, even Slower Collective Justice*

The hallmark of southern European judiciaries has been for decades their slowness. Delays and backlogs have been for a long time the characteristic feature of Italian civil justice, but the situation is not much different in a number of other southern European countries, like Greece, Portugal, Slovenia and Croatia, as well as in a number of post-Socialist countries, like Poland.[28]

The Croatian experience demonstrates that delays happen even in cases of very minor social and financial importance, for instance in small claims' litigation. After several decades of judicial reforms, it can still be safely predicted that relatively simple cases defined in law as 'urgent' – like trespassing (*Besitzstörung*, disturbance of possession) – will last for many years.

Should collective litigation devices expect any better – and faster – processing? This is not likely. Rather, what can be expected is that an increased level of complexity will bring along an increased time use. The higher level of social importance and multiplication of the people affected by the judgment could add to the need to take more evidence, and for countries like Croatia, which nurture a paternalistic and inquisitorial style of court proceedings in which the court has to take care that 'no stone should be left unturned', delays will definitely occur on a much larger scale. As shown in some Croatian anti-discrimination cases, in which the issues were quite straightforward (evaluation of a single public statement), the time needed to produce a final decision was over two years (with a very

28 See *inter alia* Uzelac 2008.

controversial final result). In addition, due to the fact that *Verbandsklagen* cannot result in any determination of compensation, such adjudicated cases serve only to cover a preliminary issue in subsequent satellite litigation, in which the determination of damages may again result in years of litigation.

### 3.2. *Lack of Finality and Effective Enforcement: Toothless Collective Justice*

In connection with the previous point is the proneness of civil justice to submit almost every judicial decision to re-examination, which may lead – according to the European Court of Human Rights – to a systemic procedural deficiency described as an 'endless cycle of remittals'.[29] In successor countries of the former Yugoslavia, for instance, the right to appeal against any judicial decision is lifted to the level of a constitutional guarantee. Until very recent times, almost every appeal suspended the enforcement of the decisions. Therefore, the first instance judgments were generally thought to be only an indication, a draft without a binding legal effect.

To that extent, even if, in a heroic and singular achievement, a first-instance judge were exceptionally to produce a well-reasoned judgment within a reasonable time (as in the earlier cited judgment of Judge Dobronić in the *Franak* case), such a decision might linger to the point of oblivion in the dockets of the higher court, with a high probability that a case would be remitted again with a 'give it another try' instruction. All the efforts in producing an exceptional piece of legal writing with convincing arguments may in the end prove to be a masochistic exercise, since the judgments of trial courts are rarely if ever published, and the reasoning of the court might ultimately remain unknown even to the circle of legal experts.[30]

And, if, at the very end of a long chain of legal remedies, all the procedural links were broken, and the judgment became *res iudicata,* another battle may be in sight – the battle for the enforcement of the decision. This battle may be equally lengthy and ineffective as the one for the final and binding judgment. As demonstrated above in the case of a gay scholar and his anti-discrimination claims, the belated victory may effectively mean ultimate defeat, since adverse judicial findings with a mild admonition issued after many months of delays may only encourage the perpetrators.

### 3.3. *No Appropriate Personal and Organizational Design for Mass Claim Processing*

Let us for a moment disregard the challenges of slow processes and their ineffective transformation into real life. One may say that these challenges are the same for individual and collective litigation, and therefore do not bring anything new into

29 See ECHR case, *Božić v Croatia*, No. 22457/02, § 36, 29 June 2006.

30 Indeed, the full text of the *Franak* judgments was never published, and the author of this contribution had to procure it upon special request addressed to the court.

the debate. But, there are still some special difficulties that may pertain solely to collective litigation devices. They relate to the fact that the personal and organizational design of the European judiciaries in several aspects collide with the ideals of appropriate decision-making regarding claims affecting interests of large groups of people.

Back in 1969 John Henry Merryman pointed to the 'quite different status of the civil law judge' as compared to the 'judicial supremacy' of the judges as 'culture heroes' of the common law tradition.[31] He described the civil law judge as 'a kind of expert clerk', whose task is 'to fit into the formal syllogism of scholastic logic' the whole process of judicial decision-making, as 'an operator' with 'a mechanical function', briefly put as 'a civil servant who performs important but essentially uncreative functions'.[32] A frank, self-critical analysis forces us to conclude that Merryman's over 45-year-old descriptions have not lost their freshness and accuracy, at least when the Judiciary of the European South is concerned. At the organizational level, similarly fresh is the description of the specific design of courts and judicial bodies by Mirjan Damaška who pointed to 'a strong attachment of the judicial apparatus to hierarchical bureaucratization'.[33] The distinctive features of judicial bureaucracy in almost all judiciaries of the 'Mediterranean' model[34] are formalism, inflexibility and concentration on the processing of individual actions in cases predominantly of private interest.

One of the clear illustrations of these features is the total absence and virtual unsuitability of judicial organizations for any form of teamwork – a feature that should be crucial for the effective resolution of large, complex matters. In Croatia, for instance, the only collaborators of judges are their typists. Even though some judicial personnel are supposed to assist judges, such as 'judicial advisors' or senior interns that used to be on the judicial career track, they never fulfilled their advisory or auxiliary role, but instead were assigned to the individual handling of less important cases in the solitary isolation of their offices.[35]

The very idea that the courts and judges should be flexible in their procedural rules and practices in order to adjust to the requirements of the case at hand is generally perceived as contrary to the strict nature of procedural legislation and the duty to apply the same rules to every case, which is generally assigned to the individual judge by random selection in a pre-set order which does not (and should not) recognize any priority. In an attempt to prevent corruption, judicial reforms are even further reducing the room for adjustment, as the need for reassignment to a

31 Merryman 1985, p. 34-35.

32 *Ibidem*, p. 37.

33 See Damaška 1986, p. 34.

34 A recently concluded EU project 'Professional development of Judicial Advisors and future Judges and State Attorneys through establishment of a Self Sustainable Training System' (IPA 2009) confirmed that the role and status of judicial advisors need to be changed, but so far has caused no reaction from the competent Croatian authorities.

35 For the concept of 'Mediterranean civil procedure' see Uzelac 2008, p. 73-75.

specially proficient judge or a group of judges may be expressly forbidden as potentially dangerous 'judge shopping'.[36]

At the level of case management and court administration, most practices are also constructed around the ideal of the rational processing of individual cases of average or below-average complexity. Sometimes such a setting creates considerable problems even in cases that are governed by conventional procedural rules. The simple multi-party and multi-claim rules (German: *Streitgenossenschaft*) in the current procedural codes originate from 19th-century codifications. Still, their application in a modern context, in a case with dozens or hundreds of claimants or respondents, becomes a nightmare for courts and individual judges. In Croatian judicial practice, therefore, the courts prefer to separate and process individually such cases wherever possible, instead of consolidating them for resolution of 'cloned' cases in joint proceedings.[37]

Additional arguments regarding the logistical unsuitability of civil justice for the processing of large, multi-party cases concern the sheer technical conditions of work, like the lack of adequate courtrooms or suitable software for case tracking. Most trial court hearing rooms in Croatia have between 10 and 20 square meters, and higher courts generally do not have hearing rooms at all when civil cases are concerned. Not surprisingly, new IT systems for case management regularly do not have modules for collective litigation.

Finally, one may ask whether southern European judges have any reason to like aggregate litigation. The reply would without hesitation be negative. The judicial resentment towards multi-party and collective litigation is not surprising, since there are very few systemic incentives for judges and judicial personnel to engage in managing and adjudicating large, complex cases. Why bother resolving hard cases when performance monitoring methods are based on quantity? For instance, the new framework criteria for the workload of judges in Croatian courts (a document that is elaborated in collaboration with an EU sponsored project of assistance to judicial reforms) provides that a judge in a commercial court should annually deliver about 200 judgments in litigation proceedings.[38] At the same time, quality measurement is centred on the percentage of quashed judgments. Under such circumstances, a judge who produced (like the one in the cited *Franak* case) a judgment of 180 pages that is likely to be set aside by the higher court as

36 Random or pre-set assignation of cases to judges is in some countries, like Germany, lifted to the level of constitutional principle (*das Recht auf den gesetzlichen Richter*) – see Art. 101, para 1(2) of the Constitution. In other European countries it is a part of statutory law (see e.g. Art. 10(1) of the Croatian Law on Courts). Quite to the contrary, the American practice of aggregate litigation contains a 'selection bias' in favour of judges who share enthusiasm for group litigation – see Marcus 2008, p. 2284-2287.

37 Such cases occurred in the practice of Croatian courts, e.g. as mass claims for payment of benefits of state employees under collective labour agreements.

38 *Okvirna mjerila za rad sudaca*, Zagreb, 6 June 2007, MoJ (<http://pak.hr/cke/propisi,%20zakoni/okvirna-mjerila-za-rad-sudaca/OKVIRNA.pdf> (last accessed in January 2014)). This was amended on 28 December 2012, when the new Framework Criteria decreased this number to 180 (but with increases in other categories).

controversial is not only irrational but is also running the risk of disciplinary proceedings at the end of the year, when the court presidents have the obligation to report all judges who significantly underperform in the statistical evaluation of their work and miss the set targets of work performance.

## 4. Why Yes? A General Test for the Desirability of Public Interest Litigation in Europe

Now, let us imagine that we are able to overcome all organizational and technical difficulties. Would that justify the generous introduction of multi-party devices into the judicial systems of European countries? Before jumping to any conclusions, it would be helpful to see whether the novelties under consideration would pass another simple test – this time not of the feasibility, but of the desirability of such a development. I would like to propose three questions that forward-thinking reformers and policy-makers might find useful to ask when assessing plans for the introduction of innovative collective litigation devices.

They are:

1. Will it make the handling of major disasters and burning social issues any better?
2. Will it improve the functioning of the Judiciary?
3. Will it be more attractive for the end users of the justice system?

Here are some thoughts regarding each of these questions.

### *4.1. Will It Make the Handling of Major Disasters and Burning Social Issues any Better?*

Today, in a global context, class actions and other collective litigation devices are associated with attempts to deal with modern challenges, like major disasters (from airplane crashes to the harmful side-effects of drugs or toxic substances). They are also used to address some burning social issues, from indirect discrimination to nicotine addiction. Indeed, the ubiquitous topic of consumer protection is among those issues as well.

What can be gained by the more proactive involvement of civil courts and judges, and by the expansion of the devices of group litigation? Indeed, group litigation inevitably has an element of policy-making, which can come close to social engineering – after all, most important conferences devoted to collective litigation speak of 'protecting supra-individual legal interests'[39] or 'public interest litigation'.

Beyond the technical tools for making group adjudication feasible and effective, and successful in dealing with supra-individual legal interests, policy matters need appropriate human substance – adjudicators who have broad

39 E.g. at the XIV World Conference of IAPL – see Ortells Ramos 2014; Kulski 2011; Verbic 2011.

experience and versatile training, and who know how to deal with matters of general, future importance. Are such individuals available in European systems of justice? The view from the European South shows us that it is increasingly difficult to find a judicial official who would correspond to these professional requirements. In stark contrast with the USA, the European career Judiciary has a number of features that are more or less inconsistent with the need for an authoritative, wise and experienced policy-maker. Judges are generally recruited shortly after graduation; they pursue only one career track, have little or no experience other than that gained in law school and in the corridors of courtrooms, and dislike discretionary decision-making as something that is adverse to legal certainty. Can we claim that young professional bureaucrats trained to resolve past disputes on the basis of highly technical legal knowledge are the best forgers of policy judgments that will determine our future? Not likely.[40] For justice in mass tort cases, what is needed is a curriculum that can match the curriculum of Judge Jack B. Weinstein[41] – and such a curriculum is almost impossible to find in Europe.

In addition, in all European judicial reforms thus far in the 21st century, one element has played a key role – the element of judicial independence. Judicial independence, in the European understanding, implies a high level of separation of the Judiciary from every other branch of power, but also from any influence of society (from the media to social sciences and economic studies). Independence also *per definitionem* implies immunity from any political responsibility (and, to a considerable degree, immunity from any responsibility at all). While independence and impartiality may be necessary for the fair and just handling of individual disputes, are they equally necessary for passing good policy decisions that affect the future rights and interests of a large number of people? Or, would we prefer to have a policy-maker that is subject to some form of democratic political responsibility?

## 4.2. *Will It Help to Improve the Functioning of the Judiciary?*

Optimistic European approaches to collective litigation often suggest that expanding devices of group litigation can cure deficiencies of the judicial system and fill in the gaps that exist in conventional litigation devices. For instance, it is often proposed to expand *locus standi* and give more leeway to various public-interest groups and associations. Yet, the causal link between the broader authority to sue in favour of diffuse public interests and the improvement of individual

40 On this point, see Rick Marcus' comment that 'there is at least some reason to feel uneasy about this "professionalized Judiciary" … that is insulated from the very public it is supposed to serve'; Marcus 2014, p. 109.

41 Judge Weinstein, who was as a judge at the very centre of the biggest mass tort cases, including Agent Orange, asbestos litigation, breast implants and tobacco producers cases (see Weinstein 1995), was throughout his career a successful lawyer, prosecutor, federal judge (appointed when he was 46 years old), law professor at Columbia Law School (from 1952 to 1998, simultaneously with his judicial career) and legal writer – author of leading treatises and numerous academic articles on legal practice, evidence and mass torts.

litigation of private claims has not been sufficiently demonstrated. Already Mauro Cappelletti was cautious:

> Opening the doors of judicial (or even legislative and administrative) proceedings to so-called public-interest groups is risky if no adequate controls are available to check abuses detrimental to either the individual or the public interests, or both.[42]

Particularly in the context of transition economies, it was argued that a possible cure for the notoriously bad quality of the legal system is a legal-reform strategy which puts enforcement of public rules in the hands of private individuals and their individual court actions.[43] But, if public justice does not produce good results with enforcement of private agreements, it will be hard to expect that private enforcement of public interests in collective or class litigation would be a magic wand that would improve the quality of the legal system. The charging of a system with additional tasks was never a good method of improving it. On the contrary, switching problems from a dysfunctional state bureaucracy to not much more functional state courts may cause them to be even less effective.

The risks of overload and further backlogs are not the only risks in this context. More dangerous is the risk of confusion. Many systems have been struggling with the definition of the proper role of the Judiciary. Finally, among various goals of civil justice, the goal of steady and rational processing of a large number of routine individual cases has emerged as dominant in many legal systems.[44] Many elements of judicial architecture were adjusted to this goal, from the court network to the requirements for the promotion of judges, from the design of court buildings to software programmes for IT support for the Judiciary.

The need to clarify the concept of the separation of powers and to build an independent and impartial Judiciary that has no political function was particularly great in the transition countries. The need still exists, because especially in the higher echelons of judicial power, which have a larger share of those who mentally and ideologically belong to past times, one can find tendencies to control the thinking of judicial peers, at least of those from the lower levels of the judicial hierarchy. Putting the emphasis on civil cases where public interest prevails over individual justice may contribute to the trends and tendencies to promote uniformity in adjudication by imposing collectivist, policy-motivated oversight. This may affect the role of the supreme courts and other highest tribunals, which could turn into centres of informal political power. In short, collective litigation may encourage the collectivist spirits of the past, and this is not necessarily good for the quality of the Judiciary.

42 Cappelletti 1975, p. 858.

43 Hey & Shleifer 1998, p. 400, focusing on the example of Russia. In their final analysis they conceded, however, that 'public enforcement is surely the ultimate goal of any legal reform', p. 402. On arguments why a Legislature would favour private enforcement see Farhang 2011, p. 3-18.

44 See Uzelac 2013, p. 3-31.

### 4.3. *Will It be More Attractive for the End Users of the Justice System?*

Finally, the last but probably most important question is what collective redress brings for the citizens as the ultimate 'consumers' of the state services for law enforcement. More effective protection of vulnerable rights holders is supposed to be the crucial argument in the discussions about collective redress.

The American experience of class actions is often invoked as a good example of private enforcement of public law. However, American enthusiasm for private enforcement may be a signal of deficiency, not of virtue.[45] Over many years, there was a consensus in comparative legal research that the American system of civil litigation was, in comparison to European systems, exceptional.[46] Whether as a blessing or as a curse, American exceptionalism was in its definition linked to a relatively compact blend of features that along with (opt-out) class actions include contingency fees, lack of fee-shifting rules, reliance on jury trial and extensive discovery, and the availability of punitive damages.[47] More importantly, the background of the rise of American class actions was not the response to specific needs of the users, but the deep distrust in public enforcement bodies and devices:

> US-style civil litigation [is] the regrettable by-product of a deep cultural hostility to the kind of robust bureaucratic administration by public regulatory bodies in Europe. … US-style tort litigation, for instance, [is] an unwieldy substitute for social insurance programs and the plaintiffs' bar [is] a useful form of privatized bureaucracy, at least in the absence of robust Euro-style public administration.[48]

Indeed, Europe is not poor on regulatory bodies. In a small country like Croatia, there are currently 44 state agencies with over 6,000 employees, out of which 34 are financed directly from the state budget.[49] And, indeed, it is often doubted whether they provide good services to the users in the fields they are supposed to regulate. Whether they provide good value for tax payers' money is also debatable. However, advocating any form of aggregate litigation, no matter whether opt-in or opt-out, usually does not go hand-in-hand with the coherent policy of the restructuring (not to speak of the downsizing) of the state regulatory bodies. It is more a sign of capitulation, the admission that the public enforcement devices do not do what they are supposed to do. What remains is to steer the users towards 'entrepreneurial litigation',[50] for which they have neither means nor incentives.

All the same, one may say that inefficient aggregate litigation is no more harmful than inefficient public administration. But, in the long run, the creation of

45 For a critical perspective on the American civil justice system among US scholars see Langbein 1985 (as a representative example of older scholarship) or Maxeiner 2011 (from a more recent perspective).

46 On American exceptionalism see e.g. Marcus 2013; Carrington 2006.

47 *Cf.* Nagareda 2009, p. 2.

48 *Ibidem*, p. 3.

49 IJF Newsletter 2014, p. 1.

50 For the notion of 'entrepreneurial litigation' in the context of US class actions, see Coffee 1987.

more 'empty boxes' that serve as fig leaves for poor governance at all levels is not a useful way of managing social affairs. For governments, it can be another temporary alibi for poor performance; for the Judiciary, it can be another source of confusion that may hamper already flimsy reforms aimed at efficient (individual) dispute resolution. Last but not least, the end users, being steered towards self-help and private initiative, may thereby be dragged into another hopeless maze of endless procedures, this time more costly and more time-consuming.

## Bibliography

**Andrews 2013**
Andrews, N., *Andrews on Civil Processes. Court Proceedings*. Vol. I., Cambridge-Antwerp-Portland: Intersentia, 2013.

**Baetge 2007**
Baetge, D., *Class Actions, Group Litigation & Other Forms of Collective Litigation – Germany*, Country Report (2007), <http://globalclassactions.stanford.edu/sites/-default/files/documents/Germany_National_Report.pdf>.

**Baretić 2009**
Baretić, M., 'Individualna i kolektivna zaštita potrošača u hrvatskom pravu', in Tomljenović, V. *et al.* (eds.), *Republika Hrvatska na putu prema europskom pravosudnom području: rješavanje trgovačkih i potrošačkih sporova*, Rijeka: Pravni fakultet, 2009, p. 260-262.

**Cappelletti 1975**
Cappelletti, M., 'Governmental and Private Advocates for the Public Interest in Civil Litigation: A Comparative Study', *Michigan Law Review*, 1975, Vol. 73(5), p. 793-884.

**Carrington 2006**
Carrington, P.D., 'Enforcing Public Law on a Global Scale: The Relevance of the American Experience', *Lecture at Gent University, presented on 27 October 2006.*

**Coffee 1987**
Coffee, J.C. Jr., 'The Regulation of Entrepreneurial Litigation: Balancing Fairness and Efficiency in the Large Class Action', *University of Chicago Law Review*, 1987, Vol. 54(3), p. 877-937.

**Damaska 1986**
Damaska, M., *The Faces of Justice and State Authority*, New Haven: Yale University Press, 1986.

**Dika 2003a**
Dika, M., 'Pravosudna legitimacija udruga za zaštitu potrošača', in Dika, M. & Pogarčić, Z. (eds.), *Obveze trgovaca u sustavu zaštite potrošača*, Zagreb: Narodne novine, 2003, p. 126-142.

**Dika 2003b**
Dika, M., 'Udružna tužba kao instrument apstraktne zaštite potrošača', *Hrvatska pravna revija*, 2003, p. 37-43.

**Dika 2011**
Dika, M., 'Postupak u sporovima za zaštitu kolektivnih interesa i prava', in Bilić, V. *et al.* (eds.), *Novela Zakona o parničnom postupku iz 2011,* Zagreb: Novi informator, 2011, p. 55-70.

**Eliantonio *et al.* 2013**
Eliantonio, M., Backes, Ch.W., Van Rhee, C.H., Spronken, T.N.B.M. & Berlee, A. (eds.), *Standing up for your Right(s) in Europe. A Comparative Study on Legal Standing (Locus Standi) before the EU and Member States' Courts,* Antwerp-Oxford: Intersentia, 2013.

**Farhang 2011**
Farhang, S., *The Litigation State. Public Regulation and Private Lawsuits in the United States,* Princeton: Princeton University Press, 2011.

**Fisch 1979**
Fisch, W.B., 'European Analogues to the Class Action: Group Action in France and Germany', *The American Journal of Comparative Law,* 1979, Vol. 27(1), p. 51-79.

**Hay & Shleifer 1998**
Hay, J. & Shleifer, A., 'Private Enforcement of Public Laws: A Theory of Legal Reform', *AEA Papers and Proceedings,* 1998, Vol. 88(2), p. 398-403.

**IJF Newsletter 2014**
IJF [Institute for Public Finances] Newsletter, No. 851 of March 2014, available at: <www.ijf.hr/upload/files/file/newsletter/85.pdf>.

**Kulski 2011**
Kulski, R., Class Proceedings in Poland. *Report at XIV World Conference on Procedural Law,* 2011 (conference materials).

**Langbein 1985**
Langbein, J., 'The German Advantage in Civil Procedure', *University of Chicago Law Review,* 1985, Vol. 52, p. 823-866.

**Lindblom 1997**
Lindblom, P.H., 'Individual Litigation and Mass Justice: A Swedish Perspective and Proposal on Group Actions in Civil Procedure', *The American Journal of Comparative Law,* 1997, Vol. 45(4), p. 805-831.

**Marcus 2008**
Marcus, R., 'Cure-All for an Era of Dispersed Litigation? Toward a Maximalist Use of the Multidistrict Litigation Panel's Transfer Power', *Tulane Law Review,* 2008, Vol. 82, p. 2245-2296, available at: <http://repository.uchastings.edu/-faculty_scholarship/466>.

**Marcus 2013**
Marcus, R., '"American Exceptionalism" in Goals for Civil Litigation', in Uzelac, A. (ed.), *Goals of Civil Justice and Civil Procedure in Contemporary Judicial Systems*, Cham-Heidelberg-New York-Dordrecht-London: Springer, *2013*, p. 123-141.

**Marcus 2014**
Marcus, R., 'Appellate Review in the Reactive Model: The Example of the American Federal Courts', in Uzelac, A. & Van Rhee, C.H. (eds.), *Nobody's Perfect. Comparative Essays on Appeals and other Means of Recourse against Judicial Decisions in Civil Matters*, Cambridge-Antwerp-Portland: Intersentia, *2014*, p. 105-126.

**Maxeiner 2011**
Maxeiner, J.R., *Failures of American Civil Justice in International Perspective*, Cambridge: Cambridge University Press, *2011*.

**Menđušić Škugor 2012**
Menđušić Škugor, E., 'Udružna tužba kao mehanizam zaštite kolektivnih prava i interesa', Zagreb: Pravni fakultet (awarded student paper), 2012.

**Merryman 1985**
Merryman, J.H., *The Civil Law Tradition*, 2nd edn., Stanford: Stanford University Press, 1985.

**Nagareda 2009**
Nagareda, R.A., 'Aggregate Litigation across the Atlantic and the Future of American Exceptionalism', *Vanderbilt Law Review*, 2009, Vol. 62, p. 1-52.

**Ombudsman Discrimination Report 2012**
Pučki pravobranitelj, Izvješće o pojavama diskriminacije za 2012, Zagreb, June 2013, <www.ombudsman.hr/dodaci/Izvješće%20o%20pojavama%20diskriminacije.pdf>.

**Ortells Ramos 2014**
Ortells Ramos, M., 'Protecting Supra-Individual Legal Interests: Enforcement Action by Public Administration Institutions, Civil Justice and a Combination of Protection Systems', in Gottwald, P. & Hess, B. (eds.), *Procedural Justice – XIV. IAPL World Congress Heidelberg 2011*, Munich: Beck, 2014, p. 319-385.

**Poljanec 2013**
Poljanec K., 'Ovlaštenici prava za tužbu za zaštitu kolektivnih interesa potrošača – Ima li prostora za nova rješenja?', in Horak, H. & Šafranko, Z. (eds.), *Potrošač na unutarnjem tržištu. Zbornik okruglog stola 'Consumer at Internal Market'*, Zagreb: Faculty of Economics, 2013, p. 56-78.

**Poretti 2014**
Poretti, P., 'Antidiskriminacijsko zakonodavstvo i sudska praksa u RH – individualna i kolektivna antidiskriminacijska tužba kao (ne)djelotvorna sredstva za ostvarenje pravne zaštite' (postgraduate student paper, unpublished), Faculty of Law, Zagreb, 2014.

**Rakić-Vodinelić 1982**
Rakić-Vodinelić, V., 'Protection of Diffuse, Fragmentary and Collective Interest in Court Proceedings', *Yugoslav Law*, 1982, No. 3, p. 43-60.

**Silvestri 2013**
Silvestri, E., 'Towards a Common Framework of Collective Redress in Europe?', *Russian Law Journal*, 2013, Vol. 1, p. 46-56.

**Tomljenović 2008**
Tomljenović, V., 'Grupne tužbe – učinkovita pravna sredstva zaštite potrošača u poredbenom pravu', in Tomljenović, V. *et al.* (eds.), *Europsko pravosudno područje u u svjetlu pristupa Republike Hrvatske europskoj uniji,* Rijeka: Pravni fakultet, 2008.

**Triva & Dika 2004**
Triva, S., Dika, M., *Građansko parnično procesno pravo*, Zagreb: Narodne novine, 2004.

**Uzelac 2008**
Uzelac, A., 'Reforming Mediterranean Civil Procedure: Is There a Need for Shock Therapy?', in Van Rhee, C.H. & Uzelac, A. (eds.), *Civil Justice between Efficiency and Quality: From Ius Commune to the CEPEJ*, Antwerp-Oxford-Portland: Intersentia, 2008, p. 71-99.

**Uzelac 2009**
Uzelac, A., 'Proceedings before the court', in Šimonović Einwalter, T. (ed.), *A Guide to the Anti-Discrimination Act*, Zagreb: Ured za ljudska prava Vlade RH, 2009, p. 95-109.

**Uzelac 2013**
Uzelac, A., (ed.), *Goals of Civil Justice and Civil Procedure in Contemporary Judicial Systems*, Cham-Heidelberg-New York-Dordrecht-London: Springer, *2013*.

**Verbic 2011**
Verbic, F., 'Aggregate Litigation in Argentina and Brazil: Principal features and some notes on the viability of enforcing American consumer class action judgments in those countries', *Report at XIV World Conference on Procedural Law*, 2011 (conference materials).

**Weinstein 1995**
Weinstein, J.B., *Individual Justice in Mass Tort Litigation. The Effect of Class Actions, Consolidations, and other Multiparty Devices,* Evanston: Northwestern University Press, 1995.

**Yeazell 1987**
Yeazell, S.C., *From Medieval Group Litigation to the Modern Class Action*, New Haven-London: Yale University Press, 1987.

A. Szalai

# BEYOND OPT-IN AND OPT-OUT: THE LAW AND ECONOMICS OF GROUP LITIGATION*

The main purpose of law and economics, or the economic analysis of law, is to analyse the expected incentive effects of legal institutions.[1] Law and economics models are based on the assumption that we are able to predict these effects, because the simple *rule of demand* remains valid in the field of the law: if a legal institution raises the cost or reduces the benefit of an activity, the level of the respective activity will decrease. (Similarly, the level of the activity will decrease if the benefits derived from an alternative activity increase.) It is well established in economic theory that benefits and costs are not only of a material, financial nature. Furthermore, decision makers are not guided only by selfish or greedy motivations; they have ethical standards and accrue a benefit (e.g. happiness) if they meet these standards.

The law and economics analysis of group litigation or collective litigation or class action follows the same path: the model attempts to demonstrate how the parties' activities in a legal procedure will change if new institutions modify the costs and benefits of lawsuits. The theory attempts to predict how these institutions influence the number of lawsuits initiated and the decisions taken in the legal procedure (e.g. the offer and acceptance of the settlement, the provision of evidence). Economic analysis of law is able to present the difference between the incentive effects related to the different forms of group litigation. Moreover, it assesses the potential effects of group litigation on the basis of the so-called *primary activity*: the incidence of illegal (or seemingly illegal) actions.

* The chapter was written within the framework of OTKA (Hungarian Scientific Research Fund) research project (registration number K-105559).

1 Many scholars of law and economics would find this definition too narrow. They would propose an additional purpose: to define socially efficient institutions. See Shavell 2004, p. 593-660; Cooter & Ulen 2012, p. 1-9; Posner 2011, p. 28-36.

## 1. Economic Theory of Group Litigation

In this section, group litigation and collective litigation will be contrasted with the representative action. The *representative action* – where authorized NGOs or public agencies may sue on behalf of the victims even if none of the victims or only a few victims participate – is not group litigation but merely a new form of *public interest litigation* managed by politically or ideologically motivated agencies, associations. For this reason, the key point is participation: why do interested parties participate in an action (opt-in or at least not opt-out)? What can they be offered in exchange for their time and effort?

It seems that the key difference between the successful and unsuccessful group litigation methods is that the successful systems (e.g. American class actions) provide some extra advantages, some extra benefits in exchange for participation. These advantages, these personal benefits are the most important features of these systems. Whether an opt-in or an opt-out mechanism is used, how litigation is funded, who has standing to sue in the name of the group: these are secondary issues. These policy issues affect the level of the extra benefits; they influence the personal decision on participation; but the most important effects come from the so-called collective action problem.

### 1.1. *The Collective Action Problem: Key Question*

Collective action problems are not distinctive features of collective lawsuits: they occur in many spheres of social life. Therefore, it is worth analysing the methods employed in other areas to deal with these problems. The key issue is: why would members of a group (or at least some members of the group) participate in a collective action?

Let us start with the economic concept of public goods and the problem of free-riding – this is the key characteristic leading to the collective action problem. Public goods are situations where two conditions are met:

1. there is a group, the members of which have a common goal (in the case of group litigation they want to overcome the defendant in the courtroom, in other examples they want clean air in a city or a successful national football team); but
2. if their common goal is achieved, it will provide a benefit (not always equal benefits, but some benefits) for all group members – and not only for those who actively participated in achieving this goal. Non-participants cannot be excluded from benefiting from the public goods.

### 1.2. *The Free-rider Problem*

This non-excludability results in the free-rider problem. If the benefit is available even without contribution, then the dominant strategy of every single member will be to refrain from taking action – why contribute if the benefit will be available independently of the personal efforts made? As will be demonstrated, in an extreme case, all members will wait for the others, everybody will attempt to free-ride; and nobody will do anything to produce the public goods (i.e. nobody will sue, nobody will fight for clean air, or nobody will take steps in order to build a strong national football team). Even if everybody will be better off with the public goods, nobody will be personally interested in fighting for them. This is the collective action problem.

**Proposition 1: Group litigation will work only if the collective action problems stemming from its public goods characteristics are solved.**

### 1.3. *The Types of Collective Actions – Different Collective Action Problems*

The basic problem of group litigation seems to be the same: the interested parties can receive their benefits without participating – as a result, they are not interested in participation. It is substantiated by European collective redress methods that interested parties will not join the action if authorized NGOs or public agencies launch the process.

However, it is worth further analysing the public goods characteristics in the legal procedure, because this may demonstrate that the collective action problem is not the same in the case of *claims for injunctions* and *compensatory collective actions*: the claim for injunctions is more likely to fail due to free-riding, while compensatory claims may be successful even if group members are basically interested in refraining from participating in the action.

### 1.4. *The Case for Injunctions*

Imagine a case where there are numerous victims of an extremely noisy music club in the neighbourhood. The public goods effect in cases of injunctions is obvious: if any group member sues to close the club or to limit its opening hours and she prevails, the other members are not required to take any further steps such as to sue, to bear litigation costs or risks. The public goods will be available for the non-participants as well: if the opening hours are constrained, then the quiet hours will be quiet hours for participants and non-participants alike. But the public goods characteristics emerge even in the case where the first plaintiff fails. In this case the others receive free information: they learn that litigation will be unsuccessful, without having to bear any litigation costs or risks. In both cases (i.e. enjoying the benefits without contributing and not participating in a failed lawsuit) they are better off, if they are not the first party to sue. And if everybody waits for the others to bring the first lawsuit, then this first suit will not be brought.

### 1.5. *Compensatory Actions – The Res Iudicata Problem*

The problem is somewhat more complicated in the case of compensatory actions. Suppose the group sues the music club for damages. In this case the decision of the court can be divided into two parts: the judgment on the liability of the club and the decision on the amount of damages payable to the plaintiffs, the group members. Obviously, damages are not public goods: the non-participants can be excluded, they will not receive compensation. They have to participate in the lawsuit or bring another suit in order to be eligible for compensation.

But what about the part of the judgment regarding liability? How does the decision on the liability (for example, negligence) of the music club affect non-participants? Can they make reference to this judgment in future lawsuits? Will the decision establishing the liability of the club have *res iudicata* effect? If the answer is yes, the decision will have clear public goods characteristics. It is worth waiting for the judgment to be rendered in the first case and then cite the decision in a second one. The decisions on liability may be referred to without any further cost – similar to the case for injunctions.

If the decision does not have *res iudicata* effect, if the judges in future cases are not bound by the first judgment on the question of liability (for example, because they are independent from other judges and not constrained by 'precedents'), the public goods effects will be weakened. The parties are less motivated to wait. But this incentive does not vanish entirely; the strategy of waiting yields clear advantages in this case as well: parties will receive free information about the successful (or unsuccessful) litigation strategy. They will be able to repeat the prevailing argument and avoid the failed ones in their own case.

In short, in a compensatory case the public goods effect depends heavily on the definition of *res iudicata* in the given legal system. But this public goods effect always exists, and the group members are always interested in waiting. And if everybody waits for others to bring the first suit, the first lawsuit will not be brought.

**Proposition 2: Public goods characteristics (collective action) are more important in the case of claims for injunctions than in the case of compensatory actions. The public goods effect in the case of compensatory collective actions depends on the definition of *res iudicata*.**

From the viewpoint of law and economics, the main function of group litigation is to cope with public goods characteristics.[2] It must reduce the incentive to free ride. But fortunately, as aforementioned, this collective action problem is not a unique feature of group litigation – it also appears in other spheres of social life. And this incidence makes it possible to borrow some solutions from other areas.

2 For similar analysis see Cassone & Ramello 2012; Cassone & Ramello 2011; Marceau & Mongrain 2003.

Two points are worth stressing:

1. The public goods characteristic does not always result in a situation where everybody follows the free-rider strategy – there are groups which are more likely to provide themselves with these public goods than others. This difference among the groups is indicated in group litigation literature as the difference between the so-called *high-value* and *low-value* lawsuits.
2. Even if the incentive for free-riding is strong enough to hinder collective action, effective regulation may provide incentives to join the groups through the so-called personal or club goods method: the participants (who do not follow the free-riders' strategy) receive some extra benefit from group membership. In this context, the most important point in group litigation regulation is to create some extra advantage for participants.

The next section will present the first point, while the subsequent section deals with the second.

## 1.6. *Remedying Collective Action Problems*

The law and economics literature of group litigation distinguishes between the groups where the parties have a high enough stake to launch lawsuits individually (but they wait for others in order to benefit from the advantages of the public goods effect) and the groups where the personal stake of each potential group member is very low, so they will not be interested in bringing a suit. The typical case for this second category is the so-called mass tort where the personal expected litigation cost of the victims is higher than the expected benefit resulting from the lawsuits.[3] Under the loser pays rule this personal 'expected litigation cost' is the cost above the amount covered by the contribution from the losing party.[4]

In terms of economic theory, the problem of high-value groups is the so-called game of 'chicken', while the low-value case can be described in terms of the prisoner's dilemma. As will be demonstrated, high-value cases are more likely to appear in the courts. In these cases, the main role of group litigation is to reduce the time lag so that the first case is filed as early as possible.

## 1.7. *Low-value Group: The Prisoner's Dilemma*

In the case of low-value lawsuits, the well-known situation of the prisoner's dilemma appears. In this case the first best option for all parties is to free ride, i.e. they do not participate in the collective action, but others provide the public goods. The second best option is when all members contribute – the cost of producing the public goods can be distributed among the participants, so the personal litigation

3 For a similar distinction, Wagner 2011, p. 62-66.
4 For similar analysis of the 'loser pays' rule, see Katz & Sanchirico 2012, p. 274.

cost will decrease. The third best option is where nobody contributes. And the worst option is the single contribution case, because the litigation cost (the cost of providing the public goods) exceeds the expected benefit resulting from the lawsuit.

In this small-claims (or mass tort) case, group litigation will be expected to fail: each potential plaintiff will wait for the others; everybody will attempt to avoid participation. The free-rider problem can be solved only if the group litigation process ensures some personal (non-public goods) benefit – advantages which are unavailable to non-participants.

## 1.8. *High-value Groups: 'Chicken Game'*

In the case of 'chicken game', the best option is to free ride on others, and the second best option is when all contribute. The sequence of the other two options is reversed. The third best option is when only the decision maker takes steps, and the worst option is when nobody takes steps. The difference comes from a feature of the high-value cases: because of the low litigation cost, bringing the first suit is better for the first mover than the case of no suits.

It is easy to demonstrate that in this case it is better to be the single contributor and bear the cost and risk of the actions than the lack of the public goods (for example the lack of injunctions against the noisy disco). Therefore, after some time, one of the group members will sue, because even a one-sided action (lacking the partners' participation) yields sufficient benefit. The only question is: who will be the contributor and who will free-ride? In this case the role of the rules of group litigation is to reduce the time lag, to induce early litigation.

**Proposition 3: Group litigation (regulatory assistance) is necessary not only in the case of low-value claims (e.g. consumer protection, cartel cases) but in high-value claims as well.**

## 1.9. *Necessary Incentives: Personal Benefits for Participants*

The legal system can cope with the collective action problem if it provides additional personal or club benefits[5] for participants (and only for the participants). This reshapes the incentives: the benefit from single or joint participation (or the cost of non-contribution) must increase – it includes not only the public goods (*res iudicata* problem), but some benefits which are unavailable outside the group.

[5] The economic literature distinguishes personal and club goods. In this case both are enough. Personal goods are benefits where the benefit is individualized – each member gets something different. For example, the money that Plaintiff A receives cannot be given to Plaintiff B at the same time. (If Plaintiff B is eligible for the same amount, she will receive different money: the defendant must pay double the damages – i.e. for Plaintiff A and for Plaintiff B.) In the case of club goods, the group members receive the same goods – but this benefit is unavailable for non-participants. (For detailed analysis of club goods: Cullis & Jones 2009, p. 68-71).

Therefore, the key issue is what kind of extra benefit group litigation can provide for the participants.

**Proposition 4: The collective action problem can be solved only if participation yields some personal benefit (non-public goods).**

The first (seemingly most obvious) potential advantage is *cost reduction*: in the case of collective action the per capita cost is expected to be lower than the litigation cost of individual lawsuits, because this litigation cost can be distributed among numerous members. But it is quite an unrealistic expectation that those who do not bring individual lawsuits will take part in a collective action just because its cost is lower. The cost of non-participation is zero - consequently it will be lower than the reduced cost of the collective action.

Moreover, in some cases, group litigation does not reduce but much rather increases costs. The group has to face many problems which are unknown to individual cases: organizational and agency problems occur. The organizational costs are obvious: the members, the parties joining the group, must be registered. But what is the agency cost? The agency cost is the problem of the conflict of interests between the principal and her agent. This conflict may also appear in the case of individual litigation, but collective action enlarges this problem. In the case of individual litigation, a single defendant (she) must control the actions of her lawyer (him) - but because she knows that she is the only principal, she will control him. However, in the case of group litigation, this issue of control causes collective action problems: if any member of the group (she) is able to monitor the actions of the group representative or the lawyer (him), and if she is able to ensure that his decisions are consistent with her own goals, then all group members are saved from his misuse of power. Therefore, the problem of free-riding is back: it is possible that everybody will wait for the others to monitor him; consequently, control will be ineffective.[6]

Moreover, the interests of the different subgroups or members may be in conflict. The subgroups can be interested in different actions of the lawyer, the representative. The group must find a solution for this conflict of interests - and finding this solution (negotiation, elaborating rules of games within the groups, etc.) will be costly.

**Proposition 5: Cost reduction is not enough to induce participation. Other additional personal benefits are needed.**

[6] The agency cost is one of the most widely discussed issues in law and economics literature on group litigation. The literature focuses on the effects of lawyer fees on the actions of the lawyer and the representative. For arguments in favour of contingent fees, see Backhaus 2012, p. 127-128; Cassone & Ramello 2012, p. 117-121; Emons & Garoupa 2006; Issacharoff & Miller 2012, p. 54-59; Macey & Geoffrey 1991. For arguments against contingent fees, see Brickman 2003a; Brickman 2003b; Cooter & Rubinfeld 1989; Gravelle & Waterson 1993; Rickman 1994; Sacconi 2012 and Swanson 1991.

The main form of these additional personal benefits is settlement payment. The expected per capita amount of the settlement offered by the defendant will be higher in the case of group litigation.

### 1.10. *The Role of Settlement: The Problem of the Enrichment of the Victim*

If cost reduction does not effectively induce participation, the increase of benefits stemming from the lawsuit can be effective. Consider first *compensatory claims*. Why would the participants receive higher damages as group members than what they could draw as individual plaintiffs in future lawsuits? Law and economics literature (and various empirical findings) demonstrate that this is possible because collective action modifies the litigation and settlement strategies of the parties. Both the plaintiff (the group) and the defendant will devote more resources to convince the court, and group litigation increases the prevailing chances of the plaintiffs.[7] The basic reason for this change is that while in the case of individual lawsuits there is an unavoidable asymmetry in the calculation of the defendant (she) and that of the individual plaintiff (he), this asymmetry decreases in the case of group litigation. In individual cases, only the defendant can recognize and consider the effects of the current lawsuit on future ones. He will know that the evidence he collects and provides in the current case regarding liability may be used in future lawsuits as well. At the same time, she deals only with the expected benefit stemming from the current case. This asymmetry in the parties' stakes increases his chances to prevail. As this asymmetry weakens, her winning chances increase in collective actions. But this increase in her winning chances is not a personal benefit – as aforementioned it has public goods characteristics (depending on the *res iudicata* effects). In order to induce participants to join, these benefits must be transformed into personal advantages. This transformation is possible through settlements: the participants can expect a higher settlement offer in the case of group litigation than in the case of individual lawsuits. The basic rationale behind this expectation is very simple: if the defendant has a higher chance of losing the case, he will offer more to avoid litigation.[8]

At first sight, this extra benefit seems to be missing in *claims for injunctions*. However, settlement is a realistic option in those cases as well. The defendant can offer some compensation for continuing the action (or reducing the activity level and paying some compensation to the plaintiffs in exchange for allowing that level of activity). In this case the effects of a settlement offer are similar to the former case: the music club promises to pay a given amount of compensation if the plaintiffs settle and allow the club to work until late into the night.

7 For the analysis of the expected litigation cost: Katz 1988.

8 For detailed analysis of the effect of this asymmetry: Rosenberg 2002, p. 853; Hay & Rosenberg 2000, p. 1379 and 1383; Coffee 1987, p. 899 and Coffee 2000, p. 416.

**Proposition 6: The most obvious benefit for participants is personal (financial) compensation through a settlement or through a higher amount of damages awarded by the court.**

However, in order to induce participation, this high amount of a settlement must be in private or club goods, it must be unavailable to non-participants. Yet, the legal system can impede the appearance of such private or club goods characteristics. Judges, and legal scholars too, may find it unacceptable that group members receive higher compensation than non-participants. The enforcement of such settlements is likely to be refused, or to be expanded to non-participants as well. In this case the appearance of such additional personal benefits necessary to induce participation will be prevented: no relevant advantage deriving from participation will remain in the system.

Moreover, because of this new balance of power, the settlement offer in the case of group litigation may be higher than what the participants are expected to receive in an individual lawsuit.[9] The defendant will be willing to pay a higher amount if she can avoid the litigation cost through settlement. But this extra payment is sensitive to the court's mistake: it is easy to be misinterpreted and declared an unjust over-compensation which is prohibited according to Sec. 31 of the EU Recommendation:[10]

> The compensation awarded to natural or legal persons harmed in a mass harm situation should not exceed the compensation that would have been awarded, if the claim had been pursued by means of individual actions.

## 2. Law and Economics of some Regulatory Problems

Sec. I demonstrated that the success of group litigation reform depends mainly on the amount of personal benefit in the collective action process. However, these personal benefits are determined basically by such features (i.e. *res iudicata*, legal acceptance of high settlement payments) which are outside of the normal area of the laws on civil procedure. Therefore, Sec. II now focuses on the incentive effects of some of these normal regulatory choices in the group litigation reforms: the formation of groups (opt-in system vs. automatic group membership), exit or opt-out options and required characteristics of the group representatives.

9 For example, Samuel Issacharoff and Geoffrey P. Miller argue that in order to induce participation the payment according to the settlement has to be higher than the damages the party would expect from an individual action. Issacharoff & Miller 2012, p. 63.

10 Recommendation 2013/396/EU, *OJ* 2013, L201/60 on common principles for injunctive and compensatory collective redress mechanisms in the Member States concerning violations of rights granted under Union Law.

## 2.1. *Opt-in or Automatic Membership*

The EU Recommendation elaborates an opt-in system:

> The claimant party should be formed on the basis of express consent of the natural or legal persons claiming to have been harmed ('opt-in' principle). (Sec. 21)

The first criticisms emphasized that this opt-in method conflicts with the current opt-out systems in several European countries (e.g. Denmark, the Netherlands, Portugal). But this contrast is misleading. The Recommendation itself requires the opt-out option, too:

> A member of the claimant party should be free to leave the claimant party at any time before the final judgement is given or the case is otherwise validly settled, subject to the same conditions that apply to withdrawal in individual actions, without being deprived of the possibility to pursue its claims in another form, if this does not undermine the sound administration of justice. (Sec. 22)

The real alternative, the real contrast to the opt-in systems is not the opt-out mechanism, but a system in which group membership is established automatically.[11] The national regulations in several European countries such as those just mentioned and the American class action system conflict with the Recommendation because they are built on automatic group membership. In the recommended European system, the potential members have two decisions: first about the entry and afterwards about the exit. This choice is made in better knowledge of the consequences of group membership and of alternative opportunities.[12]

As the opt-in and opt-out systems do not exclude each other, it is worth separating their law and economics analysis. Focus on the choice between the opt-in system and automatic group membership and start with the *advantage of automatic group formation*. Several articles[13] demonstrate the link between the success of the group litigation system and automatic membership because opt-in systems reduce the personal benefit for the group members. In the case of automatic membership the plaintiff group is expected to be larger, the larger groups are more likely to prevail and therefore the defendant will be willing to offer a higher amount per

11 It is inevitable that this view of an unavoidable choice between opt-in and opt-out mechanisms is widely accepted, and this misunderstanding influences some European reforms. For example, Fabrizio Cafaggi and Hans-W. Micklitz state that the Swedish system was transformed from an opt-out system into an opt-in system at the last moment before the enactment because the legislators feared that the unwanted consequences of the American class action system would appear if an opt-out system were established (Cafaggi & Micklitz 2007, p. 30).

12 Coffee 2000, p. 424-425.

13 See for example Issacharoff & Miller 2012, p. 59-65; Ulen 2012, p. 85.

capita as settlement – the personal benefits for participants are higher in the case of automatic membership.[14]

The other main argument for automatic membership is the reduction of the administrative cost. Remember, low-value cases are not brought, because of the very small personal benefit and high litigation cost. All forms of group litigation reduce this personal litigation cost, but the reduction in the case of automatic membership is larger because registration is not required.

But automatic group membership is not the better solution in all situations – it has its own *problems*. The choice between opt-in and automatic membership is similar to what Richard Posner has mentioned with regard to contract formulation: does the acceptance of an offer require an explicit agreement or is silence (the lack of refusal) enough?[15] In this case the 'offer' comes from the representative; the opt-in system requires explicit agreement, while the automatic group membership (with an opt-out option) is a system where silence is acceptance. According to Posner, the optimal default rule depends on whether the number of acceptances exceeds the number of refusals. This argument returns in the law and economics literature of group litigation: in case of a low level of exit the average parties are more likely to accept the 'offer', so silence should be enough for acceptance.

Analysing this regulatory choice, the literature often applies the models of *bounded rationality*. According to this theory, the default rule (group membership in the case of automatic membership, or non-membership in opt-in systems) heavily influences the result. There are potential members whose membership depends entirely on this default rule: in the case of automatic membership they will be members (they do not exit), while under the opt-in system they would not participate (they do not enter). According to bounded rationality theory, this stickiness of the default rule comes from the fact that the potential members do not understand the consequences of their choice (about entry or exit), so even if the default rule provides less benefit, they do not change the situation (they do not exit or they do not enter).

## 2.2. *Opt-Out*

Even if opt-out seems to be a necessary point in the group litigation system (especially if it is based on automatic membership), there are some group litigation (class action) systems without exit options. For example, the US class action did not know an exit option before 1966, and today there are 'mandatory classes' (meaning there is no mechanism for individual class members to opt-out). Richard A. Nagerda describes the Norwegian and Danish systems as ones where exit is possible only if the members have no real chance to join another group or start an individual action in the future.[16] And there are reform proposals which would

14 Issacharoff & Miller 2012, p. 63.
15 Posner 2011, p. 128.
16 Nagerda 2009, p. 29-30.

deprive the exiting parties of some of their rights; for example, they would have no right to file new lawsuits.[17]

The legal argument for the opt-out option is that the parties must be able to influence their own lawsuit. Since in the case of group litigation many people have to make decisions collectively, the individual plaintiff is not able to ensure that the group decisions will be the best for her. She is not able to change these decisions; but the exit option provides an opportunity to leave the group if these collective decisions (or the decisions of the representative or of the lawyer) are against her own interests. The law and economics arguments are similar, but they distinguish two problems: the conflict of interests within the group and the agency problem.

The opt-out system protects against the agency problem because each member has the right to leave the group who thinks that the representative or the lawyer accepts a settlement or will achieve a judgment that is worse for her than the expected results of an individual action or of another group litigation.[18]

However, although this opt-out mechanism exists in many legal systems, it is rarely used. The main reason is the rational ignorance and rational apathy of the group members: if the stakes in exiting the group are very low, then it is not worth gathering information about the settlements, about the expected judgment or about other options. The group member will not exit in order to ensure only a few euros of expected extra benefit. Implicitly, this rational apathy can be proved if the exit rate increases as the stakes increase – the literature presents several findings consistent with this expectation.[19]

As the last point it is worth stressing that the option to exit affects the defendant's willingness to settle. Without the option to exit (or with high costs of exit because of the aforementioned sanctions) the defendant will expect that the problem he faces with the plaintiffs will be solved once and for all with the settlement or a lawsuit. Therefore he is willing to make a higher settlement offer (higher payment per capita). This increasing willingness to settle implicitly appears in 'null and void clauses': the defendant is free to denounce the settlement, if the rate of exit reaches a given level.

## 2.3. *The Role of Non-profit Organizations as Representatives*

In Sec. 4, the Recommendation requires that the representative must be a non-profit organization.

> The Member States should designate representative entities to bring representative actions on the basis of clearly defined conditions of eligibility. These conditions should include at least the following requirements:
> (a) the entity should have a non-profit making character;

17 Issacharoff & Miller 2012, p. 63.
18 Coffee 2000, p. 422-428; Hay & Rosenberg 2000, p. 1399; Ulen 2012, p. 85.
19 Eisenberg & Miller 2004, p. 1563.

(b) there should be a direct relationship between the main objectives of the entity and the rights granted under Union law that are claimed to have been violated in respect of which the action is brought; and
(c) the entity should have sufficient capacity in terms of financial resources, human resources, and legal expertise, to represent multiple claimants acting in their best interest.

The non-profit form is mistakenly seen as a panacea in many fields of law. Contrary to the general view, the lack of dividend does not mean that non-profit organizations will not be able to abuse their position. Even if they cannot divide the extra revenue (profit) among the managers of the organization, they are able to pay it directly to the managers as a 'management fee'. They can spend this extra revenue for buying personal goods used by the managers. Therefore, these organizations can be interested in accepting far from the best settlements if it is lucrative for them. Moreover, this misunderstanding of the consequences of the lack of profit-motive may lead to an unreasonable overconfidence - while the for-profit institutions are viewed with suspicion and therefore the group members attempt to control them, the non-profit organizations are able to avoid this control because the group members do not keep in mind the danger of abuse by them.

Naturally this hidden profit-motive is often weaker, and the main motivation of these organizations is often not profit-seeking but something determined by social or ideological goals. For example, green organizations (consumer organizations) are more interested in protecting the environment (protecting the interests of consumers) than in collecting extra revenue. But this special goal may result in another form of agency problem: these organizations follow their own goals and these goals can be in conflict with the interests of the represented group. Samuel Issacharoff and Geoffrey P. Miller offer the example of chewing tobacco: the manufacturers manipulated the market, and they agreed on supra-competitive prices; but the consumer organization did not take the case to court because in their view chewing tobacco is a dangerous product and they did not want to reduce its price - even if the cartel harms the consumers.[20]

## 3. Summary

So, what is the answer to my opening question? What renders the group member interested in participating in collective actions? When will group litigation work? The key is the extra personal benefit, the advantage secured for the participants who opt-in or who do not opt-out. But does this extra benefit depend primarily on the choice between the opt-in or the opt-out system? Does this extra benefit depend primarily on the question of who has the power to sue? Does this extra benefit depend primarily on the system of funding? It seems not. Then, what does it

20 Issacharoff & Miller 2012, p. 52. See *In re Massachusetts Smokeless Tobacco Litigation* No. 30-5038-BLS1 (Mass. Cup. Ct. 7 April 2008).

depend on? It depends on the handling of settlements – especially when they 'overcompensate' the plaintiffs.

## Bibliography


**Backhaus 2012**
Backhaus, J.G., 'Class Action Finance and Legal Expense Insurance', in Backhaus, J., Cassone, A. & Ramello, G.B. (eds.), *The Law and Economics of Class Actions in Europe*, Cheltenham, UK: Edward Elgar, 2012, p. 127-130.

**Brickman 2003a**
Brickman, L., 'Effective Hourly Rates of Contingency-Fee Lawyers: Competing Data and Non-Competitive Fees', *Washington University Law Quarterly*, 2003, Vol. 81, p. 653-736.

**Brickman 2003b**
Brickman, L., 'The Market for Contingent Fee-Financed Tort Litigation: Is It Price Competitive?', *Cardozo Law Review*, 2003, Vol. 25, p. 102-165.

**Cafaggi & Micklitz 2007**
Cafaggi, F. & Micklitz, H.-W., 'Administrative and Judicial Collective Enforcement of Consumer Law in the US and the European Community', EUI Working Paper 2007/22.

**Cassone & Ramello 2011**
Cassone, A. & Ramello, G.B., 'The Simple Economics of Class Action: Private Provision of Club and Public Goods', *European Journal of Law and Economics*, 2011, Vol. 32, p. 205-224.

**Cassone & Ramello 2012**
Cassone, A. & Ramello, G.B., 'Private, Club and Public Goods: The Economic Boundaries of Class Action Litigation', in Backhaus, J., Cassone, A. & Ramello, G.B. (eds.), *The Law and Economics of Class Actions in Europe*, Cheltenham, UK: Edward Elgar, 2012, p. 101-126.

**Coffee 1987**
Coffee, J.C., Jr., 'The Regulation of Entrepreneurial Litigation: Balancing Fairness and Efficiency in the Large Class Action', *The University of Chicago Law Review*, 1987, Vol. 54, p. 877-937.

**Coffee 2000**
Coffee, J.C., Jr., 'Class Action Accountability: Reconciling Exit, Voice, and Loyalty in Representative Litigation', *Columbia Law Review*, 2000, Vol. 100, p. 370-439.

**Cooter & Rubinfeld 1989**
Cooter, R.D. & Rubinfeld, D.C., 'Economic Analysis of Legal Disputes and Their Resolution', *Journal of Economic Literature*, 1989, Vol. 27, p. 1067-1097.

**Cooter & Ulen 2012**
Cooter, R. & Ulen, Th., *Law and Economics*, 6th edn., Boston: Addison-Wesley, 2012.

**Cullis & Jones 2009**
Cullis, J. & Jones, Ph., *Public Finance and Public Choice: Analytical Perspectives,* Oxford: Oxford University Press, 2009.

**Eisenberg & Miller 2004**
Eisenberg, Th. & Miller, G.P., 'The Role of Opt-out and Objectors in Class Action Litigation: Theoretical and Empirical Issues', *Vanderbilt Law Review,* 2004, Vol. 57, p. 1528-1567.

**Emons & Garoupa 2006**
Emons, W. & Garoupa, N., 'US-Style Contingent Fees and UK-Style Conditional Fees: Agency Problems and the Supply of Legal Services', *Managerial and Decision Economics,* 2006, Vol. 27, p. 379-385.

**Gravelle & Waterson 1993**
Gravelle, H. & Waterson, M., 'No Win, No Fee: Some Economics of Contingent Legal Fees', *The Economic Journal,* 1993, Vol. 103, p. 1205-1220.

**Hay & Rosenberg 2000**
Hay, B. & Rosenberg, D., '"Sweetheart" and "Blackmail" Settlements in Class Actions: Reality and Remedy', *Notre Dame Law Review,* 2000, Vol. 75, p. 1377-1408.

**Issacharoff & Miller 2012**
Issacharoff, S. & Miller, G.P., 'Will Aggregate Litigation Come to Europe?', in Backhaus, J., Cassone, A. & Ramello, G.B. (eds.), *The Law and Economics of Class Actions in Europe,* Cheltenham, UK: Edward Elgar, 2012, p. 37-68.

**Katz 1988**
Katz, A.W., 'Judicial Decision Making and Litigation Expenditure', *International Review of Law and Economics,* 1988, Vol. 8, p. 27-143.

**Katz & Sanchirico 2012**
Katz, A.W. & Sanchirico, C.W., 'Fee Shifting', in Sanchirico, C.W. (ed.), *Procedural Law and Economics,* Cheltenham, UK: Edward Elgar, 2012, p. 271-307.

**Macey & Geoffrey 1991**
Macey, J.R. & Miller, G.P., 'The Plaintiffs' Attorney's Role in Class Action and Derivative Litigation: Economic Analysis and Recommendations for Reform', *The University of Chicago Law Review,* 1991, Vol. 58, p. 1-118.

**Marceau & Mongrain 2003**
Marceau, N. & Mongrain, S., 'Damage Averaging and the Formation of Class Action Suits', *International Review of Law and Economics,* 2003, Vol. 23, p. 63-74.

**Nagerda 2009**
Nagerda, R.A., 'Aggregate Litigation Across the Atlantic and the Future of American Exceptionalism', *Vanderbilt Law Review,* 2009, Vol. 62, p. 1-52.

**Posner 2011**
Posner, R.A., *Economic Analysis of Law,* 8th edn., New York: Aspen Law and Business, 2011.

**Rickman 1994**
Rickman, N., 'The Economics of Contingent Fees in Personal Injury Litigation', *Oxford Journal of Economic Policy,* 1994, Vol. 10, p. 34-50.

**Rosenberg 2002**
Rosenberg, D., 'Mandatory-Litigation Class Action: The Only Option for Mass Tort Cases', *Harvard Law Review,* 2002, Vol. 115, p. 831-897.

**Sacconi 2012**
Sacconi, L., 'Good Law and Economics Need Better Microeconomic Models: The Case Against "Contingent Fees" as Application of Agency Models to the Professions', in Backhaus, J., Cassone, A. & Ramello, G.B. (eds.), *The Law and Economics of Class Actions in Europe,* Cheltenham, UK: Edward Elgar, 2012,p. 178-218.

**Shavell 2004**
Shavell, S., *Foundations of Economic Analysis of Law,* Cambridge: Belknapp, 2004.

**Swanson 1991**
Swanson, T.M., 'The Importance of Contingent Fee Agreements', *Oxford Journal of Legal Studies,* 1991, Vol. 11, p. 193-226.

**Ulen 2012**
Ulen, Th., 'The Economics of Class Action Litigation', in Backhaus, J., Cassone, A. & Ramello, G.B. (eds.), *The Law and Economics of Class Actions in Europe,* Cheltenham, UK: Edward Elgar, 2012, p. 75-98.

**Wagner 2011**
Wagner, G., 'Collective Redress – Categories of Loss and Legislative Options', *Law Quarterly Review,* 2011, Vol. 127, p. 55-82.

# PART II: NATIONAL PERSPECTIVES

S. Voet

# BELGIUM'S NEW CONSUMER CLASS ACTION

## 1. Introduction

Until very recently, Belgium had no, or limited, tools to resolve mass cases.[1] In addition to joinder of claims, claims in intervention and the technique of party representation,[2] only injunctive or declaratory collective actions were possible, allowing (public or private) associations or organizations, that satisfy certain legal criteria (e.g., having legal personality for a number of years), to bring an injunctive or declaratory action on behalf of a group of people. These actions only exist in a limited number of legal fields: consumer protection, environment, and discrimination and racism. All these tools are deficient for the redress of collective harms.[3] The techniques of joinder of claims, claims in intervention, and party representation remain embedded in an individualistic context, designed for conflicts involving a limited number of people. Injunctive or declaratory collective actions are rarely used in Belgium. Their biggest shortcoming is the impossibility of claiming damages, as they can only be used for injunctive or declaratory relief. In addition, associations and organizations lack the financial means to initiate them.

In 2009 and 2010, three class action bill proposals were launched in Belgium.[4] All three failed because a political consensus could not be reached. The first proposal came from the minister of Consumer Affairs and was based on a two-tiered approach: a partially out-of-court settlement track (based on the Dutch Collective Settlements Act) and a court-based litigation track (based on the

1 Fierens & Volders 2012, p. 273-276; Storme & Terryn 2009, p. 96-101 and Taelman & Voet 2011, p. 316-325.

2 Party representation makes it possible for a natural or legal person to represent a group of individuals if the representative receives an explicit mandate from each individual. In a situation involving multiple people with a common claim against the defendant, only the group members who gave a mandate will be represented in court and will be considered a party to the proceedings.

3 Voet 2013b, p. 447-448.

4 For an analysis see Taelman & Voet 2011, p. 325-342 and Voet 2013b, p. 448-455.

Quebecian class action). It created a real opt-out class action. According to this project, the class representative could act on behalf of a class of unknown fellow-sufferers without the need for the class members to intervene in the lawsuit. Moreover, the settlement and the action would lead to a decision that was binding on all parties involved. The second proposal was drafted by the two Green opposition parties and suggested an opt-in class action that consisted of two phases: a collective phase during which the common issues were resolved and the individual class members had to opt-in, and an individual phase during which the individual issues were dealt with. The third proposal came from the Flemish Bar Council. According to this proposal, a class action was brought before the district court, which in Belgium is a special tribunal serving as an arbitrator in jurisdictional disputes among all first instance courts. The district court would only certify the class action, and would then refer the case to a competent first instance court that had to decide the merits of the case.

In the 2011 coalition agreement, the government Di Rupo aimed to put in place a procedure of collective claim settlement for consumers. In mid-December 2013, the cabinet approved a draft act introducing an action for collective redress in Belgium. The proposal was submitted to Parliament at the beginning of 2014. The Act of 28 March 2014 'Introducing a Consumer Collective Redress Action in the Code of Economic Law' was published in the Official Gazette on 29 April 2014 and entered into force on 1 September 2014.[5] The act goes hand in hand with the Act of 4 April 2014 'Regarding the Out of Court Resolution of Consumer Disputes',[6] implementing the EU Consumer ADR Directive.[7] The goal of the Directive is to establish harmonized quality requirements for ADR entities and ADR procedures. Member States must also ensure the existence of a residual ADR entity that is competent to deal with disputes for the resolution of which no existing ADR entity is competent. The Belgian Act of 4 April 2014 establishes such a residual ADR entity: the Consumer Ombudsman Service. According to the minister of Consumer Affairs, this act and the Act of 28 March 2014 both aim to reinforce consumer rights.[8]

5 Loi portant insertion d'un titre 2 «De l'action en réparation collective» au livre XVII «Procédures juridictionnelles particulières» du Code de droit économique et portant insertion des définitions propres au livre XVII dans le livre 1er du Code de droit économique [Act Introducing a Consumer Collective Redress Action in the Code of Economic Law] of 28 March 2014, *Moniteur Belge* [Official Gazette of Belgium], 29 April 2014, 35201.

6 Loi portant insertion du Livre XVI, «Règlement extrajudiciaire des litiges de consommation» dans le Code de droit économique [Act Regarding the Out of Court Resolution of Consumer Disputes] of 4 April 2014, *Moniteur Belge* [Official Gazette of Belgium], 12 May 2014, 38262.

7 Directive 2013/11 of the European Parliament and of the Council of 21 May 2013 on alternative dispute resolution for consumer disputes and amending Regulation (EC) No. 2006/2004 and Directive 2009/22/EC, 2013 *OJ* (L165) 63 (EU). See Voet 2014, p. 118-120.

8 Chambre des représentants de Belgique, Projet de loi portant insertion du Livre XVI, «Règlement extrajudiciaire des litiges de consommation» dans le Code de droit économique. Rapport [Proposal to Introduce an Act Regarding the Out of Court Resolution of Consumer →

## 2. Consumer Law Only

The first class action certification criterion is that the cause of action must be a possible infraction by the defendant on his contractual obligations or on one of the 31 European or Belgian consumer regulations or acts that are specifically enumerated in the act.[9] These regulations and acts relate to competition policy, consumer protection, credit services, product and services safety, intellectual property, electronic economics, privacy, electronic signature, market practices, prices, insurance, professional liability, health, travel, energy, transport of passengers, etc.[10] So, the class representative has to base his or her claim on one or more of these regulations or acts.[11]

Contrary to the EC Recommendation on common principles for injunctive and compensatory collective redress mechanisms,[12] that urges Member States to have such mechanisms in all areas where Union law grants rights to citizens and companies,[13] the Belgian class action procedure only applies to C2B (consumer-to-business) disputes. Amendments to expand the scope of the procedure, for example to shareholder disputes, were rejected.[14] The minister clarified that the act is a modest first step. An evaluation is planned in 2017. If this turns out positive, the procedure might be expanded to other fields of substantive law.[15]

The question arises whether the limited scope of application of the Belgian class action device puts the access to justice principle at risk.[16] For consumer disputes there is now collective access to justice. Victims of mass accidents or securities cases, who fall outside the scope of the law, only have individualized access to justice. The Belgian Constitutional Court could consider this exclusive field of application a constitutional discrimination. Moreover, the use of a limitative list was criticized, since it will have to be adjusted in case of new legislation or when existing laws are amended.[17]

Disputes. Report], 5e Session de la 53e Legislature, Doc. 3360/004, 28 February 2014, available at <www.dekamer.be/FLWB/PDF/53/3360/53K3360004.pdf> (hereafter Report), 3 (last accessed in September 2014).

9 Art. XVII.36, 1° Code of Economic Law (hereafter CEL).

10 Art. XVII.37 CEL.

11 Report, p. 46.

12 Recital (7) of the preambule of Recommendation 2013/396 of the European Commission of 11 June 2013 on common principles for injunctive and compensatory collective redress mechanisms in the Member States concerning violations of rights granted under Union Law, 2013 *OJ* (L206) 60 EU (hereafter EC Recommendation). See Hodges 2013; Silvestri 2013 and Voet 2014, p. 106-113.

13 E.g., consumer protection, competition, environment, protection of personal data, financial services legislation and investor protection.

14 Report, p. 41, 51, 63, 66, 68, 69, 71, 72 and 75.

15 Report, p. 16-17, 22, 40 and 42-43.

16 Verougstraete 2012, p. 100.

17 Report, p. 13.

## 3. Standing to Sue

The second certification prerequisite is that the class action can only be brought by an adequate class representative.[18] Only consumer associations and authorized non-profit organizations, of which the statutory aim corresponds with the collective harm, have standing to bring a class action.[19] The Consumer Ombudsman Service only has standing to initiate a class action and to negotiate a collective settlement.[20] If a settlement cannot be reached, and the court has to decide the merits of the case, a consumer association has to step in to continue the procedure.[21]

The Belgian Legislature chose for an ideological plaintiff, as having no private cause of action or grievance against the defendant.[22] This choice can be applauded.[23] When an ideological plaintiff initiates a class action, the focus from the outset will be on the class and not on the personal claim of an individual class member.[24] The collective interests of the class members as a whole will be the motivating reason to initiate a class action. During the proceedings, these interests will always come first, not those of an individual representative class member or his or her attorney. Therefore, one may expect ideological plaintiffs to pursue class actions more strongly, with more commitment and enthusiasm, which will benefit the class members. Moreover, time-consuming procedural problems will not occur when the individual claim of the class representative becomes moot or is settled by the defendant.

The law explicitly, and correctly, states that the representative also has to be adequate. Standing has to be distinguished from adequacy of representation.[25] An association or organization having class action standing is not automatically adequate to be a class representative in a specific case. When multiple associations present themselves as a class representative, the class action mechanism forces the court to determine which association or body is most adequate to represent the class in that particular case. Therefore, the adequacy of representation test can obviate potential conflicts of interest.

It is regrettable that *ad hoc* associations, under the form of a legal entity and created after a specific mass case, are not allowed to bring a class action. Amendments to give standing to Belgian *ad hoc* associations were rejected.[26]

18 Art. XVII.36, 2° CEL.
19 Art. XVII.39 CEL.
20 Art. XVII.39, 3° CEL.
21 Art. XVII.40 CEL.
22 Mulheron 2004, p. 303.
23 Voet 2013b, p. 458-459.
24 This refers to the class-entity or class-as-client theory (Shapiro 1998).
25 See Gidi 2003, p. 367-372 and Micklitz 2007, p. 21.
26 Report, p. 57.

## 4. Superiority

The third and final condition is that the class action is more suitable than (or superior to) an individual civil action.[27] In assessing this condition, the court may take into account the following elements: the potential group size, the existence of individual damages in connection with the collective harm, the complexity and judicial efficiency of the class action mechanism and the legal certainty for the group of consumers on whose behalf the action is brought. The size of the individual damages cannot be a decisive factor.[28]

## 5. Brussels Courts

The courts in Brussels have exclusive jurisdiction to decide class actions that will be binding on the whole country.[29] In the first instance, the class action can be brought before the Brussels Court of First Instance or the Brussels Commercial Court.[30] In appeal, the case is brought before the Brussels Court of Appeal.

This will lead to a specialized and experienced class action court, and will pave the way for an efficient resolution of class actions.[31] A uniform and predictable case law will develop in such a specialized area of the law. Moreover, a specialized and more experienced court will be able to deal with these cases more efficiently and swiftly. Because the total number of mass cases in European countries seems to be fairly limited, even in jurisdictions that already have class actions or class action-like tools, it would be inefficient to give jurisdiction to multiple courts in a small country like Belgium. One competent court also avoids time-consuming litigation over jurisdictional issues, as well as the disadvantages of forum shopping.

Critics argue that an exclusively competent court can be very powerful and can hinder the development of the law. It can also be perceived by class members as isolated, far, and inaccessible, which can lead to opt-outs because victims want to

27 Art. XVII.36, 3° CEL.

28 Chambre des représentants de Belgique, Projet de loi portant insertion d'un titre 2 «De l'action en réparation collective» au livre XVII «Procédures juridictionnelles particulières» du Code de droit économique et portant insertion des définitions propres au livre XVII dans le livre I du Code de droit économique. [Proposal to Introduce an Act Introducing a Consumer Collective Redress Action in the Code of Economic Law], 5e Session de la 53e Legislature, Doc. 3300/001, 17 January 2014, available at: <www.dekamer.be/FLWB/PDF/53/-3300/53K3300001.pdf> (hereafter Proposal), p. 8-9 and 21 (last accessed in September 2014).

29 Loi portant insertion des dispositions réglant des matières visées à l'article 77 de la Constitution dans le livre XVII «Procédures juridictionnelles particulières» du Code de droit économique et modifiant le Code judiciaire en vue d'attribuer aux cours et tribunaux de Bruxelles une compétence exclusive pour connaître de l'action en réparation collective visée au livre XVII, titre 2, du Code de droit économique [Act Making the Brussels Courts Exclusively Competent Regarding Collective Redress Actions] of 27 March 2014, *Moniteur Belge* [Official Gazette of Belgium], 29 April 2014, 35197.

30 The Brussels Justices of the Peace and the Brussels Labour Court have no jurisdiction.

31 Voet 2013b, p. 471-472.

enforce their rights in a closer jurisdiction. These dangers are real but can be controlled by a number of safeguards. Class action cases can be allocated to a three-judge panel. This allows discussion, and leaves room for development of the law. These class action judges also must be trained. Judicial education is essential. This training can be organized on a national and international level. A coordinating role can be reserved for the European Judicial Training Network.[32] Finally, the class action court can be made mobile and become a traveling class action court, when the particularities of the class conflict requires the court to be closer to the place of harm, or closer to the class members.

## 6. Opt-in or Opt-out

An important issue is the opt-in or opt-out feature of the class action device.[33] The EC Recommendation puts forward the opt-in system as default,[34] because it allows a class member to freely decide to participate in the proceedings or not, and therefore better preserves the principle of party autonomy. The EC also allows for opt-out class actions, but only when this is allowed by law or court order and duly justified by reasons of sound administration of justice,[35] a vague concept that is open to multiple interpretations. The Commission points out two advantages of an opt-out system: facilitating access to justice for small damages claims and offering more certainty and finality to the defendant.[36] The argument that only opt-in class actions are compatible with Article 6 ECHR, since they alone allow class members to actively participate in the proceedings, is crumbling. In the Dutch Dexia case,[37] the Amsterdam Court of Appeal ruled that if class members are duly and individually notified and have the opportunity to object or to opt-out in order to pursue their claim individually, their Article 6 rights are guaranteed.[38]

Contrary to the EC Recommendation, there is no default rule in Belgium. In its certification decision, the Belgian court can freely choose between an opt-in or opt-out system.[39] The court will make the decision in light of the underlying facts and claims of the case. For example, in small consumer damages claims, an opt-out system will be most feasible. In some (limited) cases, the court must impose an opt-

32 <www.ejtn.eu/> (last accessed in September 2014).

33 Stuyck 2009.

34 Art. 21 EC Recommendation ('the claimant party [i.e., the class] should be formed on the basis of express consent of the natural or legal persons claiming to have been harmed').

35 Art. 21 *in fine* EC Recommendation.

36 Communication from the Commission to the European Parliament, the Council, the European Economic and Social Committee and the Committee of the Regions, Towards a European Horizontal Framework for Collective Redress, COM(2013) 401/2, 12.

37 Amsterdam Court of Appeal, 25.01.2007, *JOR* 2007, 71 (*Dexia Bank Nederland NV v Stichting Platform Aandelenlease*).

38 Proposal, p. 30.

39 Art. XVII.43, §2, 3° CEL.

in system: when the class members are not residing in Belgium,[40] and when physical or moral damages are claimed.[41]

The consumer has to opt-in or opt-out after the certification decision has been notified.[42] This choice is irrevocable. If a consumer has opted-in or has not opted-out, and afterwards disagrees with a collective settlement or the decision on the merits of the case, the consumer will be bound by the *res iudicata* effect of that settlement or decision. It allows to determine the definite size of the group at an early stage of the proceedings, which can facilitate and encourage a collective settlement. The Legislature also wants to avoid that class members make their opt-in or opt-out decision in function of the result of the procedure.[43] All this could have the possible adverse effect that class members will simply not opt in or will opt out because their choice will be final. It is regrettable that there is no second opt-in or opt-out round, for example after a collective settlement is approved. At least the court should have the discretionary power to order a second opt-out. An amendment allowing class members to opt-out at any stage of the proceedings, was rejected.[44]

## 7. Procedure: Settlement Phase and Merits Phase

### 7.1. *Settlement before the Proceedings*

If the parties reach a collective settlement before the start of the proceedings, they jointly submit it to the court to have it approved (homologated).[45] The agreement has to contain the following information: a detailed description of the collective harm; a description of the class; information about the class representative and the defendant(s); the extent and the forms of collective redress; the reasons to use the opt-in or opt-out system; in case of an opt-out system, the amount of time the class members, who will not opt-out, will have after the settlement approval to come forward to obtain individual compensation; the amount of costs the defendant(s) will pay to the class representative; which party will pay the costs of notice; a possible revision procedure; additional forms of notice and the text of the collective settlement as it will be notified to the class members. If one of these elements is missing or unclear, the court sends the agreement back to the parties, who have to

40 Art. XVII.38, §1, 2° CEL.

41 Art. XVII.43, §2, 3° CEL.

42 Art. XVII.38, §1 CEL. The certification decision is published in the Official Gazette of Belgium (*Moniteur Belge*) and on the website of the Federal Public Service Economy, SMEs, Self-Employed and Energy (Art. XVII.43, §3 CEL). Generally, there is no individual notice. If necessary, the court may order additional forms of notice, for example individual notice, notice in newspapers, magazines or on websites.

43 Proposal, p. 23 and 31.

44 Report, p. 52.

45 Art. XVII.42, §2 CEL.

complete it within eight days.[46] The joint petition must contain evidence that the certification criteria are met.[47]

The court must make a decision within two months.[48] If it refuses to approve the settlement, the procedure ends; it will not proceed as a class action. There is no *pro forma* approval. The law states that the court refuses approval if:[49]

- the agreed redress is evidently unreasonable;
- the amount of time the class members, who will not opt-out, will have after the settlement approval to come forward to obtain individual compensation, is evidently unreasonable;
- the additional forms of notice are evidently unreasonable;
- the amount of costs the defendant(s) will pay to the class representative exceed the real costs the latter has made.

Again, and if necessary, the court can send the agreement back to the parties, to have it amended on one or more of these grounds.[50] If the settlement is ultimately approved, the court appoints a collective claims settler.[51] Neither the collective settlement, nor the judicial approval decision imply a recognition of liability by the defendant.[52] The approval decision and the complete text of the settlement will be published in the Official Gazette of Belgium (*Moniteur Belge*) and on the website of the 'Federal Public Service Economy, Small and Medium Enterprises, Self-Employed and Energy' (since 2002 the new name of the Belgian Ministry of Economic Affairs).[53]

## 7.2. *No Settlement before the Proceedings*

If the parties have not reached a collective settlement, the class action procedure is initiated by the class representative who submits a petition to the clerk of the court. The complaint must contain the following information: evidence that the certification criteria are met, a description of the collective harm, a detailed description of the class and the reasons to use the opt-in or opt-out system.[54] If one

46 Art. XVII.42, §3 CEL.

47 The cause of action is a possible infraction by the defendant on his contractual obligations or on one of the 31 European or Belgian consumer regulations or acts that are enumerated in the act. The class action is brought by an adequate class representative and the class action is more suitable than (or superior to) an individual civil action.

48 Art. XVII.44, §1 CEL.

49 Art. XVII.49, §2 CEL.

50 Art. XVII.49, §2 CEL.

51 Art. XVII.49, §3 CEL.

52 Arts. XVII.46 and XVII.51 CEL.

53 Art. XVII.50 CEL.

54 Art. XVII.42, §1 CEL.

of these elements is missing or unclear, the court sends the petition back to the class plaintiff, who has to complete it within eight days.[55]

The court has to make a certification decision within two months.[56] If the class action is not certified, the lawsuit is dismissed without prejudice. Otherwise, the court renders a certification decision in which it decides to impose the opt-in or opt-out system and its modalities (e.g., the opt-in or opt-out period).[57] The certification decision will be published in the Official Gazette of Belgium (*Moniteur Belge*) and on the website of the Federal Public Service Economy, SMEs, Self-Employed and Energy.[58] If necessary, the court may order additional forms of notice.

In its certification decision, the court must set a time during which the parties have to negotiate a collective settlement.[59] There is a mandatory negotiation phase, during which the parties can use an accredited mediator.[60] If a settlement is reached, the approval procedure as described above, applies.

If a settlement cannot be reached within the allotted time frame, the procedure continues so the court can decide the merits of the case.[61] Within a month after the court has been notified of the fact that no collective settlement could be reached, it orders a hearing, where the parties agree on a procedural calendar.[62] If the parties reach a collective settlement during the procedure on the merits of the case, they can ask the court to approve it and the procedure described above applies.[63] If no settlement is reached, the court decides the merits of the case. If it finds the class claim valid, the decision will contain the same elements as a collective settlement.[64] The court will also appoint a collective claims settler. The decision is published in the same manner as the approval decision.[65]

## 8. Collective Redress in Kind or by Monetary Payment

Any collective settlement and decision on the merits of the case have to determine the extent and forms of collective redress. This redress can be in kind or by monetary payment. The amount of payment can be determined on an individual basis, meaning that the defendant(s) will have to pay an individualized amount of

55 Art. XVII.42, §3 CEL.
56 Arts. XVII.43, §1 and XVII.44, §1 CEL.
57 Art. XVII.43, §2 CEL.
58 Art. XVII.43, §3 CEL.
59 Art. XVII.45, §1 CEL. This time limit cannot be shorter than three months and cannot be longer than six months (Art. XVII.43, §2, 8° CEL). The court can prolong the time limit once with maximum six months (Art. XVII.45, §1 CEL).
60 Art. XVII.45, §2 CEL. See on mediation in Belgium and the accreditation of mediators: Traest 2012.
61 Art. XVII.52 CEL.
62 Art. XVII.53 CEL.
63 Art. XVII.56 CEL.
64 Art. XVII.54, §1 CEL.
65 Art. XVII.55 CEL.

money to every consumer coming forward, or, when this is impossible or impracticable, on a global basis.[66]

Every consumer who wants to be compensated, has to come forward, even in an opt-out system. In case of a low take-up rate, the court will determine the allocation of the residual funds. The court has a wide range of options: the funds can flow back to the defendant or the defendant can be ordered to set up a cy-près scheme (e.g., an invoice discount or the distribution of coupons or a free product).[67]

Common Belgian liability law applies.[68] The guiding principle remains full and individual compensation of the damages suffered. It is by no means the intention of the Legislature to introduce punitive damages that could lead to overcompensation.[69]

## 9. Collective Claims Settler

Finally, there is a phase during which the settlement or the decision on the merits of the case is enforced under the supervision of a collective claims settler.[70] The claims settler is appointed by the court from a list drawn up by the general assembly of the Brussels Court of First Instance, the Brussels Commercial Court or the Brussels Court of Appeal. Only attorneys, ministerial public servants or judicial mandataries (who are competent in settling claims) can be appointed.[71]

The enforcement procedure is very complicated and governed by short time limits. In case of an opt-out system, the court determines a term during which the class members who have not opted-out, have to come forward before the clerk of the court, to obtain individual compensation. In case of an opt-in system, consumer class members have already opted-in with the clerk of the court. Based on the information received from the clerk of the court, and within a reasonable time, the claims settler creates a provisional list of class member who will receive compensation. When a member does not meet the class description, this is mentioned on the list.[72] The claims settler sends the list to the judge, the class representative, the defendant, and the class members he or she proposes to exclude. Within 30 days, the class representative or the defendant can challenge the inclusion or exclusion of a class member on the provisional list, with the clerk of the court. No more than 14 days later, the clerk informs the concerned class members and the claims settler. Within 14 days, the class representative, the defendant(s), the class members whose enlistment is challenged, and the claims settler have an opportunity to communicate their views to the clerk of the court.[73] Within 30 days,

66 Arts. XVII.45, §3, 6° and XVII.54, §1, 7° CEL.
67 Proposal, p. 42.
68 Proposal, p. 37.
69 *Ibidem.* See also Art. 31 EC Recommendation.
70 Art. XVII.57, §2 CEL.
71 Art. XVII.57, §1 CEL.
72 Art. XVII.58, §1 CEL.
73 Art. XVII.58, §3 CEL.

the court orders a hearing. The claims settler, the class representative, the defendants, and the class members concerned are heard, after which the court creates the final list of class members who are entitled to compensation.[74] This list is notified to all of the parties.

In case conflicts occur during the enforcement phase, the parties and the claims settler can always request the court to resolve them.[75] Every three months, the claims settler reports to the judge.[76] When the settlement or the decision are fully enforced, he or she deposits the final report, and sends a copy to the class representative and to the defendant(s). The final report contains all the necessary information for the court to decide about the closure of the procedure. The final report gives an overview of the funds that were not distributed among the class members and contains a detailed outline of the costs and fees of the claims settler.[77] In its final decision, the court determines the allocation of the residual funds and approves or reduces the costs and fees of the claims settler. By approving the final report, the court definitely ends the enforcement phase. Based on that decision, the claims settler can claim his or her costs and fees from the defendant.[78] The decision is published in the Official Gazette of Belgium (*Moniteur Belge*) and on the website of the Federal Public Service Economy, SMEs, Self-Employed and Energy.[79]

## 10. Evaluation

### *10.1. Holistic Approach*

The Act of 28 March 2014 'Introducing a Consumer Collective Redress Action in the Code of Economic Law' makes Belgium one of the European front-runners regarding consumer collective redress. The new procedure, which is limited to consumer law cases, largely complies with the EC Recommendation on common principles for injunctive and compensatory collective redress mechanisms. The act, that entered into force on 1 September 2014, will be evaluated in 2017. Possibly, the procedure might be expanded to other fields of substantive law.

A holistic approach is required to address mass harms. Optimal collective redress can only be achieved by a matrix of intertwined models. Especially with respect to small consumer claims, the potential for other redress mechanisms and models has to be underlined. Moreover, priority has to be given to an ADR model that encompasses direct negotiation, conciliation and arbitration by ADR agencies.

74 Art. XVII.58, §4 CEL. The question arises whether an excluded class member can challenge the decision that excludes him. Because he is no party to the proceeding, he cannot appeal the decision. The fact that the class member concerned is heard by the court, does not make him a party.

75 Art. XVII.60 CEL.

76 Art. XVII.59, §1 CEL.

77 Art. XVII.61, §1 CEL.

78 Art. XVII.61, §2 CEL.

79 Art. XVII.62 CEL.

In addition, the significance of regulation and possible regulatory oversight of collective restitution and restoration cannot be underestimated. Nevertheless, and to complete this set of collective redress mechanisms, the private litigation model should include a class action device.[80] In that sense, the Belgian consumer class action should be viewed as a legal protection tool that juxtaposes the new consumer ADR scheme that the Act of 4 April 2014 has set up.

### 10.2. *Bottlenecks*

The new class action procedure has some bottlenecks that could undermine its efficiency. First, there is the possibility to appeal the certification decision. According to Belgian law,[81] when a decision is appealed, all the (factual and legal) issues that were not decided by the first court, are transferred to the appellate court that will decide them. There is no referral back to the court of first instance. There are some exceptions to this rule. For example, when the appellate court affirms, on the same grounds, an investigative measure ordered by the first court, the appellate court will refer the case back to the first court. This exception does not apply when the Brussels Court of Appeals affirms a certification decision. In that case, the Court of Appeals has jurisdiction to deal with the rest of the procedure. Because the stakes in class action procedures are so high, the certification decision will almost always be appealed. This means that the procedure in first instance will be *de facto* limited to the certification issue. It will be the Brussels Court of Appeals that will approve a collective settlement reached after certification or will render a decision on the merits of the case. Because of the backlog in this court – currently, it takes sometimes 4 or 5 years to have an individual lawsuit decided – consumers will have to wait for years to get compensated.

Second, there is the complicated phase during which the settlement or decision on the merits of the case is enforced under the supervision of a collective claims settler. This complexity threatens to undermine the efficiency of the procedure.

Third and finally, no attention is given to the funding and financing issue.[82] This seems to be the biggest obstacle to the effectiveness of the Belgian class action. The Belgian Legislature assumes that the procedure can and will be financed in the same way as individual procedures.[83] Bringing a consumer class action will therefore depend exclusively on the financial willingness and power of a consumer association or the Consumer Ombudsman Service. The question arises how much financial readiness they will have. If at the end of the procedure the class representative runs the risk of also having to pay the costs of the defendant, because of the loser pays rule, there will be a disincentive to bringing class actions, which

80 Voet 2013b, p. 478-479 and Voet 2013a.
81 Art. 1068 Belgian Judicial Code.
82 See Voet 2015. See also Arts. 29-32 EC Recommendation.
83 Report, p. 25.

could create a barrier to access to legal remedies of the kind which the procedure itself aims to overcome.

## Bibliography

**Fierens & Volders 2012**
Fierens, J.-P. & Volders, B., 'Belgium', in Karlsgodt, P.G. (ed.), *World Class Actions. A Guide to Group and Representative Actions around the Globe*, New York: Oxford University Press, 2012, p. 271-285.

**Gidi 2003**
Gidi, A., 'Class Actions in Brazil: A Model for Civil Law Countries', *American Journal of Comparative Law*, 2013, Vol. 51, p. 311-408.

**Hodges 2013**
Hodges, Ch., 'Collective Redress: A Breakthrough or a Damp Sqibb?', *Journal of Consumer Policy*, 2013, Vol. 37, p. 67-89.

**Micklitz 2007**
Micklitz, H.-W., 'Collective Private Enforcement of Consumer Law: The Key Questions', in Van Boom, W.H. & Loos, M. (eds.), *Collective Enforcement of Consumer Law. Securing Compliance in Europe through Private Group Action and Public Authority Intervention*, Groningen: Europe Law Publishing, 2007, p. 11-34.

**Mulheron 2004**
Mulheron, R., *The Class Action in Common Law Legal Systems: A Comparative Perspective*, Oxford: Hart Publishing, 2004.

**Shapiro 1998**
Shapiro, D., 'Class Actions: The Class as Party and Client', *Notre Dame Law Review*, 1998, Vol. 73, p. 913-962.

**Silvestri 2013**
Silvestri, E., 'Towards a Common Framework of Collective Redress in Europe. An Update on the Latest Initiatives of the European Commission', *Russian Law Journal*, 2013, Vol. 1, p. 46-56.

**Storme & Terryn 2009**
Storme, M.E. & Terryn, E., 'Belgium', *The Annals of the American Academy of Political and Social Science*, 2009, Vol. 622, p. 95-104.

**Stuyck 2009**
Stuyck, J., 'Class Actions in Europe? To opt in or to opt out, that is the question', *European Business Law Review*, 2009, Vol. 20(4), p. 483-505.

**Taelman & Voet 2011**
Taelman, P. & Voet, S., 'Belgium and Collective Redress: The Last of the European Mohicans', in Dirix, E. & Leleu, Y.-H. (eds.), *The Belgian Reports at the Congress of Washington of the International Academy of Comparative Law*, Brussels: Bruylant, 2011, p. 305-346.

**Traest 2012**
Traest, M., 'Belgium', in Esplugues Mota, C., Iglesias, J.-L. & Moreno, G.P. (eds.), *Civil and Commercial Mediation in Europe, Vol. I. National Mediation Rules and Procedures*, Cambridge: Intersentia, 2012, p. 45-68.

**Verougstraete 2012**
Verougstraete, I., 'Class Actions: les doutes et certitudes du magistrat', *Cahier du Juriste*, 2014, Vol. 4, p. 99-103.

**Voet 2013a**
Voet, S., 'Public Enforcement and A(O)DR as Mechanisms for Resolving Mass Problems: a Belgian Perspective', in Hodges, Ch. & Stadler, A. (eds.), *Resolving Mass Disputes. ADR and Settlement of Mass Claims*, Cheltenham: Edward Elgar, 2013, p. 270-292.

**Voet 2013b**
Voet, S., 'Cultural Dimension of Group Litigation: The Belgian Case', *Georgia Journal of International and Comparative Law*, 2013, Vol. 41(2), p. 433-479.

**Voet 2014**
Voet, S., 'European Collective Redress: A *Status Quaestionis*', *International Journal of Procedural Law*, 2014, Vol. 4(1), p. 97-128.

**Voet 2015**
Voet, S., 'Funding and Financing Collective Redress Mechanisms: The Icing on the Cake', in Storskrubb, E. (ed.), *Civil Justice in the EU – Growing and Teething? Questions Regarding Implementation, Practice and the Outlook for Future Policy*, Oxford: Hart Publishing, 2015, forthcoming.

N. Andrews

# MULTI-PARTY LITIGATION IN ENGLAND

English 'multi-party' litigation can take one of four forms:[1] (I) test case litigation, supported by the staying of related individual actions; (II) consolidated litigation or joinder, so that claims are coupled together into a single but long snake of a case;[2] (III) representative proceedings;[3] (IV) numerous claims under a 'Group Litigation Order' (GLO).[4] The scheme of this chapter is as follows: after brief explanations of I and II, detailed discussion will turn to III and IV.

Representative proceedings (mode III) in England differ from modes I, II, and IV (see above) because the representative claimant brings an action on behalf of himself and others (the represented class). He is the only claimant. Members of that represented class are not parties to the action. However, Group Litigation Order litigation has become the main, but not the exclusive, means of handling claims for compensation involving large groups of similarly affected persons or entities. Group Litigation Orders are characterised by high levels of case management at all stages of the proceedings. The GLO procedure is an opt-in system.

## 1. Test Cases

Large numbers of related claims might be stayed (placed in suspense, but not dismissed) pending the outcome of a test case to be decided by the High Court.

1 For massive citation of other literature, Andrews 2013, 22.01, n. 1.

2 Andrews 2001, p. 249, 257; noting CPR 3.1(2)(g); 19.1; 19.2(3); ordinary joinder of co-claimants in *Lubbe v Cape plc* [2000] 1 WLR 1545, HL, resulted in over 3,000 claimants seeking personal injury damages against a multi-national company concerning its manufacturing activities in South Africa.

3 CPR 19, Sec. II; Andrews 2001, p. 249, 250-257.

4 CPR 19, Sec. III; and Practice Direction 19B. For comparative discussion on collective actions, see also the 2012 Buenos Aires conference papers: *Procesos Collectivos: Class Actions*, Buenos Aires, 2012 (reports submitted to the International Congress, 6-9 June 2012, Argentina). See also Eliantonio *et al.* 2013.

For example, in the bank charges litigation the English courts were asked to pronounce on a point of law. The huge financial importance of the issue, and the banks' determination to defeat the challenge to their charges, led to successive appeals from the High Court to the Court of Appeal and the Supreme Court.[5] In this test case a governmental agency, which is responsible for consumer protection and regulation of trading practices, invoked its statutory powers to seek a judicial declaration. It was hoped (although this hope proved to be misplaced) that this declaration would provide the legal basis for a vast number of bank customers to obtain relief in respect of alleged over-charging on their bank accounts. These charges, onerous and harsh, are imposed under contract when the customer exceeds a specified credit limit on her current banking account. But the test case failed when the Supreme Court held that the alleged over-charging could not be struck down under the relevant contractual regulations. This was because the contractual conditions fell within the prohibited zone of contractual freedom, as defined by the relevant legislation.

Although unsuccessful in the bank charges litigation, the test case technique remains available whenever public bodies have legal power disinterestedly to seek legal declarations (or other relief) on behalf of the community or segments of it.

## 2. Consolidation and Joinder

Consolidation and joinder of co-claimants are established means of accommodating multi-party actions. There is no limit on the number of co-claimants who can use this form of procedure. Consolidated procedure is an opt-in system of multi-party litigation.

For example, in *Weir v Secretary of State for Transport (No. 1)*,[6] the 'Railtrack' case, a group of claimants formed an 'action committee'. This committee brought a single action in which a very large group of co-claimants (nearly 50,000 shareholders in that case) were *full parties to the proceedings*. These claimants sought monetary redress against a defendant company.

Another example of a large (and successful) claim in which many individuals joined, using the well-established technique of joinder, is *Attrill v Dresdner Kleinwort Ltd* (2013).[7] In August 2008 the defendant investment bank's management had promised high-earning employees working in London a minimum pool for discretionary bonuses of Euros 400 million for the January 2009 'season'. In late December 2008 and early 2009, under pressure from the new management (a German bank which had acquired the business) management sought to resile from this. It was held that the promise was enforceable and that there were established criteria for allocation of this bonus chest.

5 *Office of Fair Trading v Abbey National plc* [2009] UKSC 6; [2010] 1 AC 696 (noted M. Chen-Wishart (2010) 126 LQR 157); on which Andrews 2011, 15.36.

6 [2005] EWHC 812 (Ch).

7 [2013] EWCA Civ 394; [2013] 3 All ER 807.

## 3. Representative Proceedings ('Opt Out')

In these proceedings, the representative claimant brings an action on behalf of himself and others (the represented class). He is the only claimant. Members of that represented class are not parties to the action. Nevertheless, those class members will receive the benefits of a *res iudicata* decision (or be subject to that decision), for example the benefit of a favourable declaration of legal entitlement. This form of proceeding is, therefore, an opt-out system. Representative proceedings are relatively uncommon in England.

The current English rule (CPR 19.6) provides:[8]

> (1) Where more than one person has the same interest in a claim – a. the claim may be begun; or b. the court may order that the claim be continued, by or against any one or more of the persons *who have the same interest* as representatives of any other persons who have that interest … (4) Unless the court otherwise directs any judgment or order given in a claim in which a party is acting as a representative under this rule – a. is binding on all persons represented in the claim; but b. may only be enforced by or against a person who is not a party to the claim with the permission of the court.

In this style of procedure, only the 'representative' is a 'party' in the full sense. Sec. 151(1) of the Senior Courts Act 1981 defines a 'party' to civil proceedings as including *any person who pursuant to or by virtue of rules of court or any other statutory provision has been served with notice of, or has intervened in, those proceedings*, and this indicates that a represented person is not a 'party', unless a rule requires him to be notified of proceedings (no such rule presently exists). In fact the represented party occupies a hybrid position. He is neither fully a party (and thus not automatically liable for costs,[9] nor is he able to demand – nor liable to provide – disclosure of documents),[10] nor is he a mere bystander uninterested in the fate of the case. Indeed, he is bound by its result: *Unless the court otherwise directs, any judgment or order given in a claim in which a party is acting as a representative under this rule (a) is binding on all persons represented in the claim …*[11]

Representative proceedings can be commenced without the court's permission (conversely, however, the court can order that pending proceedings should be continued in representative form).[12] Furthermore, the court does not approve

8 CPR 19.6.

9 *Price v Rhondda UDC* [1923] WN 228; (1923) 130 LT 156, Eve J; on which, contending that the matter should be re-considered, Waller J in *Bank of America National Trust and Savings Association v John Taylor* [1992] 1 Lloyd's Rep 484, 495.

10 *Ventouris v Mountain* [1990] 1 WLR 1370, Saville J.

11 CPR 19.6(4).

12 CPR 19.6(1)(b).

settlements of representative proceedings, unless the represented persons are either under a mental disability or are minors.[13]

It is unnecessary for the representative to have been appointed or elected by the relevant group. In short, he can be a self-appointed general. However, 'the court may direct that a person may not act as a representative'.[14] This allows the court to bar an unsuitable representative. The rule provides that 'Any party may apply to the court for [such] an order', a provision which rather begs the question whether a represented person is a 'party' to the action.[15] In *Moon v Atherton* (1972) a represented person was treated as a 'party' under the pre-CPR rules,[16] but only for the limited purpose of enabling a person to take over the role of representative when the earlier representative discontinued his claim.

Represented persons need not be informed of the representative party's intention to bring the action nor need they be informed of its progress. Furthermore, the representative claimant or defendant is *dominus litis* (Latin for 'the one who calls the procedural shots') and so it follows that the representative can compromise the claim or defence. Such a settlement will not bind represented persons unless they specifically assent and become parties to it. But a settlement which is constituted as a judgment by consent would appear to bind represented persons because: ... *any judgment or order given in a claim in which a party is acting as a representative under this rule (a) is binding on all persons represented in the claim...* However, if they are discontent with the manner in which the proceedings are being conducted by the head representative, a segment of the represented group can secede from the main group and become co-defendants.[17]

Representative proceedings can provide an efficient means of gaining 'closure' of a dispute affecting a host of persons. A good example is the *Equitable Life* case (2002), where a defendant life insurance company sponsored a representative action. Ultimately, the House of Lords issued a declaration in this action.[18] That declaration established the true interpretation of a clause in the defendant company's life assurance policy. Ninety thousand policy-holders were bound by this decision.

The representative mechanism has been used to try to obtain effective injunctive relief against a disruptive unincorporated association (a 'protest group'), but the Court of Appeal in *Astellas Pharma Ltd v Stop Huntingdon Animal Cruelty* (2011) held that the lower court had over-stretched itself by attempting to render unidentified persons subject to immediate enforcement of the injunction.[19]

13 CPR 21.10(1) (proceedings by or on behalf of a child or patient). *Cf.* the US practice where the need to obtain judicial approval for class action settlements is standard, although it has not escaped criticism: Andrews 2003, 41.90 to 41.109.

14 CPR 19.6(2).

15 CPR 19.6(4).

16 [1972] 2 QB 435, CA.

17 Andrews 1994, 7-011, considering, notably, *John v Rees* [1970] Ch 345, Megarry J.

18 *Equitable Life Assurance Society v Hyman* [2002] 1 AC 408, HL.

19 [2011] EWCA Civ 752.

Apart from declarations and injunctive relief, representative proceedings are relatively uncommon in England. Representative proceedings for pecuniary relief remain distinctly marginal. This is so for two reasons: first, costs; secondly, a tradition (now receding or even about to end) of restrictive judicial interpretation of the relevant rule. These points will now be developed.

First, there is the claimant's personal 'costs risk'. A representative must bear the entire cost of the litigation if the case is lost. He will then be required to pay the defendant's costs. Even if the representative wins the case, there is the risk that he might not succeed in recovering all his costs from the losing opponent. For these reasons, prospective representative claimants will be apprehensive about their personal liability for costs.

The second impediment to damages litigation in representative proceedings has been the courts' traditionally narrow interpretation of the statutory phrase, *where more than one person has the same interest in a claim*.[20] Until recently, the major obstruction to the award of damages in representative proceedings was the Court of Appeal's (majority) analysis in *Markt & Co Ltd v Knight SS Co Ltd* (1910).[21] In this case a ship had been sunk by the Russian navy. The reason for this attack was that it was believed to be carrying contraband goods. A representative action was brought in respect of the 44 cargo owners against the carrier, on the basis that it had been culpable in exposing the ship to this risk of Russian naval intervention. Joinder in the *Markt* case (1910) would have required recommencement of proceedings by a consolidated claim for 44 cargo owners. The court thought that this was practicable (all 44 could be contacted). Furthermore, it would be desirable, because the court considered that it might facilitate more effective discovery. Despite the manifest procedural unattractiveness of the decision (and even the possibility that claims might have become statute-barred), the court suggested that it is not enough that the suggested class of claimants is suing in respect of the same cause of action (for example, in contract or in the tort of negligence); nor that their claims raise strikingly similar factual issues, perhaps arising from the same incident. The presence, or even the possible presence, of different defences (for example, individual contractual clauses imposing limitations upon liability or, in the case of negligence claims in tort, the possible presence of different degrees of contributory negligence), would preclude a representative claim.[22] It is now apparent that the

20 CPR 19.6(1).

21 [1910] 2 KB 1021, 1030, 1035, 1040, CA. Mulheron 2005b, p. 424, 426-431, 433-435 and 437, and especially 428-430; Mulheron 2009, p. 159; Sorabji 2009, p. 498.

22 Vaughan-Williams LJ, at 1030, emphasised the possibly heterogeneous nature of the set of (contractual) bills of lading applicable between the cargo owners and the carrier. Fletcher-Moulton LJ, at 1035, took the severe view that an individual claim for damages (whether or not founded on breach of contract) is by definition not a claim for common relief, and therefore incompatible with the spirit of representative proceedings, as earlier expressed by Lord Macnaghten in *Duke of Bedford v Ellis* [1901] AC 1, 8, HL, who said: 'Given a common interest and a common grievance, a representative suit was in order if the relief sought was in its nature beneficial to all whom the plaintiff proposed to represent.' The dissentient on the representative action point in the *Markt* case, Buckley LJ, [1910] 2 KB 1021, 1048, considered →

post-CPR law has removed the long shadow first cast in 1910 by the dicta of the *Markt* case.

The new flexibility is illustrated by *Millharbour Management Ltd v Weston Homes* (2011),[23] where Akenhead J held that representative claimants can validly seek damages for their own personal loss and for the loss suffered by other members of the class, using for this purpose the English system of representative proceedings. In that case numerous purchasers of flats, and sub-purchasers of flats, each of whom had bought leasehold interests in these dwellings, complained that the defendant builder had failed to construct satisfactory accommodation. Because of these defects, expensive repair work would be required. At first the cost of this work would be incurred by the management company responsible for maintaining the accommodation on behalf of leaseholders. That cost would then be passed on to individual tenants as increased 'service charges' in accordance with the contracts between the management company and the leaseholders. The present representative action would operate to enable the representatives of these different cohorts of leaseholders to obtain compensation. That compensation would be the amount of the extra service charges payable by the leaseholders to the management company as a result of the repair costs.

According to this decision, therefore, a representative claim for damages is available if (i) the court at the time of judgment will be able to determine the total amount of damages to be awarded in favour of the represented class and (ii) the court will also be able at judgment to determine the value of an individual represented person's entitlement to damages. The same judgment emphasises the procedural efficiency which can be derived from pursuing representative proceedings. Such a claim avoids the procedural cost of each alleged victim being joined in name as a full party to the relevant proceedings. The court acknowledged in this case that procedural economies can be achieved by a representative claim. The court was keen in this litigation to facilitate such economies by rejecting the defendant's challenge to the representative proceedings.

## 4. Group Litigation Orders ('Opt In')[24]

Such orders ('GLOs') were intended to become the mainstay of the English system's treatment of multi-party litigation (an 'opt-in' system). But it is possible that relaxation of representative proceedings, to accommodate some pecuniary claims, might cause GLOs to become less important during the next decade. A GLO is a special form of joinder, by listing of claims on a group register. The Senior Master and the Law Society maintain a list of GLOs.[25]

that a representative action could proceed on the basis of a declaration of liability for breach of contract; Buckley LJ's suggestion foreshadowed Vinelott J's decision in the *Prudential* case [1981] Ch 229.

23 [2011] EWHC 661 (TCC); [2011] 3 All ER 1027.

24 Mulheron 2005a, p. 40, 45.

25 PD(19B), para 11.

The GLO system attractively expanded multi-party litigation beyond the '*same interest*' constraint of representative proceedings. CPR 19.10 states that:

> A Group Litigation Order ('GLO') means an order ... to provide for the case management of claims which give rise to common or related issues of fact or law (the 'GLO issues').

By contrast, CPR Rule 19.6 provides as follows for representative parties with same interest:

> (1) Where more than one person has the same interest in a claim – (a) the claim may be begun; or (b) the court may order that the claim be continued, by or against one or more of the persons who have the same interest as representatives of any other persons who have that interest.

In *Taylor v Nugent Care Society* (2004) Lord Woolf CJ explained the need for the GLO system:[26] '[the new procedure] provided the courts with very wide powers to manage the proceedings ... [and] in a more efficient and economic manner [in order] to provide more expeditious justice.' As for the relative speediness of GLO actions, the Senior Master of the Queen's Bench Division has stated: 'in the Group Litigation Orders with which I have been involved we have achieved settlement or decisions in half or a third of the time that normal litigation might have taken.'[27]

However, 'funding' is a fundamental problem in the field of multi-party litigation. In English civil litigation in general, 'economic access to justice'[28] is no longer significantly supported by public expenditure on legal aid (see for example, comments in *AB v Ministry of Defence* (2012)).[29] There is a general shift within English modern civil litigation towards the 'privatised' conditional fee system ('CFA') or damages-based agreements ('damages-based agreements: introduced under the Legal Aid, Sentencing, and Punishment of Offenders Act 2012).[30] This shift has also affected multi-party litigation. Formally, the rules and guidance permit public financial support of unusually deserving group litigation.[31] In fact public funding for group litigation is seldom granted.[32]

26 [2004] EWCA Civ 51; [2004] 1 WLR 1129, at [9].

27 Statement by Senior Master Robert Turner, cited in Andrews 2008, p. 302.

28 The distinction between formal and economic or 'effective' access to justice was acknowledged in *Hamilton v Fayed (No. 2)* [2002] 3 All ER 641, CA, at [65], by Chadwick LJ, and [81], by Hale LJ.

29 [2012] UKSC 9; [2012] 2 WLR 643, at [152].

30 For details, Andrews 2013, Vol 1, Ch. 20.

31 See 'The Funding Code', Part B, Sec. D, issued by the Community Legal Services Commission: <www.legalservices.gov.uk/civil/guidance/funding_code.asp> (last accessed in January 2014).

32 Mulheron 2008, Chapter 11, at p. 74.

There are six main components of the GLO system.[33] First, the court must approve a group litigation order, a two-stage procedure: first there must be an (i) application to a specified judge,[34] or (ii) the court can itself make such an order of its own initiative (on the related topic of consolidation);[35] secondly, both in situations (i) and (ii), ratification is necessary (the 'making' of the GLO), at a very senior level.[36] Secondly, group litigation involves 'opting-in' by each individual. Thirdly, a group member enjoys both membership of the group and the general status of a fully-fledged 'party to civil proceedings'. Fourthly, during the progress of the GLO, the court will exercise extensive case management and issue directions. Fifthly, if the group loses the case, each group member is liable to the victorious party both for that member's share of the common costs of the proceedings and for any individual costs specifically incurred with respect to his claim; but if the group is victorious, the defeated party is liable to pay costs attributable both to the 'common costs' and the 'individual costs'.[37] *Barr v Biffa Waste Services* (2009)[38] concerned a Group Litigation Order for damages worth c £1 million, but involving a very much larger measure of potential costs liability. In that case, Coulson J (as mentioned) held that he could not make a cost-capping order tied to the value of the claimant's ATE ('After-the-Event' legal expenses insurance) cover. But, with the claimants' consent, he made a cost-capping order based on the claimants' revised costs estimate.[39] Another major decision on the costs aspects of a GLO action is *Motto v Trafigura Ltd* (2011).[40]

Finally, decisions on 'common' issues are binding on, and in favour of, the group. A party who is adversely affected by a judgment or order can seek permission to appeal.[41] Such a 'common' issue will normally concern questions of liability or the availability of a particular head of loss.

During preparation of the GLO for trial, the court will exercise extensive case management and issue directions. The managing court's[42] orders are binding on all the cases on the register. Exercise of this power of decision is a weighty responsibility. The court's directions can include the following:[43] (i) providing for one or more claims on the group register to proceed as test claims[44] (this occurred on the question of limitation of actions in *AB v Ministry of Defence* (2012), where nine

33 See also the summary by Lord Walker in *Autologic Holdings plc v Commissioners of Inland Revenue* [2005] UKHL 54; [2006] 1 AC 118, at [86].
34 PD(19B), para 3.3.
35 PD(19B), para 4.
36 PD(19B), paras 3.5 to 3.9.
37 See also *Sayers v Merck & SmithKline Beecham plc* [2002] 1 WLR 2274, CA; noted M Goldberg (2002) New LJ 437–8 and M Mildred (2002) 65 MLR 597.
38 [2009] EWHC 2444 (TCC); [2010] 3 Costs LR 317.
39 *Ibidem*, at [53] *et seq*.
40 [2011] EWCA Civ 1150; [2012] 1 WLR 657; [2012] 2 All ER 181; [2011] 6 Costs LR 1028.
41 CPR 19.12(2).
42 PD(19B), para 8.
43 For greater detail, Hodges 2001, 5.06 and 5.07.
44 CPR 19.13(b).

slightly different lead cases were selected from a group consisting of 1011 claimants);[45] (ii) appointing the solicitor of one or more parties to be the lead solicitor for the claimants or defendants[46] (appointment to be a lead solicitor can be lucrative); (iii) specifying the details to be included in a statement of case in order to show that the criteria for entry of the claim on the group register have been met;[47] or (iv) fixing a date after which no claim may be added to the group register unless the court gives permission[48] (there is a mechanism[49] for transferring actions which should join the register and which are commenced prior to the cut-off date); or (v) considering applications for 'costs-capping' (discussed by Coulson J, in *Barr v Biffa Waste Services* (2009)).[50]

But what of late-comers, if they are not admitted to the register, or if the relevant claimant wholly fails to make an application to join the register? The short answer is that they cannot be barred or struck out. But they might become subject to special managerial orders, namely stays and costs decisions. These matters were examined by the Court of Appeal in *Taylor v Nugent Care Society* (2004).[51]

The GLO system is a versatile and wide-ranging procedure. There is no restriction on the subject-matter of the relevant claims capable of being framed as a GLO. All forms of civil wrongdoing and dishonest misconduct can form the basis of 'common issues' in a GLO. Thus the rules state (CPR 19.10):

> A Group Litigation Order ('GLO') means an order ... to provide for the case management of claims which give rise to common or related issues of fact or law (the 'GLO issues').

There has been a wide range of GLOs, including: (i) claims for personal injury arising from pharmaceutical drugs;[52] (ii) corporation tax allegedly overpaid to the UK Revenue, for example, the Supreme Court's decision on points of limitation of actions in *Test Claimants in the FII Group Litigation v Revenue and Customs Commissioners* (2012);[53] and (iii) loss of corporate 'group tax relief': some idea of the sophistication of this type of group litigation order is conveyed by this statement by Lord Nicholls in the House of Lords:[54]

45 [2012] UKSC 9; [2012] 2 WLR 643.
46 CPR 19.13(c).
47 CPR 19.13(d); on this question, Lord Woolf in *Boake Allen Ltd v Revenue and Customs* [2007] UKHL 25, at [33].
48 CPR 19.13(e); and PD(19B), para 13.
49 PD(19B), para 9.1.
50 [2009] EWHC 2444 (TCC); [2010] 3 Costs LR 317.
51 [2004] EWCA Civ 51; [2004] 1 WLR 1129; Mildred 2004, C67, C69.
52 *Sayers v Merck & SmithKline Beecham plc* [2001] EWCA Civ 2017; [2002] 1 WLR 2274, CA.
53 [2012] UKSC 18; [2012] 2 WLR 1149; see also *Boake Allen Ltd v Revenue and Customs* [2007] UKHL 25; [2007] 1 WLR 1386.
54 *Autologic Holdings plc v Commissioners of Inland Revenue* [2005] UKHL 54; [2006] 1 AC 118, at [2].

> 'six groups of companies have been selected as test cases. They represent a large number of claimant companies in proceedings started in the Chancery Division against the Commissioners of Inland Revenue. This litigation is currently being managed under a group litigation order made by the Chief Chancery Master in May 2003.'

The former Senior Master Robert Turner, in a report sent to the author in 2007 (and amplified at a Cambridge seminar in 2012), stated that he had dealt with the following GLOs:

- a hotel in Spain to which tour operators sent parties long after they allegedly knew of the serious risk of food poisoning that existed;
- the Alder Hey hospital organ removal litigation involving hundreds of deceased young children and their grieving families; the (then) Senior Master of the Queen's Bench Division sent this to mediation with huge success (as the author has explained elsewhere);[55]
- the hot drinks claims against McDonalds; these claims failed (in England);
- long distance flight thrombosis claims;[56]
- removal of indigenous inhabitants from the Chagos Islands in the Indian Ocean;[57]
- the unexploded shells cases from the Army's training areas in Kenya;
- pension cases where long-serving employees were allegedly cheated out of their final salary pension entitlements;
- Ivory Coast contamination claims, involving oil dumping: *Motto v Trafigura Ltd* (2011);[58]
- the Buncefield disaster (explosion at oil depot; devastation of vicinity; property claims; 3,400 claimants).[59]

## 5. Rejection (2009) of Generic 'Opt Out' Class Action

Rachael Mulheron's 2008 paper on 'Reform of Collective Redress in England and Wales', presented to the Civil Justice Council, noted that there have been relatively few (only 63) GLO since their introduction in 2000.[60] She suggested that this figure is low, when comparison is made with Common Law jurisdictions (notably Ontario and Australia)[61] offering 'opt-out' systems. Certainly the English GLO figures (an 'opt-in' system) are perhaps disconcerting if one takes an absolutist approach to 'access to justice'. But the figures are not surprising, because large-scale litigation will not be brought unless there is substantial private funding or public support. As

55 Andrews 2008, 10.13.
56 *Deep Vein Thrombosis and Air Travel Group Litigation* [2005] UKHL 72; [2006] 1 AC 495.
57 Scanlan 2007, p. 292.
58 [2011] EWCA Civ 1150; [2012] 1 WLR 657; [2012] 2 All ER 181; [2011] 6 Costs LR 1028.
59 [2008] EWHC 1729 (Comm); [2008] 2 CLC 258.
60 Mulheron 2008, Chapter 3.
61 *Ibidem*, Chapter 12.

for the private source, it would appear that the conditional fee system has not worked in this context. This seems to be attributable to the absence (in this especially risky context) of ATE legal expenses insurance to cover the claimants' risk of liability for the defendant's costs. As for the public source, Mulheron notes the sharp decline in public funding of such litigation since the pre-2000 peak.[62]

Mulheron noted four main reasons why potential group litigation litigants are reluctant to join such collective litigation, that is, to 'opt in':[63] (i) economic anxiety that they will become liable for substantial costs; (ii) psychological considerations, that they will be exposed to a rough-and-tumble experience; (iii) fear of reprisals, notably by employers; and (iv) basic misunderstanding of the system of civil compensation.

Mulheron compared the 'take up' levels by victims of wrongdoing who are able to 'follow on' success on the question of liability in the class action ('opt-out') systems used in some Common Law jurisdictions (notably the USA, Ontario, and Australia).[64] And she noted the rise of the class action ('opt-out') mechanism in some European jurisdictions: Hodges has made a study of these European developments.[65]

As a result of Mulheron's suggestion that the English system of civil procedure had scored low in its delivery of effective access to justice in this context,[66] the Civil Justice Council in 2008 issued a major document entitled 'Improving Access to Justice Through Collective Actions' ('the CJC's 2008 Final Report).[67] However, the Government in July 2009 opposed introduction of a generic opt-out class action in England for compensatory claims, etc.[68] The (then Labour) 2009 Government had no stomach for collective big money litigation.[69] It rejected the proposal for a generic opt-out class action mechanism. Mulheron (2011) remains unimpressed by this Governmental decision.[70]

## 6. Concluding Remarks

These are the salient points:

62 *Ibidem*, Chapter 11, p. 74. She notes that the Legal Services Commission funded 133 multi-party actions in 2000; in 2002/3 this had fallen to 45; in 2006/7 it had fallen to 4; and of the 293 actions since 2000, 156 had concerned child abuse, 34 health matters including pharmaceutical problems, and 27 prisoner claims.

63 *Ibidem*, Chapter 7.

64 *Ibidem*, Chapter 20.

65 Hodges 2008.

66 Mulheron 2008, Chapter 21.

67 <www.civiljusticecouncil.gov.uk/files/Improving_Access_to_Justice_through_Collective_-Actions.pdf> (last accessed in January 2014).

68 Ministry of Justice, July 2009: The (English and Welsh) Government's Response to the Civil Justice Council's Report Improving Access to Justice Through Collective Actions.

69 *Ibidem*.

70 Mulheron 2011, p. 288-315; see also Sorabji 2012, Chapter 3.

(1) There must be a significant number of persons who are allegedly harmed, or whose interests are threatened, in the same or a similar way.
(2) In order to protect those interests, there can be either public enforcement or private enforcement and vindication. Or there can be a combination of these.
(3) Legal systems can also offer a choice between, or a combination of, opt-in and opt-out systems. For example, England offers a combination.
(4) What of practical or economic access to justice? Without this a legal system will be creating merely empty procedural categories, procedures which shine when introduced but which, as the years pass, rust through disuse. However, public funding has fallen away. England and the USA have used contingency funding. Non-party funding is also growing in importance.
(5) Under the opt-out system, there is the central issue: who will be the representative? In the Scandinavian countries,[71] the models of public representatives, consumer association representatives, and private representative are all found. In the USA and England, the main form of representative is a private individual.
(6) What type of relief is available? Should it be confined to declarations or injunctions. If damages are available, compensatory sums must (a) involve award of the global amount and (b) provide a criterion for allocation of individual shares (not necessarily equal). Awards paid into court which are to be allocated cy-pres are not attractive. Punitive damages are not favoured in many systems. And what of actions for debts or restitution for unjust gains?
(7) This is a specialist judicial responsibility. Judges, chosen for their high ability and flexibility, should be trained to carry it out. This will promote sound practice and consistency.
(8) There is a need for transparency: (i) what are the procedures and how effective are they? (ii) is there a reliable register of such claims? (iii) what judgments have been delivered and for how much?
(9) The technique of class/group civil procedure can be combined with: (a) settlement (b) mediated settlement (c) judicially ratified settlement (as in the Dutch system)[72] (c) judgment (d) outside the USA, where adhesion arbitration clauses have been upheld, class arbitration seems a remote prospect because of the need for free consent to arbitration clauses.
(10) There are three main obstacles: (i) within Europe a 'sectorial' preference, as distinct from uniform or general introduction of private group/class procedural techniques; (ii) a tendency to sap the vitality of these methods by entrusting 'standing' to public or quasi-public bodies, by withholding or

71 As reported by Laura Ervo (surveying Sweden, Norway, Finland and Denmark) at a conference in Hungary on Multi-Party Redress Mechanisms, Budapest, November 2013.
72 As reported by C.H. van Rhee (Maastricht, the Netherlands) at a conference in Hungary on Multi-Party Redress Mechanisms, Budapest, November 2013.

restricting pecuniary remedies, and by restrictions on contingency fees or private commercial funding (it remains to be seen whether contingency fee funding, now validated in England and Wales for civil litigation, following the Legal Aid, Sentencing, and Punishment of Offenders Act 2012,[73] will inject dynamism into the representative proceedings style of litigation); (iii) a xenophobic fear of USA systems – but a fresh and objective appraisal of procedural techniques is required.

*Caution*
However, there are dangers in adopting an 'opt out' system:

(a) *abuse and overkill:* a generic opt-out class action for damages would involve claimants' rights being championed by the joint enterprise of law firms (including foreign firms fishing in England for work) and commercial funders (or syndicates of funders) interested in profiting from others' litigation; this might involve potentially aggressive collective litigation and very large gains being made by law firms;
(b) *defensive behaviour:* the fear of commercial and public entities being exposed to expensive and protracted litigation;
(c) *increase in liability costs:* inevitable increases in the cost of potential defendants' defensive measures; in particular, consumers and businesses paying more for insurance cover.

73 Andrews 2013, Chapter 20.

## Bibliography

**Andrews 1994**
Andrews, N., *Principles of Civil Procedure,* London: Sweet & Maxwell, 1994.

**Andrews 2001**
Andrews, N., 'Multi-Party Proceedings in England: Representative and Group Actions', *Duke Journal of Comparative & International Law*, 2001, Vol. 11, p. 249-268.

**Andrews 2003**
Andrews, N., *English Civil Procedure,* Oxford: Oxford University Press, 2003.

**Andrews 2008**
Andrews, N., *The Modern Civil Process: Judicial and Alternative Forms of Dispute Resolution in England*, Tübingen: Mohr Siebeck, 2008.

**Andrews 2011**
Andrews, N., *Contract Law,* Cambridge: Cambridge University Press, 2011.

**Andrews 2013**
Andrews, N., *Andrews on Civil Processes, Vol. 1, Court Proceedings and Principles*, Cambridge: Intersentia, 2013.

**Eliantonio *et al.* 2013**
Eliantonio, M., Backes, Ch.W., Van Rhee, C.H., Spronken, T.N.B.M. & Berlee, A. (eds.), *Standing up for your Right(s) in Europe. A Comparative Study on Legal Standing (Locus Standi) before the EU and Member States' Courts,* Antwerp-Oxford: Intersentia, 2013.

**Hodges 2001**
Hodges, C., *Multi-Party Actions,* Oxford: Oxford University Press, 2001.

**Hodges 2008**
Hodges, C., *The Reform of Class and Representative Actions in European Legal Systems*, Oxford: Hart Publishing, 2008.

**Mildred 2004**
Mildred, M., 'Personal Injury - Civil Procedure - Group Actions - Group Litigation Orders', *Journal of Personal Injury Law*, 2004, C67, C69.

**Mulheron 2005a**
Mulheron, R., 'Some Difficulties with Group Litigation Orders - And Why a Class Action is Superior', *Civil Justice Quarterly*, 2005, Vol. 24, p. 40-68.

**Mulheron 2005b**
Mulheron, R., 'From Representative Rule to Class Action: Steps rather than Leaps', *Civil Justice Quarterly*, 2005, Vol. 24, p. 424-449.

**Mulheron 2008**
Mulheron, R., 'Reform of Collective Redress in England and Wales: A Perspective of Need', Research Paper, Civil Justice Council of England and Wales, 2008, <www.civiljusticecouncil.gov.uk/files/collective_redress.pdf>.

**Mulheron 2009**
Mulheron, R., '*Emerald Supplies Ltd v British Airways plc*: A Century Later, the Ghost of *Markt* Lives On', *Competition Law Journal*, 2009, Vol. 8(3), p. 159-179.

**Mulheron 2011**
Mulheron, R., 'Recent Milestones in Class Actions Reform in England: A Critique and a Proposal', *The Law Quarterly Review*, 2011, Vol. 127, p. 288-315.

**Scanlan 2007**
Scanlan, G., 'The Chagos Islanders' Case – A Question of Limitation?', *Civil Justice Quarterly*, 2007, Vol. 26, p. 292-300.

**Sorabji 2009**
Sorabji, J., 'The Hidden Class Action in English Civil Procedure', *Civil Justice Quarterly*, 2009, Vol. 28(4), p. 498-514.

**Sorabji 2012**
Sorabji, J., 'Collective Action Reform in England and Wales', in Fairgrieve, D. & Lein, E. (eds.), *Extraterritoriality and Collective Redress*, Oxford: Oxford University Press, 2012, 3.01-3.45.

F. Ferrand

# COLLECTIVE LITIGATION IN FRANCE: FROM DISTRUST TO CAUTIOUS ADMISSION

## 1. Introduction - Several Previous Attempts to Introduce Group Litigation in France

Many sectors are subject to deregulation in Europe. When the State deregulates, individuals must get protection through possible aggregate litigation. But even if the State - as the French State does[1] - still tries to provide remedies by way of public regulation, this does not mean that collective redress should not be allowed as an additional remedy in cases where many individuals have suffered from the same unfair business practice or anti-competitive conduct, or where they bring claims arising out of mass contracts or based on the default of the same kind of product they had purchased.[2] Private law enforcement and group litigation appear nowadays to be a necessary counterweight to deregulation and outsourcing of risks (especially by the banks). Group litigation is aimed to guarantee effective access to justice too, especially where small claims are concerned;[3] also when large claims are at stake, a specific procedure for collective redress can enhance the procedural economy[4] and the efficiency of the proceedings.

The purpose of collective litigation is compensation and deterrence. Those two aims are also considered in France. However, the French government, the

1 See Roskis & Jaffar 2013, No. 25, p. 24: 'A la différence des Etats-Unis où l'action privée est l'instrument central de régulation des marchés, en France, et de manière plus générale en Europe, la mise en œuvre de la répression des pratiques anticoncurrentielles ou des infractions au droit de la consommation est confiée à titre principal aux autorités publiques.'

2 See Murray 2009, p. 96 *et seq.*

3 See Caponi 2011, p. 74: '[T]he new instrument serves not only the purpose of procedural economy and efficiency, but it also allows for the emergence of latent disputes that would not otherwise appear before the courts due to the disproportionality between the value of a single case, typically modest, and the cost of the individual plea before the courts or the mediation proceedings.'

4 See Deffains 2008.

employers' associations and also most scholars are reluctant to opt for a system following the American class action model that appears to them too dangerous and a door open to many abuses,[5] probably because group litigation is linked with society and the national culture. Therefore, group litigation should not be envisaged only as a procedural technique, but is also embedded in substantive law as well as in the structure of the society.[6] However, this has not been the way chosen in France. Group litigation has most of the time been presented as a procedural device, which has led to many controversies with regard to fundamental principles of procedure that could be infringed if a broad system of group litigation with the opt-out model were adopted.[7] Shall one be afraid of collective litigation?[8]

In France, the discussions on group litigation started already more than thirty years ago. They always took place in the framework of 'consumers' protection' (*protection des consommateurs*).[9] Especially non-profit consumer associations such as UFC-Que choisir (a very well-known association) argued that only through collective redress could an adequate response be provided to a demand for justice from consumers claiming small amounts of money, and also deter companies from acting illegally and harming many consumers. The consumer associations argued therefore for a procedural tool to help regulate business activities impacting the interests of a large number of individuals.

The French story of collective redress is a story of 'missed appointments' (*rendez-vous manqués*); one could also say of 'stillborn reforms'.[10] There have been several attempts to enact a law establishing group litigation, but only recently (2014) one of them has succeeded and will come into force when the necessary governmental decree is enacted.[11] However, collective redress exists in France, mostly for compensation of damage caused to the collective interest of the consumers, or in a complicated and not really effective way, in some cases also for compensation of individual harm. The problem of French law is not that it ignores collective redress but that it had not yet designed an effective group litigation scheme for compensation of individual harm caused to a group of persons by the

5 *Cf.* Azar-Baud 2012, p. 2160, who asserts that most criticisms brought in France against the American class actions are linked with the typically American context: juries, punitive damages, contingency fees ..., all aspects that are not currently contemplated in French or in European law.

6 *Cf.* Stadler 2013, p. 1801 *et seq.*

7 For *Germany*, especially in the context of international class actions, *cf.* Stürner 2009, p. 107 *et seq.*

8 See De Silguy 2012, p. 55 *et seq.*

9 For Italy, *cf.* Caponi 2011, p. 745: '[T]he introduction of the class action suit is a fundamental element of a strategy to improve the conditions of the civil justice system in the field of consumers' protection.'

10 Jeuland 2012, No. 327, p. 317 (*réformes mort-nées*), who states p. 318 that 'l'histoire de l'action de groupe en France est l'histoire d'une résistance ou d'un blocage, selon l'angle où l'on se situe'.

11 See De Silguy 2012, p. 57: 'les actions de groupe 'à la française': l'archétype du serpent de mer'.

same professional on the basis of the same infringement of his legal or contractual obligations. This has changed with the entry into force of Law No. 2014-344 of 17 March 2014.

The first step was the Law of 27 December 1973 (*loi Royer*) recognising the right of consumer associations approved for this purpose (*associations agréées de consommateurs*) to bring an action before the court in the collective interest (*intérêt collectif*) of the consumers.

Ten years later, in September 1983, the *Commission sur le règlement des litiges de la consommation* (Commission dealing with the resolution of consumer disputes) published a report suggesting for France collective proceedings called *action de groupe* influenced by two models: the American class action and the law of Québec.

In 2005, President Jacques Chirac committed himself to introducing *actions groupées* in French law[12] and the Sénat (one of the two Houses of the French Parliament) drafted a report that favoured an *action collective inspirée de la class action américaine*. However, the bill drafted in autumn 2006[13] was withdrawn at the last minute due to a lack of political will.

In 2007, a bill was drafted on request of President Sarcozy, but again withdrawn from the bill on the modernisation of the economy.

Two years later a new bill was drafted but did not become law.

In 2010, several proposals were brought. Whereas one of them advocated an opt-out system, the others opted for a classic opt-in model. Two senators (L. Béteille and R. Yung) presented a bill on consumers' protection introducing the *action de groupe*,[14] but it was stopped at an early stage when it came before the National Assembly. (The terminology can vary from one draft to another: *recours collectif, action collective, action de groupe*. The new Law No. 2014-344 of 17 March 2014 *relative à la consummation*[15] opts for the terminology '*action de groupe*'.)

During his election campaign President François Hollande promised to introduce group litigation in France. A report on collective litigation (under the title *La protection du consommateur: rationalité limitée et regulation*) was drafted in September 2012 by the Council for Economic Analysis (*Conseil d'analyse économique*, CAE) and advocated the introduction of a mechanism of collective action in France.[16] The French National Consumer Council (*Conseil National de la Consommation*, CNC) also expressed this opinion. In 2011, 85 per cent of French citizens were in favour of introducing group litigation to assert their rights before

12 See the model suggested by Guinchard 2005, p. 2180 *et seq*., who asserts that 'le droit d'un Etat est le reflet de la culture d'une société; on ne peut se contenter ici de référence à une "demande sociale", aux contours imprécis et aux retombées incertaines, pour justifier le bouleversement de nos normes juridiques et de nos principes fondamentaux de procédure'.

13 Bill No. 3430 of 8 November 2006.

14 See <www.senat.fr/rap/r09-499/r09-4991.pdf> (last accessed in June 2014).

15 *JORF* No. 0065, 18 March 2014, p. 5400.

16 Gabais *et al*. 2012 (the report can be downloaded from the website of Documentation française, <www.ladocumentationfrancaise.fr/var/storage/rapports-publics/124000494/-0000.pdf>, last accessed in June 2014).

the courts.[17] A public consultation took place in November 2012; 7,165 people answered a questionnaire online.[18]

A bill aimed to keep this promise was presented in September 2012 by the minister in charge of consumer matters, Benoît Hamon. The French Parliament started discussing the bill in June 2013. After a first vote by the National Assembly (the first chamber of Parliament) at the beginning of July 2013, the bill was sent to the second chamber (*Sénat*) that adopted it with amendments. The bill was then examined by the Commission of Economic Affairs of the National Assembly and gave rise to a second reading and vote[19] before both Houses of Parliament. Again, employers' associations started to complain and to warn that class actions cost companies €16.5 billion,[20] which means one per cent of GDP (gross domestic product) each year. According to employers' associations, French companies only budget for pending proceedings, so they would become insolvent if group litigation were started against them.[21] Eventually, the Joint Committee of the two chambers suggested a compromise which was adopted by the Sénat on 12 February 2014. The Act was passed by the National Assembly on 13 February 2014. It was immediately submitted for control to the Constitutional Council[22] and then published as *Loi no 2014-344 du 17 mars 2014 relative à la consummation* in the *Journal Officiel* of the French Republic. However, it has not yet come into force since this requires the government to enact a decree regulating many procedural issues.

## 2. Where Are We? The Current State of Affairs in France before the Coming into Force of the New Statute

### 2.1. *The Existing Procedural Devices*

In France, currently three systems of collective redress are available; however, it is generally argued that none of them is really effective. These three mechanisms are

17 *Ibidem*, p. 47.

18 See Action de groupe: les avocats ne pourraient pas initier l'action, *Contrats Concurrence Consommation* (CCC) No. 2, February 2013, alerte 6.

19 Any bill, whether tabled by the government or by a Member of Parliament, is discussed in turn by each of the two Houses of Parliament (*Assemblée Nationale* and *Sénat*) in order to reach an agreement on the clauses to be examined. This process is called the Shuttle (*la navette*). The government is empowered to stop the Shuttle after two readings in each House. The Prime Minister then calls for a meeting of the Joint Mediation Committee (*commission mixte paritaire*) which is composed of seven members from each House. They are entrusted with the task of drawing up a compromise on the clauses on which agreement has not been reached. If this mediation procedure fails, the government can proceed to a new reading in each House and then ask the National Assembly to vote on the text as presented at its final reading (this has arisen for only about 10 per cent of the laws introduced since 1958).

20 In damages paid to the claimants and lawyers' fees.

21 See De Silguy 2012, p. 57.

22 Decision No. 2014-690 DC, 13 March 2014: the provisions on group litigation do not violate the rights of the defence or freedom or any other constitutional guarantee.

not contained in the Code of Civil Procedure but in more specialised codes (Consumer Code and Monetary and Financial Code).

### 2.1.1. An Action for the Financial Compensation of the Consumers' Collective Interest (Article L. 421-1 Consumer Code)[23]

This action was provided by the Law of 27 December 1973 and aims to allow financial compensation when the collective interest of consumers has been infringed in a direct or indirect way. A lawsuit can only be brought by non-profit consumer associations which have been officially approved (*agréées*)[24] by common decision of the minister in charge of consumption matters and of the ministry of justice if the association exists at a national level; if it is a local association, the approval is given by the general administrator of the *département* (*préfet*) in which the association has its registered office (Article R. 411-2 Consumer Code).[25] Such an association can exercise the rights of a civil party in respect of events directly or indirectly harming the collective interest of consumers. The action can be brought either before a criminal court if there is a criminal offence or before a civil court (Article L. 421-2 Consumer Code). It can seek for damages or for the prohibition of illegal practices such as unfair contract terms (cease order, *action en cessation d'agissements illicites*)[26] and also for the publication of the court decision.[27] This action is better suited for reaching the judicial prohibition of illegal practices[28] than for compensation: the weak point of this mechanism is that only the *collective* interest of consumers is concerned so that the financial compensation is allocated to the association that sues; the collective interest is different from the accumulated individual interests of the consumers. The consumers themselves do not receive any financial compensation. Moreover, French courts do not allocate high damages to compensate the harm of a collective interest; often, only symbolic amounts are allocated. This kind of action is most often used in France,[29] especially to stop unfair practices, but it cannot replace group litigation when many individuals are affected

23 Art. L. 421-1, para 1 C. consommation: 'Les associations régulièrement déclarées ayant pour objet statutaire explicite la défense des intérêts des consommateurs peuvent, si elles ont été agréées à cette fin, exercer les droits reconnus à la partie civile relativement aux faits portant un préjudice direct ou indirect à l'intérêt collectif des consommateurs.'

24 With regard to the conditions to be fulfilled by the association, see Art. R. 411-1 Consumer Code.

25 The approval is given for five years and can be renewed, Art. R. 411-2, last para Consumer Code.

26 Art. L. 421-6 Consumer Code.

27 Art. L. 421-9 Consumer Code.

28 For an example, see Cass. Civ. 1, 23 January 2013, No. 10-21177 and 10-22815; Cass. Civ. 1, 3 February 2011, No. 08-14402, *Bull. Civ.* I, No. 23.

29 The country report for France (in *Evaluation of the effectiveness and efficiency of collective redress mechanisms in the European Union*, 2008, available at: <http://ec.europa.eu/consumers/-redress_cons/finalreportevaluationstudypart1-final2008-11-26.pdf> (last accessed in June 2014)) indicates 427 actions for financial compensation of the consumers' collective interest (information provided by the national consumer association UFC-Que choisir).

by the same act or omission and seek compensation for this.[30] Logically, the consumers as individuals do not bear any costs in such proceedings; costs are only involved for the non-profit organisation that sues.[31]

### 2.1.2. A Joint Representative Action for Consumers (Article L. 422-1 Consumer Code) Brought by Approved Consumer Associations (*action en représentation conjointe d'une association agréée de consommateurs*)

The joint representative action was created by Law No. 92-60 of 18 January 1992. The starting point is that several individuals (consumers) have suffered *individual* harm having the same origin (the same act or behaviour of the same person or entity) and they wish to seek financial compensation. In such a case, a consumer association approved by the competent authority may bring a lawsuit 'in any court' (*devant toute juridiction*) in order to claim compensation on behalf of at least two consumers[32] who must have appointed the association as a proxy. The association needs therefore at least the (written)[33] power of attorney of two individuals to bring an admissible action.[34] This is a clear opt-in model that does not require any criminal offence nor the consumers to be members of the association that will take legal action. A consumer who gave such power of attorney to the association may withdraw it (Article R. 422-5 Consumer Code) for example if the association does not take legal action in due time; the consumer shall then give notice of his

30 See Cass. Crim., 20 May 1985, No. 84-91606, *Bull. Crim.* No. 190: 'le préjudice direct ou indirect qui est porté par une infraction à l'intérêt collectif des consommateurs, dont une association de défense régulièrement déclarée peut demander réparation ..., ne se confond pas avec le préjudice subi personnellement par les victimes directes de l'infraction, qui seules peuvent en demander réparation'; the direct or indirect harm caused by an illegal act to the consumers' collective interest for which an association may seek compensation is different from the harm personally suffered by the direct victims who are solely entitled to claim compensation.

31 The French country report (in *Evaluation of the effectiveness and efficiency of collective redress mechanisms in the European Union*, 2008, p. 5) mentions costs of about €15,000.

32 In its statement of claim, the association shall indicate the names of the consumers on whose behalf it is acting (Art. R. 422-8, para 1 Consumer Code). The power of attorney given by the consumers extends to a first means of recourse called *appel*, while a separate power of attorney is required to bring a *pourvoi en cassation* before the highest court (*Cour de cassation*); see Guinchard, Chainais & Ferrand 2012, No. 281.

33 Art. R. 422-2 Consumer Code: 'Le mandat doit être écrit, mentionner expressément son objet et conférer à l'organisation nationale agréée de consommateurs le pouvoir d'accomplir au nom du consommateur tous les actes de procédure.'

34 See Art. L. 422-1 Consumer Code: '1. Lorsque plusieurs consommateurs, personnes physiques, identifiés ont subi des préjudices individuels qui ont été causés par le fait d'un même professionnel, et qui ont une origine commune, toute association agréée et reconnue représentative sur le plan national en application des dispositions du titre Ier peut, si elle a été mandatée par au moins deux des consommateurs concernés, agir en réparation devant toute juridiction au nom de ces consommateurs. 2. Le mandat ne peut être sollicité par voie d'appel public télévisé ou radiophonique, ni par voie d'affichage, de tract ou de lettre personnalisée. Il doit être donné par écrit par chaque consommateur.'

withdrawal to the court and the defendant and can continue the proceedings as if he had himself brought the claim. Each claim for compensation is examined separately; whereas the assistance of a lawyer is not required before the *tribunal d'instance* (which has jurisdiction when the value at stake does not exceed €10,000) and the *juridiction de proximité*, the claimant who wants to seize the *tribunal de grande instance* (which has jurisdiction when the value in controversy exceeds €10,000) has to appoint a lawyer. French law prohibits contingency fees[35] as well as a *quota litis* agreement; however, since 1991, complementary fees are allowed that depend on the outcome of the judicial proceedings, but shall remain reasonable. A party can contest the fees requested by the lawyer before the president of the bar (*bâtonnier de l'ordre des avocats*) and later on before a court.

To determine which court has jurisdiction with regard to the amount in controversy as well as the admissibility of appeal,[36] only the value of the largest claim has to be taken into account (Article R. 422-3 Consumer Code).

The main problem of this procedural mechanism is that the legal provisions do not allow the association to solicit such powers of attorney via TV or radio nor by distributing leaflets or personalised letters, but only in newspapers and magazines. In a recent decision of 26 May 2011,[37] the first chamber of the French *Cour de cassation* (Court of Cassation) even held that the law prohibits any use of mass communication means such as internet calls.[38] In this case, the French *Conseil de la concurrence* (Competition Council) ruled against several mobile telephone operators on the grounds of illegal price fixing (*entente*). A consumer brought a compensation claim (€67.20) against one of the operators; the consumer association UFC-Que choisir joined the proceedings and claimed €55,559 compensation for the harm caused to the *collective* interest of the consumers (Article L. 421-7 Consumer Code). After they requested and received help from the association, more than 3,500 consumers also intervened in the proceedings in order to receive compensation. The association pretended not to bring a joint representative action but only to play an intermediary role between the consumers and their lawyer. However, the court of appeal applied Article L. 422-1 Consumer Code (joint representative action) because the association had sought proxies in order to take legal action on their behalf and in their interest.[39] The court declared the summons, the interventions and the entire proceedings void because the association had used an illegal means to ask consumers to join the proceedings: its internet website, which is prohibited because

35 See Art. 10, para 3 of Law No. 71-1130 of 31 December 1971: 'Toute fixation d'honoraires, qui ne le serait qu'en fonction du résultat judiciaire, est interdite. Est licite la convention qui, outre la rémunération des prestations effectuées, prévoit la fixation d'un honoraire complémentaire en fonction du résultat obtenu ou du service rendu.'

36 In France, normally, appeal is only admissible if the value at stake exceeds €4,000.

37 Cass. Civ. 1, 26 May 2011, No. 10-15676, *Recueil Dalloz* (*D.*) 2011, p. 1884 with obs. Dupont.

38 '… l'article L. 422-1 du code de la consommation selon lequel, étranger à la préservation de l'image et de la présomption d'innocence, prohibe notamment tout appel public par moyen de communication de masse ou par lettre personnalisée.'

39 CA Paris, 22 January 2010, No. 08-09844.

it is a *technique d'information de masse*. The association brought a *pourvoi en cassation* (cassation appeal) and argued that only a public call through TV or radio, not via the internet, were expressly prohibited by Article L. 422-1 Consumer Code. But the Court of Cassation took into account the fact that the association was in fact the real initiator of the proceedings.[40] The Court rejected the argument of the association and made an extensive interpretation of the provision that is not favourable to the associations. A liberal *a contrario* interpretation would have admitted public calls via the internet since this means of communication is not expressly prohibited in the relevant legal provision.

The representative joint action is 'overly bureaucratic and complex'[41] which explains why it is seldom used[42] (only five cases between 1992 and 2010).[43] Moreover, the French case law prevents the approved associations from using means of mass communication or personalised letters to obtain the necessary powers of attorney. The behaviour of the associations can even be criticised if they take the initiative to contact consumers in some effective way. This case law paralyzes the proper functioning of any joint representative action. Instead of softening the conditions of admissibility, the Court of Cassation has hardened them, which shows a reluctant approach towards group litigation.

### 2.1.3. A Joint Representative Action for Investors (Article L. 452-2, para 1 Monetary and Financial Code)

This joint representative action for investors has the same features as the joint representative action for consumers and is also based on an opt-in system. Where several investors have suffered personal harm having a common origin through an act or behaviour of the same person, an approved association of investors[44] can start proceedings on behalf of at least two investors who have given written power of attorney. For ten years now,[45] the claim can also be brought by a (not approved) association of shareholders; such an association may be created if the shares of the company can be negotiated on a regulated market, the shareholders have held the

40 It had put on its website a tool to calculate the amount of the financial damage to be claimed and suggested the consumers give the association power of attorney to take legal action. See Dupont 2011, p. 1884 *et seq.*

41 See Country report France, in *Evaluation of the effectiveness and efficiency of collective redress mechanisms in the European Union*, 2008.

42 See Guinchard, Chainais & Ferrand 2012, No. 282; Fievée & Grosjean 2010 ('impraticable du fait des nécessités matérielles et financières de gestion des mandats').

43 See *Rapport Sénat, L'action de groupe à la française: parachever la protection des consommateurs*, 26 May 2010.

44 See Art. L. 452-1, para 2 Monetary and Financial Code: to be approved, an association must have existed for at least six months, have at least 200 members paying individual contributions and its executives must fulfil conditions of competence and honour; the opinion of the public prosecutor and the registration of the statutes of the association with the *Autorité des marchés financiers* (French securities regulator) are also required. See also Le Bars 2004.

45 Law No. 2003-706 of 1 August 2003. See Magnier 2004.

shares for at least two years and own together at least 5 per cent of the voting rights in the same listed company. The aim of the association is to represent the interests of its members within the company.[46]

When one compares this with the other representative action in the field of consumer law, there is an important difference with regard to the publicity that can be given to the claim brought by the association: the presiding judge in the civil or commercial court may issue a summary order authorising the association to solicit a power of attorney from the investors by means that are prohibited in the other joint representative action: TV or radio, distribution of leaflets or personalised letters (Article L. 452-2, para 3 Monetary and Financial Code), which makes a huge difference and facilitates the circulation of information and therefore the action of the association.

Also in the field of labour law, special organisations (trade unions) which are representative on a national or local level or within the company concerned may bring a claim when an employee or a job applicant has been a victim of discrimination (Article L. 1134-2 Labour Code). The organisation only has to give written notice to the victim who can oppose within two weeks; it does not have to present to the court a written power of attorney. The victim may intervene in the proceedings started by the trade union.

## 2.2. *The Insufficiencies of the Existing Mechanisms*

The recurring and ongoing debates on group litigation in France prove a lack of real and effective justice in mass cases especially where consumers are involved. They are also related to the respective room for individual and collective concerns within French society, to the role of the State and of specific groups as associations.[47]

As shown before, the existing procedural tools do not function well. The legal requirements are excessive, the prohibition of publicity through means of mass communication hinders a large and effective use of the joint representative action aimed at seeking compensation for individual harm suffered by several persons on the grounds of the same events.

However, when the subject of group litigation is raised in France, three obstacles preventing the admission in France of group litigation are often mentioned,[48] the first two of them being constitutional guarantees:

1. The legal maxim *Nul ne plaide par procureur* – which means that one can represent a person in proceedings only if this person has given power of attorney and if his or her name appears expressly in the proceedings. This maxim is based on a strictly individualistic conception of civil proceedings in France and on the

46 See Art. L. 225-120 Commercial Code.

47 *Cf.* Jeuland 2012, No. 327, p. 318: 'Le débat sur l'action de groupe est donc la forme que prend le questionnement sur l'articulation entre l'individuel et le collectif.'

48 See Jeuland 2012, No. 327, p. 316. However, some authors argue that these principles should be adapted since better social justice is needed; see Caballero 1985, p. 247.

necessary transparency of proceedings:[49] unless the law provides otherwise, the capacity to sue (*capacité d'agir*) belongs to the person who has a personal interest in the action (*intérêt personnel à agir*). The French Constitutional Council (*Conseil constitutionnel)* held in 1989[50] that a trade union may only bring a suit on behalf of an employee if it has informed the employee who shall have agreed on the representation by the trade union. However, it is not certain that the Constitutional Council would render the same decision with regard to a collective action of consumers or of an approved consumer association on behalf of harmed consumers.[51] Also the very important procedural principle *de la contradiction* should not be infringed (right to be heard).

2. The prohibition of *arrêts de règlement* (court decisions stating a general rule applying to cases other than the concrete one being adjudicated. This prohibition is formulated by Article 5 French Civil Code[52] and prevents a judgment from being binding in further proceedings dealing with similar cases. This prohibition expresses the deep fear in France of a government by judges, and this fear goes back to the time of the *Ancien Régime* when the *parlements* - courts - had arrogated themselves large powers).
3. The relative effect of *res iudicata* (*effet relatif de la chose jugée*) requires that court decisions only have effect as to the parties (and their successors or privies) to the proceedings. This could - as well as the principle of individualisation of compensation - be an obstacle to collective litigation with opt-out regime. This is probably the weakest argument against group litigation since the legislator can decide in some specific and exceptional cases to extend the *res iudicata* effect to persons that were not parties to the proceedings.

In fact, one can have the impression that in France, the hostility of employers' associations, other groups or academics regarding group litigation is based on cultural traditions as well as on the fear of the American model sometimes seen as the only possible collective redress mechanism available.[53] What would not fit in the

49 See Guinchard 2005, p. 2183.

50 *Conseil constitutionnel*, 25 July 1989, DC 89-257, *Prévention des licenciements économiques, Droit social* 1989, p. 701 with obs. Prétot: trade unions can only initiate group litigation on behalf of their members if the employee has been given the opportunity to give his assent with full knowledge of the facts and remains free to conduct personally the defence of his interests. This formula used by the Constitutional Council has led many academics to the conclusion that an opt-out system would not be compatible with the French Constitution.

51 See also Guinchard 2005, p. 2182.

52 'Il est défendu aux juges de prononcer par voie de disposition générale et réglementaire sur les causes qui leur sont soumises.' This provision was enacted in 1803 and has not been subject to any amendments until now.

53 *Cf. Sénat, Rapport d'information No. 499,* by L. Béteille and R. Yung, 29 May 2010, p. 27 *et seq.* Three main reasons to oppose collective actions are reported: the fear that the competitiveness of French companies could be endangered, the fear about possible abuses as in the United States, and the preference of French professionals for mediation of small consumer disputes.

French culture and procedural tradition are the following American features: discovery, punitive damages, contingency fees and possibly also cross examination.[54]

In the United States, class actions have been generalised in the Federal Rules of Civil Procedure and in the state procedural laws, whereas in France, group litigation tends to be embedded in specific legal provisions, especially in the *Code de la consommation* (Consumer Code) or the *Code monétaire et financier* (Monetary and Financial Code). This is the way taken by a recent French bill *relatif à la consommation* (on consumer protection). However, it can be questioned whether this is the right choice or whether it would not be more appropriate to design group litigation as a general device that could apply in all cases of mass damages and that should be contained in the Code of Civil Procedure.[55] Also the new bill brought before Parliament in June 2013 has opted for this sector-based approach and introduces an *action de groupe* in the Consumer Code and not in the Code of Civil Procedure.

## 3. Where Do We Go? The New French Act (Loi no 2014-344 of 17 March 2014 *relative à la consommation*)

### 3.1. *The Recent Introduction of an Action de Groupe*

President Hollande has promised new regulations strengthening consumer protection and introducing group litigation in French law. This is why at the end of 2012 a large bill related to consumers was drafted by the government in order to increase consumer protection, especially (but not only) by creating a new collective redress mechanism (*action de groupe*). The study[56] carried out before drafting the bill on consumers (*projet de loi relatif à la consommation*) underlines the stake of international legal competitiveness (*enjeu de compétitivité juridique internationale*) connected with collective actions and states that 'it is preferable to build a French model of group litigation in order to avoid that national disputes be indirectly dealt with by foreign courts pursuant to rules that would not necessarily be compatible with the principles of the French legal system'.

First, the French Ministry of Justice declared that a special mechanism of collective redress should not be created for each legal field such as consumer law, environmental law, construction or health sectors, but that a procedure allowing individuals to act together as a group should be provided. It was planned to be a civil procedure that would apply to all kinds of harm (except personal injury), but this only where it concerned small claims cases and within the framework of an opt-in model.

54 *Cf.* Jeuland 2012, No. 327, p. 317.

55 Sharing this view, see Guinchard 2005, p. 2186.

56 *Projet de loi relatif à la consommation, Etude d'impact* 30 April 2013, available at: <www.assemblee-nationale.fr/14/projets/pl1015-ei.asp> (last accessed in June 2014).

Then, however, the government changed its mind. In the new *Projet de loi relatif à la consommation* 2013, an *action de groupe* was planned in order to allow compensation for harm suffered by consumers because of illegal practices of professionals, such as practices in restraint of trade or contractual infringements. The bill determines the scope of the proceedings, the conditions of admissibility (e.g. standing, constitution of the group, jurisdiction). The Act was eventually passed on 13 February 2014.[57]

The method chosen is to add a new Chapter to the Consumer Code and not to integrate group litigation into the Code of Civil Procedure.

*Terms. Source of Law* – The bill adopted by the *Assemblée nationale* creates a new Chapter III in Title II of Book IV Consumer Code. The heading of Chapter III is *Action de groupe*. The first section deals with the scope of action and standing.

*Commencement of action, locus standi, limitation, admissibility conditions* – Standing is given to approved consumer associations[58] which are 'representative' at a national level in order to claim compensation for individual damage suffered by consumers who are in a similar situation where the damages have the same origin and the same grounds (infringement by a professional of his legal or contractual obligations).[59] However, group litigation is only permitted where the damage occurred in the framework of a sale of goods, a provision of services or of restrictive trade practices (*pratiques anticoncurrentielles*). Only material harm (patrimonial or financial damage)[60] can be compensated. A decree shall give details on the institution of group action proceedings (Article L. 423-2 Consumer Code).

The taking of collective action before a court suspends the limitation period related to individual actions for compensation of the damage resulting from the professional's infringements assessed in the court decision (Article L. 423-20 Consumer Code). The limitation period starts to run again for at least six months from the date on which the judgment became final (*irrevocable*).

*Parties* – The genuine nature of the new *action de groupe* is not very clear. Some argue that it is a representative action[61] since the consumer who opts in is deemed to give power of attorney to the association in order to obtain compensation. Other scholars wonder whether it is a kind of 'joint representation action', a substitutional collective action (*action collective de substitution*)[62] or collective redress in the

57 Loi No. 2014-344 of 17 March 2014 *relative à la consommation, JORF* No. 0065 of 18 March 2014, p. 5400. See Miniato 2014, p. 65 *et seq.*

58 This has been criticised since the associations can choose the cases they want to bring to court. Moreover, they do not always have legal competences and their financial means are very limited, see Rebeyrol 2014, p. 943.

59 Art. L. 423-1 Consumer Code ('réparation des préjudices individuels subis par des consommateurs placés dans une situation similaire ou identique et ayant pour cause commune un manquement d'un ou des mêmes professionnels à leurs obligations légales ou contractuelles').

60 *Ibidem*, last para: 'préjudices patrimoniaux résultant des dommages matériels subis par les consommateurs'.

61 Azar-Baud 2013a, p. 1488.

62 On the *action de substitution*, see Jeuland 2010, p. 749 *et seq.*

individual interest of consumers;[63] the nature of the action is of high relevance for many issues such as jurisdiction, admissibility, admissibility of appeal, *res iudicata* and costs. For E. Jeuland, it is not a representative action even if a consumer gives power of attorney to the claiming association to receive the compensation that will be shared among the harmed consumers. If the association were only the consumers' proxy, it would not be bound by *res iudicata* of the judgment on liability and could start new proceedings for additional consumers, which does not seem to be the case in the bill. The association would also need to obtain the permission of all represented consumers to bring an appeal or to agree to a settlement. Therefore, E. Jeuland rightly suggests analysing the *action de groupe* as an *action de substitution*: the association holds an action consisting of exercising the individual actions of the (not yet known) substituted consumers; it does not have to request their consent but shall inform them so that they can refuse and take their own individual legal action. When at a second stage of the proceedings consumers opt in, this gives power of attorney to the association to receive and then distribute the financial compensation that will be paid by the professional,[64] which transforms the substitutional action into a representative one. This explains that the *res iudicata* effect of the judgment on liability then extends to consumers that opt in.

*Opt-in model* – The new statute has chosen an opt-in model (Article L. 423-5 Consumer Code). The joining of the group by a consumer gives a power of attorney to the claiming association to receive compensation on behalf of the consumer. It is not required of the consumer to be a member of the association. In its decision on the professional's liability, the civil court sets the time-limits (from 2 to 6 months from the accomplishment of the publicity measures) and the methods to be followed by the consumers in order to opt in (*adhérer au groupe*).[65]

*Jurisdiction, Role of the Court, Evidence* – Jurisdiction is given to the civil courts (*tribunaux de grande instance*), Article L. 211-15 Judicial Code.

63 Hesitating and stressing the unclear nature and regime of the future collective action, see Jeuland 2013, p. 1609.

64 Jeuland 2013, p. 1610: 'L'action en substitution se mue en action en représentation à partir de l'adhésion du consommateur, ce qui explique que le jugement ait autorité de chose jugée à son égard.' Jeuland stresses that the notion of *action de substitution* could also allow an approved consumer association to take collective legal action together with other associations. If it were a representative action and if two different proceedings were brought before different courts that both had jurisdiction, it could be very difficult to solve the jurisdiction issue; whereas in the case of an *action de substitution*, if two different collective actions were brought, it would not be a question of jurisdiction but only of *lis pendens* or related action for which the solutions are easier to provide.

65 Art. L. 423-5 Consumer Code. The court shall determine whether the consumers shall contact directly the professional, or the association or a third person (most likely a lawyer) if the assistance of a third person has been authorised by the judge; see Art. L. 423-9 Consumer Code: 'L'association peut s'adjoindre, avec l'autorisation du juge, toute personne appartenant à une profession judiciaire réglementée dont la liste est fixée par décret en Conseil d'État, pour l'assister, notamment afin qu'elle procède à la réception des demandes d'indemnisation des membres du groupe et plus généralement afin qu'elle représente les consommateurs lésés, auprès du professionnel, en vue de leur indemnisation.'

The second section of Chapter III is dedicated to the *judgment on liability* (*jugement sur la responsabilité*, Article L. 423-3 Consumer Code). The court examines whether the conditions for admissibility of the claim are fulfilled; if this is the case, it rules on the professional's liability and defines the consumers' group towards which the professional is liable and sets the connecting factors (*critères de rattachement*). The court then determines the damage suffered by each consumer or each category of consumers building the group or at least sets the elements to be considered when evaluating the damages to be paid. In this respect, the court may at any stage of the proceedings order any legally admissible investigative measure aimed at the preservation or presentation of evidence, including evidence in the professional's possession (para 2). There is no other specific provision on evidence that would only apply for collective actions. Therefore, general rules on evidence should apply, which means that the claimant has to prove the facts leading to the professional's liability. To some authors, it is not yet clear whether the claiming association will be allowed to request from the professional that he shall produce evidence in his possession relating to the fault on the basis of which he is being sued for damages.[66] I think that the general rules contained in the French Code of Civil Procedure (CPC) allow that under the supervision of the judge: the claiming association could request an order from the judge imposing on the defendant (the professional) that he produce some pieces of evidence (Article 11, para 2 French CPC).[67] The judge could also act on his own motion since Article 10 CPC gives the judge the power to order *sua sponte* any kind of instruction measure legally admissible.[68]

The new law does not contain a preliminary stage during which the admissibility of the claim could be examined as under American law.[69] The court rules on the admissibility of the claim in the judgment on liability. The 'one-man band' (*homme orchestre*)[70] of the proceedings is the judge since he decides on the professional's liability, determines the consumers' group concerned with the action, states how their damage shall be compensated and determines the adequate publicity measures to be undertaken in order to inform the consumers and to allow them to opt in if they wish to do so. The statute does not state how the judge will appraise the common causality between the damage suffered by each consumer and the professional's infringement of his contractual or legal duties nor how he will

66 See Grandjean 2013, p. 1777.

67 Art. 11, para 2 CPC: If a party has in his/her possession a piece of evidence, the judge may at the request of the other party enjoin him/her to produce it (possibly under penalty called *astreinte*). The judge may even (at the request of a party) enjoin a third party to produce documents in his/her possession barring legitimate impediment.

68 Art. 10 French CPC: 'Le juge a le pouvoir d'ordonner d'office toutes mesures d'instruction légalement admissibles.' Pursuant to Art. 11 CPC, the parties shall give their support to the instruction measures; if they do not do so, the judge may impose adverse consequences.

69 Some scholars criticize the absence of such a preliminary stage, see Molfessis 2014, p. 949.

70 See Grandjean 2013, p. 1777.

determine the individual compensation to be paid by the professional. It is likely that the judge will seek expert testimony in this respect.

The judge shall order, at the professional's expense, adequate measures to inform in all appropriate ways the consumers likely to belong to the group with regard to which the court decision on liability has been given (Article L. 423-4). However, these publicity measures can only take place when the judgment on the professional's liability is not subject any longer to any ordinary means of recourse or to a *pourvoi en cassation*.[71] In the judgment, the court sets the time-limits (from 2 to 6 months from the accomplishment of the publicity measures) and the methods to be followed by the consumers in order to opt in.

If the consumer association that brought the lawsuit is *défaillante* (which probably means that it did not fulfil its procedural duties in due time or refrained from taking an active part in the proceedings), another consumer association which fulfils the procedural requirements may request from the court to replace the inactive one for the conduct of the collective action (Article L. 423-24 Consumer Code).

When the court holds that the professional is liable, it can impose on the defendant interim payment (*provision*) of the costs that are not strictly necessary to the pursuit of the proceedings (called *frais irrépétibles*) and that encompass especially the lawyers' fees. It can also order the deposit by the professional of part of the amounts due.

*Costs and legal aid* – The issue of costs and legal aid does not give rise to any more precise and specific legal provision. However, as mentioned above, French law prohibits contingency fees as well as *quota litis* agreements; yet, since 1991, complementary fees are allowed that will depend on the outcome of the judicial proceedings but shall remain reasonable.

No specific funding of group litigation is provided by the new statute. This issue could, however, be dealt with in a decree drafted by the government that will probably be enacted in autumn 2014.

*Appeal, legal remedy* – Means of recourse are not expressly regulated, which probably means that the general rules apply with regard to the admissibility of appeal (*appel*) and further appeal (*pourvoi en cassation*). Since standing is given only to approved consumer associations, it is likely that only the claiming association may bring an appeal, not the consumers themselves.

*Res iudicata* – The judgment on liability as well as the judgment which, in the simplified procedure, rules on the professional's liability and on the damages to be paid to the consumers do have *res iudicata* effect as to each of the group members whose damage has been compensated at the end of the proceedings (Article L. 423-21 Consumer Code).

The fact that a consumer has opted in to the collective action does not prevent him from bringing an individual lawsuit in order to obtain compensation for damage that did not belong to the scope of action (losses to be compensated)

[71] Art. L. 423-4, para 2 Consumer Code.

defined by the court in its judgment on the professional's liability or in the settlement approved by the court (Article L. 423-22 Consumer Code).

Article L. 423-25 *Code de la consommation* states that any clause aimed at prohibiting a consumer from taking part in a collective action shall be void.[72]

*Enforcement* - Sec. 4 of the new statute deals with *compensation* and *enforcement* (*liquidation des préjudices et exécution*). The professional shall compensate individually each consumer under the conditions, limits and time-limits stated in the court decision (Article L. 423-11 Consumer Code). The court that ruled on the liability also has jurisdiction with regard to the difficulties arising in the phase of liquidation of damages (Article L. 423-6). It shall decide in one single judgment on all compensation claims that the professional did not admit.

The claiming association also represents the consumers that have not been compensated in due time by the professional and will take steps in order to enforce the judgment (seizure).[73]

*Specific features* - Sec. 3 of the new statute creates a *simplified procedure* that was not proposed in the bill presented by the government.[74] The purpose of this procedure (for which the detailed rules will be clarified by a governmental decree) is to facilitate and to speed up the payment of the compensation where the consumers are already identified.[75] In that case, after ruling on the professional's liability, the court may order the defendant to directly and individually pay compensation to the consumers harmed within the time-limits set by judicial order.[76]

Sec. 5 envisages *mediation* as a possible tool in the framework of group actions. The claiming association (not the individual consumers) can take part in mediation in order to obtain individual compensation for the damages covered by the proceedings of *action de groupe*. In respect of a possible (voluntary, not compulsory) mediation, the general rules stated in Law No. 95-125 of 8 February 1995 (as amended by implementation of EU Directive No. 2058/52 of 21 May 2008)[77] apply. Where a settlement is negotiated on behalf of the consumers' group,[78] it is subject to the approval of the court (*homologation*) that makes it enforceable if the settlement is

72 'Est réputée non écrite toute clause ayant pour objet ou effet d'interdire à un consommateur de participer à une action de groupe.'

73 See Art. L. 423-13 Consumer Code.

74 Art. L. 423-10 Consumer Code.

75 *Ibidem*: 'Lorsque l'identité et le nombre des consommateurs lésés sont connus et lorsque ces consommateurs ont subi un préjudice d'un même montant, d'un montant identique par prestation rendue ou d'un montant identique par référence à une période ou à une durée.'

76 *Ibidem*, para 2: before the professional enforces the court judgment, and when it is not anymore subject to any means of recourse, the decision shall be notified individually to each consumer concerned (at the professional's costs) in order to give them opportunity to accept the compensation in the terms stated by the court decision.

77 See Ordonnance No. 2011-540 of 16 November 2011 and Décret No. 2012-66 of 20 January 2012.

78 But since the members of the group are not yet known when the settlement is agreed upon, how can the amount of damages be determined? See Rebeyrol 2014, p. 946.

in accordance with the interests of those to whom it may apply (*conforme aux intérêts de ceux auxquels il a vocation à s'appliquer*), Article L. 423-16 Consumer Code. The settlement (*accord*) shall mention the modes to be followed by the consumers to opt in to the settlement and the time-limits in this respect. The court may impose on the professional the publicity measures necessary in order to inform the consumers about the existence of the judicially approved settlement.

French companies are very eager for mediation in the framework of collective redress, probably in order to negotiate the amount of compensation to be paid and to avoid negative publicity. Some even require mediation be compulsory with regard to the determination of damages to be paid.[79] In fact, mediation should only be an option and it would be desirable that the consumers who do not wish to take part in mediation could take individual action before a court. This is not expressly stated by the new statute, it should, however, apply since if the consumers are not obliged to opt in to the court decision, they should also not be bound by a mediation settlement that they did not approve.

In recent years, mediation has gained an increased role in consumer protection. Law No. 2010/737 of 1 July 2010 created a *Commission de la médiation de la consommation* (Commission on Consumer Mediation). The CMAP (Centre de Médiation et d'Arbitrage de Paris)[80] created in 1995 by the Chamber of Commerce and Industry of Paris, instituted a few years ago a collective mediation procedure for consumer disputes aimed to favour the resolution of disputes between companies and approved national consumer associations. This initiative started with a case regarding variable-rate loan contracts between a bank (Crédit foncier) and several clients who alleged to be victims of misleading trade practices. The bank requested the CMAP provide mediation; the consumer association UFC-Que choisir and two other associations took part in the mediation procedure that ended with a collective settlement agreement in November 2009. All possibly concerned clients of the bank received notice of the settlement agreement by letter and could then individually request to benefit from it.[81]

Sec. 5 of Chapter III deals with specific features of the *action de groupe* in the field of competition law (*Modalités spécifiques à l'action de groupe intervenant dans le domaine de la concurrence*).[82] Where the professional's infringements are related to the rules contained in Title 2 of the fourth book of the French Commercial Code or to Articles 101 and 102 of the Treaty on the Functioning of the European Union (rules on competition), a collective claim (*action de groupe*) can only be brought before the court on the basis of a decision asserting the infringements which is not subject to any means of recourse anymore and which has been given by competent authorities

79 See Fievée & Grosjean 2010, No. 10.

80 See the website of the CMAP <www.cmap.fr/> (last accessed in June 2014).

81 See Ascensi & Bernheim-Desvaux 2012.

82 *Cf.* Proposal for a directive of the European Parliament and of the Council on certain rules governing actions for damages under national law for infringements of the competition law provisions of the Member States and of the European Union, COM(2013) 404 final, 11 June 2013.

or courts of France or of the European Union (so-called collective follow-up action).[83] In such a case, the professional's infringements are deemed to be proved irrefutably with regard to the collective redress proceedings (Article L. 423-17 Consumer Code).[84] The collective action shall be brought before a court within five years from the date on which the decision of the national or European competent authority became irrevocable (which means when no ordinary or extraordinary means of recourse were available anymore). These specific features in the field of competition are welcome since civil courts do not have effective investigation means with respect to economic expertise and causality issues.[85]

Article 2 of the new statute shows that neither the French government nor Parliament is very confident that the collective action designed will function well and be a success. Therefore, as Germany did with the law instituting a capital market model claim (*Kapitalanlegermusterverfahren*), 30 months after promulgation of the new law, the government shall present a report to Parliament. The report shall evaluate the implementation of the collective action procedure, suggest possible necessary adaptations and contemplate possible evolutions with regard to the substantial scope of group litigation (especially, according to the Senate, its extension to the fields of health and environment).

The new law will only come into force when the necessary governmental decree is promulgated, which will probably happen in autumn 2014.

### 3.2. *Much Criticism with Regard to the Cautious Regulation of Group Litigation*

Some have argued that the bill drafted by the government in 2013 instituting an *action de groupe* is restricted and has become less ambitious due to concessions made

83 See Commission Recommendation of 11 June 2013 on common principles for injunctive and compensatory collective redress mechanisms in the Member States concerning violation of rights granted under European Union Law (1013/396/EU), *OJ* 27 July 2013, L 201/60, Art. 3.

84 At present, when a claim is brought before a civil court after seizure of the Competition Authority (*Autorité de la concurrence*), the civil court is not bound by the decision of the Competition Authority (Cass. com., 17 July 2001, no 99-17251) so that it could theoretically deny the existence of a civil fault. However, French civil courts seldom refuse to follow the decision of the Competition Authority; see e.g. T. com. Pars, 26 April 2013, RG No. 2012002045 quoted by De Lanzac & Hochart 2013, p. 976.

85 See Roskis & Jaffar 2013, No. 25, p. 29 *et seq*. See also Vogel 2013, especially Nos. 13 *et seq*. Evidence difficulties especially arise with regard to the quantification of damage so that expert testimony is often necessary, which takes time and discourages the victims from taking legal action; see De Lanzac & Hochart 2013, p. 976. Where the victims did not take part in the procedure before the Competition Authority (*Autorité de la concurrence)* and thus do not have evidence as to the infringement they allege, the court may request from the Competition Authority the communication of documents (Law of 20 November 2012, Art. L. 462-3 Commercial Code). For critical remarks regarding the French provisions on group litigation in the field of competition law, see Molfessis 2014, p. 952 *et seq.* who argues that 1° the civil proceedings will be delayed and 2° the civil court will be deprived from any discretion.

towards employers' associations.[86] Only the financial damage suffered by consumers because of illegal practices of a professional is envisaged. Other mass losses or injuries are not covered (airplane crash, health injuries, environmental cases). Neither physical nor moral or emotional harm can be subject to the future collective action.

The 'monopoly' given to approved national consumer associations (there are currently 17 of them in France)[87] to take a collective action is strongly criticised by some legal professionals, especially by lawyers.[88] Some also argue that the new collective action should not only aim to compensate individual damage suffered by many consumers but that it should also and even primarily be a sanction of professionals' illegal behaviour.[89]

With regard to the opt-in system provided by the new statute, some scholars[90] express their doubts with regard to the distinction between opt in and opt out. According to them, opt out leads to abuse whereas opt in is a complicated and expensive choice. One should therefore follow the Model Code for collective redress of the Instituto Ibero-americano de Derecho Procesal that suggests an original solution: *res iudicata secundum eventum litis* (*système de la chose jugée selon le résultat du litige*), which means that only the effects of the court decision that admit the claim should extend to the other members of the group, which is an exception to the rule *res inter alios iudicata nec nodest nec prodest* (an action adjudged between certain parties does not harm or benefit other parties). The Model Code (*código modelo de procesos colectivos para iberoamerica*) also suggests a *res iudicata secundum eventum probationem* in order to make admissible a new collective action where the first one was rejected because of absence of evidence.[91] Other scholars[92] approve the choice of an opt-in model with publicity, which is an advancement compared with the former *action en représentation conjointe* (joint representative action) for consumer associations that were not allowed to solicit powers of attorney via TV, radio or the internet nor by distributing leaflets or personalised letters, but only in newspapers and magazines.

Another difficulty is the financial aspect of the future collective action: approved consumer associations do not have plentiful financial resources, yet only they are entitled to bring a collective action before the court. Moreover, in France insurance companies often refuse to insure an approved consumer association for

86 Azar-Baud 2013, p. 1487 *et seq.*

87 See Roskis & Jaffar 2013, No. 25, p. 28.

88 *Ibidem*. The CNB (*Conseil National des Barreaux*) advocated the possibility for lawyers to bring collective actions; see *Résolution du CNB sur l'introduction de l'action de groupe en droit français*, General Assembly, 6 and 7 July 2012, suggesting that the group could be built by several consumers who should be entitled to bring a collective action before the civil court.

89 See Mainguy & Depince 2013.

90 See e.g. Azar-Baud 2012, p. 2160.

91 See Azar-Baud 2013b.

92 See e.g. Sauphanor-Brouillaud 2013, p. 1317.

joint representative litigation.[93] It will probably be the same for the new *action de groupe*.[94]

Other criticised points are, for example, the complexity of the judgment on liability, the issues of *lis pendens* and related actions when a collective action and an individual one are concurring.[95] Some scholars[96] even suspect that the future collective action (*action de groupe*) will be 'stillborn' (*mort-née*).

### 3.3. *Comparison with the Content of European Recommendation 2013*

The European Commission has expressed its concern towards collective redress in several documents such as Green Papers,[97] a White Paper[98] and the results of a Public Consultation.[99] On 11 June 2013, it published a Recommendation on common principles for injunctive and compensatory collective redress mechanisms in the Member States concerning violation of rights granted under Union Law[100] The Recommendation – which is not a binding instrument – contains a set of principles that should apply in many fields such as consumer protection, competition, protection of the environment, protection of personal data, financial service legislation and investor protection.[101] On this first issue, the French approach is diverging since the new statute only aims at consumer protection in the framework of sale of goods, provision of services or of restrictive trade practices (competition). The French scope of group litigation is therefore much narrower than contemplated and suggested by the European Recommendation. Also with regard to the persons who can claim compensation collectively, the French bill is more restrictive than the European Recommendation: only an approved consumer association may bring the action, and it may only claim compensation for the harm suffered by *natural* persons whereas the Recommendation admits for compensatory collective redress (as well as for injunctive collective redress), that the claim for compensation can be brought 'collectively by two or more natural *or legal* persons claiming to have been harmed in a mass harm situation or by an entity entitled to bring a representative action' (Article 3a).

93 Boré 2013, p. 29.
94 Sauphanor-Brouillaud 2013, p. 1317.
95 *Ibidem.*
96 See Jeuland 2013, p. 1609.
97 Green Paper on antitrust actions for damages in 2005, COM(2005) 672; Green Paper on consumer collective redress COM(2008) 794.
98 COM(2008) 165.
99 COM(2010) 135 final. Also the European Parliament dealt with this subject and adopted a resolution called *Towards a Coherent European Approach to Collective Redress* 2011/2089(INI) which supports a horizontal approach.
100 *OJ* 27 July 2013, L201/60. See Decocq 2013.
101 See recital 7. The principles should also apply in other areas where collective claims for injunctions or damages in respect of violations of the rights granted by EU law would be relevant.

The Recommendation (Article 2) addresses both compensatory and injunctive collective redress whereas the French bill only deals with compensatory claims, since injunctive collective redress is already available under French law (Article L. 421-6 Consumer Code, *action en cessation d'agissements illicites*).

The Recommendation stresses the necessity to preserve procedural safeguards and guarantees of parties to civil actions[102] and to avoid abusive litigation. Therefore, it suggests avoiding punitive damages,[103] intrusive pre-trial discovery procedures,[104] contingency fees[105] and jury awards.[106] The French law and the new bill are in accordance with this recommendation as well as with the constitution of the claimant party by the 'opt-in' principle stated in Article 21 of the European Recommendation.[107]

The conditions for standing to bring a representative action stated in Article 4 of the European Recommendation are met by the French law (non-profit making character of the entity; direct relationship between the objectives of the entity and the rights that are claimed to be violated). Only sufficient capacity in terms of financial and human resources to represent multiple claimants is not expressly required by the French statute. With regard to funding (Articles 14 *et seq.* of the Recommendation), the new French statute does not contain specific provisions.

With regard to the admissibility of the claim, the French court shall carry out the examination on its own motion (Article L. 423-3 Consumer Code), which is advocated by the European Recommendation (Article 9).

Also the recommendations relating to the dissemination of information on a collective redress action (Articles 10 and 11 of the European Recommendation) are in accordance with the provisions of the French bill.

The European Commission and the French government both encourage the parties to a dispute in a mass harm situation to settle regarding compensation especially by means of ADR, both at the initial stages and during litigation (see Article 25 of the Recommendation). French general rules on time-limits[108] already state the suspension of any limitation period during an attempt to reach an amicable settlement through mediation or any other ADR mechanism.[109] The binding outcome of the collective settlement shall be verified by the court that shall 'take into consideration the appropriate protection of interests and rights of all parties

102 Recital 15.
103 Art. 31 of the Recommendation.
104 Recital 15 of the Recommendation.
105 Arts. 29 and 30 of the Recommendation.
106 Recital 15 of the Recommendation.
107 The French bill does not mention whether a member of the claimant party is free to leave the claimant party at any time before the final judgment is given or the case is otherwise validly settled (Art. 22 of the European Recommendation) nor whether persons claiming to have been harmed in the same mass harm situation may join the claimant party at any time before judgment is given (Art. 23 of the European Recommendation). However, if the general principles of civil procedure apply, this should be possible.
108 See Art. 2238 French Civil Code.
109 See Art. 27 of the European Recommendation.

involved' (Article 28 of the Recommendation) or, in the French statute, scrutinise 'whether the settlement is in accordance with the interests of those to whom it may apply'. This shows common concern that mediation should not lead to an unjust outcome.

The French bill does not create a national register of collective redress actions although this is recommended by the European Commission. The national registry should be available free of charge to any interested person through electronic means and otherwise (Articles 35 and 36 of the European Recommendation).

## 4. Conclusion

The new French law aims to make effective the consumers' right to compensation and to organising the coexistence between public and private enforcement.[110] However, private enforcement should not be limited to group litigation and to consumers. Therefore, in the near future France will probably need further reforms of its civil procedure.

Moreover, it can be questioned whether group litigation is the only way to strengthen consumers' protection. The French Law of February 2014 also decided to enhance the role of a public institution called *Direction générale de la concurrence, de la consommation et de la répression des fraudes* (DGCCRF, General Directorate of competition, consumer matters and the sanction of fraud). Every year, this body receives about 100,000 complaints but is not empowered to impose serious sanctions. The new law (Article 76) enlarges the scope of competence of the agents of the General Directorate (public enforcement). Also the DGCCRF itself will have broader power and will be able to impose severe administrative sanctions on professionals who do not follow its injunctions. The General Directorate will have the power too, in the field of electronic commerce, to seize the court in order to request any appropriate measure to prevent harm or to stop harm caused by the contents of a communication service online. Many new provisions aim to enhance the powers of the DGCCRF in the field of economic protection, consumers' safety and the application of competition law.[111]

Has France taken a 'giant step'[112] or only cautiously moved forward towards more effective remedies for consumers? The second assertion of a cautious first step in the right direction is probably correct[113] and one can assume that the topic of collective actions will in the future again give rise to intense debate in France.

110 See Decocq 2013.
111 See Roskis & Jaffar 2013, No. 25, p. 27; Aubry 2014, p. 11.
112 See Grandjean 2013, p. 1777 *et seq.*
113 See Boré 2013, p. 29: 'un premier pas, certes insuffisant, mais qui va dans la bonne direction'.

## Bibliography

**Ascensi & Bernheim-Desvaux 2012**
Ascensi, L. & Bernheim-Desvaux, S., 'La médiation collective, solution amiable pour résoudre les litiges de masse?', *Contrats Concurrence Consommation (CCC)*, 2012, No. 8, étude 9.

**Aubry 2014**
Aubry, H., 'La loi du 17 mars 2014 relative à la consommation: de réels apports pour la protection des consommateurs', *Revue Lamy de Droit civil (RLDC)*, 2014, No. 5404, p. 8-13.

**Azar-Baud 2012**
Azar-Baud, M.-J., 'Quel avenir pour les *class actions* en France?', *Recueil Dalloz (D.)*, 2012, p. 2160.

**Azar-Baud 2013a**
Azar-Baud, M.-J., 'L'entrée triomphale (?) de l'action de groupe en droit français', *Recueil Dalloz (D.)*, 2013, p. 1487-1488.

**Azar-Baud 2013b**
Azar-Baud, M.-J., *Les actions collectives en droit de la consommation, Etude de droit français et argentin à la lumière du droit comparé*, Paris: Dalloz, 2013.

**Boré 2013**
Boré, L., 'Le projet d'action de groupe: action mort-née ou premier pas', *Gazette du Palais (Gaz. Pal.)*, 16 May 2013, No. 136, p. 29-30.

**Caballero 1985**
Caballero, F., 'Plaidons par procureur! De l'archaïsme procédural à l'action de groupe', *Revue trimestrielle de droit civil (RTDCiv.)*, 1985, p. 247-276.

**Caponi 2011**
Caponi, R., 'Collective Redress in Europe: Current Developments of "class actions" suits in Italy', *Zeitschrift für Zivilprozess International (ZZPInt.)*, 2011, Vol. 16, p. 61-77.

**Decocq 2013**
Decocq, G., 'Le développement du *Private enforcement?*', *Contrats Concurrence Consommation (CCC)*, 2013, No. 8, repère 8.

**Deffains 2008**
Deffains, B., 'Les effets bénéfiques des actions de groupe: une approche économique', *Concurrences*, 2008, No. 2, p. 34-38.

**de Lanzac & Hochart 2013**
de Lanzac, P. & Hochart, J., 'L'action en réparation du dommage résultant d'infractions au droit de la concurrence', *Jurisclasseur Périodique édition Générale (JCP G)*, 2013, No. 976, p. 1718-1719.

**de Silguy 2012**
de Silguy, S., 'Faut-il craindre les actions collectives?', *Revue Lamy de Droit Civil (RLDC)*, 2012, No. 4914, p. 55-58.

**Dupont 2011**
Dupont, N., 'L'action en représentation conjointe des associations de consommateurs ou l'action mal aimée des juges', *Recueil Dalloz (D.)*, 2011, p. 1884-1887.

**Fievée & Grosjean 2010**
Fievée, A. & Grosjean, J., 'L'action de groupe ... ou l'introduction d'une nouvelle voie de droit - Réflexions sur les travaux en cours', *Contrats Concurrence Consommation (CCC)*, 2010, No. 12, étude 14.

**Gabais *et al.* 2012**
Gabais, X., Landier, A., Thesmar, D., Mongin, P. & Tirole, J., *La protection du consommateur: rationalité limitée et régulation*, Paris: Documentation française, 2012.

**Grandjean 2013**
Grandjean, J.-P., 'Action de groupe: petit pas ou pas de géant?', *Jurisclasseur Périodique édition Générale (JCP G)*, 2013, No. 1007, p. 1777-1778.

**Guinchard 2005**
Guinchard, S., 'Une class action à la française?', *Recueil Dalloz (D.)*, 2005, p. 2180-2184.

**Guinchard, Chainais & Ferrand 2012**
Guinchard, S., Chainais, C. & Ferrand, F., *Procédure civile, Droit interne et droit de l'Union européenne*, 31st edn., Paris: Dalloz, 2012.

**Héron & Le Bars 2012**
Héron, J. & Le Bars, T., *Droit judiciaire privé*, 5th edn., Paris: Montchrestien, 2012.

**Hodges 2008**
Hodges, C., *The Reform of Class and Representative Actions in European Legal Systems, A New Framework for Collective Redress in Europe*, Studies of the Oxford Institute of European and Comparative Law, Oxford: Hart Publishing, 2008.

**Jeuland 2010**
Jeuland, E., 'Quelques questions sur l'action de substitution «à la française»', in *Justices et droit du procès, Mélanges en l'honneur de S. Guinchard*, Paris: Dalloz, 2010, p. 749-758.

**Jeuland 2012**
Jeuland, E., *Droit processuel général*, 2nd edn., Paris: Montchrestien, 2012.

**Jeuland 2013**
Jeuland, E., 'Substitution ou représentation? A propos du projet d'action de groupe', *Jurisclasseur Périodique édition Générale (JCP G)*, 2013, No. 927, p. 1609-1610.

**Le Bars 2004**
Le Bars, B., *Les actions de défense d'actionnaires et d'investisseurs*, Paris: LGDJ, 2004.

**Magnier 2004**
Magnier, V. (ed.), *L'opportunité d'une action de groupe en droit des sociétés*, Paris: PUF, 2004.

**Mainguy & Depince 2013**
Mainguy, D. & Depince, M., 'Pour l'action de groupe en droit français', *Jurisclasseur périodique Entreprises (JCP E)*, 2013, Act. No. 355.

**Miniato 2014**
Miniato, L., 'L'action de groupe à la française est née', *Revue Lamy de Droit civil (RLDC)*, 2014, No. 5445, p. 65-67.

**Molfessis 2014**
Molfessis, N., 'L'exorbitance de l'action de groupe à la française', *Recueil Dallot (D.)*, 2014, p. 947-953.

**Murray 2009**
Murray, P., 'Class Actions in a Global Economy', in Stürner, R. & Kawano, M. (eds.), *Current Topics of International Litigation*, Tübingen: Mohr Siebeck, 2009, p. 95-106.

**Notte 2013**
Notte, C., 'Projet de loi relatif à la consommation', *Jurisclasseur Périodique édition Générale (JCP G)*, 2013, No. 664, p. 970-973.

**Paisant 2013**
Paisant, G., 'A propos des vingt ans du Code de la consommation', *Jurisclasseur Périodique édition Générale (JCP G)*, 2013, No. 621, p. 1061-1068.

**Prieto 2011**
Prieto, C., *Cohérence européenne des recours collectifs, Réponse à la consultation publique de la Commission européenne*, Paris: Société de législation comparée, Coll. TEE, Vol. 2, 2011.

**Rebeyrol 2014**
Rebeyrol, V., 'La nouvelle action de groupe', *Recueil Dalloz (D.)*, 2014, p. 940-946.

**Roskis & Jaffar 2013**
Roskis, D. & Jaffar, S., 'L'introduction de l'action de groupe à la française, «Une justice plus proche des citoyens?»', *Cahiers droit de l'entreprise* July-August 2013, No. 25, p. 23 *et seq*.

**Sauphanor-Brouillaud 2013**
Sauphanor-Brouillaud, N., 'Une refonte du Code de la consommation s'impose', *JCP G* 2013, No. 757, p. 1317.

**Simon 2008**
Simon, J., 'L'action de groupe, panacée ou cheval de Troie', *Concurrences,* 2008, No. 2, p. 25-29.

**Stadler 2013**
Stadler, A., 'Collective Redress Litigation – A New Challenge for Courts in Europe', in *Festschrift R. Stürner zum 70. Geburstag*, Tübingen: Mohr Siebeck, 2013, p. 1801-1816.

**Stürner 2009**
Stürner, R., 'International Class Actions From a German Point of View', in Stürner, R. & Kawano, M., *Current Topics of International Litigation,* Tübingen: Mohr Siebeck, 2009, p. 107-117.

**Vogel 2013**
Vogel, J., 'Stratégies et moyens de défense face à une action en dommages-intérêts pour atteinte au droit de la concurrence', *Jurisclasseur périodique Entreprise,* 2013, No. 12, p. 1172-1174.

M. Bakowitz

# THE GERMAN EXPERIENCE WITH GROUP ACTIONS - THE *VERBANDSKLAGE* AND THE CAPITAL MARKETS MODEL CASE ACT (KAPMUG)

When it comes to mass litigation in Germany, a lot has changed in recent years. The Capital Markets Model Case Act has entered the stage and caused a stir that has not faded away yet. In comparison, the *Verbandsklage* functions without attracting much attention, which does not lessen its significance, especially for consumer protection. This article will give an overview of the *Verbandsklage*, before examining the Capital Markets Model Case Act in more detail.

## 1. The *Verbandsklage*

### 1.1. *Prohibitory Injunctions Act (UKlaG)*

The *Verbandsklage* is an action brought by a *Verband* (an association) on behalf of a group of victims. The *Verbandsklage* has its roots in the 1976 *AGB-Gesetz* (Act on Standard Contract Terms). At first, the suing association could obtain prohibitory injunctions only against undertakings that used contracts with unlawful standard terms. Since 2000, the Act has also covered infringements of consumer protection provisions by undertakings. In the course of the *Schuldrechtsmodernisierung* (the modernisation of the law of obligations) in 2001 the *Verbandsklage* was incorporated in the new *Unterlassungsklagengesetz* (UKlaG, Prohibitory Injunctions Act) and replaced the AGB-Gesetz. Actions against the use of unlawful standard terms in contracts are now covered by Sec. 1 UKlaG, actions against infringements of consumer protection provisions by Sec. 2 UKlaG.[1]

In accordance with Sec. 3, para 1 UKlaG, three types of associations have legal standing to bring an action: qualified institutions listed on special indices by either the *Bundesamt für Justiz* (the Federal Office of Justice) or the European Union; a

1 Micklitz 2013, Vorbemerkung zu den §§ 1 *et seq.* UKlaG, No. 8 *et seq.* for the historical development.

limited number of non-listed associations that have to fulfil stringent criteria; and the *Industrie- und Handelskammern* as well as the *Handwerkskammern* (chambers of industry and commerce, chambers of crafts).

Publicly funded consumer associations can be listed on the index of qualified institutions if they meet the requirements of Sec. 4, para 2 UKlaG (for instance, they must have a certain number of members and act on a non-profit basis). There is a non-rebuttable presumption that the *Verbraucherzentralen* (the organisations for the protection of consumers' rights) fulfil all requirements and are thus qualified, Sec. 4, para 1 UKlaG. Currently, 77 associations are listed,[2] the majority being 37 renters' associations and 16 *Verbraucherzentralen*, one for each of the 16 *Bundesländer* (the federal states).

Instead of consumer interests, the non-listed associations pursue the professional interests of their members. The requirements are listed under Sec. 3, para 1, sentence 1, No. 2 UKlaG.[3]

## 1.2. *Act Against Unfair Competition (UWG) and Act Against Restraints on Competition (GWB)*

In different contexts, other acts refer to Secs. 3 and 4 UKlaG. Particular mention should be given to the *Gesetz gegen den unlauteren Wettbewerb* (UWG, Act Against Unfair Competition) and the *Gesetz gegen Wettbewerbsbeschränkungen* (GWB, Act against Restraints on Competition).[4] According to the two acts, associations may bring actions to protect free competition against unfair practices, Sec. 8, para 3 UWG, or against cartel infringements, Sec. 33, para 2 GWB.

However, these actions are not to be confused with actions for damages such as those brought by *Cartel Damage Claims (CDC)*, for example in the cases of the German Cement cartel[5] in 2002 or the Hydrogen Peroxide cartel[6] in 2009. In its business model, CDC brings actions for damages in cartel infringement cases in its own name. It does so because the individual parties have bundled and assigned their claims to CDC; if it succeeds with the action, CDC receives roughly 20 per cent of the damages and forwards the rest to the injured parties.[7] In contrast, when

2 As of 2 January 2014, <www.bundesanzeiger.de> search criterion: BAnz AT 02.01.2014 B2, alternatively via <www.bundesjustizamt.de/DE/Themen/Buergerdienste/Verbraucherschutz/Verbraucherschutz_node.html> (last accessed on 7 March 2014).

3 Micklitz 2013, § 3 UKlaG, No. 19 *et seq.*

4 For English translations see <www.gesetze-im-internet.de/englisch_uwg/index.html> and <www.gesetze-im-internet.de/englisch_gwb/index.html> (last accessed on 7 March 2014).

5 The Landgericht (LG) Düsseldorf dismissed the action as unsubstantiated on 17 December 2013 - 37 O 200/09 (Kart) U, WuW (*Wirtschaft und Wettbewerb*) 2014, 183. The claimants have appealed. For background and analysis in English see Pavlova 2014.

6 LG Dortmund, 13 O (Kart) 23/09, the case has been partly settled, Seitz 2012, p. 141 fn. 45, the continued case has been forwarded to the ECJ for preliminary references on 29 April 2013, GRUR Int. (*Gewerblicher Rechtsschutz und Urheberrecht – Internationaler Teil*) 2013, 842.

7 LG Düsseldorf, 37 O 200/09 (Kart) U, WuW 2014, 183. The Court took the view that the assignments were invalid because they violated public policy. On this ground it dismissed →

bringing a *Verbandsklage*, the associations can obtain injunctions only; they sue on behalf of their members or the consumers; they always act on a non-profit basis.

A common feature of actions by associations under both the UWG and the GWB is the possible aim of the legal action. So far, an association can obtain a prohibitory injunction. In competition cases, it can additionally demand that the infringing undertaking surrender the economic benefit gained at the expense of consumers or competitors to the federal budget, Secs. 10 UWG, 34a GWB. This possibility was introduced into the UWG in 2004 and the GWB in 2005.[8]

### 1.3. *Practical Application*

In theory, the confiscation of profits appears to be a reasonable claim for associations to make. In practice, however, it has no relevance at all. In the nine years since its introduction, only a handful of claims have been successfully raised. Listed associations can effectively reach their goals with prohibitory injunctions. For non-listed professional associations the main reason not to bring such actions is the risk of legal cost. They would have to bear the procedural risk under the German 'loser pays all' principle,[9] yet the benefits are surrendered to the federal budget. Therefore, there is no incentive to bring this kind of action.[10]

The pure prohibitory injunction is of greater significance and is frequently obtained in court. One pending example is a case by the *Verbraucherzentrale* Hamburg against Deutsche Telekom,[11] which had advertised a smartphone in newspapers for €50. Only the small print conveyed that a two-year contract was required. The small print in dark colours on a dark background was illegible without magnifying glasses. The Regional Court issued the injunction on the ground that due to the advertisement's misleading character it infringed on consumer protection provisions.

the action as unsubstantiated. This had to do with the financial structure of CDC and the inability to cover the costs of the defendant in case CDC lost; Pavlova 2014. The decision is under appeal, but even if it is upheld this business model can be kept up only if the financial risks are distributed among the assignors. Alternatively, a company like CDC could be endowed with more capital; Uphoff 2014, 149.

8 For the historical developments see Köhler 2014, § 10 UWG, No. 1, and Lübbig 2008, § 34a GWB, Nos. 3-5.

9 For an overview of German cost rules see Jackson 2009, p. 555-565; briefly Pavlova 2014.

10 Goldmann 2013, § 10 UWG, No. 5; Lübbig 2008, § 34a GWB, No. 20.

11 LG Bonn, judgment of 5 August 2011 - 11 O 35/11.

## 2. The Capital Markets Model Case Act

The Capital Markets Model Case Act has been the subject of debate right from the beginning. With no historical experience in genuine group actions, comprehensive literature has developed dealing with the Act[12] and its application.

### 2.1. *Emergence of a Group Action*

#### 2.1.1. The Starting Point: The *Telekom* Case

When dealing with the formation of the Capital Markets Model Case Act it is impossible to bypass the landmark *Telekom* case.[13] Deutsche Telekom passed into private hands in 1995 and went public in 1996. At that time it had accumulated debts approximating 60 billion euros. It issued 500 million shares and signed the prominent German TV actor Manfred Krug to advertise them as the '*Volksaktie*' (the people's share) across the media. A decade later, Mr Krug declared his involvement in the 50-million-euro campaign his 'biggest professional mistake'.[14] Initially the development was positive, but instead of the promised bright future the stock turned out to be one of the biggest let-downs in German stock market history.

The shares, five times oversubscribed, were sold mainly to private investors. While the first shares were listed at €14.57, Telekom offered a second contingent in 1999 at a price of €39.50. The third contingent in June 2000 was offered at €66.50 and was still three times oversubscribed. This time it did not live up to the expectations and the stock continuously lost value, mainly due to failed buyouts, bad investment decisions and bad publicity, reaching its all-time low of €8.14 in June of 2002. In early 2001, Telekom had to correct its opening balance sheet from 1995: the company's real estate value had been rated too high and therefore the balance sheet was adjusted by 2.5 billion euros.

Shareholders brought actions for damages against Telekom in 2001 and 2002. Allegedly, Telekom had insufficiently disclosed the risks in its prospectuses regarding the second and third share contingents. Within a few months, 17,000 shareholders brought 2,650 actions in one single court, the Regional Court of Frankfurt. This court had jurisdiction[15] because Telekom has its registered seat in Frankfurt. Not surprisingly, the court was not prepared for such a number of

12 For English publications see e.g. Fairgrieve & Howells 2012, p. 26 *et seq.*; Feess & Halfmeier 2012; Hodges 2008, p. 76-80; Micklitz & Stadler 2006, p. 1485-1488.

13 For a background to the case see Hodges 2008, p. 77 *et seq.*; Guldner 2011.

14 Krug 2007, summarised at <www.stern.de/lifestyle/leute/schauspieler-krug-entschuldigt-sich-bei-t-aktionaeren-581528.html> (last accessed on 7 March 2014).

15 See Sec. 17, para 1 ZPO (*Zivilprozessordnung*, Code of Civil Procedure) for venue and Sec. 71, para 2, No. 3 GVG (*Gerichtsverfassungsgesetz*, Courts Constitution Act) for subject matter jurisdiction. English translations available at <www.gesetze-im-internet.de/-englisch_zpo/index.html> and <www.gesetze-im-internet.de/englisch_gvg/index.html> (last accessed on 7 March 2014).

lawsuits and was flooded with so many documents that fax machines would run out of paper and mailboxes would overflow.[16] There were days when the statements of claim had to be delivered by trucks. Understandably, the court was completely overburdened at first.

After an intervention by the *Bundesverfassungsgericht* (the Federal Constitutional Court)[17] the first hearing took place in late 2004. It was nevertheless already clear that under the procedural framework at that time it was impossible to manage all cases within a reasonable time period.[18]

### 2.1.2. Legislative Procedure

Among scholars there had been discussions on the implementation of collective redress mechanisms before,[19] but it required the *Telekom* mega case to substantially further the development and finally move the legislator to introduce such an instrument. Faced with the problems at the Regional Court of Frankfurt it took only one year from the Federal Ministry of Justice's first discussion draft in April 2004 to the enactment by the Bundestag and by the Bundesrat (the Federal Parliament and the Federal Council) in July 2005.[20] The result was *KapMuG*, the *Kapitalanleger-Musterverfahrensgesetz* (Capital Markets Model Case Act).

Considering the procedural novelty of the Act in Germany, the legislative procedure was very fast. The Act went into effect on 1 November 2005 and was provided with a sunset clause for 1 November 2010 for further review and amendment, which has now been extended to 1 November 2020, Sec. 28 KapMuG (2012). An official English translation of the 2005 version is available online.[21] Unfortunately, the 2012 recast with its clarifications has not been translated.

### 2.1.3. Limited Scope

The 2005 Act covered damages regarding wrong or misleading public capital markets information, Sec. 1, para 1 KapMuG (2005). Not only was this a limitation to capital markets cases, but according to the restrictive interpretation by the courts,[22] it only covered damages caused directly by capital markets information, damages resulting from faulty investment consulting were outside the KapMuG's

16 Kurz 2012, p. 8.

17 BVerfG, decision of 27 July 2004 - 1 BvR 1196/04, NJW (*Neue Juristische Wochenschrift*) 2004, 3320.

18 Hess 2014, Einleitung KapMuG, No. 19.

19 Notably at the 1996 and 2002 *Deutscher Juristentag* (German Conference of Jurists); Hess 2014, Einleitung, No. 17 *et seq*.

20 Promulgated in the *Bundesgesetzblatt* (Federal Law Gazette), BGBl. 2005 I, p. 2437.

21 <www.bmj.de/SharedDocs/Downloads/DE/pdfs/KapMuG_english.pdf> (last accessed on 7 March 2014).

22 BGH, decision of 30 August 2008, NJW 2009, p. 513; BGH, decision of 30 November 2010, NJW-RR 2011, p. 327.

scope.[23] In the 2012 recast a new Sec. 1, para 1, No. 2 KapMuG was introduced, including cases regarding *the use* of wrong or misleading public capital markets information or the failure to clarify that such information was wrong or misleading. Liability for faulty investment consulting is now covered, as well as liability for information contained in prospectuses.[24]

The sectoral capital markets approach is owed to the Act's still being in the stage of field testing. In the recast materials the legislator cautiously announced that he might consider introducing horizontal model proceedings if the Model Case Act stands the test of time.[25]

## 2.2. *Mechanics of the Act*

### 2.2.1. Constitution of the Civil Courts in Germany

Courts of different levels are involved in the KapMuG procedure. It is therefore appropriate to give an overview of the constitution of German civil courts.

There are four levels of civil jurisdiction, *Amtsgerichte* (Local Courts), *Landgerichte* (Regional Courts), *Oberlandesgerichte* (Higher Regional Courts) and the *Bundesgerichtshof* (Federal Court of Justice).[26] A party to a case might be able to appeal twice, but it will never have more than three courts hearing the case. If the claimant begins at the Local Court, the *Berufung* (appeal on points of law or facts, Secs. 511, 513 ZPO) leads to the Regional Court. If the case is commenced at the Regional Court, a Higher Regional Court will hear the *Berufung*. A *Revision* (appeal on points of law following a *Berufung*, Secs. 542, para 1, 545 ZPO) is always dealt with by the Federal Court of Justice, Sec. 133 GVG.

Whether the first instance is a Local or Regional Court depends on the value in litigation or the subject matter. Local Courts hear cases valued up to €5,000, Sec. 23, No. 1 GVG, Regional Courts hear cases with higher values, Sec. 71, para 1 GVG. Certain subject matters are allocated to the courts regardless of monetary value, Secs. 23, para 2, Nos. 2, 72 GVG. According to Sec. 71, para 2, No. 3 GVG, capital markets cases are assigned to the Regional Courts.

### 2.2.2. Three Phases

The Capital Markets Model Case Act consists of only 28 sections. The specific procedure as regulated by the Act unfolds in three phases.[27] Phase 1 takes place at the Regional Court of the *Ausgangsverfahren* (the initial proceeding for damages

23 BT-Drs. (*Bundestags-Drucksache*, Parliamentary Publication) 17/8799, p. 16; Kruis 2014, § 1 KapMuG, No. 4.

24 BT-Drs. 17/8799, p. 16; Hess 2014, Einleitung, No. 22; Kruis 2014, § 1 KapMuG, No. 4.

25 BT-Drs. 17/8799, p. 14.

26 Secs. 22 *et seq.*, 59 *et seq.*, 115 *et seq.* and 123 *et seq.* GVG, English translation available at: <www.gesetze-im-internet.de/englisch_gvg/index.html> (last accessed in March 2014).

27 Hess 2014, Einleitung KapMuG, No. 27 *et seq.*; Feess & Halfmeier 2012, p. 9 *et seq.*

brought by an individual). A party to an action for damages can make a request for a model case to be commenced. The court will submit a specific subject matter to the respective Higher Regional Court if the prerequisites are met. In phase 2, the Higher Regional Court decides on the contended subject matter and delivers a binding ruling. In phase 3, the subject matter returns to the Regional Court, where cases are dealt with on an individual basis.

The initial action for damages marks the beginning of phase 1, Secs. 2-8 KapMuG. Then, either the claimant or the defendant can make a request for a *Musterverfahren* (a model case). They have to show that their claim has significance for other similar cases beyond the individual dispute concerned, Sec. 2, para 3, sentence 2 KapMuG. The application is published in a complaint registry on the internet,[28] Sec. 3, para 2 KapMuG. If nine other claimants join the application within six months, the court phrases the precise subject matter that shall be dealt with in the model proceeding, Sec. 6, para 1 KapMuG. It forwards a question to the Higher Regional Court and stays its own proceeding, Sec. 5 KapMuG. If cases pending in other courts depend on the decision in the model case, these courts will stay their proceedings as well, Sec. 8, para 1 KapMuG.

In phase 2, Secs. 9-21 KapMuG, the Higher Regional Court picks one *Musterkläger* (the model claimant), Sec. 9, para 2 KapMuG; all other claimants become *Beigeladene* ('interested parties summoned' in the official English translation of Sec. 8, para 1, No. 3 KapMuG (2005)) to the model case, Sec. 9, para 3 KapMuG. This selection entails considerable consequences for the procedural situation of the claimants: only the model claimant is considered a party to the model proceedings, the other co-claimants are not formal parties, but have a limited procedural role enabling them to participate in the model proceedings with the aim of supporting the model claimant. They may, for example, object to a decision, and they must do so if they do not want the objection to be excluded at a later point, namely in their individual cases, Sec. 22, para 1, sentence 2 and para 3 KapMuG. The court adjudicates upon the submitted subject matter by way of a *Musterentscheid* (a Model Case Ruling), Sec. 16, para 1 KapMuG.

The model claimant and the model defendant can also make a joint proposition for a court settlement, Sec. 17, para 1, sentence 1 KapMuG. Likewise, the court can suggest a settlement itself and it is obliged to do so, Sec. 11, para 1, sentence 1 KapMuG and Sec. 278, para 1 ZPO. In case of a settlement the court will verify that the agreement is fair and balanced, Sec. 17, para 1, sentence 3 and Sec. 18 KapMuG. The 'interested parties summoned' must be heard (Sec. 17, para 1, sentence 2 KapMuG) and – if the court gives permission to the model parties' agreement – this time they may opt out of the settlement, Sec. 19, para 2 KapMuG. The settlement becomes binding for all remaining 'interested parties summoned' only if less than 30 per cent have opted out within a month, Sec. 17, para 1 sentence 4 and Sec. 23, para 1 KapMuG. If the quota is exceeded, fairness and balance are

28 <www.bundesanzeiger.de> (last accessed in January 2014).

called into question,[29] and the entire settlement is void. It is another question whether the model defendant will agree to a settlement when it has to expect ongoing proceedings with up to 30 per cent of the claimants. The settling model parties will probably only agree on a lower quota, if at all.

In phase 3, Secs. 22-26 KapMuG, the Regional Courts resume their proceedings, but now they are bound by the decision of the Higher Regional Court, be it a Model Case Ruling, Sec. 22, para 1, sentence 2 and para 3 KapMuG, or a settlement, Sec. 23, para 1 KapMuG. If the model case was decided in favour of the claimants, the courts now have to assess the amount of individual damages, Sec. 22, para 4 KapMuG. In case of a settlement the Regional Court dismisses the individual actions and decides on the costs, Sec. 23, para 3 KapMuG.

### 2.2.3. Registration of a Claim

In the 2005 Act, an injured party did not have the option to wait for the Model Case Ruling and to then bring its own action for damages. The limitation periods were too short for that. If the party sued and lost, it would have had to bear the legal cost. This risk would prevent many parties from suing at all.

The 2012 recast therefore introduced a 'registration of claim', Sec. 10, para 2 KapMuG.[30] For six months after the model proceeding has started, injured parties can register their claim and in doing so suspend the limitation period until the Model Case Ruling is issued, Sec. 204, para 1, No. 6a BGB (*Bürgerliches Gesetzbuch*, Civil Code).[31] The only condition is that their case is not already pending in another court, Sec. 10, para 2, sentence 2 KapMuG. Apart from suspension, the registration has no other effect. Once there is a Model Case Ruling the party still has to bring an individual action, where the validity of the claim will be assessed.

A settlement of the model case has no legal effect on the registered claims, because they are not included in the list of parties to the model proceeding, Sec. 9, para 1 KapMuG for whom the settlement becomes binding according to Sec. 23, para 1 sentence 4 KapMuG.[32]

A party must be represented by a lawyer in order to register its claim,[33] Sec. 10, para 2, sentence 3 KapMuG.

### 2.2.4. Costs

There is no separate order for payment of costs in the first instance model proceeding. The parties are not required to pay in advance,[34] since the *Gerichtskasse*

29 BT-Drs. 17/10160, p. 26.

30 Suggested before by Bergmeister 2009, p. 330 *et seq.*; similarly Braun & Rotter 2004, p. 299 *et seq.*; in detail Reuschle 2014, § 10 KapMuG, No. 11 *et seq.*

31 English translation available at <www.gesetze-im-internet.de/englisch_bgb/index.html> (last accessed on 7 March 2014).

32 Halfmeier 2012, p. 2150.

33 Critically Halfmeier 2012, p. 2147.

(the court cashier) will temporarily cover the costs until the model proceeding is finished,[35] Secs. 9, para 1, sentence 2, 17 para 4, sentence 1, 22 para 4, sentence 1 GKG (*Gerichtskostengesetz*, Court Fees Act).

Instead, expenses of the model claimant and 'the interested parties summoned' are contained in the orders for payment of costs in their respective initial proceedings, Sec. 24, para 1 KapMuG.[36] Likewise, expenses of the model defendant are dealt with by the order for payment in the initial proceeding, Sec. 24, para 2, sentence 1 KapMuG. In the latter case, however, the claimant has to cover the defendant's expenses only at the percentage of his claim to the total sum claimed in all stayed proceedings, Sec. 24, para 2, sentence 2 KapMuG.

In other words: while the defendant's costs are calculated on the basis of the total sum of all claims brought against him, the losing model claimant has to cover the costs based on the sum he claims in his individual proceeding. The defendant has to pay for the difference himself, namely for court fees and for his *Prozessbevollmächtigten* (his lawyers of record). The provision intends to minimise the procedural risk for claimants,[37] but also faces criticism for discrimination of the defendant, who will in large part be burdened with his costs.[38]

In case of an appeal Sec. 26 KapMuG governs costs independently without allocating them to the initial proceedings. According to Sec. 26, para 5 KapMuG, once again, the defendant might not get fully reimbursed.[39]

The court also temporarily covers fees for expert opinions, Sec. 13, para 5 JVEG (*Justizvergütungs- und entschädigungsgesetz*, Judicial Compensation Act); they are allocated *pro rata* to the costs of the initial proceedings.[40]

There is a fee for the registration of a claim, which is taken into account if the registration is followed by an action for damages, Appendix 1 to the GKG: No. 1210, para 2 *Kostenverzeichnis* (schedule of values).[41]

### 2.2.5. Nature of the Model Proceeding

Group actions can be described as 'procedures which in effect provide case management tools to handle mass litigation'.[42] The *Telekom* case and the subsequent legislative procedure illustrate that model proceedings under the Capital Markets Model Case Act have exactly this goal. However, a model case only deals with a specific question phrased by the Regional Court, Sec. 6, para 1 KapMuG. Therefore,

34 BT-Drs. 15/5091, p. 2.
35 Kruis 2014, GKG, No. 11.
36 Kruis 2014, § 24 KapMuG, No. 4.
37 BT-Drs. 15/5091, p. 19.
38 Kruis 2014, § 24 KapMuG, No. 8 deems the provision unconstitutional.
39 BT-Drs. 15/5091, p. 32 *et seq.*
40 BT-Drs. 15/5091, p. 37; Kruis 2014, JVEG, No. 1.
41 Kruis 2014, GKG, No. 14.
42 Fairgrieve & Howells 2012, p. 18.

the KapMuG procedure is often referred to as *begrenzte Gruppenklage*[43] (limited group action) or *begrenztes Gruppenverfahren*[44] (limited group procedure).

The model procedure also takes a unique position when it comes to opt-in and opt-out regimes.[45] We have seen that 'interested parties summoned' can opt out of a settlement between the model parties, Sec. 19, para 2 KapMuG. Such an option does not exist in the case of a Model Case Ruling. It becomes binding for all stayed proceedings, Sec. 22, para 1 KapMuG. When looking at the initiation of the model proceeding and a possible opt-in, we have to differentiate. The nine claimants who join the application for a model case, Sec. 6, para 1 KapMuG, clearly opt into the action.[46] However, once the quota of ten applications is reached and the case is forwarded to the Higher Regional Court, not only are their cases stayed until the end of the proceedings in the model case, Sec. 5 KapMuG, but so are all other pending cases that raise the same subject matter question, Sec. 8, para 1 KapMuG. The claimants in those other actions have no choice whether to participate in the model proceeding or not,[47] and considering the long duration of some of the proceedings, it is conceivable that many claimants may prefer their individual actions to continue. It can therefore be concluded that in its nature the Model Case Act is neither an opt-in nor an opt-out procedure.[48]

## 2.3. *Practical Application*

How does the Capital Markets Model Case Act function in practice? The first case which ended with a Model Case Ruling was decided by the Higher Regional Court of Munich on 30 December 2011 (*Medienfonds VIP 4*);[49] three more were adjudicated in 2012 (*Medienfonds VIP 3*,[50] *MLP*[51] and *Informatec*).[52] The courts are also dealing with the aftermath of the recent financial crisis via the KapMuG procedure, notably in a case concerning *Hypo Real Estate*.[53]

43 Söhner 2013, p. 10.
44 Lange 2011.
45 Micklitz & Stadler 2006, p. 1481, define opt in as a model in which 'the affected persons join the procedure voluntarily', whereas in an opt-out model 'the group plaintiff is granted the right to enforce the rights of all affected persons without their explicit consent'.
46 Hess 2014, Einleitung KapMuG, No. 33, identifies additional features that resemble an opt-in procedure.
47 Feess & Halfmeier 2012, p. 10.
48 Söhner 2013, p. 10; Feess & Halfmeier 2012, p. 10.
49 OLG München, decision of 30 December 2011 - KAP 1/07 (published at <www.bundesanzeiger.de> on 9 January 2012).
50 OLG München, decision of 8 May 2012 - KAP 2/07 (published 11 May 2012).
51 OLG Karlsruhe, decision of 16 November 2012 - 17 KAP 1/09 (published 20 November 2012). An appeal is pending.
52 OLG München, decision of 8 May 2012 - KAP 1/08 (published 21 May 2012).
53 OLG München, KAP 3/10. The oral hearings began on 3 February 2014, DW.de 2014; Scally 2014.

### 2.3.1. Geltl v Daimler Chrysler

A striking case is *Geltl v Daimler Chrysler*,[54] Geltl being the model claimant in this case. In 2005, the supervisory board of Daimler decided that the then CEO Jürgen Schrempp should be replaced by Dieter Zetsche (who holds this position at the time of writing). Allegedly, this was inside information which the company had not immediately released to the public. If correct, injured parties had a claim for damages according to Sec. 37b *Wertpapierhandelsgesetz* (WpHG, Securities Trading Act).[55] The Regional Court published the application for a model case in the Complaint Registry in April 2006. The Higher Regional Court selected the model claimant in August of the same year and dismissed the petition by way of a Model Case Ruling in February 2007.[56] In its opinion, Daimler had published the necessary information without delay.

This could have been the prime example of an efficient model proceeding that was undertaken in just ten months. But the model claimant appealed. The Federal Court of Justice annulled the decision in 2008 due to a procedural error and referred the case back to the Higher Regional Court for additional fact-finding.[57] On the merits the Higher Regional Court came to the same conclusion as earlier and dismissed the petition in 2009.[58] The model claimant appealed again. This time, in 2010 the Federal Court of Justice submitted the case to the European Court of Justice for preliminary references.[59] It received the Court's reply in 2012[60] and, based on that, annulled the second Model Case Ruling as well and referred the case back in 2013.[61] The case is still pending at the Higher Regional Court of Stuttgart. From this timeline we can expect another ruling in 2014. After that, the Regional Court will have to adjudicate on each individual case, if we discount the possibility of further appeals. Who would have expected that after such a good start this case would keep the courts busy for that long?

### 2.3.2. The *Telekom* Case – A Never-Ending Story

Was the *Telekom* case processed more smoothly? In 2006 the Higher Regional Court picked one model claimant for each of the two model cases (for the initial public

54 For summaries see Meller-Hanich 2011, p. 189 (factual and legal problems up to the BGH decision to refer to the ECJ in 2010); Di Noia & Gargantini 2012, p. 494, fn. 29 (factual background); Hess 2014, Einleitung, No. 60 (procedural process).

55 English translation available at: <www.bafin.de/SharedDocs/Aufsichtsrecht/EN/Gesetz/-wphg_101119_en.html> (last accessed on 7 March 2014).

56 OLG Stuttgart, decision of 15 February 2007 - 901 Kap 1/06, ZIP (*Zeitschrift für Wirtschaftsrecht*) 2007, p. 481.

57 BGH, decision of 25 February 2008 - II ZB 9/07, NJW-RR 2008, p. 865.

58 OLG Stuttgart, decision of 22 April 2009 - 20 Kap 1/08, ZIP 2009, p. 962.

59 BGH, decision of 22 November 2010 - II ZB 7/09, NJW 2011, p. 309.

60 ECJ, judgment of 28 June 2012, *Geltl v Daimler* - C-19/11.

61 BGH, decision of 23 April 2013 - II ZB 7/09, NJW 2013, p. 2114.

offerings in 1999 and 2000, respectively).[62] The first oral hearings took place in 2008.[63] Further delay was necessary due to ten related decisions by the Regional Court between 2009 and 2013. In each of these *Erweiterungsbeschlüsse* the court amended or expanded the subject matter that the model proceeding was dealing with. The Higher Regional Court was bound by these decisions under Sec. 13, para 2 KapMuG (2005) and thus had to constantly adapt to the modifications. This has since been changed for future cases in the 2012 recast. Under Sec. 15, para 1 KapMuG the Higher Regional Court now has discretion concerning the adoption of the modifications, for example it can refuse to adopt them if they have no relevance for the model case.

In 2012 and 2013, respectively, the two model cases were decided upon.[64] The court ruled that the sales prospectuses neither contained any errors nor had been misleading. In both cases, as one would expect by now, appeals are pending.[65] It can hardly be predicted when this case, which commenced more than ten years ago, will come to an end. This is especially true for the stayed individual cases waiting for the Model Case Rulings to become binding. The Local Court of Frankfurt will probably be occupied with processing the individual cases for several years.

## 2.4. *First Conclusions*

The first model case was adopted in late 2011 and together with the pending cases it can be concluded that model cases typically deal with the accuracy of ad hoc disclosure or prospectuses, the construction of indefinite legal terms or the standard of care in capital markets cases.[66]

The KapMuG of 2005 revealed some shortcomings which have been addressed in the 2012 recast. Whether the amendments suffice to make the KapMuG a strong instrument in the handling of mass litigation still remains to be seen. It may seem odd that eight years after its entry into effect, no clear answer can be given yet as to whether the Act is a success or not. But the first model case was finally decided in late 2011 and the 2012 amendments are currently being put to the test.

It was the intention of the legislator to promote settlements.[67] It is, however, still too early for an evaluation of the parties' willingness to settle, as the first model case was finally decided in late 2011. We will also have to see whether the Act needs

62 OLG Frankfurt, 23 Sch 2/06 and 23 Sch 1/06.

63 Tilp 2009, p. 352.

64 OLG Frankfurt, decision of 16 May 2012 - 23 KAP 1/06 (published 29 May 2012) and decision of 3 July 2013 - 23 KAP 2/06 (published 10 July 2013).

65 The BGH ordered the publication of the appeals in the Complaint Registry, BGH XI ZB 12/12, NJW-RR (*Neue Juristische Wochenschrift – Rechtsprechungs-Report*) 2013, 235 and BGH XI ZB 9/13.

66 Meller-Hanich 2011, p. 189.

67 BT-Drs. 17/8799, p. 14 *et seq.*

more comprehensive adaptations and whether the legislator will have the courage to expand the system of model proceedings to other areas of law.[68]

Time will also show how the new registration of claims will be used. It is supposed to minimise the risk for those parties who might otherwise be discouraged by the risk of costs. Having said that, it could offer an incentive for law firms to register the majority of their cases and to bring only a few cases in order to inexpensively test the prospect of success.[69]

## 3. Summary

German procedural law essentially provides two types of collective actions. The *Verbandsklage* is brought on behalf of others and covers prohibitory injunctions in different areas of law, namely consumer protection and competition law. As a means of regulation and market control it has proven its worth.

The Capital Markets Model Case Act does not conform with conventional categories of group actions. While it has opt-in and opt-out elements, it does not fit into either of the two categories. At first glance, the Act might not have withstood the initial scrutiny, as the cases keep dragging on. But we have to bear in mind that the concept of model proceedings was new to German procedural law and that the Act was drafted under immense time pressure. Hopefully, legal practice has acquainted itself with the procedure by now and with the incorporation of the 2012 amendments we should consider awaiting the handling of cases commenced more recently, like *Hypo Real Estate*, before reaching our final verdict.

68 The legislator announced he might consider an expansion if the new KapMuG stands the test, BT-Drs. 17/8799, p. 14.

69 Wardenbach 2013, p. 37; von Bernuth & Kremer 2012, p. 891; Schneider & Heppner 2012, p. 2712; there is no such risk according to Halfmeier 2012, p. 2147.

## Bibliography


**Bergmeister 2009**
Bergmeister, F., *Kapitalanleger-Musterverfahrensgesetz (KapMuG). Bestandsaufnahme und Reformempfehlung aus der Perspektive von Recht und Praxis der US-amerikanischen Securities Class Action*, Tübingen: Mohr Siebeck, 2009.

**von Bernuth & Kremer 2012**
von Bernuth, W.H. & Kremer, R.M., 'Das neue KapMuG: Wesentliche Änderungen aus Sicht der Praxis', *Neue Zeitschrift für Gesellschaftsrecht (NZG)*, 2012, p. 890-895.

**Braun & Rotter 2004**
Braun, F. & Rotter, K., 'Der Diskussionsentwurf zum KapMuG - Verbesserter Anlegerschutz?', *Zeitschrift für Bank- und Kapitalmarktrecht (BKR)*, 2004, p. 296-301.

**Di Noia & Gargantini 2012**
Di Noia, C. & Gargantini, M., 'Issuers at Mindstream: Disclosure of Multistage Events in the Current and in the Proposed EU Market Abuse Regime', *European Company and Financial Law Review (ECFR)*, 2012, p. 484-529.

**DW.de 2014**
Deutsche Welle Business, 'Germany's HRE Bank in the Dock over Alleged Misinformation', 3 February 2014, <www.dw.de/germanys-hre-bank-in-the-dock-over-alleged-misinformation/a-17405120?maca=en-rss-en-bus-2091-rdf>.

**Fairgrieve & Howells 2012**
Fairgrieve, D. & Howells, G., 'Collective Redress Procedures: European Debates', in Fairgrieve, D. & Lein, E. (eds.), *Extraterritoriality and Collective Redress*, Oxford: Oxford University Press, 2012, p. 15-41.

**Feess & Halfmeier 2012**
Feess, E. & Halfmeier, A., 'The German Capital Markets Model Case Act (KapMuG) - A European Role Model for Increasing the Efficiency of Capital Markets? Analysis and Suggestions for Reform', 2012, available at: <http://papers.ssrn.com/-sol3/papers.cfm?abstract_id=1684528>.

**Goldmann 2013**
Goldmann, M., in Harte-Bavendamm, H. & Henning-Bodewig, F. (eds.), *Gesetz gegen den unlauteren Wettbewerb (UWG)*, 3rd edn., München: Verlag C.H. Beck, 2013.

**Guldner 2011**
Guldner, J., *Die verflixte Volksaktie*, 18 November 2011, <www.handelsblatt.com/-finanzen/aktien/aktien-im-fokus/15-jahre-telekom-boersengang-die-verflixte-volksaktie/5861838.html>.

**Halfmeier 2012**
Halfmeier, A., 'Zur Neufassung des KapMuG und zur Verjährungshemmung bei Prospekthaftungsansprüchen', *Der Betrieb (DB)*, 2012, p. 2145-2151.

**Hess 2014**
Hess, B., in Hess, B., Reuschle, F. & Rimmelspacher, B. (eds.), *Kölner Kommentar zum KapMuG*, 2nd edn., Köln/Berlin/München: Carl Heymanns Verlag, 2014.

**Hodges 2008**
Hodges, C., *The Reform of Class and Representative Actions in European Legal Systems. A New Framework for Collective Redress in Europe*, Oxford/Portland: Hart Publishing, 2008.

**Jackson 2009**
Jackson, R.M., *Review of Civil Litigation Costs: Preliminary Report. Volume Two*, Norwich: TSO, 2009, available at: <www.judiciary.gov.uk/publications-and-reports/review-of-civil-litigation-costs/reports/civil-litigation-costs-review-preliminary-report >.

**Köhler 2014**
Köhler, H., in Köhler, H. & Bornkamm, J., *Gesetz gegen den unlauteren Wettbewerb*, 32nd edn., München: Verlag C.H. Beck, 2014.

**Krug 2007**
Krug, M., Interview by von Bülow, U. & Kühn, A., 'Ich vermisse mich auch ein bisschen', Stern, 1 February 2007.

**Kruis 2014**
Kruis, F., in Hess, B., Reuschle, F. & Rimmelspacher, B. (eds.), *Kölner Kommentar zum KapMuG*, 2nd edn., Köln/Berlin/München: Carl Heymanns Verlag, 2014.

**Kurz 2012**
Kurz, A., 'Der Prozess', *Financial Times Deutschland*, 15 May 2012, p. 8.

**Lange 2011**
Lange, S., *Das begrenzte Gruppenverfahren. Konzeption eines Verfahrens zur Bewältigung von Großschäden auf der Basis des Kapitalanleger-Musterverfahrensgesetzes*, Tübingen: Mohr Siebeck, 2011.

**Lübbig 2008**
Lübbig, T., in Hirsch, G., Montag, F. & Säcker, F.J. (eds.), *Münchener Kommentar zum Europäischen und Deutschen Wettbewerbsrecht (Kartellrecht). Band 2. §§ 1-96, 130, 139 GWB*, München: Verlag C.H. Beck, 2008.

**Meller-Hanich 2011**
Meller-Hanich, C., 'Das Kapitalanleger-Musterverfahrensgesetz (KapMuG) - Eine Zwischenbilanz', *Zeitschrift für Bankrecht und Bankwirtschaft (ZBB)*, 2011, p. 180-191.

**Micklitz 2013**
Micklitz, H.-W., 'Gesetz über Unterlassungsklagen bei Verbraucherrechts- und anderen Verstößen (Unterlassungsklagengesetz - UklaG), in Krüger, W. & Rauscher, T. (eds.), *Münchener Kommentar zur Zivilprozessordnung. Band 3. §§ 1025-1109*, 4th edn., München: Verlag C.H. Beck, 2013.

**Micklitz & Stadler 2006**
Micklitz, H.-W. & Stadler, A., 'The Development of Collective Legal Actions in Europe, Especially in German Civil Procedure', *European Business Law Review (EBLR)*, 2006, p. 1473-1503.

**Pavlova 2014**
Pavlova, P., 'Is Private Enforcement of Competition Law Still an Option in Germany?', Conflict of Laws.net, <http://conflictoflaws.net/2014/is-private-enforcement-of-competition-law-still-an-option-in-germany/>.

**Reuschle 2014**
Reuschle, F., in Hess, B., Reuschle, F. & Rimmelspacher, B. (eds.), *Kölner Kommentar zum KapMuG*, 2nd edn., Köln/Berlin/München: Carl Heymanns Verlag, 2014.

**Scally 2014**
Scally, D., 'Hypo Real Estate Investors Seek Compensation for Bank's Losses', 4 February 2014, <www.irishtimes.com/business/sectors/financial-services/hypo-real-estate-investors-seek-compensation-for-bank-s-losses-1.1678476>.

**Schneider & Heppner 2012**
Schneider, B. & Heppner, H., 'KapMuG Reloaded - das neue Kapitalanleger-Musterverfahrensgesetz', *Betriebs-Berater (BB)*, 2012, p. 2703-2713.

**Seitz 2012**
Seitz, C., 'Public over Private Enforcement of Competition Law? Zugleich Besprechung von AG Bonn, Beschluss v. 18 Januar 2012 - 51 Gs 53/09 - Pfleiderer', *Gewerblicher Rechtsschutz und Urheberrecht, Rechtsprechungs-Report (GRUR-RR)*, 2012, p. 137-142.

**Söhner 2013**
Söhner, M., 'Das neue Kapitalanleger-Musterverfahrensgesetz', *Zeitschrift für Wirtschaftsrecht (ZIP)*, 2013, p. 7-14.

**Tilp 2009**
Tilp, A.W., 'Das Kapitalanleger-Musterverfahrensgesetz: Stresstest für den Telekom-Prozess', in Blaurock, U., Bornkamm, J. & Kirchberg, C. (eds.), *Festschrift für Achim Krämer*, Berlin: De Gruyter Recht, 2009, p. 331-360.

**Uphoff 2014**
Uphoff, B., 'BB-Kommentar zu LG Düsseldorf vom 17.12.2013', *Betriebs-Berater (BB)*, 2014, p. 149.

**Wardenbach 2013**
Wardenbach, F., 'KapMuG 2012 versus KapMuG 2005: Die wichtigsten Änderungen aus Sicht der Praxis', *Gesellschafts- und Wirtschaftsrecht (GWR)*, 2013, p. 35-38.

V. Harsági

# THE NEED FOR FURTHER DEVELOPMENT OF COLLECTIVE REDRESS IN HUNGARY*

## 1. Introduction

Multi-party litigation may be an effective legal instrument in situations where the interests of a large number of persons should be protected, for example against a tortfeasor or a distributor of harmful products. Such situations increasingly arise in a consumer-based society. The various forms of multi-party litigation, which include class actions, group litigation and representative proceedings, enable lawsuits to be brought by or on behalf of many persons whose interests are so closely related that they can be decided in a single proceeding much more effectively than in many individual proceedings. Examples of this are often seen today not only in consumer protection cases, but also in environmental protection cases, in competition matters, in cases relating to misleading advertising and unfair contract terms, as well as in labour law and in equal opportunity disputes. As Professor Stürner has written: 'Class actions are a sharp weapon of consumers, shareholders, copyright owners, or victims of mass accidents against big corporations or mighty firms mostly acting as global players.'[1]

In Hungary, two environmental disasters that occurred in the span of ten years drew attention to the existing regulatory gap to provide for collective redress. At the end of January 2000, a cyanide spill in Romania at the Baia Mare gold mine owned by Aural - a joint-venture between Esmeralda Exploration of Perth, Australia and a Romanian state-owned company called Remin - resulted in devastating pollution of the Tisza, Hungary's second biggest river.[2] Ten years later, public opinion in Hungary was shocked by another industrial accident and the resulting loss of life and injuries, and environmental pollution: the so-called red

* This chapter was written within the framework of OTKA (Hungarian Scientific Research Fund) research project (registration number K-105559).

1 Stürner 2009, p. 107.

2 For more details, see Harsági 2014, p. 221-222.

mud disaster caused by the collapse of a tailings dam of mining waste at the Ajkai Timfoldgyar plant near Kolontár on 4 October 2010. For the latter disaster, a number of lawsuits are still pending in the courts. Because of the lack of regulatory provisions providing for group litigation, each lawsuit was brought individually and separately by the inhabitants of the villages in the areas affected by the disaster who suffered damage to their property and/or suffered non-pecuniary damage (for example, they were injured or a relative of theirs died). According to then and current Hungarian law, claims for damage can be brought in single cases only, and the joinder of parties and the joinder of actions are not considered appropriate legal instruments to treat these cases in an effective way before the courts (the main reason for this is that the parties have - in practice - their own representatives and they may act in different ways, so they cannot conduct the lawsuit with one common purpose).

In addition to the above, the issue of unfair terms and conditions, and lack of consumer information, of bank loans denominated in foreign currencies, particularly in Swiss francs, and the growing indebtedness of individual consumers due to the difficulty they have in repaying such loans, have in recent times grown to the level of a social problem in Hungary. This has provoked much discussion among politicians and legal scholars on which procedural method (here again the regulatory gap to provide for collective redress appears) might be most effective to group many individual cases of possible unfair lending practices together in one action before the courts. The situation remains unresolved.

Multi-party litigation in Hungary is sporadic (as compared to, for example, Poland where group litigation in a general sense was introduced in 2010)[3] and typically sectoral regulation is applied, which means the regulation covers only specific areas of law such as consumer protection, equal opportunity, equal treatment, competition law, environmental protection, animal welfare and protection against unfair standard contract terms and conditions. Moreover, it does not take the form of class actions or group litigation in the sense applied in the common law countries or in other European Union countries, but is merely an *actio popularis*. In the existing forms of public interest litigation, principally the following persons, organizations and authorities may bring a case before the courts: public prosecutors, NGOs, private interest groups, ministers, town clerks (the highest career civil servants of local government) or other authorities (e.g. the Hungarian Competition Authority (*Gazdasági Versenyhivatal*)).[4] The newest change was brought in 2013 by an Act that guarantees for the Hungarian National Bank the right to bring an action to enforce the civil law claims of consumers.

Public interest litigation (*actio popularis*) in Hungary has several subtypes, but they all share the common characteristic that the filing of this kind of action is possible only on the basis of statutory authorization; therefore, only organizations and persons defined by the law are entitled to bring such an action. The person

3 Kulski 2011; Małgorazata 2010, p. 24-25.

4 Kengyel & Harsági 2013, p. 332.

authorized to file a public interest action does not sue for his or her own benefit. The law lays down the violation of which rights and the enforcement of which claims may give rise to the institution of a public interest action.[5]

It is worth mentioning that there was an attempt in 2009 to pass a law on group litigation in a general sense (Bill No. T/11332 of December 2009 on the amendment of Act III of 1952 on the Code of Civil Procedure). Following a motion put forward by two MPs - without proper consultation with experts - Parliament passed the bill that would have expanded the possibility of collective redress, granting the right to initiate an action to any private individual or legal person as well. The then President of the Republic, László Sólyom, himself a professor of law, sent the bill back to Parliament for reconsideration before the general elections, following which the newly elected Parliament removed the question from the agenda.

## 2. Present Areas of Collective Rights Protection (*actio popularis*)

### 2.1. *Public Interest Litigation on Unfair Standard Contract Terms*

In Hungarian civil law, the resolution of the main problems relating to standard contract terms, including the invalidity of unfair contract terms, is built on the conceptual system of a European Union Directive (93/13/EEC).[6] § 102(5) of Book Six of the new Hungarian Civil Code,[7] which entered into force on 15 March 2014, created the legal basis for the injured party to contest any unfair contract terms that have been incorporated into the contract as a standard contract term. Based on the authorization of § 6:105, regarding contracts that involve a consumer and a business entity, a case may be brought in court for the annulment of an unfair contract term that has been incorporated into a contract by third persons or organizations defined by the Act.[8] Concerning the regulation of public interest actions relating to unfair standard contract terms, the new Civil Code incorporates the enumeration of organizations entitled to file a public interest action, further specifying and supplementing this list.[9] The earlier Civil Code did not include such a list, which instead was contained in a separate Act. Those entitled to bring a public interest action under the present regulation include: public prosecutors, government ministers, autonomous organs of public administration, government agencies, the heads of the central administrative offices, chambers of economy, associations of professionals, public interest groups, associations for the protection of consumers' interests within the scope of the consumer interests they protect and organizations set up for the protection of consumers' interests under the laws of any Member

5 Kecskés & Wallacher 2012, p. 283.
6 Vékás 2013, p. 575; for more details, see Harsági 2014, p. 225.
7 Act V of 2013.
8 *Cf.* Wopera & Nagy 2010, p. 2 *et seq.*
9 Vékás 2013, p. 575.

State of the European Economic Area. Even if all the conditions for the filing of an action are met, the above-mentioned organizations have no obligation to commence a lawsuit; they are only entitled to do so. In these proceedings the court annuls the unfair standard contract term with regard to any parties involved in a contractual relationship with the user of the unfair term (with *erga omnes* effect). The expression 'any parties' does not solely mean persons who are parties to already existing contracts, but also all parties entering into a contract in the future. At the same time, it means only parties deemed to be consumers may do so having regard to the fact that the right to file a public interest action is restricted to consumer relationships.[10] Organizations entitled to public interest litigation have the right to bring an action merely for a declaration of the unfairness of standard contract terms and, therefore, their annulment. However, they have no right to apply to the court for a declaration of the invalidity of a specific contract concluded between the user of the unfair term and a consumer, because these organizations are not involved in the legal relationship giving rise to the legal action.[11] Therefore, the legal consequences of invalidity established by the court in the framework of public interest litigation are to be enforced by the consumer as the injured party individually, in an individual action.[12]

The specified organizations initiate these lawsuits - based on statutory authorization - in their own name, but in the interests of consumers, which is indicated by the name of these proceedings as established in the academic literature (public interest actions). However, neither the person nor the number of consumers is identified in the proceedings. Since these organizations are not subject to the disputed contract term, the real legal dispute is not between them and the party using the contract term, but between the latter and the consumers. The effect of the judgment delivered in such actions extends to all the parties entering into a contract with the user of the annulled term, which means that the effect of a judgment dismissing such a claim also extends to them too. Therefore, if it can be established that an organization having the right to file a public interest action has already instituted proceedings against the same defendant for a declaration of the unfairness of the same contract term based on the same cause or if a final judgment has been delivered relating to the same subject matter, then a statement of claim filed by another organization entitled to file a public interest lawsuit must be dismissed without the issue of a summons (*in limine litis*) or the proceedings must be discontinued. All this does not prevent the organization entitled to file a public interest action from intervening in the pending public interest proceedings on the side of the claimant to assist him or her with winning the lawsuit. Under the Civil Code, the party's legal interest attached to this must be regarded as given.[13] This

10 Source: Bírósági Határozatok, 2010, No. 149; Wellmann 2013b, p. 166-167.

11 Source: 3/2011. *PK vélemény a fogyasztói szerződéssel kapcsolatos közérdekű kereset elbírálásának egyes kérdéseiről*; Source: Bírósági Határozatok 2012, No. 3.

12 Wellmann 2013a, p. 156.

13 Source: 3/2011. *PK vélemény a fogyasztói szerződéssel kapcsolatos közérdekű kereset elbírálásának egyes kérdéseiről*. Source: Bírósági Határozatok 2012, No. 3.

interpretation was developed by judicial practice concerning the text of the earlier Civil Code, but these ideas also apply to the new Civil Code.

Moreover, pursuant to § 6:105(3) of the Civil Code, a public interest action may be brought to have a standard contract term that has been defined for consumer contracts and made available to the general public declared unfair by the court, regardless of whether the term or condition in question has in fact been applied or not. If the court finds the contested standard term and condition unfair, in its judgment it will prohibit the person who has published the term from using it. The action may be brought against any party that publicly recommends the use of any unfair standard contract terms and conditions. This preventive public interest action under § 6:105(4) of the Civil Code may also be initiated against the person who publicly recommends the use of an unfair standard contract term that has been made available to the general public. In this case, the judgment will contain an injunction prohibiting the party from recommending that contract term.[14]

The court orders the user of the contract term to have a notice published at his or her own expense about the fact that the contract term has been declared unfair by the court. The wording of the public notice and the mode of publication should be specified by the court. It should contain the precise description of the contract term in question, an indication that it has been found unfair and arguments proving its unfair nature. The annulment does not affect those contracts that have been performed prior to their being contested. This rule is applicable even in situations where the court has established the unfairness of a standard contract term that has not been used in a contract before. Publication must be arranged by and at the expense of the person who has made the general contract term concerned available or who has recommended it for use.

Proceedings for the annulment of standard contract terms fall within the competence of courts of justice (formerly county courts) having regard to the complexity of these actions (§ 23(1) point k of the Hungarian Code of Civil Procedure).[15]

The new Civil Code has brought a series of essential changes in the field of the *actio popularis*, the most conspicuous of which is the insertion of § 6:106, which has extended the regulation of public interest actions relating to unfair contract terms also to lawsuits between business entities. These provisions conform to the rules laid down by Directive 2011/7/EU. The transposition of this Directive has been carried out, for example, by the provisions of § 6:106, Subsec. (1) of which, in compliance with Article 7(4) and (5), ensures that an organization representing the interests of business entities may also contest – as an unfair standard contract term – a term incorporated into a contract between business parties relating to the deadline for performance of the payment obligation, the amount of interest on late payment and the due date for payment of that interest, if that term is deemed contrary to good faith and fair dealing, and as such regarded as unilaterally and unjustifiably

14 Wellmann 2013a, p. 157.
15 Act III of 1952.

unfair to the obligee business association. This option is available alongside the obligee's own right to challenge the contract term as unfair.[16] As regards the payment deadline for monetary obligations that have been incorporated as a standard contract term into a contract between a contracting authority and a party other than a contracting authority, the organization representing the interests of business entities may also apply to the court (a) to declare null and void the part exceeding 60 days, where a term lays down a deadline of more than 60 days or (b) to annul – as being unfair – a term laying down a deadline not exceeding 60 days, where it has been defined as being in conflict with what is laid down in the Act relating to contracting authorities and it is deemed contrary to good faith and fair dealing, and as such regarded as unilaterally and unjustifiably unfair to the party other than a contracting authority. If the petition is deemed well founded by the court, the court will declare the term void or invalid with regard to all parties entering into a contract with the user of that term. The declaration of nullity or invalidity does not apply to contracts that have already been performed.

The organization representing the interests of business entities may request the court to declare unfair or null and void a standard contract term referred to in Subsecs. (1) and (2) that has been defined for contracts and made available to the general public, regardless of whether the term in question has in fact been used or not. If the court finds the contested standard contract term unfair and declares it null and void, it will prohibit the person having published the term from using it.

In the proceedings the court orders, at the request of the person enforcing a claim, that the person by whom the contract term has been used, published and recommended for use shall, at his or her own expense, arrange for the publication of a notice about the fact that the contract term has been found unfair and declared null and void. The wording of the public notice and the mode of its publication are decided by the court. The public notice shall contain the precise description of the contract term in question, an indication that it was found unfair and that it was annulled, including the reasons and the arguments in support of such finding.

The organization representing the interests of business entities may apply to the court to declare null and void: (a) a standard contract term incorporated into a contract between business entities that excludes the obligation to pay interest on late payments or excludes or limits the obligation to cover the costs incurred in connection with the recovery of claims; (b) a standard contract term incorporated into a contract between a contracting authority and a business entity other than a contracting authority that defines – as the deadline for the payment of interest on late payments – a date different from the one laid down in the Act concerning the performance of monetary obligations, or excludes or limits the obligation to provide compensation for recovery costs relating to interest on late payment and/or other claims (Civil Code, § 6:106).

The two main fields of public interest litigation share the common feature that public interest claim enforcement refers to taking action against unfair standard

16 Wellmann 2013a, p. 157-158.

contract terms with *erga omnes* effect. However, there is a difference that in a legal relationship with a consumer, the legal consequence of the unfair standard contract term is nullity, while in legal relations between business entities, the possibility of public interest claim enforcement in some cases means only a right to challenge the contract term (which is a significant difference because of the fixed time limits available for challenging a contract term).[17]

## 2.2. *Further Means of Consumer Protection*

The Hungarian Consumer Protection Act[18] regulates further means of claim enforcement. Under § 38, a consumer protection authority or the associations for the protection of consumers' interests may file a case on behalf of consumers against any person who was found guilty by the consumer protection authority of any violation of the consumer protection regulations set out under Sec. 45/A, where such illegal action affects a wide range of - personally unknown - consumers whose general identity, however, can be established relying on the circumstances of the infringement. Under § 45/A, with the exception of the regulations pertaining to the conclusion, validity, legal effects and termination of contracts, the consumer protection authority shall monitor compliance with and shall take action in the event of any infringement of the provisions of this Act and other decrees adopted for the implementation of this Act relating to (a) marketing and the provision of services, (b) the protection of children and young people, (c) consumer groups, (d) complaints handling and customer service, and the employment of a consumer relations officer, and (e) the business entity's obligation to file a response in proceedings before the arbitration board. It also monitors compliance with the provisions set out in other specific legislation pertaining to consumer protection and shall take action in the event of any infringement. In addition to this, the consumer protection authority shall monitor compliance with the provisions relating to (a) goods supplied to consumers, (b) the quality, composition, packaging of products supplied to consumers, (c) the measurement of goods offered and supplied to consumers, and the official price and the mandatory price of such goods, (d) the handling of consumer complaints, (e) warranty claims and associated guarantees relating to certain aspects of the sale of consumer goods, (f) enforcing the principle of equal treatment in connection with the supply of products and services, and (g) consumer information; and it shall take action in the event of any infringement.

No action may be brought after three years following the time of commission of the aforementioned infringement (or following the statutory limitation period prescribed in a separate Act for the civil claims of consumers, if this is shorter). Failure to comply with this time limit results in loss of the right to file a claim.

If, with respect to the consumers affected by the infringement, the legal grounds for the claim and the amount of damages demanded or the overall contents

17 Wellmann 2013a, p. 155.
18 Act CLV of 1997.

of the claim in the case of other claims can be clearly established, the consumer protection authority or the associations for the protection of consumers' interests may request the court to award such claims and order the business entity in question to satisfy these claims or, alternatively, they may request the court to establish the fact of the infringement with regard to all consumers indicated in the claim. If according to the court's decision the violation was established with regard to all consumers indicated in the claim, the consumers affected may file a claim against the infringer, and they are only required to verify the extent of the damage and to prove that the damage is the direct result of that infringement.

The court's decision shall specify the consumers who are affected by the violation and who are therefore entitled to demand satisfaction based on the judgment, and shall determine the data required for their identification. In the case of an action for a declaratory judgment, the court does not simply establish the fact of the infringement, but also defines the circle of affected consumers. Thus the judgment does not have *erga omnes* effect, but applies only to the specified circle of consumers.[19]

If the decision, apart from having established the violation, also orders the business entity to provide satisfaction for a specific claim, the business entity shall be required to satisfy the claim of the consumer on whose behalf the judgment was awarded. If the consumer's claim is not satisfied voluntarily, the consumer may request judicial enforcement. The court (upon the plaintiff's request) may order the business entity to take measures to have a public notice published at its own expense. The wording of the public notice and the mode of publication shall be decided by the court. Publication shall include, in particular, the posting of the notice in a newspaper of nationwide circulation, or on the Internet (Consumer Protection Act, § 38). The Act does not enumerate the possible modes of publication. Apart from dailies with nationwide circulation it mentions only the Internet, but in cases of high importance, publication may take place also through a television channel.[20]

The enforcement of a claim through a consumer protection authority or association does not affect the consumer's right to enforce an individual claim against the infringer separately.

The entitlement to file for legal action shall be afforded to all qualified organizations established under the laws of any Member State of the European Economic Area - with respect to the consumer interest they protect - that are included in the list published in the Official Journal of the European Communities pursuant to Article 4(3) of Directive 2009/22/EC of the European Parliament and of the Council, provided that the claim for which the action is filed pertains to the infringement of a regulation transposing European Union legislation listed in Annex I to Directive 2009/22/EC of the European Parliament and of the Council

19 Sík-Simon 2013, p. 2.
20 Benedek 2007, p. 798-799.

where the ensuing proceedings fall within the jurisdiction of the consumer protection authority (Sec. 38, Consumer Protection Act).

Where the illegal actions of a business entity affect a wide range of (personally unknown) consumers whose general identity, however, can be established relying on the circumstances of the infringement, or where such illegal actions cause substantial harm, and the proceedings fall within the jurisdiction of the court, the public prosecutor or the associations for the protection of consumers' interests shall have the right to bring action. If the proceedings relating to the infringement of a regulation transposing European Union legislation listed in Annex I to Directive 2009/22/EC of the European Parliament and of the Council fall within the jurisdiction of the court, the entitlement to file for legal action shall be afforded to all qualified organizations established under the laws of any Member State of the European Economic Area - with respect to the consumer interests they protect - that are included in the list published in the Official Journal of the European Communities pursuant to Article 4(3) of Directive 2009/22/EC of the European Parliament and of the Council. The organizations entitled to bring action may also demand: (a) the termination of the infringement and the prohibition of the offender from any further violation of the law; and (b) the termination of the injurious situation and the restoration of the previous state. Such actions do not affect the consumers' right to bring civil action independently against the infringer (Sec. 39, Consumer Protection Act).

Under § 10(1) of the Act on Chambers of Economy,[21] in order to establish, preserve and improve the security of business transactions and the fairness of market practices, chambers of economy shall issue a warning to member business entities pursuing their business activities in violation of the interests of consumers and thereby damaging and endangering the reputation of a wide range of business entities, and publish this warning in situations and ways defined by their code of ethics, or in more serious or repeated cases they may initiate the taking of measures to suspend the economic activities of the business entity for a specific period. If the economic activity of the business entity also has a detrimental impact on a broad range of consumers or is of a substantial magnitude, they may take legal action with a view to enforcing a civil claim on behalf of consumers.

## 2.3. *Actions against Financial Service Providers*

The Act on the National Bank of Hungary[22] adopted by Parliament in 2013 contains a chapter on actions in the public interest, which constitutes a novelty in this field. In the performance of its tasks, the National Bank of Hungary (MNB) may file a civil action on behalf of consumers against a financial service provider that is engaged in any violation of the provisions of specific Acts and, furthermore, that is allegedly engaged in the use of any unfair standard contract terms as defined by the Civil

21 Act CXXXI of 1999.
22 Act CXXXIX of 2013.

Code in connection with its activities, where such illegal action affects a wide range of consumers that can be established relying on the circumstances of the infringement.

No action may be brought after the end of three years from the time the infringement was committed. Failure to comply with this time limit shall result in the loss of the right to file a claim. For continuous infringements, the time limit shall commence at the moment the infringement is terminated. Where an infringement consists in the failure to terminate a situation or circumstance, the aforementioned period shall not commence as long as such situation or circumstance continues to exist.

Where, with respect to the consumers affected by the infringement, the legal basis of the claim and the amount of damages demanded or – in the case of other claims – the overall contents of the claim can be clearly established irrespective of the individual circumstances of the consumers affected by the infringement, the MNB may request the court to order the defendant to satisfy such claims, or failing this, it may request the court to establish the fact of the infringement with regard to all of the consumers indicated in the claim. If the court's decision established the fact of the infringement with regard to all of the consumers indicated in the claim, the consumers affected shall be required, in an action filed against the financial service provider, to prove exclusively the amount of their damage and the existence of a causal link between the infringement and such damage.

In its judgment, the court shall specify the group of consumers with respect to whom the fact of the infringement was established and who therefore are entitled to demand performance of the court order, and shall determine the data required for their identification. In its ruling, the court may authorize the MNB to publish the court's decision in a national daily newspaper or to make it available to the general public by means consistent with the nature of the infringement at the infringer's expense.

If in its judgment the court, in addition to establishing the infringement, also ordered the defendant to provide satisfaction for a specific claim, the infringer shall be required to satisfy the claim of the consumer in compliance with the judgment. In the absence of voluntary compliance, the consumer may request judicial enforcement of the court judgment.

The action brought by the MNB does not affect the consumer's right to file a civil action independently against the infringer in accordance with the rules of civil law.

The right to file a civil action is afforded to (a) associations for the protection of consumers' interests under the Act on consumer protection and (b) all authorized entities established under the laws of any Member State of the European Economic Area that are included in the list published in the Official Journal of the European Union pursuant to Article 4(3) of Directive 2009/22/EC of the European Parliament and of the Council – with respect to the consumer interests they protect – provided that the claim to be enforced by the legal action pertains to the infringement of legal provisions transposing EU directives (§ 164).

### 2.4. *Other Areas of Collective Redress under the Hungarian Regulations in Force*

In the present Hungarian regulations, one may find a similar possibility for collective claim enforcement in the field of competition law, the protection of the environment and nature, equal treatment, equal opportunity and in legal instruments protecting the interests of non-smokers,[23] the majority of which are being dealt with in detail in other chapters of this volume.

## 3. On the Lack of Group Litigation

As has been pointed out, collective redress in Hungary is limited today to a certain narrow area. In the case of mass damages (which are not governed by the regulations listed above), the joinder of parties or joinder of actions may provide a solution for the enforcement of claims, or there is the possibility to resort to the legal instrument of assignment (if the preconditions for this are met).[24] However, these solutions may also give rise to numerous difficulties that may hinder collective claim enforcement. For example, the permissive joinder of parties renders possible, to some extent, the collective enforceability of diffuse interests. At the same time, the legal framework for this is limited: it is a disadvantage of the joinder of parties that although the parties may authorize one common legal representative, this does not (necessarily) happen in practice. Hence they will not speak with one voice. The claims remain independent, and the acts of one party do not necessarily have an effect on the other parties.

## 4. Outlook for the Future

The experiences of the last several years (serious environmental pollution cases, increasing consumer protection problems) are forcing the experts to rethink the adequacy of the present regulation relating to multi-party litigation in Hungary. The result of this reconsideration could be the expansion by the Legislature of the scope of group litigation. This process may receive a further impetus from the European legislator. It is still an open question as to how far one must (or may) go with the amendments during the codification process. Obviously, the answer to this question could be given only following a thorough comparative study carried out in the area of law and in the economic analysis of law.

The question as to which direction the Hungarian legislator should set out is not an easy one to answer. It may be stated, though, that under the present regulation the *actio popularis* designed for the enforcement of the public interest fulfils its role, but there is a need for the introduction of new procedural means to supplement it. The kind of instrument that is needed is one that would be suitable

23 For more details, see Harsági 2014, p. 230-232.

24 For more details, see Harsági 2014, p. 234-236.

for managing the cases that cannot be managed today due to their dimensions or that appear in the justice system in a scattered form, one by one (in the absence of procedural solutions), in spite of the fact that it might be justified to 'join' these cases. It seems also indispensable to extend the scope of regulation to claims of negative expected value, which cannot be enforced effectively by the present means (and therefore often remain unenforced).

Future legal regulation must be elaborated also having regard to Recommendation 2013/396/EU.[25]

The limits and main principles of the new regulation could be constituted by the following. Priority should be given to new solutions of collective redress over individual lawsuits. Under the new regulation, the possibility to form a group (or class) would be restricted to claimants. The basis for group formation should be defined taking into consideration questions of fact and law and the time factor. Lawyers would have to bear a higher administrative burden (e.g. they would keep a register of those who opt in; they would obtain the documents, initiate a person's classification as a group member – the latter would be checked by the court in the final analysis). It is also to be taken into account that the opt-out system requires less administration, which could be an important aspect with regard to cases of a lower expected value. Thought must be given to whether it is possible to define a maximum and/or minimum amount as a limit.

The future regulation could basically be founded on the opt-in model, but in cases where the value of the claim is so low (with respect to the individual cases) that it is not worth the higher administrative costs of the opt-in system – as indicated above – the system must be supplemented with a model based on opt-out. The former (opt-in) system would serve the enforcement of claims that appear in the system today as well, but which cannot be enforced with sufficient effectiveness within the framework of present procedures. Here the primary aim would be to reduce the workload of the courts by joining the appropriate cases. The latter category could cover cases that do not even appear in the justice system at present. These are claims the enforcement of which is given up by law-seekers due to the lack of effective procedural means. Concerning claims of lesser value, one must have regard to the fact that there are some effective systems in the present regulation as well (e.g. the order for payment procedure); therefore, proposals would extend only to cases which do not appear in the present system. Consequently, the new regulation would be applicable to specific areas of substantive law, for example, relating to the claims of parties adversely affected in cartel cases, actions for compensation for damage resulting from unfair contract terms and data protection claims.

For both models, registration as a lawsuit would be based on the court's permission and there would be increased judicial control at numerous stages of the

25 Commission recommendation of 11 June 2013 on common principles for injunctive and compensatory collective redress mechanisms in the Member States concerning violations of rights granted under Union Law (2013/396/EU), *OJ* L201 of 26 July 2013, p. 60.

proceedings (e.g. the court would decide on admissibility, it would approve settlements). From the aspect of jurisdiction, some sort of concentration would be absolutely necessary. A system oriented toward court settlements should be developed, which would be both encouraged and controlled by the judge. Prior to approving the settlement, the judge would have to examine it for compliance not only with legal provisions, but also with the interests of the group or class.

These ideas could serve as a foundation for a future Hungarian regulation.

## Bibliography

**Benedek 2007**
Benedek, K., 'A szerződés megkötése', in Gellért, G. (ed.), *A Polgári Törvénykönyv magyarázata,* Vol. 1, Budapest: Complex, 2007, p. 750-831.

**Harsági 2014**
Harsági, V., ,Kollektiver Rechtsschutz - Ungarn und der Einfluss der Europäischen Entwicklung', in Schulze, G. (ed.), *Europäisches Privatrecht in Vielfalt geeint - Der modernisierte Zivilprozess in Europa/Droit privé européen: l'unité dans la diversité - Le procès civil modernisé en Europe,* München: Sellier, 2014, p. 221-237.

**Kecskés & Wallacher 2012**
Kecskés, L. & Wallacher, L., 'A csoportos jogérvényesítés formái a választottbíráskodás keretében a magyar jogban', in Kecskés, L. & Lukács, J. (eds.), *A választottbírók könyve,* Budapest: HVG-Orac, 2012, p. 280-306.

**Kengyel & Harsági 2013**
Kengyel, M. & Harsági, V., 'Hungary - Civil Law', in Eliantionio, M., Backes, Ch.W., Van Rhee, C.H., Spronken, T. & Berlee, A. (eds.), *Standing up for Your Right(s) in Europe. A Comparative Study on Legal Standing (Locus Standi) before the EU and Member State Courts,* Cambridge/Antwerp/Portland: Intersentia, 2013, p. 322-344.

**Kulski 2011**
Kulski, R., 'Class Proceedings in Poland', XIV World Conference: International Association of Procedural Law, Heidelberg, 25-30 July 2011, [online] <http://iapl-2011-congress.com/Sites/papers.html>.

**Małgorazata 2010**
Małgorazata, K., 'Gruppenklagen bald in Polen', *Deutsch-Polnische Juristen-Zeitschrift*, 2010, Vol. 2, p. 24-25.

**Sík-Simon 2013**
Sík-Simon, R., '*A környezetvédelmi törvény kollektív jogérvényesítéssel kapcsolatos törvény kollektív jogérvényesítéssel kapcsolatos szabályozási hiányosságai', Manuscript*, 2013, p. 1-3.

**Stürner 2009**
Stürner, R., 'International Class Actions from a German Point of View', in Stürner, R. & Kawano, M. (eds.), *Current Topics of International Litigation,* Tübingen: Mohr Siebeck, 2009, p. 107-117.

**Vékás 2013**
Vékás, L., 'A szerződés általános szabályai', in Vékás, L. (ed.), *A Polgári Törvénykönyv magyarázatokkal,* Budapest: Complex, 2013, p. 543-588.

**Wellmann 2013a**
Wellmann, G., 'Az érvénytelenség', in Petrik, F. (ed.), *Polgári jog. Kommentár a gyakorlat számára. III. Kötet,* Budapest: HVG-Orac, 2013, p. 96-184.

**Wellmann 2013b**
Wellmann, G., 'Az érvénytelenség', in Wellmann, G. (ed.), *Polgári jog - Kötelmi jog. Az új Ptk. magyarázata. V/VI,* Budapest: HVG-Orac, 2013, p. 113-192.

**Wopera & Nagy 2010**
Wopera, Z. & Nagy, A., '"Class Action". National Report of Hungary', 18th International Congress on Comparative Law, Washington D.C., 2010, Manuscript, p. 1-7.

T. Tóth
P. Szilágyi

## PRIVATE ENFORCEMENT IN HUNGARY WITH A VIEW ON CLASS ACTIONS*

## 1. Introduction

Group litigation still has a long way to go before it can exercise its full preventive force against infringers of competition rules in Hungary. As we will show below, neither the Hungarian Competition Authority nor public interest representative bodies and not even consumers are in a position to bring damages claims in competition cases successfully and effectively. However, in

> modern-day societies, when citizens are confronted with particularly complex administrative decisions, recourse to collective bodies such as associations is one of the accessible means, sometimes the only means, available to them whereby they can defend their particular interests effectively. Moreover, the standing of associations to bring legal proceedings in defence of their members' interests is recognised by the legislation of most European countries.[1]

Sec. 92 of the Hungarian Competition Act (HCA) allows the Hungarian Competition Authority (in Hungarian: *Gazdasági Versenyhivatal*, or: GVH) to bring representative actions before the courts. According to paragraph (1):

> [T]he Hungarian Competition Authority may file an action to enforce civil law claims of consumers where activities infringing the provisions of this Act, or unlawful practices in relation to which the Hungarian Competition Authority has the power to proceed under UCPA, of an undertaking concern a large group of individually not known consumers that can be defined based on the circumstances of the infringement, though the identity of the individual consumers is not known.

* This chapter was written within the framework of OTKA (Hungarian Scientific Research Fund) research project (registration number K-105559).

1 ECtHR, *Gorraiz Lizarraga and others v Spain* (App. No. 62543/00), § 38, 27 April 2004.

It is interesting to note that not only injunctions but also damages can be awarded. It is the judge who defines the group; the 'individualization' of the plaintiffs occurs only in the enforcement stage.

There are no other legal instruments under Hungarian competition law that would allow for collective redress. There are no representative actions by public bodies nor class actions, just the usual association of plaintiffs ('joinder'), which is not an effective way to organize mass claims cases. The position of the Hungarian government expressed on the European Commission's questionnaire (2011) showed serious concerns against the introduction of a US-style class action and opted for the promotion of alternative dispute resolution methods.[2]

## 2. The Proposed Directive on Actions for Damages

At the time of the submission of this chapter, following an eight-year-long discussion, the proposed directive on damages claims in competition cases[3] has been accepted by the European Parliament with some amendments in the first reading and the draft directive is waiting for the Council of the European Union's deliberation. The European Commission is very optimistic that it will be adopted by the EU institutions soon.[4] Once adopted, Member States will have two years to implement the directive in their national legal systems.

On 11 June 2013, the EU Commission published a proposal for a directive on how claims for damages under EU antitrust rules can be brought.[5] The suggested measures feature expanded access to evidence for claimants, rules on limitation periods, rules confirming the respondent's ability to claim the passing-on defence and rules on the quantification of harm. The directive covers both individual and collective actions, the latter being currently available in only about half of the EU Member States.

Alexander Italianer, Director-General for Competition, points out that over the past eight years only 25 per cent of the antitrust infringements found by the Commission were followed by civil claims, with most of them brought in the UK,

2 One of the typical sources for guidance on experience in private competition litigation is the US practice. Looking, however, to the other side of the Atlantic has its own dangers. See Lande 2014.

3 Directive of the European Parliament and of the Council on certain rules governing actions for damages under national law for infringements of the competition law provisions of the Member States and of the European Union, COM(2013) 0404. On the road to the draft directive, see e.g. Ashton *et al.* 2013, p. 136-146 or Delatre 2011, p. 29-58 and Hegymegi-Barakonyi and Horányi 2013.

4 European Commission - IP/14/455 - 17/04/2014.

5 The Commission adopted a non-binding recommendation encouraging Member States to set up collective redress mechanisms for victims of violations of EU law in general, including the antitrust rules. The third element of the package is another soft law instrument, this time a communication on the quantification of antitrust harm supplemented by a detailed practical guide. See the elements of the package on: <http://ec.europa.eu/competition/antitrust/-actionsdamages/documents.html> (last accessed on 20 June 2014).

Germany and the Netherlands where procedures are perceived to be more favourable. He emphasizes that there are two aims: (i) to remove existing barriers to effective redress for victims of antitrust infringements and (ii) to regulate the interaction between public and private enforcement of EU antitrust rules, in particular to protect the effectiveness of EU and national leniency programmes.[6]

The directive aims to achieve the following:

- It is assumed that a cartel causes damage in the form of a relative price increase; it will be for the cartel members to rebut this presumption.
- Cartel members are liable to pay not only the actual damage caused, but also the profits lost and appropriate interest from the time the damage occurred (principle of full compensation).
- Infringers may invoke the passing-on defence, i.e. that their direct customers offset at least a part of the overcharge resulting from the infringement by raising the prices they charged to their own customers. However, this defence will be unavailable if it is 'legally impossible' for the persons to whom the overcharge is passed on to bring a claim for damages.
- Leniency applicants with full immunity will only be liable for harm to their own direct or indirect customers (exception from the general rule of collective liability), unless the injured parties were not able to obtain full compensation from the other infringers.
- Parties are encouraged to agree on compensating the harm through consensual dispute resolution mechanisms, such as out-of-court settlement, arbitration and mediation.
- A claimant may obtain a court order for the disclosure of evidence that is in the hands of other parties or third parties if the claimant can show that the evidence is relevant to substantiate its claim.
- Leniency statements and other submissions prepared by the company during the competition law proceedings admitting guilt should not be used in civil actions against the companies that made them.
- The decision of National Competition Authorities (NCAs) will be binding on courts.

## 3. The European Way: Collective Redress instead of Class Actions

In 2013, the European Commission adopted recommendations on cross-border collective redress.[7] One of the considerations behind the document was the furthering of competition group litigation.[8] The Commission urges Member States

6 See Italianer 2013, available at: <http://ec.europa.eu/competition/speeches/text/-sp2013_06_en.pdf> (last accessed on 20 June 2014).

7 2013/396/EU, Commission Recommendation of 11 June 2013 on common principles for injunctive and compensatory collective redress mechanisms in the Member States concerning violations of rights granted under Union Law, *OJ* L201 of 26 July 2013, p. 60-65.

8 See *ibidem*, Preamble (3).

to adopt and introduce collective redress mechanisms at the national level for both injunctive and compensatory relief[9] in the form of representative actions by representative bodies and/or public authorities. The wording of these documents carries a clear message: European policy makers are not fond of copying the American type of class actions. The broader phrase of 'collective actions' is preferred, possibly including class actions, but expressly excluding its most efficient form, opt-out class actions.

The recommendation is an excellent example showing how difficult the introduction of collective actions in EU Member States is. Hungary has already introduced many important suggestions of the recommendation. The GVH is authorized to bring representative actions; the legal costs of the winning party have to be reimbursed (loser pays principle); the rules on legal representation fees do not facilitate unnecessary litigation; there are no contingency fees,[10] no punitive damages; follow-on actions are possible; etc. Despite this, even though a very committed NCA, the GVH basically refrains from such claims, either due to lack of resources or interest in bringing a case, or both. There has been only one case so far: the Municipal Court ruled in May 2012 that some provisions of the general terms of contracts drafted by Ingatlandepo, the operator of a real estate website, were null and void. This case, which ended in a court decision imposing a fine of HUF 6 million for misleading advertising, did not involve damages claims.

Even if the proposed directive is adopted, the lack of opt-out class actions and of contingency fees will be – according to recent empirical studies – a great barrier for the wide adoption of the 'class-action' type of litigation.[11]

## 4. Experience in Hungary Regarding Private Enforcement – Stand-alone Actions

There have been some cases before national courts in Hungary where the antitrust rules were used either as a sword or as a shield. The number of cases is, however, very limited (less than 20),[12] especially if we take into consideration that in Germany alone there were close to 2,000 cases between 2004 and 2009.[13] We assume that Hungarian courts follow the legal obligation imposed on them by Regulation 1/2003.[14] Article 15(2) of the regulation requires Member States to forward to the Commission a copy of any written national court judgment on the application of

9 *Ibidem*, Art. 2.
10 It is worth noting that one of the reasons for the successes of antitrust litigation in the US is the availability of contingency fees. See e.g. Rodger 2014b, p. 59. As the author phrases it, there is 'strong academic evidence' for this.
11 See e.g. Lande 2014, p. 6.
12 See Szilágyi 2013.
13 See Peyer 2013. For an overview of a recent report on competition litigation in EU Member States and the conclusions from the project, see Rodger 2014a.
14 Council Regulation (EC) No. 1/2003 of 16 December 2002 on the implementation of the rules on competition laid down in Arts. 81 and 82 of the Treaty, *OJ* L1 of 4 January 2003, p. 1-25.

Article 101 or 102 TFEU. These judgments must be sent 'without delay after the full written judgment is notified to the parties'. The European Commission publishes these reports,[15] but unfortunately we can only find one case from Hungary referring to a review of a GVH decision.[16]

It is obvious from the cases available at the public register of Hungarian courts[17] that most occasions where competition issues were raised in private litigation had no merit. There were just a few cases where the courts evaluated the arguments in more than a few sentences, but those considerations also lacked substantial analysis of the issues raised. Of course this is partly the result of the meritless claims of the parties, but we can also observe that some judges have only a limited knowledge of the vast amount of case law at the EU level or of the available soft-law instruments governing the application of competition law. A careful observer would also ask whether or not most of these courts followed the express obligation imposed on them by the Hungarian Competition Act in Article 88/B, para 2, which states that 'the court shall notify, without delay, the Hungarian Competition Authority of lawsuits before it, which are to be assessed under the provisions laid down in Chapters III to V of this Act'.

Without going into further detail, we can state that the courts are fairly inexperienced in the application of EU or Hungarian competition law. Below, we will explain that even if they had some notable experience, the procedural rules and the legal environment do not really favour group litigation in competition cases. These rules will, however, be further relaxed, since empirical evidence suggests that the most successful private cases have not been follow-on but stand-alone actions.[18]

## 5. Experience in Hungary Regarding Private Enforcement - Follow-on Actions

There are no published judgments on damages awarded on the basis of the infringement of competition law. The only case that reached the supreme court in Hungary - currently called the *Curia*, the Supreme Court at the time of the judgment - faltered on procedural issues, and therefore there is no reliable guidance on any substantial competition law issues relating to actions for damages.

One of the difficulties hindering collective actions in follow-on competition litigation is the time dimension: it takes years to reach a final decision. A typical cartel investigation by the GVH lasts for 2.5 to 3 years. Review courts deal with a case for another 4 to 6 years. In one clear-cut cartel case (*EGÚT*), the procedure before the courts took 4.5 years. If a preliminary rulings procedure is also involved, we might end up with more than 10 years before a final judgment is reached.

15 See here: <http://ec.europa.eu/competition/elojade/antitrust/nationalcourts/> (last accessed on 20 June 2014).

16 Case No. 7 K 34364/2006/16.

17 See <http://birosag.hu/ugyfelkapcsolati-portal/anonim-hatarozatok-tara> (last accessed on 20 June 2014).

18 Lande 2014, p. 10-11.

The situation is not better in the case of a follow-on action after a decision of the European Commission. An investigation by the Commission might take an extremely long time. Once a case reaches – and basically all the cartel cases do reach – EU courts, the General Court might deal with the case for 4 to 5 years, later the ECJ might also take additional time. After a final verdict, one must also take into account the time needed by a national court to come to a decision on the facts of the case, the amount of the damage and the causal link. One may reasonably ask: who will sue for a cartel overcharge of a 'replica shirt' knowing that the wait to receive compensation is likely to be 10 to 15 years?

## 6. Practical Difficulties with Antitrust Claims

Many cartels have a cross-border or even a global scope. In such cases private plaintiffs prefer to choose the best jurisdiction available for them to sue. According to many observers, the following criteria are of great importance to any reasonable private litigation culture in competition law:

- the court's language capabilities;
- the duration of proceedings;
- some understanding of economic reasoning; and
- the attitude towards EU law.

These factors suggest that Hungary will not draw many plaintiffs in international cases. The most likely situation is that plaintiffs in class actions in Hungary will only be consumers harmed by national cartel in this country.

Added to this is the fact that as of the date of the submission of this chapter the experience of Hungarian courts with private competition claims is rather limited, and only a handful of judges currently have an up-to-date understanding of the most important competition law developments. Generalist judges in Hungary[19] who have to deal with divorces, property claims, contractual disputes, etc. will have to make a lot of effort to familiarize themselves with notions such as cross-elasticity, comparator-based methods of harm quantification, individual data observations, interpolation and simple adjustments, regression analysis, simulation models, etc.[20]

19 We have to note that there is a general recognition of the benefits of specialist competition law tribunals in such cases. Rodger 2014b, p. 24-32.

20 For the guidance of the European Commission to the national courts, see Practical Guide: Quantifying Harm in Actions for damages based on breaches of Arts. 101 or 102 of the Treaty on the Functioning of the European Union SWD (2013) 205.

## 7. Rules Supporting Private Enforcement

This lack of a meaningful enforcement practice is surprising if one looks at just the legislative background. Several provisions of Hungarian competition law aim to further private litigation. According to Sec. 88/C of the HCA:

> [I]n the course of civil proceedings for any claim conducted against a party to a restrictive agreement between competitors aimed at directly or indirectly fixing selling prices, sharing markets or setting production or sales quotas that infringe Article 11 of this Act or Article 81 of the EC Treaty, when proving the extent of the influence that the infringement exercised on the price applied by the infringer, it shall be presumed, unless the opposite is proved, that the infringement influenced the price to an extent of ten per cent.

This was a revolutionary development some years ago, yet there have been no reported cases interpreting this rule. Even if we deem this rule beneficial,[21] there are many other factors which must be proven by the plaintiff in order to prevail. Finally, this is also only a presumption which can be rebutted, thus it simply reverses the burden of proof at the initial stage of a lawsuit.

It is interesting to note that even though the rule was intended as a 10 per cent damage presumption,[22] the actual wording of the Act refers only to price increase, which of course cannot be equated to a 10 per cent damage, one reason being the passing on of the price increase, another being the negative effect on the quantities sold at a higher cartel price.

Sec. 88/B (6) of the HCA regulates the link between public and private enforcement with a view to making the plaintiff's position more comfortable: '... the statement on the existence or absence of an infringement, made in the decision of the Hungarian Competition Authority against which no action has been filed or in the decision of the review court, shall be binding on the court hearing the lawsuit.' New rules will enter into force in July 2014, since the Curia narrowed the reach of this paragraph in a recent judgment.[23] The basic content and goal remains the same: judges deciding a private lawsuit should not contradict the public authority's final decision as to the existence or non-existence of a competition law infringement.

There is another unique provision in the HCA benefiting the leniency applicant, but at the same time restricting quick success of a follow on private lawsuit. According to Sec. 88/D of the HCA, the leniency applicant with full immunity may 'refuse to pay damages ... until the claim can be recovered from any other persons responsible for causing harm by the same infringement'. This

21 Some Member States (e.g. the UK) also considered such a presumption, but dropped the idea. See e.g. Ashton *et al.* 2013, p. 105-107.

22 This was reinforced by the representatives of the GVH at the public consultation of the amendment introducing the rule to the HCA.

23 See Hegymegi-Barakonyi & Horányi 2012. The new rules will oblige the judge to suspend the court proceedings until the GVH has come to a conclusion not challenged or approved by an administrative court.

provision may postpone the date when the plaintiff may effectively get compensation, since cartel members without a full leniency award tend to fight their case through the courts for quite a number years.

## 8. Conclusions

As Barry Rodger noted in a recently published book on the experience of private litigation in EU Member States:

> [H]istorically a range of institutional factors and mechanisms have combined to ensure that private enforcement of US antitrust law is effective. These are the wider litigation culture, the significant period of development of antitrust law and economics and the specific characteristics of US civil procedure: the rules on discovery, funding of actions, the availability of class action (and modification) by the courts of the legal position in relation to issues such as the passing-on defence and standing for indirect purchasers.[24]

Looking at these factors we can see that many of them are not present in Hungary to the extent that would be necessary to reach the threshold to induce a flourishing competition litigation environment.

In our opinion, the national courts in Hungary do not deliver judgments fast enough to make consumers interested in bringing small claims cases. The courts lack the capabilities to shorten delivery times mainly due to legal rules, but also due to practical considerations in dealing directly with complex economic arguments in complex competition damages cases. They also have only a limited possibility to inform themselves directly about EU case law and practice.[25]

To sum up: we have some doubts about whether even more sophisticated procedural rules favouring antitrust damages litigation would lead to more cases before Hungarian courts, even if the legislator adopted more rules to further that goal.[26] The introduction of US-type class actions would change the landscape and the litigation culture in a hardly predictable way, but only if procedural rules relating to the financing of these class actions were also carefully prepared. That, however, would require a significant shift among Hungarian legal scholars and judges, away from the precept of providing full compensation to injured persons, to the goal of taking away the unlawful enrichment from the cartel members (and compensating the victims as far as possible).

24 Rodger 2014a, p. 5.

25 Only 16 antitrust judgements prior to 2004 are available in Hungarian and basically none of the lengthy European Commission decisions. There are, however, some case law books in Hungarian that ease the pain a bit.

26 E.g. the 10 per cent price increase presumption rule based on Art. 88/C of the HCA.

## Bibliography


**Ashton et al. 2013**
Ashton, D., Henry, D., Maier-Rigaud, F. & Schwalbe, U., *Competition Damages Actions in the EU*, Cheltenham: Edward Elgar, 2013

**Delatre 2011**
Delatre, J.G., 'Beyond the White Paper: Rethinking the Commission's Proposal on Private Antitrust Litigation', *Competition Law Review*, 2011, Vol. 8(1), p. 29-58.

**Hegymegi-Barakonyi & Horányi 2012**
Hegymegi-Barakonyi, Z. & Horányi, M., 'A Gazdasági Versenyhivatal határozatainak kötõereje polgári perekben', *Versenytükör*, 2012, Vol. VIII(2), p. 18-21.

**Hegymegi-Barakonyi & Horányi 2013**
Hegymegi-Barakonyi, Z. & Horányi, M., 'A Bizottság versenyjogi jogsértéseken alapuló kártérítési perekre vonatkozó irányelvtervezete', *Versenytükör*, 2013, Vol. IX(2), p. 4-18.

**Italianer 2013**
Italianer, A., 'Competition Law within a Framework of Rights and the Commission's Proposal for a Directive on Antitrust Damage Actions', 12th Annual Conference of the Association of European Competition Law Judges (AECLJ), Luxembourg, 14 June 2013, <http://ec.europa.eu/competition/speeches/-text/sp2013_06_en.pdf>.

**Lande 2014**
Lande, R.H., 'The Proposed Damages Directive: The Real Lessons from the United States', *CPI Antitrust Chronicle*, 2012, Vol. 2, p. 2-12.

**Peyer 2013**
Peyer, S., 'Germany – Comparative Private Enforcement & Consumer Redress in the EU', in Rodger, B. (ed.), *Application of competition law in the national courts of the European Union Member States*, 2013, <www.clcpecreu.co.uk/pdf/final/-Germany%20report.pdf>.

**Rodger 2014a**
Rodger, B., *Competition Law, Comparative Private Enforcement and Collective Redress across the EU*, Alphen a/d Rijn: Kluwer Law International, 2014.

**Rodger 2014b**
Rodger, B., 'Institutions and Mechanisms to Facilitate Private Enforcement', in Rodger, B. (ed.), *Competition Law, Comparative Private Enforcement and Collective Redress across the EU*, Alphen a/d Rijn: Kluwer Law International, 2014, p. 23-71.

**Szilágyi 2013**
Szilágyi, P., 'Private Enforcement of Competition Law and Stand-alone Actions in Hungary', *Global Competition Litigation Review*, 2013, Vol. 6(3), p. 136-142.

E. Silvestri

# CLASS ACTIONS IN ITALY: GREAT EXPECTATIONS, BIG DISAPPOINTMENT

## 1. Introduction

In the early 1970s, this author's *Alma Mater*, the University of Pavia, hosted the first Italian conference on the judicial enforcement of collective interests.[1] The conference was organized by the late Professor Vittorio Denti, who was the founder of the Italian school of comparative civil procedure, together with his world-wide acclaimed colleague and friend, the late Professor Mauro Cappelletti. In the years that followed, the topic of collective interests surfaced here and there in scholarly writings devoted to subjects such as environmental protection or labour law. American class actions became a popular topic to study with the view to exploring whether their example should be followed and, if so, to what extent their 'transplantation' into the Italian legal system could be possible.[2]

The interest of the academic community in the variety of problems concerning the redress of mass harms and, in general, the judicial protection of the rights and interests belonging to groups of individuals was met by the indifference of the national legislators. Later on, under the pressure of European Union institutions and in compliance with the duty to implement EU directives, collective actions for injunctive relief were provided for in the field of consumer protection, and these actions outlined the pattern to be followed in other fields, such as anti-discrimination law and environmental protection.

Only in the early 2000s did the debate on the need to provide for group actions for damages as well seem to regain momentum, as a consequence of the many financial scandals that, around the end of the last century, had originated in Italy (for example, the *Parmalat* case, just to mention one of the most infamous) and that had affected thousands of investors, both Italian and foreign. Finally, in January 2010 the statute regulating a 'class action' (*azione di classe*) available to groups of

1 See the proceedings of the conference: Facoltà di Giurisprudenza 1976.
2 See, for instance, Giussani 1996.

individuals that claim damages as compensation for the harm suffered as a consequence of the wrongdoing perpetrated by the same defendant entered into force. Around the same time, another form of collective redress first saw the light of day in the form of a special action (conventionally known in Italy as 'public class action') that groups of citizens could initiate against public bodies when they had failed to take action in spite of a specific duty to do so.

Therefore, if one looks at the Italian law currently in force, one could reach the conclusion that while it took the legislator a long time to realize the importance of devising procedural tools suitable for affording collective rights and interests appropriate levels of judicial enforcement, the time was well spent, since eventually the Italian legal system was able to offer its citizens quite a number of group actions, for both injunctive and compensatory redress. Unfortunately, though, this conclusion is based only on a theoretical evaluation of the statutes in force, that is, it is based on the appearance of the law, and not on its practical application and the results this application brings about. Appearances can be deceiving, and that holds true with reference to Italian group actions, since the assortment of legal instruments available 'on paper' is offset by an egregious lack of success of these very legal instruments.

## 2. Collective Actions for Injunctive Relief

Collective actions for injunctive relief are provided for by Italian statutes in several areas of law. In the field of consumer protection, these actions are direct 'filiations' of European Union legislation, since their introduction in the national legal system took place as implementation of several Directives issued by EU institutions, in particular the Directive on unfair terms in consumer contracts[3] and the so-called Injunctions Directive.[4] At present, the actions at issue are governed by the Italian Consumer Code; for unknown reasons, the Code distinguishes between a general model of action for injunctive relief available 'for the protection of collective interests belonging to consumers and users',[5] and a special action that consumers can bring against sellers or suppliers so as to have a court ordering the defendant to refrain from continuing to use unfair terms in the contracts professionals conclude with consumers.[6]

3 Council Directive 93/13/EEC of 5 April 1993 on unfair terms in consumer contracts, *OJ* L095, 21 April 1993, 0029–0034.

4 Directive 98/27/EC of the European Parliament and of the Council of 19 May 1998 on injunctions for the protection of consumers' interests, superseded by Directive 2009/22/EC of the European Parliament and of the Council of 23 April 2009 on injunctions for the protection of consumers' interests (Codified version), *OJ* L110, 01 May 2009, 0030–0036.

5 Consumer Code, Art. 140.

6 Consumer Code, Art. 37.

In spite of the fact that these actions have been around for almost two decades,[7] they have never been very popular, to the point that the case law is limited to a handful of decisions issued by courts of first instance but often reversed on appeal. It is hard to say why these collective actions for the protection of consumers' interests have not taken off. One may speculate that it depends on a combination of factors that one can only try to guess at: in fact, to the best knowledge of this author, no studies have looked into the reasons explaining the limited relevance of injunctive collective redress in the field of consumer law. It does not seem unconscionable to say that, to a certain degree, consumer associations are to blame for the modest success of collective actions. The associations that are accredited by the Italian Ministry of Economic Development and have standing to commence these actions are 19 (as of December 2013): it is difficult to judge whether they are too many or too few for a country of over 60 million inhabitants. What can be said with a high degree of certainty is that consumer associations are not very active in disseminating information about the judicial initiatives they could take on behalf of consumers, so that the role they play often turns out to be 'much ado about nothing': most Italians are not even aware of the existence of consumer associations, nor have they any idea of what collective actions for injunctive relief are about.

A few words on the procedural structure of these actions are in order, most of all in light of the fact that collective actions in the field of consumer protection represent a sort of general model followed in other areas of law, with some minor changes due to the specificity of the group rights at stake: as examples, one can mention the actions provided for by various statutes aimed at preventing a wide range of gender-based, race-based or religion-based discriminations, as well as statutes addressing issues concerning immigration law. Actually, it is worth mentioning also other collective actions for injunctive relief that are older than the ones in the field of consumer law, the most important one being the action for the protection afforded to employees whenever their rights as members of trade unions are infringed by the employer.[8]

Consumer collective actions are representative actions, since standing to sue is granted to the consumer associations accredited by the Ministry of Economic Development which keeps a special record of these associations. Consumer associations must meet a number of requirements as far as their bylaws, budget, and number of members are concerned; have the protection of consumers and users as their unique mission; and be organized as non-profit entities.[9] With reference to the 'special' collective action whose aim is to prevent the continued use of unfair terms in contracts concluded with consumers, professional associations and Chambers of Commerce have standing as well.

7 The Consumer Code dates back only to 2005; previously the actions at issue were governed by the Civil Code.

8 No literature in English is available on the collective actions referred to in the text, while the bibliography in Italian is extensive. Good starting points are Donzelli 2007, p. 1-16; Menchini 2008; Belli 2007; Giussani 2007, p. 132-152; Lanfranchi 2003.

9 Consumer Code, Art. 137.

Procedurally speaking, no special features are provided for. Injunctions, when granted by the court, can order the defendant (1) to refrain from any further 'acts and behaviours prejudicial to the interests of consumers and users'; (2) to adopt all the measures that are necessary to cure the prejudicial effects of past violations, keeping in mind that these measures by definition do not include any awards of damages; (3) to have a notice of the injunctive order published in national or local newspapers, when that could be useful with a view to removing or mitigating the negative effects of past violations.

Before the commencement of the judicial proceeding the parties can attempt to reach an out-of-court settlement according to the conciliation procedures set up by various entities, including the Chambers of Commerce. If a settlement is arrived at, it is made enforceable by a court order. The fact that an attempt at conciliation is provided for is interesting, since it is in line with a trend followed by the administration of Italian civil justice more and more frequently, that is, the reliance on facilitative ADRs, such as conciliation and mediation, as a way out of the problems connected with an overloaded judicial system. It is worth emphasizing that in the field of consumer collective actions at issue, conciliation procedures are optional, while at present the backdrop of Italian civil and commercial litigation at large is characterized by mandatory mediation, which means that in most lawsuits an attempt at mediation is a compulsory step the parties must take either before the beginning of adjudication or even when adjudication is already pending, if the court so orders.[10]

The injunction can be reinforced with penalties whose purpose is to foster compliance, since the penalties are incremental, so that they increase insofar as compliance is delayed or new violations take place. The amount of the penalties can range between a minimum and a maximum threshold established by the relevant regulation: the court shall determine the amount of the penalty on a case-by-case basis, having regard to the 'seriousness' of the failure to comply with the injunctive order. Penalties shall be paid into a special public fund, which is supposed to support initiatives advancing the cause of consumers. The collective settlement, too, can include penalties for the defaulting compliance with the obligations it lays down, but, in order to make the penalties operational, the interested party will have to lodge a new, special application to the court.

Italian scholars have discussed extensively the problems of the binding effects of injunctive orders issued in collective actions, on the background of the rule according to which *res iudicata* binds only the parties to a case. It is beyond the purpose of this chapter to summarize this debate, even though, by applying an unsophisticated rule of thumb, one is inclined to think that whenever the injunctive order is granted and its obligations are complied with, consumers at large (and not only those who are members of the association that initiated the lawsuit) will benefit. At the same time, it is easy to understand that if the injunctive order is

10 On Italian mediation and the problems stemming from the regulations that make it mandatory, see Silvestri & Jagtenberg 2013, p. 29-45.

served on one professional-defendant, many other professionals will remain unaffected, and therefore nothing will prevent them from perpetrating the very infringement of the consumers' rights for whose protection the first injunction has been issued.

As mentioned above, the success of collective actions for injunctive relief has not been stellar. Evidence of that can be found in a new rule adopted in 2012.[11] According to this rule, in the field of unfair terms in standard consumer contracts, the Italian Competition Authority (*Autorità Garante della Concorrenza e del Mercato-AGCM*) can take action even *ex officio* and start a special investigative procedure aimed at declaring the terms unfair so as to give public notice (for example, through national newspapers) of the results of the investigation. Public notice of 'bad behaviour' perpetrated by sellers or suppliers is supposed to deter them from further unlawful activities, but it should also encourage consumer associations to take a stand and bring the appropriate collective actions, since the findings of the Authority *per se* do not affect unfair terms, nor do they make them ineffective. In short, the idea underlying this rule seems to be that consumer associations must be somehow persuaded to be more proactive: whether this is the proper way to make consumer associations become more involved in the judicial enforcement of the rights belonging to the individuals they are expected to represent is disputable and, in any event, it does not appear that - at least to this author's knowledge - the new rule has brought about any significant changes in the cautious attitude (and limited activism) of consumer associations.

## 3. Class Actions Italian Style

Group actions for damages, a recent addition to Italian law, are officially labelled as '*azioni di classe*': the literal translation into English of the Italian name is 'class actions', which is a glaring misnomer, since the Italian actions have almost nothing in common with American class actions. As already mentioned, the rule governing them came into force at the beginning of 2010; previous versions of the rule - Article 140-*bis* of the Consumer Code - are not worth examining due to the fact that they only existed on paper, and never became applicable law. The rule was significantly amended in 2012, probably with the view to making it more 'palatable' and user-friendly. Unfortunately, class actions Italian-style were born with incurable defects that reforms may somewhat mitigate, but not correct completely.[12]

In order to clarify the reasons why this author thinks that the legal instrument devised by the Italian legislator for compensatory collective redress is nothing but 'a damp squib',[13] data seem more enlightening than words.[14] Since January 2010 (and

11 Consumer Code, Art. 37-*bis*.

12 On class actions for damages, rivers of ink have been written by Italian scholars. Luckily for readers not proficient in the language of Dante Alighieri, a few references in English exist: see, for instance, Quarta 2012, paras 15.01-15.40; Caponi 2011, p. 1-17; Nashi 2010, p. 147-172; Silvestri 2009, p. 138-148.

13 The expression is borrowed from Hodges 2014, p. 67.

as of April 2014) 40 actions have been commenced; 15 have been declared inadmissible at a preliminary stage (a sort of stage for the certification of the action), nine have been declared admissible; 23 are still pending; and only one has been decided on the merits, in February 2013. The first judgment finding for the class (if you are willing to define as a class a group of 12 individuals only) concerned an all-inclusive vacation package to Zanzibar;[15] the action was brought against the tour operator that had sold the vacation package. The damages awarded to the plaintiff and the remaining class members who joined the suit (since Italy has adopted an opt-in system, as it will be explained later on) were strictly compensatory.

In August 2013, the press reported the news that, in another class action for damages, an appellate court had reversed the judgment by which a court of first instance had found for the defendant, and had imposed huge penalties on the class members for frivolous and abusive litigation. The appellate judgment has not been made public (at least to this author's best knowledge), but is worth mentioning all the same, because it highlights a problem that is typically Italian, that is to say the problem of delay: the case at issue[16] began in 2009 (when another version of the rule allowing for compensatory collective redress was in force) and in 2013 it was still pending, since the judgment issued by the court of appeal is, in principle, subject to a further appeal to the Italian Court of Cassation, namely, the Italian Supreme Court. It is beyond the point to expand on further procedural technicalities: what needs to be emphasized is that the problem of the excessive length of Italian judicial procedures has a bearing on the limited success of class actions for damages, for the awareness of this problem certainly does not increase the attractiveness of these actions.

Another element worth accentuating is the limited number of class members who have decided to opt-in so as to join the actions that have commenced. As mentioned, in the only class action decided in favour of the class only 12 individuals became parties to the lawsuit, but there have been cases in which one single consumer joined the action brought by a consumer association. Again, this is partially due to the fact that consumer associations do not do a good job in disseminating information, to the point that they seem more interested in bringing group actions merely for demonstrative purposes or to justify their very existence. In reality, though, consumer associations are not the only ones to blame: the main responsibility for the less than modest success of the Italian class actions for damages lies on the scheme devised by the legislators.

14 An official register of class actions for damages is lacking; in spite of that, the data provided in the text come from a reliable source: see <www.osservatorioantitrust.eu/it/azioni-di-classe-incardinate-nei-tribunali-italiani/> (last accessed on 22 April 2014).

15 The judgment was issued by the court of first instance in Naples: see Tribunale di Napoli (XII Sezione Civile), 18 febbraio 2013, available (in Italian) at: <www.consumatori.it/-images/stories/sentenza_tribunale_di_napoli.pdf> (last accessed on 22 April 2014).

16 The case originated from the action brought by a consumer association against the medical corporation in charge of distributing a do-it-yourself test for the diagnosis of swine flu, on the allegation that the test was not reliable.

The action can be commenced for 'the judicial enforcement of both the homogeneous individual rights of consumers and users, and collective interests'. The first lines of the rule (that this author has tried to translate in the most faithful way) show that the choice of words is bound to generate a variety of problems. For example, when can one say that two or more rights are 'homogeneous'? According to the Mirriam-Webster Dictionary, 'homogeneous' is an adjective meaning 'of the same or a similar kind or nature'. Does this definition, if applied in a legal context, mean that the rights actionable through the class actions must be simply similar, for instance because they arise out of the same transaction, or – since we are talking about actions for damages – have been equally infringed by the same unlawful behaviour perpetrated by the defendant? Do homogeneous rights have to be identical, but, if so, may one say that two or more rights can ever be identical? And what is the difference between the sum of a plurality of 'homogeneous individual rights', on the one hand, and collective rights, on the other? Needless to say, these questions have kept legal scholars very busy, but it seems pointless to expand on the many interpretations circulating in the Italian legal market. What is important to emphasize is that the scope of the Italian class action for damages is identified in a very precarious way. More doubts arise when it has to be determined which subjects can be identified as 'consumers' and 'users'; yet more problems spring out of the question as to whether the rights that can be asserted must arise out of contracts or torts as well.

Each class member can commence the proceeding, but associations and committees can be granted standing too, insofar as they are designated by one or more class members to allegedly represent the whole class. Which class, one may wonder, and rightly so, since the idea of a 'class' comes out of the blue, so to speak. More precisely, the rule introduces the concept of a 'class' without any further explanations, and therefore, with an effort at creative interpretation, one must infer that the members of the 'class' at issue are the bearers of the 'homogeneous individual rights' or 'collective rights' mentioned above. In any case, the event of a class action brought by a single consumer (or user) has turned out to be the exception, the rule being the initiative of consumer (or user) associations on behalf of one or more class members, which makes perfectly good sense, considering that individuals could hardly bear the costs of a complex and time-consuming procedure, and that in Italy third-party litigation funding is unheard of.

As noted above, Italy has adopted an opt-in system: class members can join the proceeding, and therefore become bound by its outcome, by lodging with the court a mysterious motion called a 'statement of adhesion'. It is mysterious to the extent that it is not a pleading in the conventional sense, nor is it an application to intervene in a proceeding already pending, due to the fact that Article 140-*bis* of the Consumer Code openly forbids intervention in class actions. Nowhere else in the rules governing Italian civil justice is a 'statement of adhesion' contemplated as the procedural tool by which individuals can become parties to an existing lawsuit, and therefore be bound by the judgment: one may wonder whether it was truly necessary to add yet another type of motion to the many kinds that both the Code of Civil Procedure and special statutes contemplate already, most of all in light of the goals of simplification that legislators constantly proclaim to pursue every time they address issues concerning the judicial enforcement of rights, whether individual or collective. At any rate, by lodging with the court their 'statements of adhesion' class members become subject to the effects of the judgment by which the court shall find for the class or for the defendant; they also relinquish their rights to bring individual actions against the same plaintiff based on the same cause of action.

The procedure laid down for class actions is quite complex, since it develops along two stages that can multiply if certain interlocutory decisions (such as the decision by which the action is declared admissible or inadmissible at the outset of the proceeding) are appealed against. The first stage is devoted to a sort of certification of the action: if the action is declared admissible, the court shall order appropriate measures aimed at giving public notice of the class action, so that interested class members can lodge their 'statements of adhesion'.

As far as the second stage of the procedure is concerned, it is worth acknowledging an interesting rule that entrusts the court with case management powers. According to the rule at issue, the court 'shall determine the development of the proceeding so as to ensure a fair, effective, and expedited decision of the case, paying due attention to the principle of equality of arms'; with this objective in mind, the court 'shall adopt the measures that are appropriate to avoid undue complications or repetitions in the taking of evidence' (my translations), so as to dispense with any superfluous formalities that could hinder the disposition of the case. This is a very intriguing rule, and in a civil procedural system impervious to case management, such as the Italian one, it would be interesting to see what practical results the wide managerial powers granted to the court in class actions could have: unfortunately, though, it seems that the rule either has not been applied yet, or, if it has been applied, it has not produced any significant case law.

A few words on the judgment on the merits are in order. When it finds for the class, the court has two options: (1) it can determine *ex aequo et bono* the damages awarded to each class member; or (2) it can establish only the criteria according to which the damages to be awarded to each class member will be calculated. That being the case, the court shall set a deadline for the parties to reach an agreement on the amount of damages; it no agreement is reached, the issue goes back to the court that shall liquidate the damages each class member is entitled to receive. The reference to an agreement the parties can reach as regards the amount of damages is the only clue pointing to a possible collective settlement; that aside, complex issues are likely to arise if one or more class members reach separate settlements with the defendant.

Finally, it seems pertinent to mention that no special provisions on financing or funding class actions are provided for. As far as costs are concerned, the general rule applicable to judicial proceedings across the board, that is, the 'loser pays' principle, applies.

Article 140-*bis* of the Consumer Code comprises no less than 15 sections, and therefore a variety of complex and finicky rules, but it seems meaningless to expand on them: after all, they are essentially 'empty boxes', bare rules subject to every kind of doctrinal interpretation, but on which courts, at least so far, have not produced any relevant amount of 'black letter law'.

Clearly, there is something wrong with class actions Italian-style, if the great expectations that their advent raised have not yet come true. This could depend on the opt-in system that is notoriously not very class member-friendly, but in this regard Italy is not different from the majority of European systems that have provided for mechanisms of compensatory collective redress. Also, it could depend on the lack of financial incentives for prospective plaintiffs and, most of all, for their lawyers, since contingent fee agreements are not allowed under Italian law, but again, this situation is common to many other jurisdictions. The list of possible 'culprits' could continue, but the blame game is a futile exercise: the rules described above are the law in force and, short of radical changes, class actions will remain a source of big disappointment for Italian consumers.

## 4. 'Public Class Actions'

As mentioned, 'public class action' is the conventional name given to a special group action available against public bodies in order to 'promote the efficiency of public entities and providers of public services',[17] so as to 'restore the proper course of administrative functions or the proper distribution of public services', whenever the interests of consumers or users have been adversely affected by conduct amounting to non-compliance with specific duties to act. Standing is granted to the 'holders of interests that are legally relevant and homogeneous with respect to a plurality of consumers and users': it is easy to notice that Italian legislators have a strong liking for the adjective 'homogeneous', whose meaning (as pointed out above, with reference to the 'homogeneous individual rights' that allegedly can be restored through 'private' class actions for damages) is far from settled. In spite of that, public class actions probably are the most successful form of collective redress in Italy, at least in terms of numbers. Unfortunately, though, since public class actions fall within the category of injunctive collective redress, problems arise when the judgment finding for the class must be enforced. These actions are dealt with by administrative courts and, according to the rules of Italian administrative law, if a public entity fails to comply with a judgment, a special procedure, always before administrative courts, must be commenced; furthermore, damages - if any - can be claimed only by resorting to yet another judicial procedure.

## 5. Conclusions

After the overview of the Italian forms of collective redress offered above, a comprehensive evaluation seems in order, and - based upon what has been described in the preceding paragraphs - the evaluation cannot be positive. There is

17 This is the goal pursued by group actions against public entities, according to the heading of the statutory instrument by which they are provided for: see Decreto Legislativo 20 dicembre 2009, n. 198, Attuazione dell'art. 4 della legge 4 marzo 2009, n. 15, in materia di ricorso per l'efficienza delle amministrazioni e dei concessionari di servizi pubblici.

room for improvement in the law in force, but this author is persuaded that any improvements are bound to have no practical effects in the access of individuals to group litigation unless the entire Italian system of judicial redress is affected by a true paradigm shift. In the field of group actions (as in many other areas of law, and most of all in procedural law), Italy represents a perfect example of hyper-legislation that has met with a disheartening lack of practical (and positive) results. After all, collective redress is just a detail in the big picture, the picture that recently the European Commission, in its Communication laying the basis for a pan-European framework for collective redress has described as 'a sound legal environment and (an) efficient judicial system'.[18] This author thinks that the cause of collective redress in Italy will advance only when Italians are able to count on a sound legal environment and an efficient judicial system: regrettably, this is not likely to happen any time soon.

18 Communication from the Commission to the European Parliament, the Council, the European Economic and Social Committee and the Committee of the Regions, 'Towards a European Horizontal Framework for Collective Redress', COM(2013) 401/2, para 1.1, available at <http://ec.europa.eu/justice/civil/files/com_2013_401_en.pdf> (last accessed on 22 April 2014): see Silvestri 2013, p. 46-56.

## Bibliography

**Belli 2007**
Belli, C. (ed.), *Le azioni collettive in Italia. Profili teorici ed aspetti applicativi*, Milano: Giuffrè Editore, 2007.

**Caponi 2011**
Caponi, R., 'Collective Redress in Europe: Current Developments of "Class Action" Suits in Italy', *Zeitschrift für Zivilprozess International* (*ZZPInt*), 2011, Vol. 16, p. 1-17.

**Donzelli 2007**
Donzelli, R., 'Interessi collettivi e diffusi', in *Enciclopedia giuridica Treccani*, Roma: Istituto dell'Enciclopedia Italiana, 2008, p. 1-16.

**Facoltà di Giurisprudenza 1976**
Università degli Studi di Pavia, *Le azioni a tutela di interessi collettivi, Atti del convegno, Pavia, 11-12 giugno 1974*, Padova: Cedam, 1976.

**Giussani 1996**
Giussani, A., *Studi sulle 'class actions'*, Padova: Cedam, 1996.

**Giussani 2007**
Giussani, A., 'Azione collettiva', in *Enciclopedia del Diritto, Annali*, I, Milano: Giuffrè Editore, 2007, p. 132-152.

**Hodges 2014**
Hodges, C., 'Collective Redress: A Breakthrough or a *Damp Squib*?', *Journal of Consumer Policy*, 2014, Vol. 37, p. 67-89.

**Lanfranchi 2003**
Lanfranchi, L. (ed.), *La tutela giurisdizionale degli interessi collettivi e diffusi*, Torino: Giappichelli Editore, 2003.

**Menchini 2008**
Menchini, S. (ed.), *Le azioni seriali*, Napoli: Edizioni Scientifiche Italiane, 2008.

**Nashi 2010**
Nashi, R., 'Italy's Class Action Experiment', *Cornell International Law Journal*, 2010, Vol. 43, p. 147-172.

**Quarta 2012**
Quarta, F., 'Foreign Punitive Damages Decisions and Class Actions in Italy', in Fairgrieve, D. & Lein, E. (eds.), *Extraterritoriality and Collective Redress*, Oxford: Oxford University Press, 2012.

**Silvestri 2009**
Silvestri, E., 'Italy', in Hensler, D.H., Hodges, C. & Tulibacka, M. (spec. eds.), *The Globalization of Class Actions, The ANNALS of the American Academy of Political and Social Science*, 2009, Vol. 622(1), p. 138-148.

**Silvestri 2013**
Silvestri, E., 'Towards a Common Framework of Collective Redress in Europe? An Update on the Latest Initiatives of the European Commission', *Russian Law Journal*, 2013, Vol. 1, p. 46-56.

**Silvestri & Jagtenberg 2013**
Silvestri, E. & Jagtenberg, R., 'Tweeluik – Diptych: Juggling a Red Hot Potato: Italy, the EU, and Mandatory Mediation', *Nederlands-Vlaams tijdschrift voor mediation en conflictmanagement*, 2013, Vol. 17, p. 29-45.

C.H. van Rhee
I.N. Tzankova

# COLLECTIVE REDRESS IN THE NETHERLANDS

## Introduction

In the present chapter we will focus on collective redress in the Netherlands regarding (1) the interests of a group of persons (aggregated individual interests), (2) general (public) interests (*actio popularis*), as well as on (3) collective settlement procedures in the Netherlands.[1] For reasons of convenience, we will refer to (1) and (2) as 'collective litigation'; (1), (2) and (3) together will be referred to as 'collective redress'. Beyond (1), (2) and (3) no other types of collective redress exist in the Netherlands apart from what has been called the 'assignment model' in legal literature.[2] This model will not be discussed here. It suffices to say that given the fact that collective litigation cannot be brought in the Netherlands in order to obtain damages, a different model of litigation is used (currently often in antitrust and securities cases) based on the assignment of claims or, to a lesser degree, mandates. In this model, members of a group having suffered harm assign their claims to a special purpose vehicle, often controlled by a claims funder, which will act as claimant in the proceedings. The compensation in case of a settlement or judgment that will be paid to the assignors is lowered by a percentage agreed with the claims funder.

In Dutch collective settlement procedures, an 'interested party' can be defined as a party who would have an entitlement as a result of the settlement agreement. Organisations acting in the interest of parties whose interests are at stake may also be brought under the heading of 'interested party'.[3] In collective litigation the situation is different. Those whose interests may be involved cannot be called 'interested parties' *tout court* since they are not a party to the lawsuit; only non-profit organisations such as foundations can be parties. Nevertheless, we will occasionally refer to these individuals as 'interested parties' below since the

1 For information in English on the Dutch law on collective settlement, see also Krans 2014.
2 Tzankova *et al.* 2014, p. 232-233.
3 Tzankova 2012, p. 562.

judgment in the case brought by the non-profit organisation may later be used as a kind of precedent in cases of individuals litigating for their own interests. No specific registers other than the ordinary court registers are held of interested parties and of the collective settlement proceedings in which they are involved. Interested parties may only qualify for legal aid under the Dutch legal aid scheme if they are natural persons. Apart from legal aid, the main ways of financing collective redress are before-the-event legal expense insurance and after-the-event third-party funding (the latter is a relatively new development in the Netherlands).[4] Members of the Dutch bar are not allowed to work on the basis of a contingency fee arrangement (others may provide legal assistance on this basis, however).

## 1. Collective Litigation

### *1.1. Sources of Law and Scope*

In 1994, the Netherlands was one of the first countries in Europe to introduce collective litigation.[5] By 2012 this had given rise to more than 288 collective litigation cases (more recent data are not yet available).[6] Twenty-one of these cases were declared inadmissible, whereas the remaining cases have resulted in judgments on the merits. Appeal against first instance judgments has been filed in 65 cases.

The cases are based on a set of articles in the Dutch Civil Code on collective litigation (Articles 3:305a-b), more specifically on civil actions brought by foundations, associations or legal persons under public law aimed at safeguarding the interests of other persons. These articles may also be used for general public interest litigation.[7] It should be noted that special rules on collective litigation are available where it concerns consumer protection (Articles 3:305c-d) and allegedly unreasonably burdensome general terms and conditions in a contract (Article 6:240).[8] In this chapter, collective litigation as regards general terms and conditions will not be discussed.

In Dutch collective litigation, there are no specific rules on the size of the group of persons whose interests are involved. However, its size should be sufficiently large to justify the collective action. There are no specific rules of procedure on collective litigation either, which means that in principle the ordinary procedural rules, including those on the role of the judge, evidence, the burden of proof and the publication of the judgment, apply. The same is true for the costs rule

4 For more information on the funding of collective redress in the Netherlands, see Tzankova 2012.

5 Tzankova & Van Lith 2012, p. 67.

6 Marris 2013.

7 Eliantonio *et al.* 2013, p. 434.

8 Art. 6:240 was introduced as a result of Directive No. 93/13 EEC, 5 April 1993, on unfair terms in consumer contracts, and Directive No. 98/27/EC, 19 May 1998, on injunctions for the protection of consumers' interests.

(in principle, the loser pays costs, also the extra-judicial costs of the foundation or association or legal person under public law)[9] and means of recourse against judgments. Since those for whose interests collective litigation is brought are not a party to the action (see below), enforcement of a judgment resulting from collective litigation can only be instigated by others, i.e. those who are a party to the action (the foundation, etc.).

Originally, claims brought by organisations aimed at safeguarding the interests of other persons would be declared inadmissible by the courts, since the rule was that a claim can only be brought where it concerns the claimant's own personal interests. Later, claims concerning the interests of others were sometimes allowed in case law and by legislation concerning particular types of cases.[10] Finally this gave rise to legislation on collective litigation in general (horizontal) in which foundations, associations with full legal personality and legal persons under public law have legal standing where they aim at protecting the interests of a group.

## 1.2. *Content of the Rules*

The first general rules on collective litigation in the Netherlands were provided for by the law, of 6 April 1994,[11] which introduced Articles 3:305a and 3:305b in the Civil Code. A collective action must be brought before the first instance court (there are 11 of such courts in the Netherlands) of the place where the defendant has its seat or its place of residence unless specific rules on jurisdiction apply.[12] Usually, the court, at its discretion, will hear the case with a panel of judges. Representation by a lawyer is compulsory unless the case can be brought before the small claims judge of the first instance court where legal representation is not compulsory (the small claims judge is not only competent as regards small claims, but also as regards specific subject matters such as labour contracts).[13] Litigation is commenced by way of a writ of summons served on the defendant by a (semi-private) bailiff (*huissier de justice*).[14] The group members whose interests are at stake do not have to be notified of the action being brought before the court.

According to the first clause of Article 3:305a, only a foundation or association with full legal personality (and not an individual injured party)[15] may bring a (civil) action in its own name (so not as a representative of others) but nevertheless in the interest of a collectivity (the foundation or association bringing the action must also have an interest in the action itself, but for this it suffices that this appears from the documents by which the legal person was created (i.e. its articles of association; in

9 Vie d'Or, Amsterdam Court of Appeal, 29 April 2009, *NJ* 2009, 448.

10 Eliantonio *et al.* 2013, p. 434; Tekst & Commentaar Burgerlijk Wetboek, Art. 3:305a (Stolker).

11 Dutch Official Journal 269.

12 Arts. 99 *et seq.* Dutch Code of Civil Procedure.

13 Arts. 93 and 79(1) Dutch Code of Civil Procedure.

14 This may change in the near future due to new legislation prescribing that group litigation should be started by way of a petition.

15 Tzankova & Van Lith 2012, p. 69.

Dutch: *statuten*)). Conditions are (1) that the interests of those for whom the action is brought must be 'similar' in nature (this means that the interests in question can be grouped together, meaning that no individual issues have to be decided),[16] and (2) that the aim of representing their interests is expressed in the articles of association.

It is not necessary that all those in whose interest the action is brought or a majority of them have agreed to the action. For example, where an action was brought against a political party that did not allow women on the list of candidates for the elections, the fact that the majority of women that were affected did not agree with the action did not prevent the action from being admissible.[17]

Article 3:305b provides that a legal person under public law (such as the State, provinces and municipalities) may also bring a (civil) action in the interest of a collectivity. The aim of representing the interests at stake must be part of the tasks of such legal persons. This usually appears from the legislation by which they are governed. But this is very rarely done, if at all.

In bankruptcy proceedings Article 3:305a may also be used.[18]

That alternative dispute resolution is preferred by the Legislature over collective litigation appears where it is laid down that the claim in collective litigation is not admissible if 'in the given circumstances' a sufficient attempt to achieve a settlement has not been made (Article 3:305a (2)). The expiry of a two-week period from receipt by the defendant of a request for consultations about a settlement giving particulars of the claim suffices for this purpose, which obviously is not a very long period of time. Preliminary settlement attempts are not required if it is clear that they are of no avail, e.g. if the defendant states positively that he does not want to settle. The claim is also inadmissible where the judge is of the opinion that the interests of those for whom the action is brought are insufficiently protected by the action (Article 3:305a (2)).

An important feature of Article 3:305a is that damages cannot be claimed (Article 3:305a (3)) since this would give rise to individual issues which would hinder the grouping together of the interests at stake (currently, however, a legislative proposal has been submitted for consultation which introduces the possibility to claim damages).[19] For the rest, the types of claim that may be submitted are not limited (e.g. claims based on contract law or tort law). If a declaratory judgment is being asked for, it is important to note that this judgment can subsequently be used as a kind of precedent in order to obtain damages in actions brought by individual claimants.[20] Injunctions may also be requested (between 1994 and 2012 an injunction was claimed in 156 of a total of 288 cases, in many cases combined with a claim for a declaratory judgment),[21] e.g. an injunction

16 *Ibidem*, p. 70.

17 HR 9 April 2010, *NJ* 2010, 388. See also HR 26 February 2010, LJN: BK5756, B9 8638 (*Stichting Baas in Eigen Huis v Plazacasa B.V. (Jaap.nl)*).

18 HR 15 September 1995, *NJ* 1996, 629.

19 See <www.internetconsultatie.nl/motiedijksma> (last accessed on 30 July 2014).

20 Tzankova & Van Lith 2012, p. 70.

21 Marris 2013.

ordering the defendant to publish the judgment resulting from the collective action or have it published in a manner to be determined by the court and at the expense of a party or parties to be designated by the court. In most cases, after a declaratory judgment has been issued which is detrimental for the defendant, the defendant seeks to resolve individual cases by means of a settlement, including the collective settlement discussed below (in that sense, collective litigation and collective settlement procedures are interrelated in the Netherlands).[22]

It should be noted that the procedure of Article 3:305a may be combined with the assignment of claims to the organisation which has brought the collective action in the interest of others (on assignation see above). If this happens, the organisation may also claim damages in an ordinary civil action, i.e. not by way of a collective action.[23]

The person who is affected by the acts of someone else may object to these acts being taken into consideration in a collective action (Article 3:305a (4)). However, if the same acts have affected other members of the group, the acts may be taken into consideration as long as these other members of the group do not object. Also, after the judgment has been rendered, those whose interests are at stake may file an objection, this time in order to make sure that the judgment will not affect them in any way, unless the judgment, due to its very nature, does not allow the exclusion of particular persons (Article 3:305a (5)). This is the case where, for example, the action was brought in the interest of the environment (*actio popularis*; such actions were brought in 32 of the 288 cases in the period 1994-2012; 23 of these concerned animal rights or the environment).[24] It should be noted that the provision allowing the filing of an objection against the judgment in collective litigation cannot be considered to be an opt-out provision. Opting out is not necessary since the judgment by its very nature only has *res iudicata* effect between the organisation that has brought the collective action and the defendants; the parties whose interests are at stake retain the right to bring individual actions to safeguard their individual interests (individual actions may be brought both pending a collective action and after judgment; rules of *lis pendens* do not apply as regards the collective action and individual actions).[25] Also, the party against whom a judgment has been given as a result of a collective action may at all times, i.e. even after the judgment, try to settle the case with those in whose interest the collective action was brought even in a manner different from that judgment.[26]

On 1 January 2001, a new Article 3:305c was introduced in the Dutch Civil Code to implement Directive EC No. 98/27/EC on injunctions for the protection of consumers' interests.[27] It lays down that an organisation or public body with its registered office outside the Netherlands that is placed on the list referred to in

22 Tzankova & Van Lith 2012, p. 70 and 75.

23 For further particulars, see Hoes-Weishut *et al.* 2008, p. 139.

24 Marris 2013.

25 Tekst & Commentaar Burgerlijk Wetboek, Art. 3:305a (Stolker).

26 *Ibidem.*

27 *OJ* EC No. L166.

Article 4, para 3 of the Directive, may institute a collective action in the Netherlands for the protection of collective consumer interests if the consumers have their habitual residence in a country where this organisation or public body is established. This is only allowed if the objective of the organisation is to represent such collective interests or where the promotion of such interests has been entrusted to the public body. It should be noted that the article does not only implement the Directive; it may also be used for the protection of consumer interests other than the ones resulting from EU legislation.[28] Litigation is commenced by way of a writ of summons served on the defendant by a bailiff (*huissier de justice*). The ordinary rules on jurisdiction apply. Usually the court will hear the case, at its discretion, with a panel of judges. Representation by a lawyer is compulsory.[29]

Finally, in 2006 Article 3:305d Civil Code was introduced. It provides that the Court of Appeal in The Hague may issue an injunction to stop acts that are in contravention of various legal provisions resulting from various Directives and a Regulation in the area of EU consumer protection, at the request of:

a. the Netherlands Authority for Consumers and Markets (*Autoriteit Consument en Markt*);
b. the Netherlands Authority for the Financial Markets (*Autoriteit Financiële Markten*); or
c. a foundation or association with full legal personality which according to its articles of association aims at protecting the interests of persons that are similar in nature.

This procedure may also be used for obtaining a court order aimed at the amendment of a code of conduct if this code promotes unfair commercial practices (Article 3:305d (2)).

At the request of the claimant, the court may order that its ruling on the basis of Article 3:305d will be published by or on behalf of the defendant. If unfair commercial practices are at stake, the court may also order the rectification of the information provided within this context. All this has to be done at the expense of a party or parties designated by the court (Article 3:305d (3)).

Litigation according to Article 3:305d may only be brought before the Court of Appeal in The Hague, where a panel of judges hears the case. The action has to be brought by way of a petition (Article 3:305d (5)). The Court of Appeal in The Hague is also competent as regards conflicts about the execution of court rulings resulting from this article and rulings ordering an *astreinte* (money penalties) in these cases (Article 3:305d (6)). Representation by a lawyer is compulsory. Only cassation appeal is available, since the Court of Appeal and not the first instance court hears the case at first instance.

28 Tekst & Commentaar Burgerlijk Wetboek, Art. 3:305c (Stolker).
29 Arts. 93 and 79(1) Dutch Code of Civil Procedure.

In 2013, new legislation introduced a preliminary ruling procedure at the Supreme Court of the Netherlands (*Hoge Raad*) which is very relevant in case of collective litigation (the procedure is not available in the collective settlement procedure discussed below).[30] Panels of judges at the court of first instance and the court of appeal have been granted the right to submit preliminary questions to the Supreme Court (1) in cases of 'mass claims', (2) where legal questions arising in many 'similar' legal actions are at stake and where legal unity would be served by an expedient answer to these questions, and (3) as regards legal questions arising from new legislation.[31] It was felt that this procedure and especially the answers provided by the Supreme Court would prevent individual litigation and contradictory case law, promote settlement agreements after collective litigation has been brought and prevent opting-out of such agreements.

## 2. Collective Settlement Procedures (*Wet Collectieve Afwikkeling Massaschade* or *WCAM*)

### 2.1. *Sources of Law and Scope*

The collective settlement procedure available in the Netherlands has been inspired by the US class settlement regime.[32] Seven collective settlements have been declared binding since the introduction of the relevant legal provisions in 2005 (the last one was the second DES settlement, declared binding on 24 June 2014).[33] In the near future (most likely in October 2014) this may happen in an eighth case (DSB Bank).[34] Five out of seven settlements concerned financial products and services and three out of seven concerned non-Dutch claimants and the global resolution of securities claims.[35] It has been claimed that the Dutch collective settlements to date 'demonstrate that within the Netherlands, being a small country, effective pressure on unwilling defendants to settle a mass claim can be created in different ways, including the exertion of political pressure and pressure from the media'.[36]

Collective settlement procedures are regulated both by the Dutch Civil Code and by the Code of Civil Procedure. Their principal aim is damages for wrongful behaviour (there are no limitations as regards the amount of damages that may be

30 Ozmis & Tzankova 2012, p. 38.
31 Arts. 392-394 Dutch Code of Civil Procedure.
32 Tzankova & Van Lith 2012, p. 73.
33 DES, Amsterdam Court of Appeal, 01 June 2006, *NJ* 2006, 461; Dexia, Amsterdam Court of Appeal, 25 January 2007, *NJ* 2007, 427; Vie d'Or, Amsterdam Court of Appeal, 29 April 2009, *NJ* 2009, 448; Shell, Amsterdam Court of Appeal, 29 May 2009, *NJ* 2009, 506; Vedior, Amsterdam Court of Appeal, 15 July 2009, *JOR* 2009, 325; Converium, Amsterdam Court of Appeal, 12 November 2010, *NJ* 2010, 683; DES II, Amsterdam Court of Appeal, 24 June 2014, see: <http://dossier.rechtspraak.nl/ResultPage.aspx?dossier=DES-regeling#> (last accessed in August 2014).
34 Tzankova & Hensler 2013, p. 99.
35 Tzankova 2012, p. 558; Tzankova & Van Lith 2012, p. 69.
36 Tzankova & Van Lith 2012, p. 70.

asked in these procedures). These rules have been introduced as a result of a specific case, the so-called DES-case concerning a hormone taken by pregnant women that caused serious damage to the children born from their pregnancies.[37] It was decided that this case against the producer of the drug at issue would not be regulated on an ad hoc basis, but that legislation would be introduced governing this and similar mass claims cases.

As previously stated, the relevant articles (Articles 7:907-910 Dutch Civil Code and Articles 1013-1018 Dutch Code of Civil Procedure) were introduced in 2005. These articles govern situations in which a large number of individuals suffer harm due to an act or related acts of one or more natural or legal persons. The number of injured or interested parties is not fixed by law; the number should, however, be sufficient to justify the collective settlement (see also below).[38]

## 2.2. *Content of the Rules*

The articles open the possibility for the natural or legal persons having caused the harm and a foundation or association (or the Consumer Authority) representing the interests of those who have suffered harm to reach an agreement which can be submitted to the Court of Appeal in Amsterdam (Article 1013(3)) in order to have it sanctioned as an agreement binding for all who have suffered harm in the context of the agreement, except for those who decide to opt out. This has to be done by way of a mutual petition of the organisation(s) acting in the interest of the victims and the natural or legal person(s) being responsible for the harm (all of whom have to be represented by a lawyer). The submission of the petition to the court stops periods of prescription (statute of limitations) from running (Article 7:907(5)). At the request of the party from whom damages are being claimed, the Amsterdam Court of Appeal may decide to stay pending individual actions for damages, including those that are started during the collective settlement procedure (Article 1015(1)).

Due to a recent amendment in legislation, the collective settlement procedure now can be used in bankruptcy proceedings as well.[39]

Unlike collective litigation which does not know a representation requirement, collective settlement procedures are only available when the organisation entering the settlement is sufficiently representative of the interests of the injured persons who are to benefit from the settlement.[40]

The interested parties will be informed of the submission of the petition in order to have the agreement approved by the court of appeal. If their address is known, they will be informed by way of ordinary mail (the letter does not have to be registered) unless the judge decides otherwise (Article 1013(5)), whereas the use of email has also been allowed in case law, but only when the interested parties

37 DES, Amsterdam Court of Appeal, 01 June 2006, *NJ* 2006, 461.

38 Tzankova & Van Lith 2012, p. 69.

39 Stb. 2013, 25: <http://njb.nl/Uploads/2013/10/stb13_255.pdf> (last accessed in August 2014).

40 Tzankova & Van Lith 2012, p. 71.

have their place of residence in the Netherlands.[41] Additionally, publication in one or more newspapers is a requirement (in the event that the number of interested parties is very large, this may be the only manner of announcement). The court may also decide that other manners of publication are needed (Article 1013(5)). In the Shell and Converium global settlements the Hague Service Convention was followed.[42]

A panel of judges will hear the case. Statements of defence may be submitted to the court by interested parties, also by a foundation or association having full legal personality acting in the interest of those for whom the agreement has been concluded (Article 1014). This foundation or association is obviously different from the foundation or association that is involved in the settlement agreement. Interested parties may be heard in court (Article 1013(5)). The court is very active in settlement procedures to the extent that party autonomy is not observed. The court may *ex officio* appoint one or more expert witnesses (Article 1016(1)). Although the court cannot alter the terms of the settlement agreement, it can make clear that it will not approve the settlement unless certain terms are changed.[43] Obviously, the active role of the court is the result of the fact that the group of persons whose interests are involved is large and may even consist of persons who are unknown at the time of the ruling by which the agreement is declared binding for all group members.

Recent legislation provides that the court should be involved at an early stage in collective settlement procedures. Originally, the court would only be involved after the parties had reached an agreement, its task being to check whether the agreement could be declared binding for all those who had suffered harm. It was felt, however, that this meant that the court would be involved in too late a stage and that there should be a possibility to have the court also involved in the stage where the agreement was negotiated (the pre-action stage). In 2013, therefore, Article 1018a was introduced in the Code of Civil Procedure. This article provides that if large numbers of individuals are affected by an event or similar events, the court may order the foundation or association and those who are considered to be responsible for the event or events to make an appearance in court in order to attempt to reach a settlement agreement. The court may *not* do this *ex officio*, but only at the request of the foundation or association representing the interests of those who have been harmed or on behalf of those who are responsible for the damage, or at the joint request of these parties

41 E.g. Dexia, Amsterdam Court of Appeal, 25 January 2007, *NJ* 2007, 427, and recently DES II, Amsterdam Court of Appeal, 24 June 2014, see: <http://dossier.rechtspraak.nl/-ResultPage.aspx?dossier=DES-regeling#> (last accessed in August 2014).

42 <www.hcch.net/index_en.php?act=conventions.text&cid=17> (last accessed in August 2014).

43 Tzankova & Van Lith 2012, p. 72-73. This is also the case in the DSB settlement where the court suggested to the parties that they reconsider certain parts of the settlement, a suggestion that the parties conditionally followed: <www.rechtspraak.nl/-Organisatie/Gerechtshoven/Amsterdam/Nieuws/WCAMVerzoekschriftDSBBankNV/brief%20WCAM%20DSB%2026%20juni%202014.pdf> (last accessed in August 2014).

The contents of the settlement agreement itself are regulated by the Civil Code. Article 7:907 of the Code provides that an agreement aimed at the compensation of damage that has been caused by a single event or related events and that has been concluded by one or more foundations or associations having full legal personality (or the Consumer Authority) and one or more other parties, who have committed themselves in this agreement to compensate the damage, may at the mutual request of these foundations, associations and the parties having committed themselves to compensate the damage be declared binding by the court for those persons who have suffered damage. This may, however, only be done if the foundations or associations, according to their articles of association, have as their aim to protect the interests of the persons having suffered the harm. When the court has declared the agreement binding, all of those having an entitlement to compensation are considered to be a party to the agreement (Article 7:908(1)).

The agreement needs to meet specific requirements (Article 7:907(2)). It needs to contain:

a. A description of the event or events having caused the damage that is covered by the agreement;
b. A description of the group or groups of persons for the benefit of whom the agreement has been concluded. These groups need to be defined based on the character and severity of the damage they have incurred (i.e. 'damage scheduling');
c. An indication of the number of persons belonging to this group or these groups, as accurately as possible;
d. The amount of compensation granted to these persons;
e. The requirements these persons need to meet in order to be entitled to compensation;
f. The way in which the amount of compensation will be established and in which manner it can be obtained;
g. The name and place of residence of the person to whom an opt-out declaration can be communicated.

The court may decline to declare the settlement agreement binding (Article 7:907(3)), amongst other things,[44] if:

a. The agreement does not meet the requirements stipulated in Article 7:907(2);
b. The amount of compensation is not reasonable;
c. It is insufficiently guaranteed that the claims resulting from the agreement can indeed be settled by the party having caused the damage;
d. The agreement does not provide for the independent resolution of disputes that may arise from the agreement (e.g. concerning the amount of

[44] The enumeration in this article is not meant to be exhaustive.

compensation) other than by the judge who would be competent according to the ordinary rules of jurisdiction;

e. The interests of the persons for the benefit of whom the agreement has been concluded are sufficiently protected in a manner other than by way of a collective settlement;
f. The foundations or associations acting on behalf of these persons are insufficiently representative for the interests at stake;
g. The group of persons for whose interest the agreement has been concluded is too small to justify a collective agreement. The test is whether the collective agreement results in a more efficient settlement of the claims than in the absence of such an agreement. There is no objective test as regards the number of persons involved; everything depends on the specific circumstances of the case. Collective settlement procedures may also be justified where, for example, a group is limited in size but where the money available for compensation is not sufficient for full coverage, as a result of which the money has to be divided in a fair manner amongst the members of the group;
h. The agreement stipulates that damages will be paid by a legal person that is *not* a party to the agreement.

The court does not have to deny declaring the agreement binding when relevant criteria are not met. Before taking a decision, it may amend the agreement with the consent of the parties by whom it has been concluded, or allow the parties to amend the agreement themselves. If this happens and if consequently the court declares the agreement binding, it has to mention the amendments in its ruling (Article 7:907(4)).

When an agreement has been declared binding for all members of a group, this ruling will be delivered to the parties that applied for the court ruling. Additionally, at the time the ruling acquires force of *res iudicata* (meaning that the period of time for lodging an appeal has expired), the ruling will be delivered to known group members. Also, an announcement will be published in one or more newspapers. In practice, public advertisements have been found sufficient to meet the notice requirements in this second stage and, consequently, individual notification has been omitted.[45] The court may order that notification will be made by other means as well (Article 1017(3)). The court has discretionary powers to decide who has to pay costs (Articles 1016(2) and 289 Code of Civil Procedure).

After notification, the court will establish a timeframe – in no case less than three months – within which those who are entitled to compensation may decide to opt out. In order to opt out, the person appointed for opting-out purposes (see above) has to be notified (Article 7:908(2)).

After the Amsterdam Court of Appeal has delivered its ruling, final cassation appeal at the Dutch Supreme Court on points of law is allowed (no other appeal is available, apart from extraordinary appeal known as 'herroeping' (Article 1018(2)),

[45] Tzankova & Van Lith 2012, p. 72.

which will not be discussed here). This appeal may only be lodged if the request to declare the agreement binding has been denied. The appeal should be brought jointly by all parties that have requested the agreement to be declared binding (Article 1018(1)).

Those who are entitled to damages and who have not opted out, as well as the foundation or association having negotiated the agreement, may ask the natural or legal person that is liable for the damages for performance of its obligations (i.e. payment). The person who is entitled to damages may, however, object to this if the foundation or association asks for performance on his behalf (Article 7:909).

As already mentioned, three out of seven collective settlements in the Netherlands concerned non-Dutch claimants and the global resolution of securities claims. For injured parties from within the EU especially two cases, Shell and Converium, are of interest.[46] These cases are discussed in depth by Tzankova & Van Lith 2012. These authors mention that in these cases the court based its jurisdiction on what they call a 'creative interpretation and application' of the jurisdiction rules under the Brussels I Regulation.[47] The Amsterdam Court of Appeal primarily focused on the settlement agreement itself and did not consider the underlying obligation of the settlement when it applied the provisions of the Brussels I Regulation. Consequently, the concepts used in the relevant Dutch legislation such as 'interested parties' and 'petitioners' do not seamlessly fit within the terminology of the Brussels I Regulation, which is based on the traditional concepts of 'defendants' and 'claimants'. This leads to a problematic application of the territorial scope of the Brussels I Regulation and the jurisdiction rules under Articles 2 and 6(1) Brussels I Regulation.

In Shell and in Converium, the Court applied the Brussels I Regulation by equalling the 'interested parties' with the persons 'to be sued' under Article 2. The Court accepted jurisdiction on the basis of Articles 2 and 6(1) Brussels I Regulation by taking into consideration the place of domicile of the interested parties. For the interested parties domiciled in the Netherlands, the court considered itself to have jurisdiction in accordance with Article 2 and regarded all other foreign interested parties domiciled outside the Netherlands, but within a European Union Member State or European Free Trade Association State as 'one of a number of co-defendants' to be sued for the purpose of Article 6(1) Brussels I Regulation.

This application of Article 6(1) in conjunction with Article 2 would, according to Tzankova & Van Lith, lead to the far-reaching consequence that the Amsterdam Court has jurisdiction even when only one of the interested parties for whose benefit the settlement agreement is concluded is domiciled in the Netherlands. In the Converium case, the Court moreover applied as an additional jurisdiction rule

46 Shell, Amsterdam Court of Appeal, 29 May 2009, *NJ* 2009, 506; Converium, Amsterdam Court of Appeal, 12 November 2010, *NJ* 2010, 683.

47 This paragraph and the two that follow are based on Tzankova & Van Lith 2012, p. 84. See also Kramer 2014.

Article 5(1) by stating that the place of performance of the obligation to pay compensation is in the Netherlands.

The above (internationally) problematic interpretations of the relevant articles of the Brussels I Regulation can, according to Tzankova & Van Lith, be avoided and even become unnecessary if parties would decide to incorporate a choice of forum clause in favour of the Amsterdam Court of Appeal in their settlement agreement declaring it binding on the interested parties for whose benefit it was concluded. After all, the application of Article 23 of the Brussels I Regulation merely requires that one of the parties be domiciled in the Netherlands.[48] It remains to be seen, however, whether this clause is also binding on interested parties who are not parties to the settlement agreement.

## 3. Final Remarks

Over the last few decades, the Netherlands has been able to introduce a series of successful procedures for collective redress. An estimated 288 cases have been litigated under the collective litigation procedure since the time of its introduction in 1994 until 2012 and it is likely that soon the 8th large case will be settled by way of the 2005 collective settlement procedure. It is important to note that Dutch collective redress procedures should not be looked at in isolation. Although up to now collective litigation cannot result in an award of damages (this may change in the near future), the judgment resulting from such litigation may help parties in subsequent individual litigation for damages (or in litigation after the assignment of claims to a third party) and may also be an incentive for reaching an individual or a collective settlement, the latter being certified by the Amsterdam Court of Appeal. Due to the fact that the collective settlement procedure is an opt-out procedure, it is highly efficient since there are no big expenses nor other difficulties involved in starting this procedure. In addition, due to the 'creative' interpretation of the Amsterdam Court of Appeal of the Brussels I Regulation, the Dutch collective settlement procedure is also available for international parties (which may be beneficial to these parties given the absence of well-working collective redress procedures in various other EU Member States). However, since it is not clear whether this interpretation will hold, it has been suggested to insert a jurisdiction clause in the collective settlement agreement in order to make sure that the procedure remains available internationally, which is especially needed in a European legal landscape where efficient and well-working procedures for collective redress are scarce in most EU Member States. It can rightly be claimed that as in many other legal areas the Dutch approach can be classified as a business-like, pragmatic approach which may help opening up a European legal services market,[49] which can still be classified as rather conservative up to the present day. It is hoped that EU initiatives will not hinder this Dutch development, for example by

48 Tzankova & Van Lith 2012, p. 85.

49 See also Arons & Van Boom 2010.

prescribing opt-in procedures which are an inefficient and often unsuccessful approach to matters in the majority of the more conservative EU Member States. It remains to be seen, however, whether the Dutch approach will indeed lead the way in Europe. The signals from Europe up to now[50] are not very encouraging, which may also be due to the fact that in a variety of EU Member States the pragmatic Dutch approach is problematic due, *inter alia,* to a Judiciary and legal services market which, with few exceptions, is still not entirely up to modern standards.

50 See EU Commission Recommendation of 11 June 2013, 2013/396/EU, *OJ* 2013, L201/60. See also Stadler 2013 and Hodges 2013.

## Bibliography


**Arons & Van Boom 2010**
Arons, T. & Van Boom, W., 'Beyond Tulips and Cheese: Exporting Mass Securities Claim Settlements from the Netherlands', *European Business Law Review,* 2010, p. 857-883, also available at SSRN: <http://ssrn.com/abstract=1715847>.

**Eliantonio *et al.* 2013**
Eliantonio, M., Backes, Ch.W., Van Rhee, C.H., Spronken, T.N.B.M. & Berlee, A. (eds.), *Standing up for your Right(s) in Europe. A Comparative Study on Legal Standing (Locus Standi) before the EU and Member States' Courts,* Antwerp-Oxford: Intersentia, 2013.

**Hodges 2013**
Hodges, C., 'Collective Redress: A Breakthrough or a Damp Squib?', *Journal of Consumer Policy,* 2014, p. 67-89.

**Hoes-Weishut *et al.* 2008**
Hoes-Weishut, S., Lunsingh Scheurler, D., Speyart, H., 'Het Witboek Schadevergoeding afgezet tegen de huidige Nederlandse B.228.36 situatie: verworvenheden en vernieuwingen', *Actualiteiten Mededingingsrecht,* 2008, p. 137-149.

**Kramer 2014**
Kramer, X.E., 'Securities Collective Action and Private International Law Issues in Dutch WCAM Settlements: Global Aspirations and Regional Boundaries', *Pacific McGeorge Global Business & Development Law Journal,* 2014, p. 235-279.

**Krans 2014**
Krans, B., 'The Dutch Act on Collective Settlement of Mass Damages', *Pacific McGeorge Global Business & Development Law Journal,* 2014, p. 281-301.

**Marris 2013**
Marris, S., *De Collectieve Actie, Artikel 3:305a BW. Het Gebruik van de Collectieve Actie in de Praktijk,* Unpublished Master's Thesis, Tilburg University, September 2013.

**Ozmis & Tzankova 2012**
Ozmis, D. & Tzankova, I., 'De evaluatie van de WCAM: de kernthema's uitgelicht', *Tijdschrift voor Civiele Rechtspleging,* 2012, p. 33-42.

**Stadler 2013**
Stadler, A., 'The Commission's Recommendation on Common Principles of Collective Redress and Private International Law Issues', *Nederlands Internationaal Privaatrecht,* 2013, p. 483-488, also available at: <www.nipr-online.eu/-upload/documents/20140113T103840-NIPR%202013-4_Stadler.pdf>.

**Tzankova 2012**
Tzankova, I., 'Funding of Mass Disputes: Lessons from the Netherlands', *George Mason University School of Law Journal of Law, Economics and Politics,* 2012, p. 549-591.

**Tzankova & Hensler 2013**
Tzankova, I. & Hensler, D., 'Collective Settlements in the Netherlands: Some Empirical Observations', in Stadler, A. & Hodges, C. (eds.), *Resolving Mass Disputes: ADR and Settlement of Mass Claims*, Cheltenham: Edward Elgar, 2013, p. 91-105.

**Tzankova & Van Lith 2012**
Tzankova, I. & Van Lith, H., 'Class Actions and Class Settlements Going Global: The Netherlands', in Fairgrieve, D. & Lein, E. (eds.), *Extraterritoriality and Collective Redress,* Oxford: Oxford University Press, 2012, p. 67-91.

**Tzankova *et al.* 2014**
Tzankova, I., Van Maanen, M. & Rijnhart, M., 'A Dutch View on Discovery: Short and Sweet', *Defense Counsel Journal,* 2014, p. 229-237.

R. Kulski

# POLISH PERSPECTIVES AND PROVISIONS ON GROUP PROCEEDINGS

## 1. Introductory Notes

The introduction of group proceedings into the Polish legal system had been under consideration for several years. A vigorous discussion concerning this instrument began in January 2007 during a conference on collective litigation.[1] In the successive years numerous scholarly papers and studies concerning group proceedings were published in Poland.[2]

The draft Act on enforcing claims in group proceedings was prepared by the Polish Council of Ministers[3] and it was handed over to the Parliament on 26 March 2009 (document No. 1829).[4] The Act was finally adopted on 17 December 2009. *Vacatio legis* lasted six months and the Act entered into force on 18 July 2010.[5]

The Act on enforcing claims in group proceedings (Act on Group Action, hereinafter: the Act) introduced a new device into Polish civil procedural law, a device which has not been clearly defined in the Polish legal system thus far.[6] This

1 Conference Materials on Group Proceedings, Warsaw, Ministry of Justice, 18-19 January 2007.

2 E.g. Kulski 2009a; Świczewska 2008; Pogonowski 2009; Pogonowski 2010.

3 It is worth noting that the works on the draft act were accompanied by a comparative study of legal solutions in other countries which had been introduced or were being elaborated. The Polish Act is not, however, based on any particular foreign legal act. Obviously, some similarities can certainly be noted, but Polish solutions can be described as innovative.

4 See Kulski 2009b; Kubas & Kos 2009; opinion available at the following website: <http://orka.sejm.gov.pl/rexdomk6.nsf/Opdodr?OpenPage&nr=1829> (last accessed in January 2014).

5 What needs to be emphasised is that it was a good decision to make a separate act governing group proceedings (instead of including it in the Polish Code of Civil Procedure (CCP)) because of a multiplicity of problems and complexity of issues related to group proceedings. It is still possible, though, that the question of regulating group proceedings in the CCP will have to be reconsidered when a new CCP is being prepared.

6 Group proceedings cannot be compared with joint participation in civil proceedings (Art. 72 CCP), with bringing an action by an NGO or another entity in the interest of a third party (Art. 61 CCP) or with combining cases for joint examination (Art. 219 CCP). The analysed new type of civil procedure is classified as group of proceedings including claims or charges →

Act only includes solutions which are procedural by nature and it is not the source of new claims. Polish group proceedings allow pursuing claims arising from substantive law.[7]

The introduction of a new regulation concerning group proceedings leads to a modification of the protective function of civil procedure through the widening of the scope of protection of collective interests in this procedure.[8] It may also bring positive social results as for example facilitating access to justice to many subjects who would not claim damages in a civil action individually. A significant number of people do not file a lawsuit in such matters (up to about €50) because the input of work is considered incommensurate with potential gains. Moreover, group proceedings may turn out useful to the system of justice, allowing one to settle many civil cases in one action.[9] The goal of introducing the Act on Group Action was to accelerate the examination of civil cases and to unify the judgments passed on the basis of either the same or similar factual backgrounds. Another goal was to impact market behaviour by introducing a civil procedure mechanism of sanctioning infringements of the law which bring significant profits to influential businesses.[10] Consequently, the most important goal of the Act is demonstrated in increasing access to justice and enhancing the effectiveness of legal protection before the court. Group proceedings should serve not only potential creditors but also the interests of the Judiciary.

The benefits of such proceedings are appreciated in other countries, where they have already been put into practice or where their implementation is in

submitted by many people to obtain a uniform resolution (aggregate proceedings). See Kulski 2008.

7 At the same time, the Act does not introduce any changes in the substantive law along with the introduction of a new procedure of enforcing claims.

8 On the protective function of civil procedure and on the growing importance of the protection of collective interests as a function of this procedure, see Cieślak 2009, p. 43 *et seq.* and p. 60. We also need to make a distinction between proceedings serving to protect the collective interests of a certain group, which are a form of public interests, and proceedings serving to provide collective protection of a sum of individual interests of group members. There are different models of legal solutions (lawsuit mechanisms) applicable for both these types of proceedings which are to be used for the purpose of fulfilling the goals of these proceedings. The protection of collective interests in Polish civil procedure can be observed in the procedure of declaring the terms of a standard contract illegal (Art. 479[36]-479[45] CCP). See Weitz 2007, p. 173 *et seq.* An example of violation of the rule of individual protection of subjective rights in Polish civil procedure is also Art. 323(2) of the Environmental Act dated 27 April 2001 (*Dz. U.* [Journal of Laws] of 2008, No. 25, item 150 as amended), which states that if a threat or violation concerns the natural environment as a common good, the State Treasury, a local authority as well as an environmental organisation may file a claim to restore the situation in compliance with the law and to undertake preventive measures, in particular through installing fittings or devices which protect against the threat or damage to the environment, and possibly to cease the activity which causes threat or damage to the environment.

9 See e.g. Friedenthal, Kane & Miller 1999, p. 736-738; Andrews 2001, p. 263-264.

10 Ereciński & Grzegorczyk 2013, p. 26-27.

progress. Therefore, we should approve of the introduction of group proceedings in Poland.[11]

As mentioned earlier, group action is a new institution in Polish civil procedure and references to it in existing legislation are scarce. The philosophy of group proceedings is different from traditional proceedings focused on protecting individual interests. Therefore, due to the large number of problems and complexity of issues related to group proceedings they are regulated in a separate act and were not incorporated into the Polish Code of Civil Procedure (CCP).[12] Nonetheless, pursuant to Article 24 of the Act, the provisions of the Code are applicable to an extent which was not regulated in the Act. A court examining a group action case should apply the provisions of the Code either directly or accordingly.[13] However, some provisions of the Code are not applied because they were deliberately excluded from group proceedings, for example provisions concerning the participation of a public prosecutor (Article 7 CCP) and non-governmental organisations (Article 8 CCP) in the proceedings; provisions related to appointing an attorney or a legal advisor by the court and the provisions of the Act on Costs in Civil Proceedings related to the exemption of a party from court costs; and provisions concerning counterclaims (Articles 204 and 205 CCP).

## 2. Key (Basic) Issues Related to the Act on Enforcing Claims in Group Proceedings

### 2.1. *The Scope of Matters that can be dealt with in Group Proceedings (Article 1, Sec. 2 of the Act)*

Under the draft Act, group proceedings could be brought in a large number of cases. The universal scope of application was supposed to be one of the main premises of the Act. The draft originally did not contain any exclusions relating to subject matter. Group actions were meant to apply to all civil cases. Such a wide range of application raised doubts of some institutions and in legal doctrine. All in all, currently the newly introduced Act on enforcing claims in group proceedings only covers positively defined categories of cases. The cases that can be examined in group proceedings include:

a) claims for consumer protection;
b) claims arising from liability for damage caused by a dangerous product (Article 449[1] *et seq.* of the Polish Civil Code);

11 On the Polish regulation on group proceedings, see in particular: Jaworski & Radzimierski 2010; Piasecki 2010, p. 775 *et seq.*; Grzegorczyk 2011; Rejdak & Pietkiewicz 2011.

12 Group proceedings differ in many aspects from individual proceedings governed by the CCP.

13 See also: *Resolution of the Supreme Court of 13 July 2011, III CZP 28/11*, OSNC (Judgments of the Civil Law Chamber of the Polish Supreme Court) 2012, No. 1, item 9.

c) claims arising from prohibited acts (torts); this includes claims other than those arising from liability for damage caused by a dangerous product, with the assumption that this liability qualifies as arising from a tort.

The Act excludes, generally, cases related to claims for the protection of personal interests. This exclusion needs to be criticised.[14] However, we ought to note that not every harm is related to the violation of personal interests. As a result, group proceedings will be applied in cases concerning damage inflicted to property by a prohibited act, (private) nuisance and other violations of ownership or of rights that are protected in the same manner as ownership (limited rights in property). Group proceedings will also be applicable in disputes between shareholders and public companies (e.g. in the case of failing to fulfil the obligation to provide information on a company). The Act does not apply to cases connected with employees' claims, claims against the State Treasury, claims against the purveyors of mass services and banks.

For the first category of cases, it is the protected subject that is of importance (violated interests of a consumer require protection, regardless of the source of violation and the legal basis). In the second and third categories, it is only the object of protection that is important.

## 2.2. *Admissibility of Group Proceedings*

Whether a particular action (which also includes group proceedings) can be admitted by a given court for consideration and adjudication depends on the

14 In the Polish Civil Code there is no definition of personal interests. The concept that definitely prevails in the doctrine and is uniformly adopted in judicial decisions is the objective concept, according to which personal interests are non-property rights which are connected to an individual's personality and are commonly acknowledged in society (as e.g. Szpunar 1979, p. 106). Issues that matter for a personal interest to exist and to state that it has been breached are social evaluation and an analysis made from the point of view of a sensible person. However, a subjective opinion of the person concerned is of no importance (see also the judgment of the Supreme Court of 16 January 1976, II CR 692/75, OSNC 1976, No. 11, item 251; judgment of the Supreme Court of 11 March 1997, III CKN 33/97, OSNC 1997, No. 6-7, item 93 judgment of the Supreme Court dated 25 April 1989, I CR 143/89, OSP 1990, issue 9, item 330). We also need to add that the concept of personal interests is normative by nature. Personal interests may only be those which are protected by law. According to Art. 23 of the Polish Civil Code, the list of personal interests is very long and it includes health and life. These interests are very susceptible to violation in situations for which the Polish group proceedings have been regulated and which are usually protected abroad by group action. Consequently, a narrow scope of the new legal device did not meet social expectations regarding this Act. Moreover, it seems that the scope of application of the Act on Group Action may lead to significant interpretation problems, because the provisions of the Act comprise several terms relevant to private law, which, until now, were not used to define the admissibility of procedural matters. Exclusion of claims connected to the protection of personal interests also generates controversies. Katner & Krakowiak 2011, p. 351.

prerequisites for court proceedings.[15] Independently of the prerequisites for court proceedings, the admissibility of group proceedings depends on some additional circumstances. There are three elements which define the borders of admissibility of group proceedings (regardless of the nature of the claim):

- the claims are of the same type (one-type claims);[16]
- the claims are raised by at least 10 persons (a group);[17]
- the claims arise from the same or identical factual basis (Article 1, Sec. 1 of the Act).[18]

Moreover, in actions on pecuniary claims it is indispensable to unify the amount of the claim for every member of the group, taking the common circumstances of a particular case into consideration (it is possible to make unification in subgroups). For example, a group of persons who were exposed to the adverse effects of a medication agree that they will demand a particular sum of money, regardless of how harmful the medication proved to be to each of them. Rules on unifying amounts of claims are left to the discretion of the group members and representatives. If a group action is initiated as a result of a train crash, unification might occur depending on the kind of injuries suffered by the victims. In the case of damage resulting from great tumult, commotion or other disturbances, standardisation can be achieved depending on the location of a house or a flat in relation to the source of the disturbance.

The Act introduced an instrument which may be applied even if standardisation is impossible to achieve. In other words, a group action can still achieve some of its goals even without standardisation of claims. In such situations, a plaintiff's claim will be limited to establishing the responsibility of the defendant (Article, 2 Sec. 3 of the Act). The lawsuit will not result in awarding a particular sum of money, rather it will be limited to establishing the responsibility of the defendant. Such a judgment will be legally binding in the subsequent trial.

It is not necessary for the claims to be based on the same legal provision. Consequently, conceivable situations might include, for instance, involvement in a train accident or a plane crash, drinking polluted water, taking the same medicine or even – theoretically – several medicines of the same producer, falling victim to the faulty functioning of a product, for example a car accident caused by a faulty car

15 On the prerequisites for court proceedings in Polish legal literature, see Broniewicz, Marciniak & Kunicki 2014, p. 189-191; Jodłowski *et al.* 2009, p. 60.

16 As a matter of fact, based on the actual circumstances of the case it can be stated that a claim is monotypic. See Rejdak 2010, p. 23.

17 Proceedings with a smaller number of people can be satisfactorily conducted by means of the joint participation in an action.

18 As compared with the definition of group proceedings used in other countries, it is quite striking that when defining additional grounds for admissibility of group proceedings in Poland there is no reservation saying that such proceedings may be initiated when enforcing claims in group proceedings is more effective than in individual (standard) proceedings.

part, damage caused by an exploding airbag, travelling by the same delayed means of transport, etc.[19]

The court decides in a hearing on the admissibility of group proceedings[20] (Article 10 of the Act). If the court acknowledges group proceedings as admissible, it issues a decision on examining the case in group proceedings. If the court decides that a particular case cannot be admitted for group proceedings (and also if the case exceeds the objective scope of the proceedings), it will refuse to allow the claim. It is possible to appeal against both decisions, i.e. the decision to examine a case in group proceedings and the refusal to allow a claim in group proceedings. If, after issuing a decision on examining a case in group proceedings, the number of group members decreases to fewer than 10 persons (for instance, when a member of the group withdraws), then the court will dismiss the action.

## 2.3. *The Model of Group Membership*

The method of defining group membership is one of the crucial (conclusive) and probably the most controversial issues in the group proceedings model. The key question here is whether the rights of an individual, which are defined by law, ought to be executed without the individual's express consent and entrusted to someone else, so that the individual can participate in litigation. The methods (regimes) of defining group membership include opt-in and opt-out models. The Polish Act on Group Action has adopted the opt-in model. Subjects who have not joined the group may assert their claims in line with the general principles of Polish civil procedure (Article 1, Sec. 3 of the Act).

The opt-out model, especially characteristic for the USA, but also for some EU Member States as the Netherlands and England & Wales, was rejected by Polish lawmakers mainly because of constitutional reasons and the rule that parties have the prerogative to individually manage their procedural rights. If a member of a group that does not typically participate in the proceedings in the opt-out model (does not have the rights of a party to the proceedings) wants to take advantage of the constitutional right to be heard, he or she would have to step out of the group. Imposing the burden of leaving the group upon a person and the risk of being bound by a potentially unfavourable judgment would clash with the right to access to court (Article 45 of the Polish Constitution).[21]

The fundamental argument for the opt-in regime was the protection of the freedom of an individual to participate in court proceedings only if he is willing to do so.[22] Group members who do not wish to take part in the proceedings should not be included in the group due to their remaining silent. A person who is actually interested in the proceedings may bring his claim in group proceedings if he

19 Ereciński & Grzegorczyk 2013, p. 33.

20 Jaworski 2009.

21 See also Grzegorczyk 2011, p. 33-36.

22 Kulski 2010, p. 171-174.

belongs to the group as defined by the court. However, the court does not force litigants to bring their claims; the court will wait until the party asserts his claim. The court decides whether there are actually grounds for the claim, i.e. it decides on material and legal issues, in the final judgment. If a person does not join the group, whether willingly or even because of ignorance, he is entitled to institute an action individually. The judgment is binding (*res iudicata*) for all the persons who have opted in as if they actually participated in the litigation.

Though the Act has, in fact, adopted the opt-in model, a member of a group who has opted in may later opt out from the group, as stipulated in Article 1, Sec. 3 of the Act, and the declaration of a group member to opt out from the group may be filed until the decision on the composition of the group is issued.[23] If a group member opts out from the group, the proceedings relating to this particular member ought to be discontinued since issuing a decision including such a member is inadmissible (Article 355 CCP).

## 2.4. *The Possibility of Introducing the Opt-out Model into the Polish System of Court Proceedings*

It seems admissible to allow instituting an action without the knowledge of the person whose rights are subject to protection, but imposing an obligation of performing a particular action in order to be excluded from the proceedings on a person who is not willing to pursue judicial protection by the agency of a group representative may raise doubts from the constitutional perspective (see below). What we need to realise, however, is that opting out does not depend upon fulfilling additional requirements by the individual concerned - a group member does not have to justify his or her decision. Moreover, we need to consider whether as a result of an opt-out regime the assertion of claims of lesser value would become easier, especially if we think of traditional barriers that impede access to the court. As a consequence, it is worth considering whether the opt-in model should not be supplemented with an opt-out regime in the Act in relation to group proceedings on small claims initiated by some public entities (e.g. by the Consumer Advocate).[24]

23 The usability of the opt-in model depends to a large extent on notification (announcement) of initiating group proceedings and on the class (group) itself. The point is to notify every individual who is interested in a group proceeding and to enable him to join the group if he is willing to do so. The opt-in model may, however, turn out to be little effective, if we allow for some typical models of social behaviour - people, in particular consumers, are afraid of joining a group because of costs and time as well as procedural complexity of a case. There is a common conviction that individual proceedings give better profits.

24 According to Grzegorczyk 2011, p. 38 we also ought to think that the combined model will have to be considered in Poland in the future.

## 3. Parties to Group Proceedings

### 3.1. *Competence and Composition of the Court in Group Proceedings*

Concerning jurisdiction, Council Regulation (EC) No. 44/2001 of 22 December 2000 on jurisdiction and the recognition and enforcement of judgments in civil and commercial matters (*OJ* 2001 L12, p. 1) applies. Territorial competence is established on the basis of the general provisions of the Polish Code of Civil Procedure (Article 27 *et seq*. CCP). Polish group proceedings lie within the competence of a regional court (the higher court of first instance) notwithstanding the value of the claim (Article 3, Sec. 1 of the Act). Cases are examined by three professional judges. Such a regulation of the court in group proceedings proves that the legislator took the meaning and importance of cases dealt with in these proceedings into consideration. Generally, in Polish civil procedure at first instance civil cases are resolved before district courts (the lower courts of first instance) by a single judge.

### 3.2. *Plaintiff*

In Polish group proceedings a court action is brought by a representative of a group who can be either a group member or a *poviat* (district) Consumer Advocate, but in group proceedings the Consumer Advocate may only act in cases concerning consumer protection-related claims.[25] Members of a group have the right to independently bring proceedings and to assert claims in group proceedings. However, declarations of intent of group members are necessary for the proceedings to be initiated as group proceedings.

The representative must be agreed upon by every member of the group.[26] We need to note that the right to act as a claimant in the case of the Consumer Advocate is not in any way materially related to the private claims which are asserted in group proceedings. The public nature of such a substitute is reflected in his or her rights and obligations.[27]

It is also worth noting that it is possible to appoint a representative for the group on the basis of a court decision upon the request of more than half of the group members.

Group representatives, if they are not advocates or counsellors at law, grant an advocate or counsellor at law power of attorney to represent the group in court proceedings[28] and conclude a contract with the attorney defining his or her

[25] Kuberska 2012, p. 92. In light of a proposed amendment to the law, it is worth considering the possibility of extending the potential circle of representatives, allowing, in particular, for such categories of individuals for whom participation in group proceedings arises for achieving public goals (e.g. acceptance of the insurance ombudsmen).

[26] The relation between the group representative and group members ought to be regulated separately by the parties in the form of an appropriate contract.

[27] Kuberska 2012, p. 95 *et seq.*

[28] Tomaszek 2010, p. 666.

remuneration.[29] The Polish Supreme Court has stressed that the obligatory representation of a claimant by an advocate or legal counsel is also applicable to the Consumer Advocate, who is a group representative. A statement of case submitted without observing the obligation of legal representation is returned without notice for correction of defects.[30]

In general, the relations between group members (or a group), the representative and the attorney are formed on the basis of the freedom-of-contract rule. We should also mention one more category of contracts, namely the contract that a group concludes with the law firm of the attorney involved in the case.

As far as the functions of representatives are concerned, some of their activities require particular attention in group proceedings. First of all, persons whose claims may be included in group proceedings submit a written declaration on joining the group to its representative. Second, the group representative prepares a list of persons who have joined the group and presents the list to the court together with the declarations on joining the group. Third, the representative may oblige a group member joining the group to provide, within an indicated time limit, additional evidence or explanations. As is stated in Article 16, Sec. 1 of the Act, in actions on pecuniary claims it is the burden of the plaintiff to prove (and in other cases, to make probable) group affiliation.

Members of the group are generally devoid of procedural rights, except for activities connected with the subject of the proceedings (Article 19 of the Act) and a change of representative (Article 18 of the Act). The position of members of a group is additionally defined by special provisions. For instance, Article 14 of the Act stipulates that acting in the capacity of an intervener is inadmissible and Article 20 of the Act assumes that members of a group will be heard as a party to the proceedings (not as a witness).

### 3.3. *Defendant*

The Act on enforcing claims in group proceedings does not envisage the possibility of carrying out group proceedings with the participation of a group representative of the defendant. Lack of clear regulation and of a detailed provision defining such proceedings lead to the conclusion that he will be inadmissible. However, several entities may act together as defendants (e.g. if they bear joint and several liability, such as a manufacturer and an importer).

29 The duties a representative has even before group proceedings start (though not explicitly regulated) also include: group formation, agreeing on the rules of participation in the group and possibly providing financial resources.

30 See also Resolution of the Polish Supreme Court of 13 July 2011, III CZP 28/11, OSNC 2012, No. 1, item 9 and Broniewicz 1963, p. 157.

## 4. Stages in the Course of Group Proceedings

### 4.1. *Introductory Remarks*

In general, group proceedings include: (1) proceedings concerning admissibility of the action and (2) the actual group proceedings (group proceedings *sensu stricto*).[31] Several other stages can be distinguished in each of the mentioned proceedings.

### 4.2. *Proceedings on Admissibility of Group Proceedings*

#### 4.2.1. Instituting an Action

The initiation of the proceedings takes place by filing a group action lawsuit. The statement of claim in group proceedings needs to comply with all the conditions envisaged for a statement of claim in general (Article 126 *et seq.* CCP; Article 187 CCP), and with special conditions envisaged for this type of action in the Act (i.e. a petition to examine the case in group proceedings, indicating the circumstances justifying the admissibility of a group action, declaration of the plaintiff stating that he or she is acting as a group representative and, in actions on pecuniary claims, the amount of claim of every group member). Moreover, the declarations of all the group members on joining the group and their consent to a particular group representative ought to be provided together with the statement of claim, as well as the contract made between the group representative and an attorney, defining the attorney's remuneration.[32]

#### 4.2.2. Delivering a Copy of the Group's Statement of Claim to the Defendant and Submitting a Reply to a Statement of Claim

The defendant's reply to a statement of claim ought to include the possible objections concerning the admissibility of group proceedings and objections to the legitimacy of the claim as well as a grounded request to secure the costs of court proceedings.

#### 4.2.3. Court's Decision on Admissibility of Group Proceedings

As mentioned earlier, admissibility of group proceedings is decided by the court at a hearing, and it is enough that the court decides on the basis of claims of at least 10 persons, because the decision on whether there are grounds for admitting group

31 Pogonowski 2010, p. 156; Ereciński & Grzegorczyk 2013, p. 38-39.

32 In group proceedings it is not enough to specify the features of a model group in whose interest the proceedings will be carried out, its members have to be specified by name, and their number must be indicated. Thus, one must emphasise that protection of group claims combines, on the one hand, some issues related to the protection of collective interests and, on the other hand, issues related to the protection of individual interests.

proceedings for the assertion of claims of all the group members is taken by the court later, when establishing the composition of the group.

## 4.3. *The Actual Group Proceedings*

### 4.3.1. Announcement of Initiation of Group Proceedings

Once the decision on examining the case in group proceedings becomes final and unappealable, the court *ex officio* adjudicates to announce the initiation of group proceedings. The announcement is the first activity in the second stage of group proceedings. The function of this announcement is to provide the public with the most detailed information possible in reference to the subject matter of the case and the regulations under which the claim is being asserted by the group representative. This announcement is, in fact, a form of notifying the potential group members of the possibility of joining the group, and thus it ought to have the broadest dissemination possible, so that all the individuals who are interested in a particular claim can be included in the group proceedings.

The announcement is usually made in the national mass media and provides a specific deadline up to which an interested person can join the group.

The announcement is not the only method that can be applied. The Act does not exclude other ways of disseminating the news, for instance on national television or online, or by individually communicating with people who bought a faulty product or fell victim to an accident.

### 4.3.2. Submitting Declarations on Joining the Group to the Group Representative by Parties whose Claims might be included in Group Proceedings

Apart from the submission of the declarations, a list of persons who have joined the group has to be prepared by the group's representative[33] and this list has to be presented (together with the declaration on joining the group) by the group representative to the court.

The Act does not define the time limit for presenting this list. The representative ought to present the list, however, without delay.[34] The moment of the presentation of declarations on joining the group to the court is the moment at which the consequences of instituting an action arise with reference to the parties that are joining the group and it results in the pendency of the case. Such a solution is problematic; the composition of the group is defined by the court (see below), which means that the declaration submitted to the group representative is not

33 Although the Act does not directly stipulate whether a group representative is entitled to reject some of the declarations, such an interpretation should be approved. The representative administers the case.

34 Jaworski & Radzimierski 2010, p. 306.

effective and it is not the document which produces the legal consequence of becoming a group member, but membership depends on the decision of the court, which constitutes the composition of the group.[35]

#### 4.3.3. Delivering the List of Persons who have joined the Group to the Defendant and Defining the Time Limits for the Defendant to Submit Objections as to Group Membership

It is worth noting that the plaintiff has the possibility of responding to the objections of the defendant as to group membership within a time limit defined by the court.

#### 4.3.4. Decision on the Composition of the Group

The court will proceed to pass a decision concerning the composition of the group independent of whether the defendant has submitted any objections in this respect. Making such a decision requires that the court examine the claims of respective members of the group. The court may decide that a group action will only be admissible in reference to particular persons or it may divide the group into subgroups.[36] Once the decision becomes final and unappealable,[37] the group composition is consolidated and 'fixed', and a future exit from the group by individual group members is ineffective.

The Act does not contain any specific provisions concerning the course of group proceedings after the composition of the group is established. It should be assumed that group proceedings will be carried out according to the general rules of the Polish Code of Civil Procedure. The court will not examine individual claims and it will limit, in fact, the scope of examination to the claim of the group as a whole.

## 5. Judgment in Group Proceedings

There are two situations which should be distinguished if the plaintiff wins the case for pecuniary claims. The first one occurs when the court restricts itself to recognising the claims as justified in principle, deciding only on the defendant's liability (Article 2, Sec. 3 of the Act). Then, each member of the group mentioned in the judgment may bring an individual action in order to determine the exact amount of the claim. The second situation takes place when the court enumerates all members of the group or subgroups and the sum of money which is awarded to

35 More on this subject in Grzegorczyk 2011, p. 74.

36 This is the crucial moment of the proceedings from the defendant's point of view.

37 The decision on group composition is subject to parties' complaint. A question arises whether the right to file a complaint will also be vested in persons who were trying to obtain the status of group members but were not included in the decision on group composition. In reference to such persons, the decision on group composition is also a decision which terminates proceedings in a case.

each of them (Article 21, Secs. 1 and 2 of the Act). Thanks to this, a judgment will directly serve as an enforcement order for individual members of a group or subgroups (Article 22 of the Act).

If non-pecuniary claims are adjudged, the content of the decision should include the names of all the members of the group or subgroups (Article 21, Sec. 1 of the Act).

Under Article 21, Sec. 3 of the Act a final judgment is effective with respect to all members of the group. The judgment allowing the action as well as dismissing it is legally binding for all members of the group (or subgroups) who are indicated in the decision on the composition of the group. Consequently, a final judgment is characterised by its *res iudicata* effect and binding force (in relations between each member of the group and the defendant). It is inadmissible to assert claims examined in a group action individually if the action has been dismissed.

From 2010 until mid 2013, 102 group (class) actions were filed in Polish courts; 41 cases reached a negative resolution. In general, we see that proceedings concerning establishing rules of liability prevail over actions for compensation. The cause for this is mainly the practical difficulty in unifying financial claims within a group (or subgroup). So far the courts of first instance have only delivered a few judgments in group actions. The most famous judgment was delivered on 3 July 2013 by the Regional Court in Łódź in case No. II C 1693/10 filed by the Municipal Consumer Advocate in Warsaw against BRE Bank Spółka Akcyjna. The court determined that the defendant bank was liable for damages to 1,247 persons due to its improper performance of credit agreements concluded with persons specified in the judgment.

## 6. Enforcement proceedings

If a group action concerns pecuniary claims, the Act allows the members of the group to take advantage of the enforcement order without the mediation of a representative. This solution, however, raises doubts as to the economic worth of initiating individual enforcement, in particular, if the adjudicated benefits are of small amounts.

A different solution was adopted with regard to the enforcement of non-pecuniary claims (e.g. an order to refrain from particular activities or to perform some activities). In this case, in order to avoid multiplicity of creditors in enforcement proceedings, the group representative files a motion to initiate the enforcement procedure (Article 23, Sec. 1 of the Act). The exclusive right (authorisation) of a group representative to initiate enforcement proceedings is temporary by its very nature. If the motion is not filed effectively within six months from the day on which the judgment has become final, each creditor (group member) acquires the right to file a motion (individually) on appending an enforcement clause and to initiate the enforcement procedure (Article 23, Sec. 2 of the Act). The scope of this regulation is to protect the interests of members of the group in such a way that it will protect them from any detrimental outcome that might result from the representative's idleness.[38]

## 7. Appeal

The Act does not contain any special regulations concerning the way of appealing against a judgment in group proceedings. Therefore, an appeal against the judgment may be filed with the court of appeal according to the general rules of the Code of Civil Procedure. A judgment rendered by the court of appeal can be further contested by a cassation complaint at the Supreme Court.

## 8. Costs of Group Proceedings

In the analysed proceedings, the envisaged court fees are lower than in an ordinary procedure regulated in the Polish Code of Civil Procedure.

In the case of group proceedings concerning proprietary rights, a proportional fee is charged in the amount of 2 per cent of the value of the object in dispute, no less, however, than PLN 30 and no more than PLN 100,000.[39] In the case of group proceedings concerning proprietary rights where the value of the object in dispute cannot be established at the time of initiating the proceedings, a temporary fee is defined between PLN 100 and PLN 10,000; the amount of the fee may be conclusively determined after the group composition is defined by the court.

In the case of an action on the protection of non-property rights asserted in group proceedings, a fixed fee in the amount of PLN 600 is collected.

At the defendant's request the court may oblige the plaintiff to submit a cash (security) deposit (in an amount not higher than 20 per cent of the value of the object in dispute) to secure the costs of the proceedings (Article 8, Secs. 1-6 of the Act). At the defendant's request the court will order the use of the deposit to satisfy the costs adjudicated to the defendant.

The Act provides the possibility of concluding a contract defining the attorney's remuneration and specifying the remuneration in relation to the amount adjudged in favour of the plaintiff (Article 5 of the Act).[40]

Costs are adjudged according to the outcome of the proceedings. Either the group representative has to pay in the interest of the defendant or the defendant has to pay in the interest of the group representative.[41]

38 Katner & Krakowiak 2011, p. 372.

39 The euro exchange rate is more or less at the level of PLN 4.20.

40 A commission fee stipulated in Art. 5 of the Act is not included in the costs of court proceedings and it is not to be reimbursed by the defendant if he loses the case.

41 The Act does not envisage charging the expenses of the proceedings of the court directly to particular members of the group. The question of collecting the funds required to carry out group proceedings as well as the source of these funds is left to the discretion of a group representative and the internal organisation of the group.

## Bibliography

**Andrews 2001**
Andrews, N., 'Multi-party Proceedings in England: Representative and Group Actions', *Duke Journal of Comparative & International Law*, 2001, Vol. 11, p. 249-267.

**Broniewicz 1963**
Broniewicz, W., 'Podstawienie procesowe', *Zeszyty Naukowe Uniwersytetu Łódzkiego*, 1963, issue 31, p. 145-170.

**Broniewicz, Marciniak & Kunicki 2014**
Broniewicz, W., Marciniak, A. & Kunicki, I., *Postępowanie cywilne w zarysie*, Warsaw: LexisNexis, 2014.

**Cieślak 2009**
Cieślak, S., *Formalizm postępowania cywilnego*, Warsaw: C.H. Beck, 2009.

**Ereciński & Grzegorczyk 2013**
Ereciński, T. & Grzegorczyk, P., 'Effective Protection of Diverse Interests in Civil Proceedings on the Example of Polish Act on Group Action', in Ereciński, T. *et al.* (eds.), *Recent Trends in Economy and Efficiency of Civil Procedure*, Vilnius: Vilnius University Press, 2013, p. 23-50.

**Friedenthal, Kane & Miller 1999**
Friedenthal, J.H., Kane, M.M. & Miller, A.R., *Civil Procedure*, St. Paul, Minn.: West Group, 1999.

**Grzegorczyk 2011**
Grzegorczyk, P., *Ustawa o dochodzeniu roszczeń w postępowaniu grupowym. Ogólna charakterystyka*, Warsaw: LexisNexis, 2011.

**Jaworski 2009**
Jaworski, A., 'Dopuszczalność postępowania grupowego', *Przegląd Sądowy*, 2009, No. 11-12, p. 50-71.

**Jaworski & Radzimierski 2010**
Jaworski, T. & Radzimierski, P., *Ustawa o dochodzeniu roszczeń w postępowaniu grupowym. Komentarz*, Warsaw: C.H. Beck, 2010.

**Jodlowski *et al.* 2009**
Jodłowski, J., Resich, A., Lapierre, J., Misiuk-Jodłowska, T. & Weitz, K., *Postępowanie cywilne*, Warsaw: LexisNexis, 2009.

**Katner & Krakowiak 2011**
Katner, W.J. & Krakowiak, M., 'Polska class action - wybrane zagadnienia prawa materialnego i postępowania cywilnego', in Gudowski, J. & Weitz, K. (eds.), *Aurea Praxis Aurea Teoria. FS for Professor Tadeusz Ereciński*, Vol. I, Warsaw: LexisNexis, 2011, p. 341-373.

**Kubas & Kos 2009**
Kubas, A. & Kos, R., 'Opinia w sprawie projektu ustawy o dochodzeniu roszczeń w postępowaniu grupowym', Sejm paper 1829, 2009.

**Kuberska 2012**
Kuberska, W., 'Ustawa o dochodzeniu roszczeń w postępowaniu grupowym - pierwsze doświadczenia praktyczne', *Przegląd Sądowy*, 2012, issues 7-8, p. 83-100.

**Kulski 2008**
Kulski, R., 'Aggregate Proceedings as Tools for Providing Efficiency in Civil Procedure', in Carpi, F. & Ortells Ramos, M. (eds.), *Oral and Written Proceedings: Efficiency in Civil Procedure, Vol. II: Presentations*, Valencia: Universitat de Valencia Press, 2008, p. 425-446.

**Kulski 2009a**
Kulski, R., 'Powództwo grupowe w świetle amerykańskiego federalnego prawa procesowego cywilnego', in *Ewolucja polskiego postępowania cywilnego wobec przemian politycznych, społecznych i gospodarczych. Materiały konferencyjne Ogólnopolskiego Zjazdu Katedr Postępowania Cywilnego, Szczecin-Niechorze 28-30 September 2007*, Warsaw: C.H. Beck, 2009, p. 189-204.

**Kulski 2009b**
Kulski, R., 'Opinia o rządowym projekcie ustawy o dochodzeniu roszczeń w postępowaniu grupowym', Sejm paper No. 1829, 2009.

**Kulski 2010**
Kulski, R., 'Modele określenia członkostwa w grupie w postępowaniu wszczętym na podstawie class action', in Pogonowski, P. *et al.* (eds.), *Współczesne przemiany postępowania cywilnego*, Warsaw: Oficyna Wolters Kluwer Business, 2010, p. 158-174.

**Piasecki 2010**
Piasecki, K. (ed.), *Kodeks postępowania cywilnego. Vol. II: Komentarz do artykułów 367-505[37]*, Warsaw: C.H. Beck, 2010.

**Pogonowski 2009**
Pogonowski, P., 'Ochrona roszczeń rozproszonych w Anglii i USA - dwa modele regulacji postępowań grupowych', *Przegląd Sądowy*, 2009, No. 6, p. 102-119.

**Pogonowski 2010**
Pogonowski, P., *Postępowanie grupowe. Ochrona prawna wielu podmiotów w postępowaniu cywilnym*, Warsaw: LexisNexis, 2010.

**Rejdak 2010**
Rejdak, M., 'Jednorodzajowe roszczenia w postępowaniu grupowym', *Przegląd Prawa Handlowego*, 2010, No. 8, p. 22-26.

**Rejdak & Pietkiewicz 2011**
Rejdak, M. & Pietkiewicz, P., *Ustawa o dochodzeniu roszczeń w postępowaniu grupowym. Komentarz*, Warsaw: LexisNexis, 2011.

**Świczewska 2008**
Świczewska, A., 'Class action oraz inne postępowania zbiorowe', *Przegląd Sądowy*, 2008, No. 4, p. 22-44.

**Szpunar 1979**
Szpunar, A., *Ochrona dóbr osobistych*, Warsaw: PWN, 1979.

**Tomaszek 2010**
Tomaszek, A., 'Pełnomocnik powoda w polskim postępowaniu grupowym', *Monitor Prawniczy*, 2010, No. 11, p. 666.

**Weitz 2007**
Weitz, K., 'Postępowanie w sprawach o uznanie postanowień wzorca umowy za niedozwolone', in Wiśniewski, T. (ed.), *Postępowanie sądowe w sprawach gospodarczych*, Vol. 7, Warsaw: C.H. Beck, 2007, p. 173-217.

L. Ervo

# GROUP ACTIONS IN SWEDEN – A MODERATE START

## 1. The Scope of Group Actions

Group actions were introduced in Sweden in the 2003 Group Proceedings Act (*Lag om grupprättegång* 2002:599). Group actions cover all civil cases that can be brought before the general first instance courts as well as cases concerning environmental damage, which can be brought before the environmental courts. Three types of group actions can be distinguished, namely private, public, and organizational group actions.[1] The Group Proceedings Act consists of 50 sections and if no specific rules can be found in the Act, the rules of the Code of Judicial Procedure and the Environmental Act should be followed.[2]

The Group Proceedings Act aims at deciding cases by way of a court judgment. The legislator did not put much effort into providing for settlement or mediation procedures in group actions, thus while the Act covers the procedure from its very beginning until judgment, there are only a few rules on settlement and mediation. Settlement and mediation are, however, possible and especially settlement has been used in practice. For instance, the very first group action in Sweden resulted in a friendly settlement of the case, which was confirmed by the court.[3]

It is well-known that group actions can be used as a tool to increase the effectiveness of negotiations aimed at resolving a dispute and to motivate the defendant to settle the case. ADR, friendly settlement and mediation are currently popular topics, not only in the European Union[4] but also in the world at large. Taking this into consideration, it is unfortunate that the Swedish legislator has not

1 Group Proceedings Act (GPA), Sec. 2 and Code of Environmental Matters, Chapter 32, Sec. 13; Lindblom 2008a, p. 257 and Lindblom 2008b, p. 833.

2 GPA, Sec. 2.

3 Aer Olympic, Stockholm District Court, T 3515-03.

4 Directive 2013/11/EU of the European Parliament and of the Council of 21 May 2013 on alternative dispute resolution for consumer disputes and amending Regulation (EC) No. 2006/2004 and Directive 2009/22/EC.

focused more on settlement and mediation in group actions. In addition, since about 60 per cent of ordinary civil cases are settled during the preparatory stage of litigation,[5] group actions should not be an exception to this rule; nevertheless, mediation is not very common in Sweden.[6] Settlement and mediation in group actions should be developed in Sweden in order to meet European Community demands[7] and to realize the idea of a multi-door courthouse.[8]

Consumer protection in Sweden is the concern of the National Board for Consumer Disputes (ARN), a public authority that functions similar to a court. The Board delivers recommendations on how consumer disputes should be resolved, and although the Board's recommendations are not binding, the majority of companies follow them. Group complaints have been possible since 1991, and the Consumer Ombudsman, i.e. the Director General and head of the Swedish Consumer Agency, and consumer associations or wage-earners can bring a group complaint to the ARN. The operation of the ARN is not based on the opt-in model; rather, the recommendations cover all consumers who could have identical demands based on the same grounds against the same business entity.[9] Traditionally, boards have had great significance in Scandinavia as a means of access to justice in a prompt and affordable way without a trial. Such a system is cheap and 'light'. The problem, however, is that it does not fulfil the right to have access to the courts and the result is not a judgment, but a recommendation. If the losing party does not voluntarily follow the recommendation, the winning party has to turn to the courts anyway in order to get an enforceable judgment. Therefore, the power of the recommendations made by the boards is only 'political', that is to say, the recommendations exert pressure against the economic interests of the losing party, and companies when a consumer has been found the winner in the case. Despite these apparent weaknesses, the boards have been useful and the losing parties normally follow their recommendations.[10]

There are no other tailored group action procedures for consumer cases in Sweden, but the Consumer Ombudsman can act as a representative of individual consumers before ordinary courts in proceedings between a consumer and a company. The requirements are that the case should be of particular importance for legal interpretation *de lege lata* and that there should be a general consumer interest

5 According to court statistics, the percentage of civil cases at district courts where the case was decided by a judgment is: in 2008 40.5 per cent, 2009 40.2 per cent, 2010 40.4 per cent, 2011 42 per cent and 2012 41.2 per cent. <www.domstol.se/Publikationer/Statistik/-Domstolsstatistik%202012.pdf> (last accessed on 11 March 2014). Similar results appear also in Lindell 2012, p. 303 and in SOU 1982/26, *Processen i tingsrätt, del B. Statens offentliga utredningar*, p. 137, which shows us that the trend has quite a long tradition now.

6 Ervo & Sippel 2012, p. 378.

7 Directive 2013/11/EU of the European Parliament and of the Council of 21 May 2013 on alternative dispute resolution for consumer disputes and amending Regulation (EC) No. 2006/2004 and Directive 2009/22/EC.

8 See Autio 2014, p. 303-311.

9 See Lindblom 2008a, p. 251.

10 Viitanen 2003, p. 438.

for taking the case before the court.[11] The Consumer Ombudsman can also act to protect the collective consumer interests in market law and unfair contract terms by prohibition orders or information disclosure orders or by initiating proceedings.[12] In addition, municipal consumer advisers can mediate between an individual consumer and a company in individual cases, and even if this function is voluntary for communities, it seems to be very effective whenever it is ordered. About 95 per cent of these types of mediations lead to friendly settlements.[13] There are no tailored group action procedures in anti-trust cases, but the Swedish Competition Authority may issue prohibition orders within the area of competition.[14]

## 2. The Nature of Group Actions

Group actions in Sweden can be private (individual) group actions, public (governmental) group actions as well as lawsuits brought by consumer organizations.[15] An individual, i.e. a natural or legal person, who is a member of the group concerned can bring a lawsuit against a defendant in the case of a private group action.[16] In lawsuits by organizations, the plaintiff is a non-profit association of consumers or employees.[17] In environmental cases, non-profit associations can bring group actions if they work for the interests of nature or environmental conservation. Also the associations of fishermen, farmers and reindeer management and forest societies can bring an organizational lawsuit in environmental issues.[18] A public group action is possible in cases where a lawsuit has not been brought as a private group action or by the organizations described above.[19] The authorities that can bring a public lawsuit are the Consumer Ombudsman and conservation authorities in environmental cases.[20] It should be emphasized that the ranking the legislator has given to private and public group actions prioritizes private group actions – the most favourable way to bring a lawsuit – and a public group action is possible only in those cases where a private group action has not been brought. To make a comparison with Finland, the situation there is the opposite. In Finland, only a public group action is allowed by the Group Action Act (444/2007) and the only authority that can bring the action is the Consumer Ombudsman. This extremely cautious start was made to guarantee safeguards against the abuse of group actions and to reach consensus for the acceptance of group actions in

11 Act on Participation of the Consumer Ombudsman in Certain Disputes 2011:1211, Sec. 2.
12 Market Act or Unfair Contract Terms Act at the Market Court, Secs. 23, 24, 28 and 47.
13 Bakardjieva Engelbrekt 2007, p. 588–589.
14 Competition Act 2008:579 and Ervo, Persson & Lindblom 2013.
15 GPA, Secs. 1, 4, 5 and 6.
16 *Ibidem*, Sec. 4.
17 *Ibidem*, Sec. 5.
18 Code of Environmental Matters, Chapter 32, Secs. 13 and 14.
19 Government bill 2001/02:107, *Regeringens proposition 2001/02:107, Lag om grupprättegång*, p. 54.
20 GPA, Sec. 6, and Decisions 1995:868 and 2001:1096 of the Council of State.

Finland.[21] However, this also means that group actions are merely the law on the books. Up to now, no group actions have been brought in Finland despite the fact that the Act has been valid since 1 October 2007. The current situation has caused quite a lot of political discussion, but in spite of that there are no pending reforms to change the situation.[22] To avoid the Finnish problems, it is important for Sweden not to render the Group Proceedings Act useless by minimizing the tools it includes. It is also an important signal to society of whether private or public group actions are the most desirable.

In Sweden, the court determines according to normal rules the admissibility of group actions – there is no multi-stage process (nor, for that matter, is there a common register for pending group actions, but only the normal register of all court cases).[23] A group action may only be considered if (1) the action is founded on circumstances that are common or of a similar nature to the claims of the members of the group, (2) group proceedings do not appear to be inappropriate owing to some claims of members of the group as regards grounds differing substantially from other claims, (3) a larger part of the claims to which the action relates cannot be pursued equally well by personal actions by the members of the group, (4) the group is appropriate for group litigation given its size and ambit and is appropriately defined, and (5) taking into consideration the plaintiff´s interest in the substantive matter, the plaintiff´s financial capacity to bring a group action and generally the circumstances, the plaintiff is appropriate to represent the members of the group in the case.[24] A private group action and an organizational group action must be brought through an attorney who is an advocate. However, if there are special circumstances, the court may allow the action to be brought without an attorney or through an attorney who is not an advocate.[25]

The Group Proceedings Act does not regulate how many members the group should have (point 4 above) nor how large or small their interest should be (point 3 above), but the court may consider what is appropriate, and if the court finds these requirements are not met, the action is inadmissible as a group action. The criteria are that the group action should be the most appropriate tool for the proceedings compared with the individual action and joinder actions. As far as the interest is concerned, one barometer is that the interest of one group member should not

21 See Ervo 2009 and 2011 and Ervo & Martinez 2012.

22 <www.om.fi/Etusivu/Ajankohtaista/Vastauksetkirjallisiinkysymyksiin/Kysymysarkisto/-Vuoden2012kysymykset/1342537252611> and <www.kuluttajaliitto.fi/ajankohtaista/-kuluttajaliitto_esittaa_ryhmakannelainsaadantoa_uudistettava_pikaisesti_vastaamaan_nykypaivan_tarpeita.html> (both last accessed on 11 March 2014).

23 It is unfortunate that a common register is lacking and even statistics on pending group actions do not exist. This makes observation and research very difficult because the only way to get information is by way of newspapers or contacting each court that has jurisdiction in group actions. To carry out follow-up studies, a common register should exist in each country that introduces collective redress. Only in this way can the development of the system be maximized.

24 GPA, Sec. 8.

25 *Ibidem*, Sec. 11.

exceed the amount (about €2,000) which is the limit for small claims proceedings. However, this is not the only indicator and even larger interests may be covered by a group action. How the interest should be measured is not established in practice.[26] In the recent *Habo Finans* case,[27] the Supreme Court unfortunately did not grant leave to appeal in a situation where the court dismissed a group action because of the lack of the superiority principle. According to the Court, the claims could proceed as individual cases due to their large amounts (about €14,000 on average). It is unfortunate that group actions can be used only as a small claims tool, because collective and representative actions can have many procedural advantages for all actors, especially when group actions are effective and working well in practice.

## 3. Opt-in

The Swedish group action procedure is based on the opt-in model only. There are no situations where the opt-out procedure could be allowed. Therefore, if the plaintiff´s application to commence group proceedings is not dismissed, the members of the group shall be notified of the proceedings.[28] The notification shall contain a brief description of the application and details of the names and addresses of the plaintiff and his attorney. The notification also includes general information about the group action procedure and the role of the members. Namely, it shall contain the information about group proceedings as a form of processing the case, the opportunity for the members to personally participate in the proceedings, the legal effect of a judgment in group proceedings and the rules applicable for litigation costs, as well as additional information about other circumstances that are important for the rights of the members of the group. Because the procedure is based on the opt-in model, the court will also provide notification about the final date for the opt-in procedure. To opt in a member of the group has to give notice to the court in writing within the time period determined by the court.[29] The application for a group action presented by the plaintiff to the court should include the names and addresses of the members of the group. Such details may be omitted if they are not necessary for processing the case. The plaintiff shall also provide details of circumstances that are otherwise important for notification to the members of the group.[30]

The notification can occur by different means and the court has broad discretionary powers to find the most suitable one. In this consideration, practical and economic reasons are the most important factors. The court may order a party to appear in person before the court for notification provided this has significant advantages for the processing of the case. This possibility covers both the plaintiff and the defendant. However, the party is in such a case entitled to compensation

26 Lindblom 2008a, p. 356-406.
27 Göta Court of Appeal, 3 June 2013, Ö 3152-12.
28 GPA, Sec. 13.
29 *Ibidem*, Secs. 13 and 14.
30 *Ibidem*, Sec. 9.

from public funds for expenses. The court may use, for instance, letters, emails, notice boards, newspapers, TV, radio, social media or the court's webpage to give the notification. Furthermore, the possibility to use the parties, especially the defendant, to do this is a very practical way for the court to provide notification whenever the defendant still has regular correspondence with the group members, for example in the form of invoicing. In that case, the notification can be done at the same time and only the extra costs caused by the notification are compensated from public funding to the party. The party has to cover the normal invoicing costs even in that case. The court may use fines as a coercive measure to force the party to fulfil his duties with regard to notification.[31]

The possibility to ask the defendant to take care of the notification has been used in practice to compensate for the problems caused by the lack of discovery. Before the trial it can be difficult to obtain the information on potential group members needed in order to fill in their names in the application. While there is no discovery in Sweden, a court order to produce a document is possible, but that possibility is not often used in practice. The use of the order requires that the applicant can identify the documents he wants to obtain from the defendant. In those situations, one extra tool is to fill in the names of the potential group members collectively in the application and in this way delegate the duty to define the group to the defendant himself.[32]

## 4. The Role of Group Members

In Sweden, a group action has been defined as an action that a plaintiff brings as the representative of several persons who will be bound by the judgment although they are not parties to the case.[33] This means that there cannot be multiple defendants in the Swedish group action. However, the joinder of actions is allowed and therefore the court may join other group actions or also other pending cases to the group proceedings.[34] Additionally, third-party intervention is allowed according to normal rules. In the case of third-party intervention, the intervenor receives party status even in group proceedings.[35]

As explained above, group actions in Sweden are framed as an opt-in procedure. A member of the group who does not give notice to the court in writing within the time period determined by the court that he wishes to be included in the group action shall be deemed to have withdrawn from the group.[36]

The idea of a group action is that one plaintiff is involved in the proceedings and the group members do not have to use their own time and energy for this. Therefore, they usually do not participate in the proceedings as the parties do.

31 *Ibidem*, Sec. 50; Lindblom 2008a, p. 572-578 and Government bill 2001/02:107, p. 181-182.
32 Code of Judicial Procedure (CJP), Chapter 38, Secs. 2-5 and Lindblom 2008a, p. 577-578.
33 GPA, Sec. 1.
34 Lindblom 2008a, p. 502-503.
35 CJP, Chapter 14.
36 GPA, Sec. 14.

However, a member of the group shall be equated to a party when applying the rules of the Code of Judicial Procedure on disqualification situations, pending proceedings, joinder of cases, examination during the proceedings and other issues relating to evidence. The list has been interpreted not to be comprehensive, since even other situations where the group member will be equated to a party may exist.

The role of the group member seems to be something between a party and an outsider. He can be an active player in the situations mentioned above. In addition, the group member is kept informed by the court, in the beginning to give him the possibility to opt in, and on several occasions during the proceedings to update him.[37] The *res iudicata* effect and in some situations the responsibility for legal expenses signal that the group member is not an outsider. Furthermore, he may appeal. However, to obtain full rights as a party he has to intervene into the group proceedings.[38]

Moreover, the group member can affect the proceedings via the plaintiff. Namely, on important issues, the plaintiff shall afford the members of the group an opportunity to express their views, if this can be done without great inconvenience.[39]

As far as the *res iudicata* effect is concerned, there is only one specific rule in the Group Proceedings Act according to which *res iudicata* covers all the group members who have opted in.[40] For the rest, the rules on *res iudicata are the same as in other cases*. Only the *dictum* in the group action requires *res iudicata* effect. This is not the case as regards the facts and the grounds of the judgment. *Res iudicata* only covers the claim and the decision of the court itself. However, facts can be subject to the so-called 'proof effect' in a subsequent procedure even if they are not binding.[41]

The group members who have opted in cannot start a subsequent lawsuit in the same case; they have already obtained a final decision based on their claims. If they have different or new claims based on the same facts, these claims are not precluded and the facts established in the earlier judgment can have evidentiary value in the new lawsuit.

37 According to the GPA, Sec. 49, the court shall, in addition to what is prescribed by other provisions, notify each member of the affected group of a judgment or a final decision and also of a settlement that is subject to a request for confirmation, in accordance with Sec. 26. If it is necessary to take into consideration the importance the information may be deemed to have for the rights of the member, the court shall also notify each member of the affected group when (1) the plaintiff has been replaced by a new plaintiff, (2) the plaintiff has appointed a new attorney, (3) the plaintiff has waived the action, (4) an issue has arisen concerning the approval of a risk agreement, (5) a judgment or decision has been appealed against and, furthermore, of (6) other decisions, measures and the overall situation.

38 Lindblom 2008a, p. 499.

39 GPA, Sec. 17, para 2.

40 *Ibidem*, Sec. 29.

41 CJP, Chapter 17, Sec. 11, Ekelöf, *Bylund & Edelstam 2009*, p. 174-240 and Lindell 2012, p. 341-364. See also Männistö 2009, p. 144-169 and Männistö 2013.

## 5. Evidence

There are no specific rules in the Group Proceedings Act concerning evidence and the burden of proof; rather, the normal rules in the Code of Judicial Procedure are valid also for group actions.[42] However, there is one specific problem in the Swedish law of evidence that can have more weight for group actions compared with individual actions, namely the lack of discovery.[43]

It is typical for the Scandinavian procedural systems that discovery and disclosure procedures do not exist. Because of this, the parties may have difficulties in estimating their possibilities to win a case. Furthermore, the parties may encounter difficulties in collecting evidence and organizing testimonies. However, this 'problem' has not been found to be a problem in Scandinavia, and there has not been any discussion on this topic lately.[44] In spite of numerous and very broad procedural reforms in Scandinavian countries, the rules on 'disclosure' have not been amended. The obligation to produce a document or an object has been found to be sufficient.

That is to say, a party is not the only one obliged to produce evidence in his possession. Any holder of any document which may be presumed to have evidentiary value may be ordered by the court to produce the evidence. This obligation applies also to persons who are not parties to the dispute. The difficulty is, however, the fact that to obtain a court order the applicant will have to identify the document with such clarity that, if need be, the order can be enforced by a bailiff. The courts tend to uphold this identification requirement to prevent fishing expeditions. The result is that disclosure of unknown documents becomes difficult. One of the ways in which the identification problems may be solved is for the requesting party to ask the court for permission in the course of the preliminary proceeding to call witnesses who may be privy to the existence and the contents of relevant documents. This tends to make the documentary discovery rules more efficient.[45] Namely, it is possible – for special circumstances – that a witness should give testimony before the hearing. Examples of special circumstances include witnesses who for good cause are unable to attend the hearing or where the cost of bringing the witness to appear at the hearing would be exorbitantly high relative to the value of the testimony. This possibility is infrequently used, as the courts are reluctant to deviate from the basic procedural rule that the proceedings should be confined to one hearing and that the judgment should be based solely on what transpires in the course of the hearing.[46] However, this possibility can be used

42 CJP, Chapters 35-41.

43 This problem has not been taken up in the follow-up report (Ds 2008:74, *Utvärdering av lagen om grupprättegång*), which has been criticized by Lindblom who sees the lack of discovery as one problem for the ineffectiveness of group actions. Lindblom 2008a, p. 845.

44 Leppänen 1998.

45 CJP, Chapter 42, Sec. 8, para 1 and Lundblad 1990, p. 151-152.

46 Lundblad 1990, p. 152.

especially when the assistance of the defendant is needed for identifying the potential members of the group.

## 6. The Role of the Court

The district courts designated by the government shall be competent to process cases under the Group Proceedings Act. There shall be at least one competent district court in each county,[47] and at main hearings in civil cases the district court shall consist of three qualified judges.[48]

It is the duty of the plaintiff to protect the interests of the members of the group when conducting the action.[49] This duty is mentioned in the Act, even though it should be obvious without mention in representative cases. Nevertheless, this clear expression of the duty of the plaintiff also shows that it is not a duty of the court. Of course, the court has to follow all procedural safeguards as usual and to respect, for instance, the rules of fair trial; but there are no extra duties placed on the court to actively promote the interests of the group members, notwithstanding the situations where the court has to notify the group members[50] or, for instance, when confirming the settlement where the court has a longer checklist compared with individual civil cases (see below).[51]

As explained above, friendly settlement as well as mediation are allowed in group actions as in other civil cases. A settlement that the plaintiff concludes on behalf of a group is valid provided the court confirms it by a judgment. The court shall examine the contents of the friendly settlement in a more extensive way in the case of group actions compared with individual actions. The court shall examine whether the settlement is proper and covers all claims and disputed questions. It shall also examine whether the settlement is discriminatory from the individual group member's point of view or otherwise manifestly unfair. The court shall, however, not examine whether the settlement is good enough or whether it is more or less advantageous for some group members compared with others. The settlement shall at the request of the parties be confirmed if it fulfils these requirements.[52]

In addition to the rules in Sec. 26 of the Group Proceedings Act, the normal regulation on friendly settlement will apply. This regulation is contained in the Code of Judicial Procedure. Because friendly settlement covers the members of the group, it is not possible to confirm the settlement before the requirements for the group action have been examined. For the same reason, it is not possible to make an agreement before the trial in the case of group actions.[53]

47 GPA, Sec. 3.
48 CJP, Chapter 1, Sec. 3a.
49 GPA, Sec. 17, para 1.
50 *Ibidem*, Sec. 49.
51 *Ibidem*, Sec. 26.
52 *Ibidem* and Lindblom 2008a, p. 127-128.
53 Lindblom 2008a, p. 127.

If necessary, the settlement can cover only some of the group members. While the representative of the group may make that kind of agreement, he may not make an agreement that covers only individual members. The distinction between these two possibilities seems to be unclear.[54]

The court shall inform the group members of the friendly settlement, in accordance with Sec. 49 of the Act. If they do not accept the friendly settlement, they can continue the proceedings as parties. If the requirements of a group action are fulfilled, even a new group action is possible.[55]

As to mediation, this also is possible in group actions.[56] In this situation, the court will appoint a special mediator for the case according to Chapter 42, Sec. 17, para 2 of the Code of Judicial Procedure.

## 7. Funding and Costs

In Sweden, the normal rule covering legal expenses is that the losing party shall reimburse the winning party litigation costs, unless otherwise provided.[57] The same rule also covers group actions. However, the group member who is not a party is not responsible for legal expenses.[58] If the group member is a party, for instance by becoming an intervenor or by appealing the judgment, the normal rule will apply. However, when appealing, he is responsible only for the costs associated with the appeal.[59] Otherwise the group member should indemnify only those costs he is found to have brought on by the action without the opposing party's having given cause for it, or if he has otherwise intentionally or negligently caused unnecessary litigation. In that event, he will reimburse the opposing party his litigation costs or, if the circumstances so justify, each party will bear his own costs.[60] In addition, if the party fails to appear or to comply with a court order, or he presents a claim or defence that he knew or should have known to be without merit, or his carelessness or oversight in other respects has occasioned adjournment of the case or has otherwise caused costs for the opposing party, then he must reimburse the opposing party such costs.[61]

Another situation where the group member who is not a party is liable for the costs is the situation where the defendant has been ordered to compensate the plaintiff litigation costs the defendant cannot pay. In that situation, the members of the group affected are liable to pay these costs. Each member of the group is liable

54 *Ibidem.*
55 *Ibidem*, p. 128.
56 *Ibidem.*
57 CJP, Chapter 18, Sec. 1.
58 GPA, Sec. 33.
59 CJP, Chapter 18 and GPA, Sec. 36.
60 GPA, Sec. 35 and CJP, Chapter 18, Sec. 3.
61 GPA, Sec. 35 and CJP, Chapter 18, Sec. 6.

for his share of the costs but is not, however, liable to pay more than he has gained through the proceedings.[62]

Risk agreements are in principle allowed, but there are some restrictions in the legislation to prohibit the abuse of the system. First of all, a risk agreement must be approved by a court. Otherwise, it is not binding among the group members.[63] A risk agreement may only be approved if the agreement is reasonable, having regard to the nature of the substantive matter. The agreement must be concluded in writing. The agreement must indicate the way in which it is intended that the fees will deviate from normal fees if the claims of the members of the group were to be granted or rejected completely. The agreement may not be approved if the fees are based solely on the value of the subject of a dispute.[64]

In addition, when considering what litigation costs are indemnifiable according to Chapter 18, Sec. 8 of the Code of Judicial Procedure, regard will not be taken to such additional costs that have arisen owing to a risk agreement,[65] which means that the group member is always responsible for the additional costs in the case of a risk agreement, and the defendant does not have to compensate that part of costs in any situation. Those extra costs will be paid out of the damages awarded.[66]

Legal aid, which also covers group actions and legal insurance have been privatized in Sweden. In principle, everyone should have legal insurance to cover the costs of potential litigation. Legal aid is just a supplement for insurance. In the case of group actions, legal aid does not have much significance because almost all legal insurance policies include coverage for group actions.[67]

In short, as long as the group member is not a party and he acts in a prudent and reasonable way without causing any unnecessary extra costs to the parties, there is no risk to him of having to pay the costs of litigation. To cover the costs of litigation the damages awarded may be used, even in the case of a risk agreement and in those situations where the defendant has the duty to pay but is without the means to do so. These solutions can be criticized from the 'loser pays' perspective. Nevertheless, the group action seems to be favourable for a defendant who loses the case. In normal individual actions, the loser should pay all indemnifiable costs, including the attorneys' fees. Therefore, a group action becomes much cheaper, and more favourable, for the losing defendant compared with individual actions by all of the group members as plaintiffs whenever the defendant loses the case. The reason for all of this is, of course, to guarantee reimbursement for the plaintiff and the attorney so as to encourage them to start group actions. At the same time, this benefits the defendant as well, which can be found unfair compared with regular procedural, legal and social principles: Why should the defendant who loses and

62 GPA, Sec. 34.
63 *GPA*, Sec. 38.
64 GPA, Sec. 39.
65 GPA, Sec. 41.
66 Lindblom 2008a, p. 559.
67 Act on Legal Aid (1996:1619), Sec. 9, para 1 and Lindblom 2008a, p. 152.

who caused the problem (for such a large number of people that the group action is the superior means to resolve the dispute) receive benefits for that type of business behaviour?

## 8. Enforcement

There are no special rules for the enforcement of a judgment in group actions; the usual enforcement procedures apply. In other words, no special enforcement is possible; the judgment is enforceable only by the members of the group who have opted in. The group members who did not opt in are outsiders, they have no rights based on the judgment, and the judgment has no *res iudicata* effect as regards them. Therefore they can start a new action if they wish and obtain an enforceable title for themselves.

Swedish legislation distinguishes between condemnatory, declaratory and constitutive judgments. It distinguishes also between enforcement of non-monetary sanctions and monetary sanctions. All of these different types of judgments are enforceable. It does not matter whether the judgment is based on a group action or not. A settlement can be enforced as long as it has been confirmed by a court.[68]

The judgment is based on fixed amounts only or at least it should include the fixed rules on how to calculate the amount. The latter is possible if, for instance, the interest is running. In this situation, the bailiff can calculate the fixed amount based on the rules given in the judgment. Otherwise, the amount is always fixed in the judgment, and the bailiff has no power to interpret the judgment.[69]

The subjects in enforcement are always the group members who have opted in. The representative cannot be a party at the enforcement level; enforcement takes place in the name of each member of the group. The reason is that in the judgment the representative cannot be named the recipient of, for instance, an award of damages, since the judgment always has to be issued in the name of group members directly and separately. Therefore in enforcement, the group members have the role of a full party even if during the proceedings it is the representative of the group who represents the members and the latter have only a restricted party role.[70] This can be criticized from the access to justice perspective. This kind of individual enforcement procedure is also very bureaucratic. There has been discussion on these problems in Sweden and it has been suggested that the procedure should be changed in the future in order to strengthen group actions. In the *travaux préparatoires*[71] group enforcement in the name of the representative of a group was suggested, but the proposal did not go through.[72]

68 Act on Enforcement (19981:774), Chapter 3, Sec. 1 and Lindell 2012, p. 599-600.

69 Heuman 2014, p. 118.

70 The Swedish GPA, Secs. 15 and 29 as well as the Finnish Group Action Act, Secs. 4 and 11.

71 SOU 1994:151, *Grupprättegång Del A – Sammanfattning, lagtext och behovsanalys*, p. 459-462.

72 For this discussion, see, for instance, Lindblom 2008a, p. 103-104.

## 9. Case Law and Evaluation

Sweden has a long tradition of group actions, not just in the Nordic countries but in all civil law countries, and has had all in all 17 cases brought before the courts, some of which were successful group action cases, and a number of which were dismissed, cancelled or ended with a friendly settlement or arbitration. One of the cases was a public lawsuit brought by the Consumer Ombudsman, while the others were private lawsuits.

The summaries of the cases are listed below.[73]

**1. Göta Court of Appeal, 3 June 2013, Ö 3152-12, *Habo Finans***
Private group action. Damages were due to the negligence of the defendant at revision. The court dismissed the group action because of the lack of the superiority principle. The claims could proceed as individual cases due to their large amounts (about €14,000 on average). The Supreme Court did not grant leave to appeal.

**2. The Supreme Court, 3 May 2012, T 2045-12, *Vinimport***
Private group action. Question of damages due to alcoholic beverages being confiscated by the state. Question about restitution. The action was rejected by the District Court of Nacka; Svea Court of Appeal affirmed the judgment. Appealed to the Supreme Court. Case on-going.

**3. The Court of Appeal for Northern Norrland, 4 November 2011, T 154-10, *Kraftkommission***
Public group action. Damages due to the defendants' failure to supply electric power. On-going case. Intermediate judgment was delivered, affirmed by the Court of Appeal for Northern Norrland. Damages were found grounded in the intermediate judgment and the Supreme Court denied review permit for the intermediate judgment. The next step will be that the court has to confirm the amounts for the group members.

**4. Svea Court of Appeal, 21 December 2009, T 3552-09, *Veterinärutbildningen***
Private group action. Damages due to discrimination regarding university entrance. Affirmed by Svea Court of Appeal.

**5. Svea Court of Appeal, 25 September 2006, Ö 6868-06, *Telia***
Private group action. Refunding of the difference between the amount being billed during a particular period and the agreed rate. Case dismissed due to the fact that the members of the group could not be defined. Appealed to Svea Court of Appeal, but was later withdrawn.

**6. Svea Court of Appeal, 5 January 2005, Ö 810-05, *Aftonbladet***
Private group action. Compensatory damages when participants could not participate in online gaming due to data transmission problems. Claim was denied

[73] The list is based on the national report 'Sweden' written by Laura Ervo, Annina H. Persson & Tomas Lindblom for the EU project 'Focus on collective redress' organized by the British Institute of International and Comparative Law. Tomas Lindblom has drafted the list of case law. The results of the project can be found at: <www.collectiveredress.org/collective-redress/> (last accessed on 10 March 2014).

due to procedural hindrance. Svea Court of Appeal remanded T 10992-04 to the District Court of Stockholm. Svea Court of Appeal denied the appeal of T 17333-04.

7. **District Court of Gothenburg, 10 February 2012, T 7211-03, *NCC***
Private group action. Demand for performance of contractual obligation. Action withdrawn.

8. **District Court of Nacka, 17 June 2011, T 3385-09, *Handelsbanken***
Private group action. Damages due to the negligence of the bank when an unauthorized person withdrew money from an account.

9. **District Court of Malmö, 4 March 2010, T 9330-09, *Psykologutbildningen***
Private group action. Damages due to discrimination regarding university entrance. Settled out of court.

10. **District Court of Nacka, 22 March 2009, T 5127-09, *Norrtäljeanstalten***
Private group action. Claim for refunding of the difference between the actual price of goods in the prison kiosk and the price that would have been fair. Case dismissed due to procedural hindrance. Review permit denied by Svea Court of Appeal, also claim for restitution of time lost.

11. **District Court of Gothenburg, 4 March 2009, T 271-09, *Parkeringsservice***
Private group action. Claim of repayment of parking fine due to ambiguous contractual terms. The case was first filed at the District Court of Solna as T 5918-08. The case was transferred to the District Court of Gothenburg, where the case was dismissed due to the larger part of the claims being held to be equally well pursued through private actions by the individual members of the group.

12. **District Court of Stockholm, 26 June 2006, T 9593-06, *Stulen barndom***
Private group action. Question of compensatory damages due to poor care in municipal orphanages. Case was dismissed due to the special investigation that was needed for each member of the group, which would go against the intent of the law.

13. **Environmental Court of Nacka, 29 August 2006, M 1931-07, *Arlanda***
Private group action. Question of damages due to aviation noise. On-going case, proceedings are stayed, to be resumed on request of the litigant.

14. **District Court of Gothenburg, July 2005, T 7247-05, *Fjärrvärme***
Private group action. Question as to the ownership of an electric power facility. Settled out of court.

15. **District Court of Stockholm, 5 January 2004, T 97-04, *Skandia***
Private group action. Right to compensation due to the fact that policyholders of a company suffered injury when the proceeds of sales were transferred to another company. An arbitration tribunal settled the case, and the group action was withdrawn.

16. **District Court of Stockholm, April 2003, T 6341-03, *Dataregister 1***
Private group action. Information collected regarding suspected, but not convicted, taggers. An action regarding the right of registration of personal data. Case was appealed to Svea Court of Appeal by the defendant, but was later withdrawn.

17. **District Court of Stockholm & Nacka, January 2003, T 3515-03 & T 1281-07, *Aer Olympic***
Private group action. Damages due to several hundred passengers having been left stranded at the airports when the company went bankrupt. Settlement was made in 2007.

## 10. Conclusion

The Swedish experience with group actions has been moderate, and the amount of case law is small. While follow-up reports show there has not been abuse of group actions, it also appears that they have not been as effective as hoped for. Especially the requirements for admissibility in Sec. 8 of the Group Proceedings Act have been found difficult to interpret and apply in practice. Also, funding has been seen to be problematic[74] as group actions are very time-consuming.[75] A number of amendments have been suggested which have caused considerable discussion in the legal literature.[76] The proposals are seen as illogical compared with the results given in follow-up reports and it has been argued that they would make the group action even less effective in the future rather than more effective. In contrast, other amendments have been suggested that would strengthen group actions: namely, those proposing the opt-out procedure.[77] The result is that the Group Proceedings Act has not been reformed since its birth.

Nevertheless, group actions are alive and working in Sweden and the reason for this is clear: private group actions are allowed and even prioritized over public group actions by the legislator. If the goal is to promote access to the courts through group actions, then it is necessary to allow private or at least organizational lawsuits. To strengthen group actions in Sweden, the opt-out procedure should be adopted and the requirements for procedural admissibility should not be as strict as they still are. According to Lindblom, opt-in is out and opt-out is in.[78]

The current Swedish group actions model was a proper start, but it could have been bolder.

74 Ds 2008:74, *Utvärdering av lagen om grupprättegång*, p. 15-17 and 154.
75 Lindblom 2008a, p. 257.
76 Heuman 2007 and Lindblom 2008b.
77 Lindblom 2008b, p. 840.
78 Lindblom 2008b, p. 843.

## Bibliography

**Autio 2014**
Autio, A.-L., *Lainkäyttö yritysten riidanratkaisussa,* Helsinki: Lakimiesliiton Kustannus, 2014.

**Bakardjieva Engelbrekt 2007**
Bakardjieva Engelbrekt, A., *'Från matieriella regler till genomföranderegrel: en ny fas i det europeiska rättssanarbetet på konusmentsskyddsområdet', Europarättslig tidskrift, 2007, Vol. 3, p. 578-607.*

**Ekelöf, Bylund & Edelstam 2009**
Ekelöf, P.O., Bylund, T., Edelstam, H., *Rättegång, tredje häftet,* Sjunde upplagan, Stockholm: Norstedts Juridik, 2009.

**Ervo 2009**
Ervo, L., 'Class Actions - Scandinavian Novelties', in Stürner, R. & Kawano, M. (eds.), *Current Topics of International Litigation,* Tübingen: Mohr-Siebeck, 2009, p. 118-126.

**Ervo 2011**
Ervo, L., 'Class Actions in Consumer Cases - A Finnish Start', in Stürner, R. & Kawano, M. (eds.), *Comparative Studies on Business Tort Litigation,* Tübingen: Mohr-Siebeck, 2011, p. 203-212.

**Ervo & Martinez 2012**
Ervo, L. & Martinez, E., 'Class Action - A Solution to Access to Justice Problems in Consumer Cases? Some Thoughts between the North, South and Europe', *Zeitschrift für Zivilprozess International,* 2012, Vol. 17, p. 207-229.

**Ervo, Persson & Lindblom 2013**
Ervo, L., Persson, A.H. & Lindblom, T., 'Sweden'. The national report for the EU project 'Focus on collective redress' organised by the British Institute of International and Comparative Law. The report can be found on the website: <www.collectiveredress.org/collective-redress/>.

**Ervo & Sippel 2012**
Ervo, L. & Sippel, L., 'Scandinavian Countries', in Esplugues, C., Iglesisas, J.L. & Palao, G. (eds.), *Civil and Commercial Mediation in Europe,* Antwerp: Intersentia, 2012, p. 371-425.

**Heuman 2007**
Heuman, L., 'Bör reglerna om grupptalan ändras?', *Juridisk Tidskrift,* 2007-2008, Vol. 4, p. 829-842.

**Heuman 2014**
Heuman, L., *Specialprocess Utsökning och konkurs,* 7th edn., Stockholm: Norstedts Juridik 2014.

**Leppänen 1998**
Leppänen, T., *Riita-asiain valmistelu todistusaineiston osalta,* Helsinki: Suomalainen Lakimiesyhdistys, 1998.

**Lindblom 2008a**
Lindblom, P.H., *Grupptalan i Sverige,* Stockholm: Norstedts Juridik, 2008.

**Lindblom 2008b**
Lindblom, P.H., 'Utvärdering av lagen om grupprättegång', *Svensk Juristtidning,* 2008, Vol. 10, p. 833-847.

**Lindell 2012**
Lindell, B., *Civilprocessen,* 3rd edn., Uppsala: Iustus, 2012.

**Lundblad 1990**
Lundblad, C., 'Sweden', in Platto, Ch. (ed.), *Pre-Trial and Pre-Hearing Procedures Worldwide,* London/Boston: Graham & Trotman and International Bar Association, 1990, p. 151-152.

**Männistö 2009**
Männistö, J., 'Effects of Judgments - Res iudicata', in Ervo, L. (ed.), *Finnish Civil Justice,* Tokyo: Jigakusha 2009, p. 144-169.

**Männistö 2013**
Männistö, J., *Theory of Preclusion,* Helsinki: Ajatuspaja Käräjä, 2013.

**Viitanen 2003**
Viitanen, K., *Lautakuntamenettely kuluttajariitojen ratkaisukeinona,* Helsinki: Suomalainen Lakimiesyhdistys, 2003.

**IUS COMMUNE EUROPAEUM**

A peer-reviewed book series in which the common foundations of the legal systems of the Member States of the European Union are the central focus.

The *Ius Commune Europaeum* series includes horizontal comparative legal studies as well as studies on the effect of treaties within the national legal systems. All the classic fields of law are covered. The books are published in various European languages under the auspices of METRO, the Institute for Transnational Legal Research at the Maastricht University.



Recently published:

Volume 120: *The Effects of Judicial Decisions in Time*, P. POLULIER, S. VERSTRAETEN, D. VANHEULE and B. VANLERBERGHE
Volume 121: *The Position of Small and Medium Sized Enterprises in European Contract Law*, I. SAMOY and M.B.M. LOOS (eds.)
Volume 122: *Property Law Perspectives II*, B. AKKERMANS, E. MARAIS and E. RAMAEKERS (eds.)
Volume 123: *The Treaty on European Union 1993-2013. Reflections from Maastricht*, M. DE VISSER and A.P. VAN DER MEI (eds.)
Volume 124: *Inside Policy Custody. Training Framework on the Provisions of Suspects' Rights*, T. SPRONKEN, J. BLACKSTOCK, E. LLOYD-CAPE, J. HODGSON, A. OGORODOVA and M. VANDERHALLEN
Volume 125: *Coordinating Ombudsmen and the Judiciary. A Comparative View on the Relations between Ombudsmen and the Judiciary in the Netherlands, England and the European Union*, M. REMAC
Volume 126: *Legal Evolution and Hybridisation. The Law of Shares Transfer in England*, M. SOLINAS
Volume 127: *The Role of EU State Aid Law in Promoting a Pro-Innovation Policy. A Review from the Perspective of University-Industry R&D Cooperation*, M. CISNEROS
Volume 128: *Tradition, Codification and Unification. Comparative – Historical Essays on Developments in Civil Law*, J.M. MILO, J.H.A. LOKIN and J.M. SMITS
Volume 129: *Nobody's Perfect. Comparative Essays on Appeals and Other Means of Recourse Against Judicial Decisions in Civil matters*, A. UZELAC and C.H. VAN RHEE (eds.)
Volume 130: *Legal Aid in the Low Countries*, B. HUBEAU and A. TERLOUW (eds.)
Volume 131: *State Aid and Public Procurement in the European Union*, S. SCHOENMAEKERS, W. DEVROE and N. PHILIPSEN (eds.)
Volume 132: *Property Law Perspectives III*, A. APERS, S. BOULY *ET AL.* (eds.)

www.ingramcontent.com/pod-product-compliance
Ingram Content Group UK Ltd.
Pitfield, Milton Keynes, MK11 3LW, UK
UKHW051926100926
8556IPUK00022B/1400

9 781780 682778